NYC GUIDE
FOR **INSTAGRAMMERS**

SILVIE BONNE

WHAT?

New York City is one of the most Instagrammed cities in the world. The different neighborhoods with their distinctive characters, the architectural masterpieces (high – higher – highest) and the city's eye-popping skyline on which you can feast your eyes from every perspective, are the ultimate paradise for Instagrammers and photographers.

This guide offers 100 suggestions for impressive or special Instragrammable spots in New York City. It includes the usual suspects such as Central Park, the Empire State Building and the Statue of Liberty as they never disappoint. In addition to these classics, you'll also find a lot of "hidden gems" that are popular with locals but attract fewer tourists. And finally, the book contains some "new classics", spots that are bound to become classic landmarks in the future.

The 100 Instagrammable spots in this book were personally selected by Silvie Bonne, the photographer and author of this book. It goes without saying that there are many more Instagrammable places in New York. What's more, the city is continually changing, which explains why works of art, shops and restaurants may disappear and new hotspots may emerge.

HOW?

Every Instagrammable spot comes with some background information, a few fun facts and lists some other photogenic spots in the neighborhood as well as the address and the nearest subway station.

Every spot is numbered so you can find it on the map at the beginning of each chapter. The maps provide an overview of where the spots are positioned.

The pictograms on the left of the page provide an instant overview of the type of spot that is described.

Each picture features hashtags that allow you to find more examples on Instagram.

There is also an "Instatip" under each picture, which explains how the photo was taken.

WHO?

Silvie Bonne, a Belgian photographer, currently lives in New York with her husband and teenage son. She has lived in Hell's Kitchen, a rough and tumble neighborhood and now lives in Long Island City (Queens). Every day, Silvie explores the concrete jungle, armed with her Nikon and her iPhone. And every day, the city manages to surprise her over and over again. You can follow her city adventures on Instagram (@bonnesilvie) and share your favorite spots with her.

#neverstopexploring

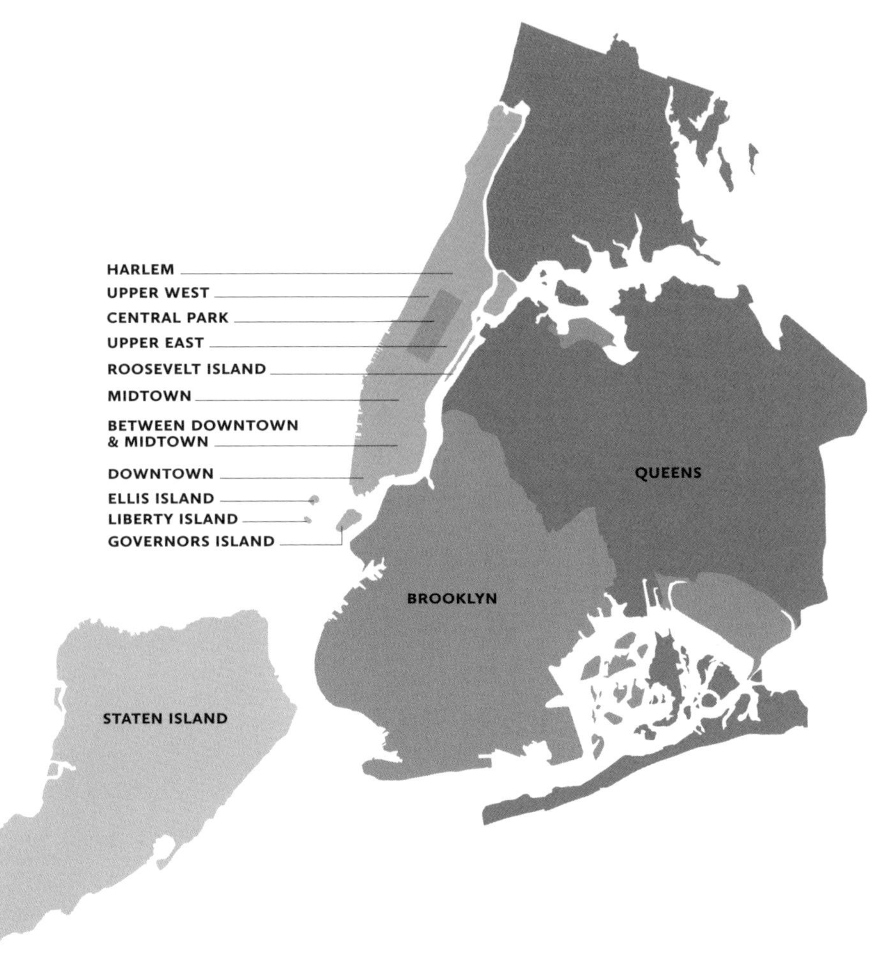
HARLEM
UPPER WEST
CENTRAL PARK
UPPER EAST
ROOSEVELT ISLAND
MIDTOWN
BETWEEN DOWNTOWN & MIDTOWN
DOWNTOWN
ELLIS ISLAND
LIBERTY ISLAND
GOVERNORS ISLAND
QUEENS
BROOKLYN
STATEN ISLAND

TABLE OF CONTENTS

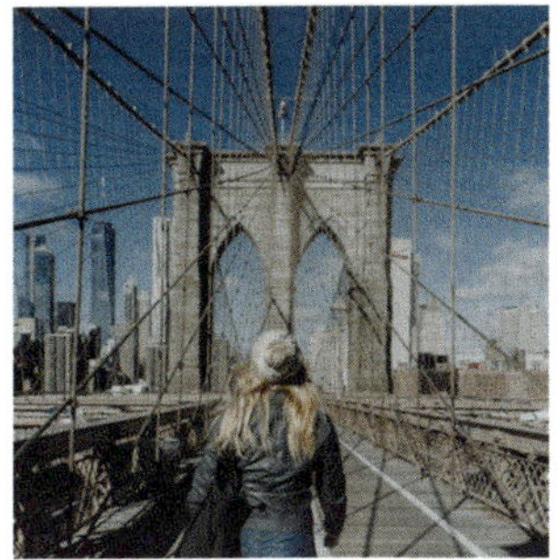

DOWNTOWN

1 Brooklyn Bridge • *10*
2 Manhattan Bridge • *12*
3 Battery Park • *14*
4 Financial District • *16*
5 Charging Bull • *18*
6 Brookfield • *20*
7 Freedom Tower • *22*
8 Oculus • *24*
9 The Irish Hunger Memorial • *26*
10 South Street Seaport • *28*
11 Economy Candy • *30*
12 Metrograph • *32*
13 Taiyaki • *34*
14 Chinatown • *36*
15 Little Italy • *38*
16 Soho • *40*
17 Washington Square Park • *42*
18 Strand Bookstore • *44*
19 The Bowery Mural • *46*

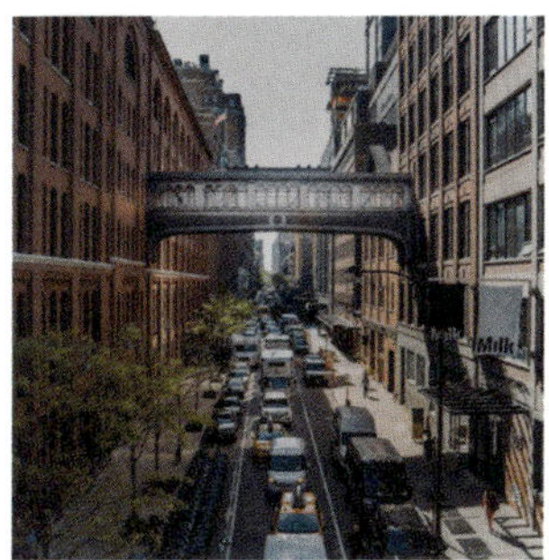

BETWEEN DOWNTOWN & MIDTOWN

20 Chelsea • *50*
21 Chelsea Market • *52*
22 Whitney Museum of American Art • *54*
23 Life Underground • *56*
24 The High Line • *58*
25 Flatiron building • *60*
26 Flatiron Room • *62*
27 Union Square • *64*
28 The Frying Pan • *66*
29 Billy's Bakery • *68*

PARK
OUTSIDE
INSIDE
CLASSIC
NEW CLASSIC
FREE
PAYING
BRIDGE
BUILDING
MONUMENT
HIDDEN GEM
NEIGHBORHOOD
FOOD
ART
SHOP
BAR
STATUE
ISLAND
ATTRACTION

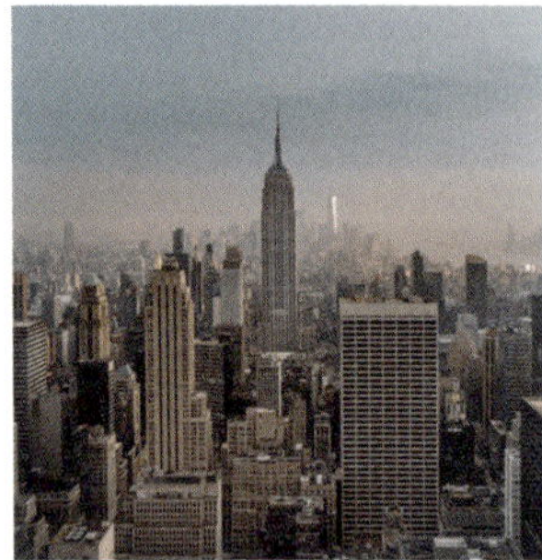

MIDTOWN

30 Hudson Yards & Vessel • *72*

31 Macy's • *74*

32 Empire State Building • *76*

33 The Morgan Library and Museum • *78*

34 Grand Central • *80*

35 Chrysler Building • *82*

36 Love & Hope Sculptures • *84*

37 New York Public Library • *86*

38 Bryant Park • *88*

39 Times Square • *90*

40 Broadway – The Theater District • *92*

41 Hudson River Park – Pier 84 • *94*

42 Rockefeller Center • *96*

43 Radio City Music Hall • *98*

44 Waterfall Tunnel • *100*

45 Moma • *102*

46 Spyscape • *104*

47 Museum of Arts and Design (MAD) • *106*

48 Columbus Circle • *108*

49 Time Warner Center • *110*

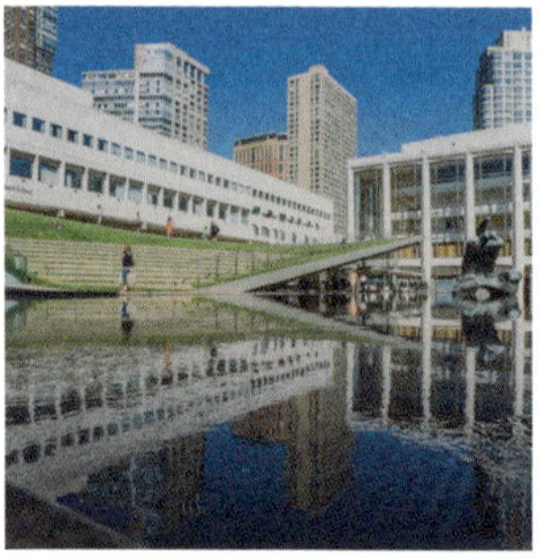

UPPER WEST, CENTRAL PARK, UPPER EAST & HARLEM

50 Lincoln Center • *114*

51 Pier i cafe • *116*

52 American Museum of National History • *118*

53 Bethesda Fountain • *120*

54 The Mall and Literary Walk • *122*

55 Loeb Boathouse • *124*

56 Alice in Wonderland statue • *126*

57 Belvedere Castle • *128*

58 Jaqueline Kennedy Onassis Reservoir • *130*

59 The Conservatory Garden • *132*

60 Dylan's Candy Bar • *134*

61 Sprinkles Cupcake ATM • *136*

62 The Metropolitan Museum of Art • *138*

63 Guggenheim Museum • *140*

64 Bluestone Lane at the Church of the Heavenly Rest • *142*

65 Cooper Hewitt design museum • *144*

66 Graffiti Hall of Fame • *146*

67 Red Rooster • *148*

68 Apollo Theater • *150*

69 Columbia University • *152*

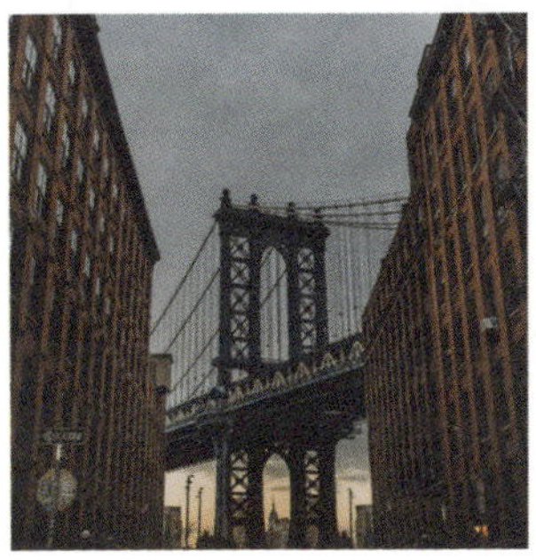

BROOKLYN

70 Goodbye Rhinos • *156*

71 Jane's Carousel • *158*

72 Tom Fruin's Watertower • *160*

73 Brooklyn Bridge Park • *162*

74 Brooklyn Heights • *164*

75 Smorgasburg Prospect Park • *166*

76 Brooklyn Botanic Garden • *168*

77 Industry City • *170*

78 The Bushwhick Collective • *172*

79 Smorgasburg Williamsburg • *174*

80 The Sketchbook Project • *176*

81 Mister Dips • *178*

82 WNYC Transmitter Park • *180*

83 The OY/YO sculpture • *182*

84 Domino Park • *184*

85 Williamsburg Bridge • *186*

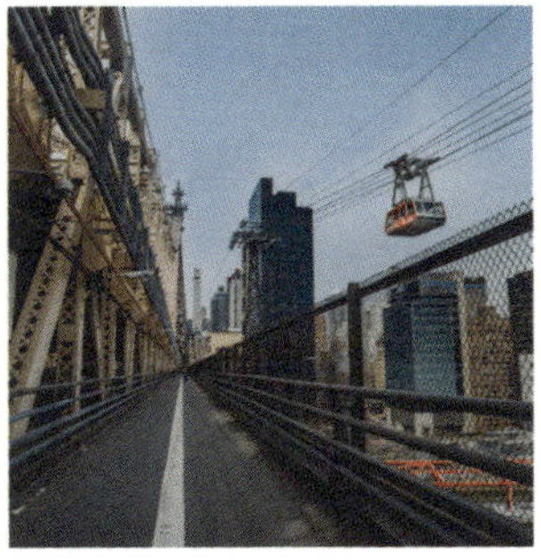

QUEENS & THE ISLANDS

86 Gantry Plaza State Park • *190*

87 Pepsi Cola Sign • *192*

88 MoMA PS1 • *194*

89 Socrates Sculpture Park • *196*

90 Welling Court Mural Project • *198*

91 Queensboro Bridge • *200*

92 Silvercup Studios • *202*

93 Museum of The Moving Image • *204*

94 Corona Park • *206*

95 Unisphere • *208*

96 Roosevelt Island Lighthouse • *210*

97 Governors Island • *212*

98 Staten Island Ferry • *214*

99 Coney Island ferris wheel • *216*

100 Ellis Island/Liberty Island • *218*

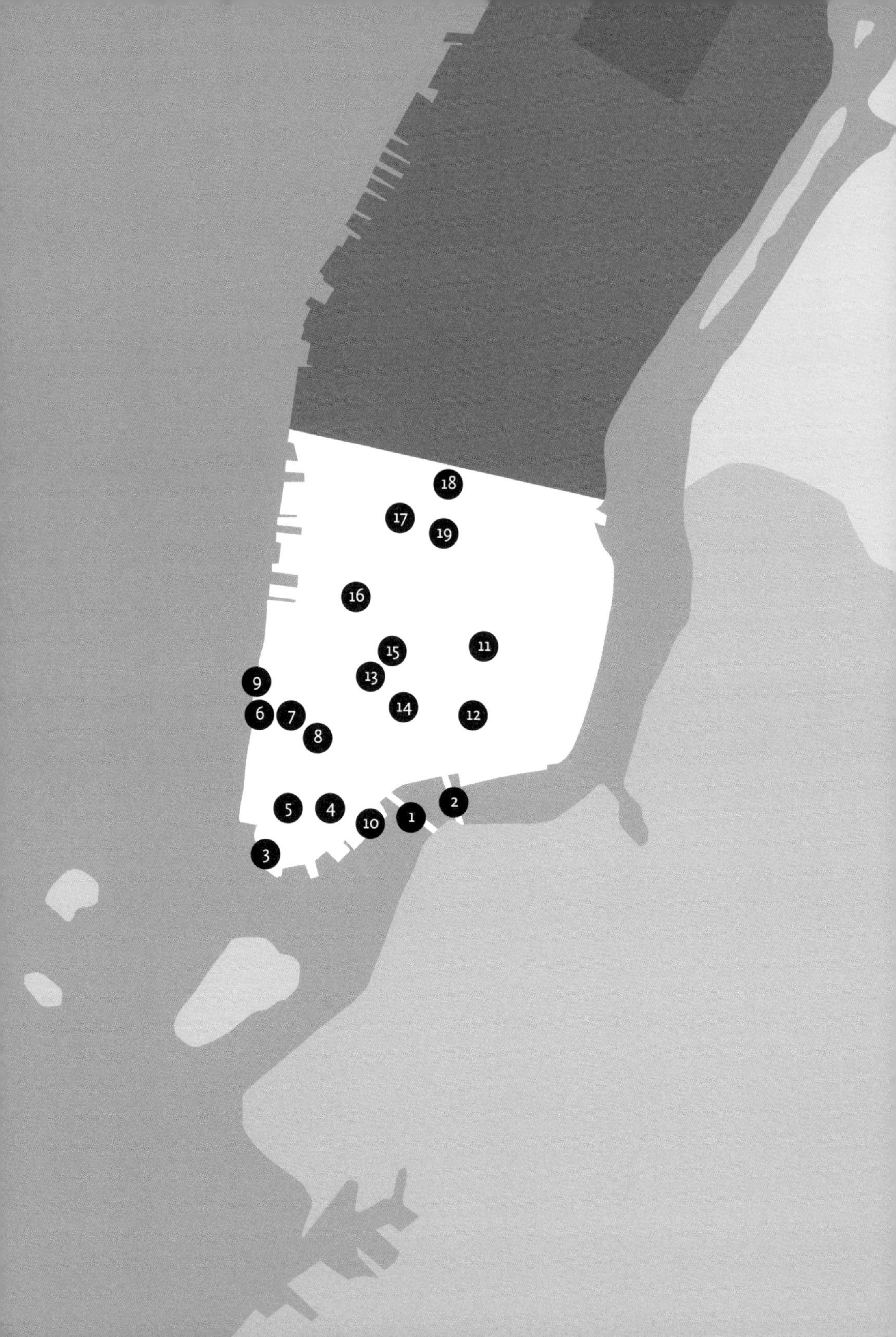
18
17
19
16
15
11
13
9
6
7
14
12
8
2
5
4
1
10
3

DOWNTOWN

❶ BROOKLYN BRIDGE

Brooklyn Bridge

HOW TO GET THERE
Manhattan
Subway 4, 5 or 6 (green) Brooklyn Bridge City Hall Station

Brooklyn
Subway A or C (blue) High Street Brooklyn Bridge (Brooklyn)

The Brooklyn Bridge is definitely New York's most iconic monument. This impressive, monumental bridge connects Manhattan and Brooklyn, spanning the East River.

The bridge took more than fourteen years to build (from 1869 until 1883) and more than 20 men died during its construction, including John August Roebling, the bridge's architect. At the time it opened, and for several years, the bridge was the world's tallest structure. Although it no longer holds this title, it is still one of New York's most popular and most photographed sights.

The pedestrian and bike lanes on the Brooklyn Bridge start next to City Hall Park in Manhattan. It will take you about 30 minutes to walk to Brooklyn (depending on how many times you stop to take photos as you go). If you start from the Manhattan side of the bridge, don't forget to look back now and then during your walk to snap some shots of the sweeping views of this borough.

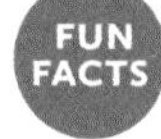

On 17 May 1884, 21 elephants, 7 camels and 10 dromedaries crossed the bridge into lower Manhatten to demonstrate how safe the bridge was. What a sight that must have been!

The vaults under the bridge were rented out as cellars for liquid stashes. The conditions were perfect for storing wine and champagne and the rent was used to pay off the bridge. A win-win situation!

INSTAGRAMMABLE PLACES IN THE NEIGHBORHOOD

COFFEE	*Manhattan*	Birch Coffee: 8 Spruce Street
FOOD	*Brooklyn*	Shake Shack: 409 Fulton Street
SEE	*Manhattan*	New York City Hall
		Brooklyn Banks Skatepark under the bridge
	Brooklyn	Brooklyn Bridge Park
		Dumbo

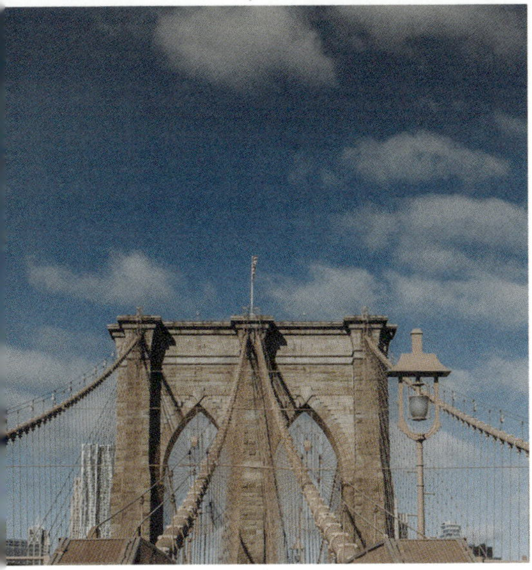

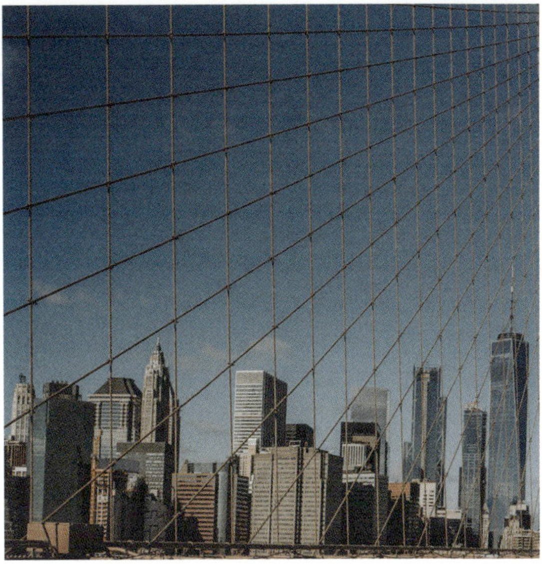

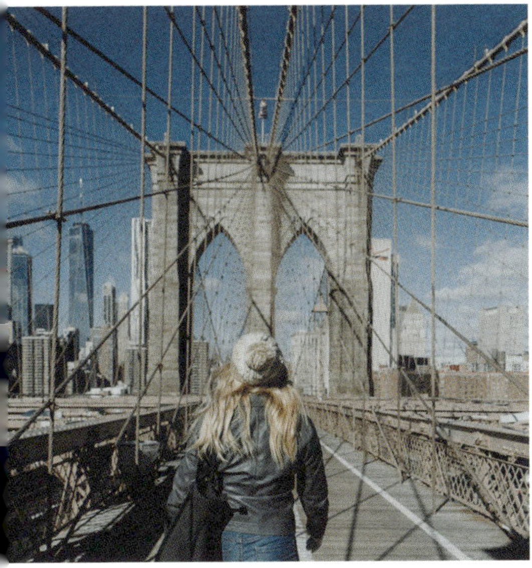

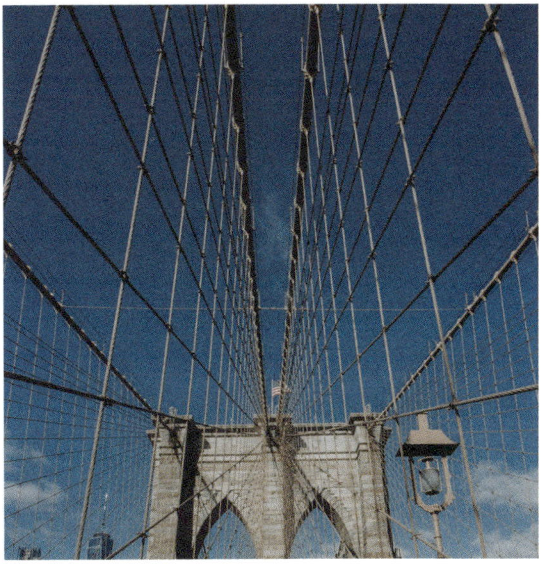

#brooklyn #brooklynbridge #brooklynbridgeview #nycview #eastriver

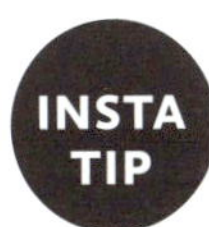

Many tourists walk halfway across the bridge and then turn back. If you want to take some nice "grammable" photos, you should walk almost all the way to the end. The closer you come to Brooklyn, the easier it is to use Manhattan's amazing skyline as your backdrop. The bridge has countless instagrammable features, including its typical stone structure and the steel cables that add a cool graphic dimension to your snapshots.

❷ MANHATTAN BRIDGE

Manhattan Bridge

HOW TO GET THERE

Manhattan
Subway
D (red),
Grand Street

Brooklyn
Subway
F (orange),
York Street Subway Station

You can find the Manhattan Bridge next to the Brooklyn Bridge. While it is less popular and attractive than the Brooklyn Bridge (meaning less overrun by tourists), you can enjoy the same amazing views of Manhattan's skyline from the Manhattan Bridge. What's more, you get a nice view of the Brooklyn Bridge too.

The Manhattan Bridge was, just as the Williamsburg Bridge, built because the Brooklyn Bridge was a victim of its own success, and was unable to cope with the traffic between Brooklyn and Manhattan.

The neighborhood between the Brooklyn Bridge and the Manhattan Bridge in Manhattan is called Two Bridges. If you're looking to take some spectacular photos however, you should head over to Dumbo (the neighborhood in between the two bridges in Brooklyn). In summertime, this neighborhood can sometimes be very busy with people who want to take in the sunset, but don't be deterred. The view (and your amazing photos) is definitely worth it!

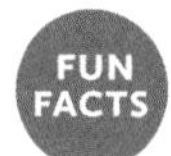

The Manhattan Bridge starred in several films including *The Lonely Guy* (Steve Martin), *I Am Legend* (Will Smith) and *Once Upon A Time in America* (Robert De Niro).

Originally the bridge was supposed to be called Bridge 3 as it was the third bridge to connect Manhattan and Brooklyn, spanning the East River. The first bridge to be built was the Brooklyn Bridge, followed by the Williamsburg Bridge. The Manhattan Bridge is in the middle and is a great place to see the two other bridges (and photograph them).

INSTAGRAMMABLE PLACES IN THE NEIGHBORHOOD

FOOD	*Manhattan*	Eggloo: 60 Mulberry Street (4 min. walk)
COFFEE	*Brooklyn*	Bluestone Lane: 55 Prospect Street (3 min. walk)
SEE	*Manhattan*	Chinatown
	Brooklyn	The Yes Murals under the bridge, between the subway and the pedestrian path
		Tom Fruin's Watertower: 20 Jay Street

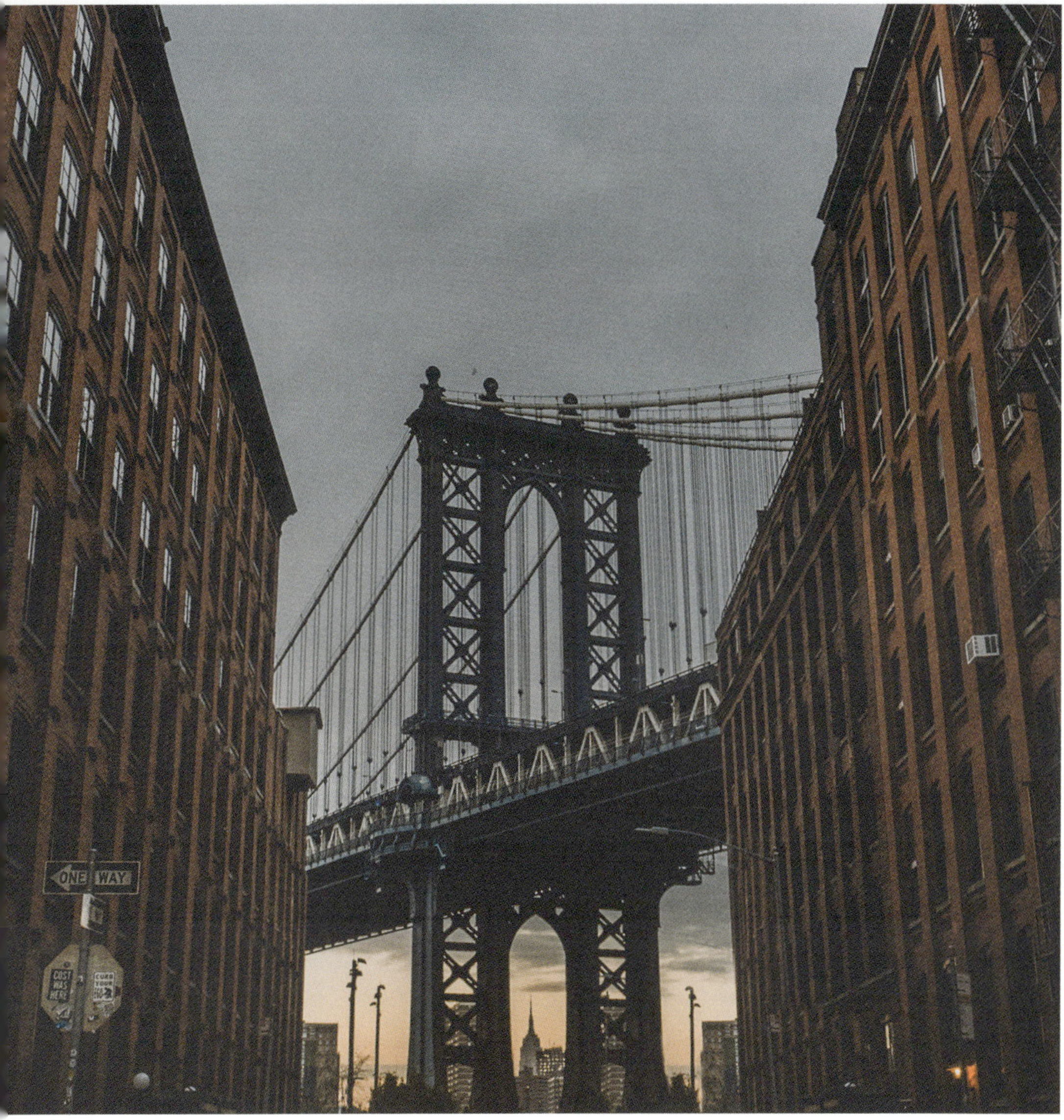

#dumbo #dumbonyc #manhattanbridge #manhattanbridgeview #nycview #eastriver
@dumbobid

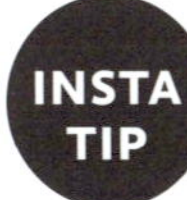

The most iconic location to take a great photo of the Manhattan Bridge is in Dumbo, at the intersection of Washington and Front Street.

The colors of the sunrise and sunset obviously paint a pretty picture in the sky, but you can also take some stunning pictures here during daytime.

Make sure the Empire State Building is aligned with the towers of the Manhattan Bridge for a nice flourish.

❸ BATTERY PARK

Battery Park

HOW TO GET THERE
Subway 4 or 5 (green), Bowling Green Subway Station

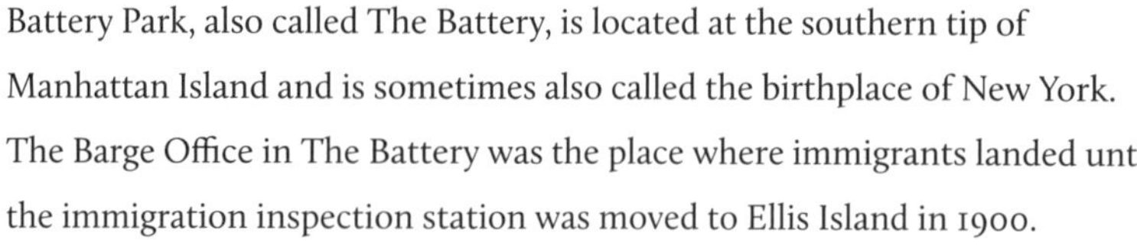

Battery Park, also called The Battery, is located at the southern tip of Manhattan Island and is sometimes also called the birthplace of New York. The Barge Office in The Battery was the place where immigrants landed until the immigration inspection station was moved to Ellis Island in 1900.

Nowadays this is a peaceful park with nice views of the Hudson River, Liberty Island and Ellis Island. It's the perfect park for a leisurely afternoon, with plenty of activities for people of all ages. The park has a nice bicycle trail, a dreamy SeaGlass Carousel, various war monuments, stunning landscaped gardens, a labyrinth and even an urban farm.

You can take a ferryboat to Liberty Island and Ellis Island from the Battery. Do you want to take a Circle Line cruise to one of these islands? Then be prepared for some long queues. The ferry terminal, from where you can take the (free) ferry to Staten Island or Governor's Island, is right next to the park. These ferries don't sail as close to the Statue of Liberty as the Circle Line cruises, which explains the shorter waiting times.

Whichever cruise or ferry you take, don't forget to enjoy the stunning view of Manhattan's skyline on your return trip to Manhattan.

Many oyster, mussel and other seafood species inhabited the port of New York in the 19th century. They could be easily shipped out of the port, making seafood the city's most important export product at the time.

Unfortunately water pollution destroyed their natural habitat. Nowadays the pollution is so bad that selling seafood from New York's port is banned.

INSTAGRAMMABLE PLACES IN THE NEIGHBORHOOD

COFFEE AND FOOD	a beautiful view of The Battery Gardens at the Battery Garden Cafés
	Pier A Harbor House
KIDS	The SeaGlass Carrousel & The Bosque Fountain
SEE	The National Museum of the American Indian
	Ferry's to Staten Island and Governors Island

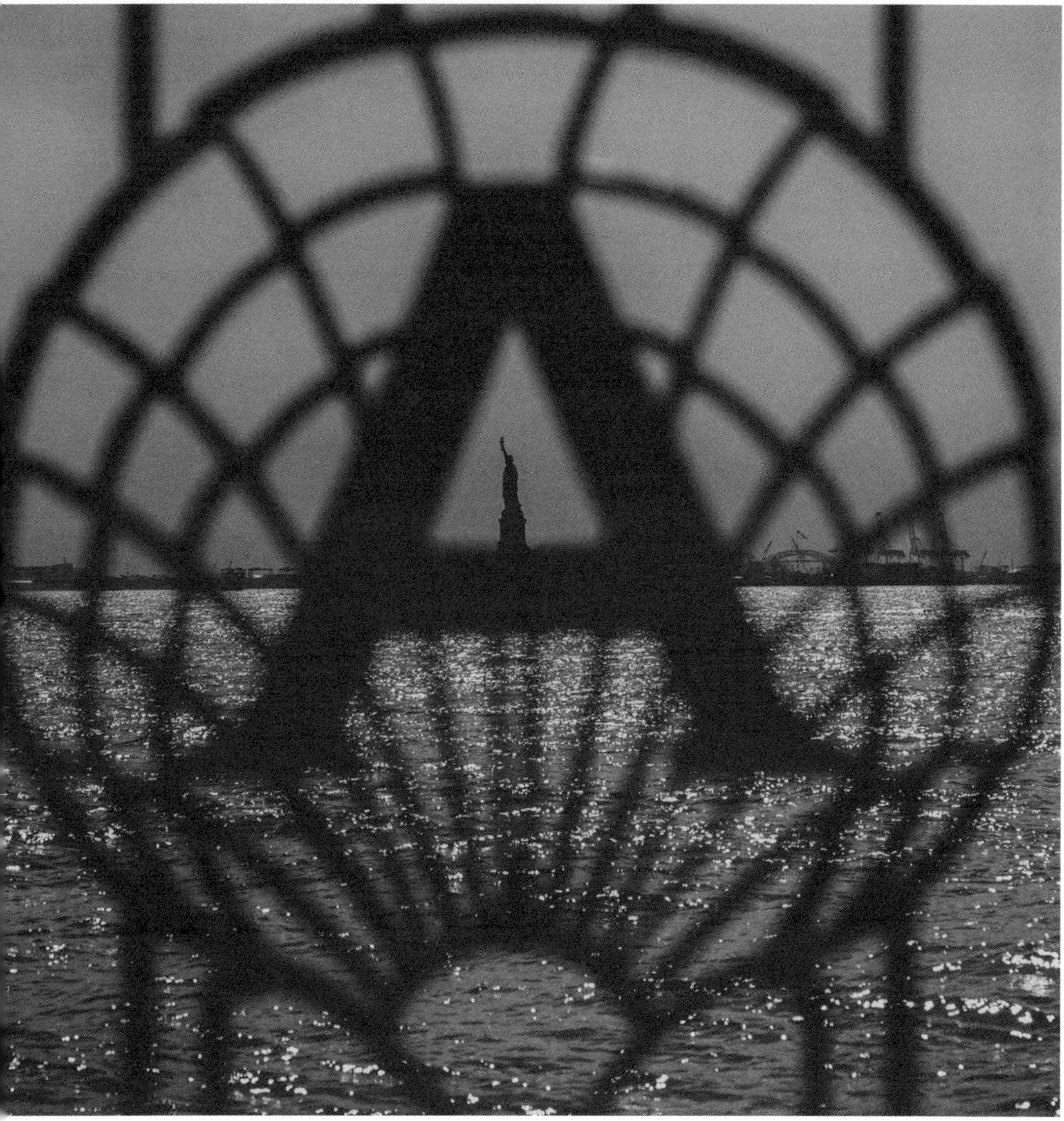

#batterypark #thebattery #brooklynbridge #hudsonriver #statueofliberty

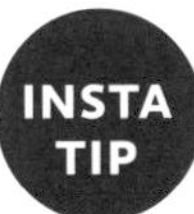

Try to frame the Statue of Liberty in an exciting frame. For this picture I used the balustrade of the Pier A terrace.

❹ FINANCIAL DISTRICT

Financial District

HOW TO GET THERE
Subway 4 or 5 (green), Bowling Green Subway Station

The Financial District is the financial center of the United States and comprises the offices of the New York Government. Some of the city's oldest buildings are located here, making it New York City's most historic and most famous neighborhood.

The Financial District is the financial epicenter of the United States and home to the city's first paved street and some of the city's oldest buildings, including Saint Paul's Chapel of Trinity Church (1764). This neighborhood is not laid out in a grid pattern, with numbered streets, like the rest of Manhattan. The street names in the Financial District often refer to the city's history. Fulton Street for example is named after Robert Fulton, the inventor of the steamship who also designed the first submarine. Beaver Street pays tribute to the once flourishing trade in beaver pelts. The most famous street of all, Wall Street, is named after the wall the Dutch built to protect the city.

New York's financial district also comprises the headquarters of many of the world's major financial institutions. They all have offices here in the modern glass skyscrapers or in the old brick buildings. But the district's most important building is the New York Stock Exchange. While the building looks quite impressive, you'll soon realize it's very difficult to take a good picture of it because of its location. Check the Instatips to find out how you can pull this off.

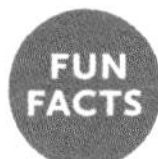

At 55 Water Street, you can find a staircase in between two office buildings that leads to a hidden park called The Elevated Acre. This tiny oasis, with its panoramic view, is definitely worth checking out!

The film *Trading Places* (1983) inspired the Eddie Murphy Rule in the Wall Street Transparency and Accountability Act, banning insider trading using non-public information that was misappropriated from a government source.

INSTAGRAMMABLE PLACES IN THE NEIGHBORHOOD

COFFEE AND FOOD	Lots of charming indoor & outdoor options at Stone Street
SEE	The Wall Street Bull
	The Broad Street facade of the New York Stock Exchange
	Federal Hall

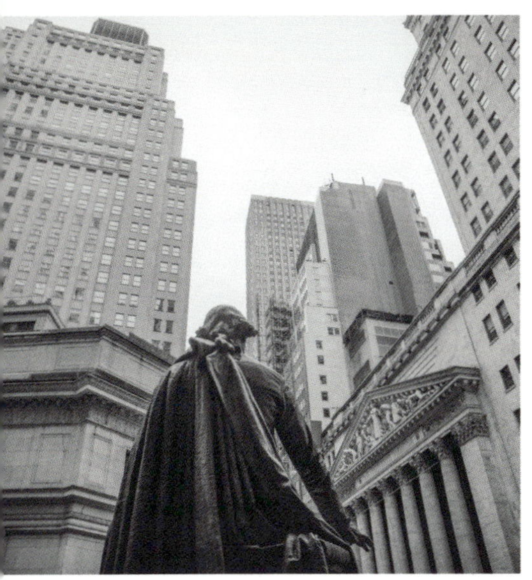

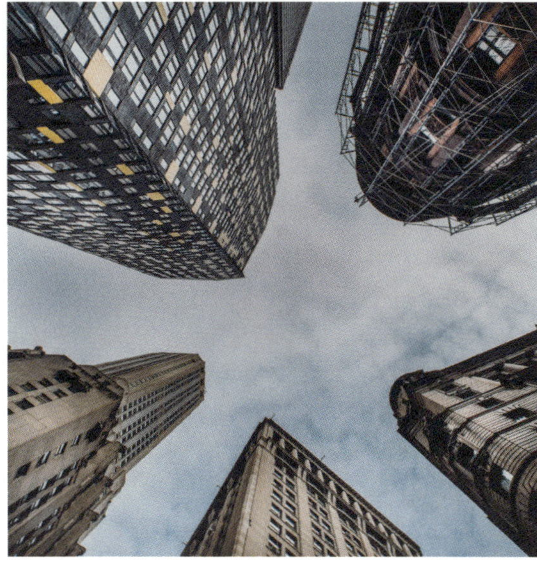

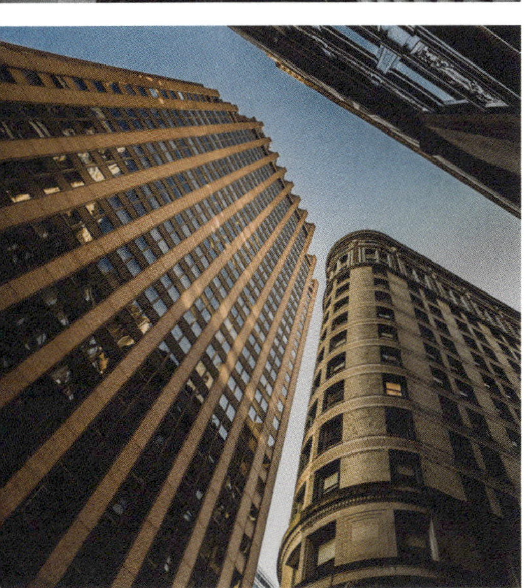

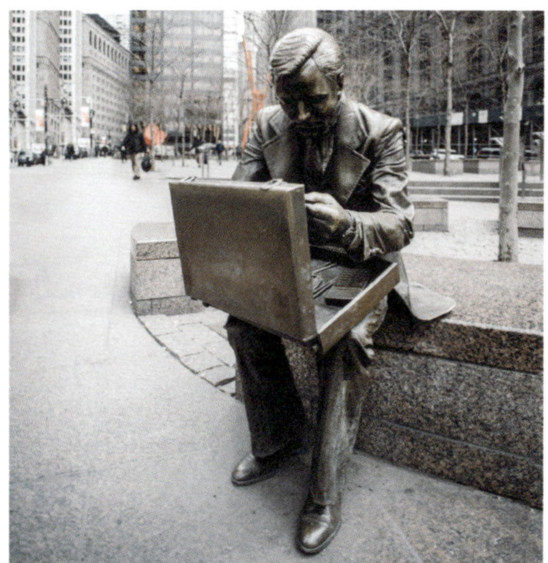

#financialdistrictnyc #fidi #downtown #lowermanhattan #wallstreet

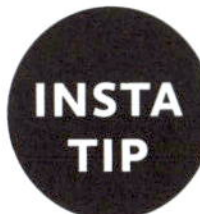

Picture 1: most people take pictures in front of Federal Hall. You can try another point of view by climbing the stairs and take a picture from behind the statue of George Washington. This way you will also capture the New York Stock Exchange in the picture.

Pictures 2 and 3: Never forget to look up! At the crossing of William Street and Beaver Street, you can find a beautiful collection of amazing skyscrapers and historical buildings.

Picture 4: At the corner of Trinity Place and Liberty Street you can find the statue Double Check. After 9/11 this statue became a memorial.

5 CHARGING BULL

Broadway & Morris Street

HOW TO GET THERE
Subway 4 or 5 (green), Bowling Green Subway Station

While the Charging Bull or the Wall Street Bull originally was an act of guerilla art, it soon became a permanent feature and a New York icon.

In 1989, the artist Arturo Di Monica installed his work of art under the Christmas tree in front of the New York Stock Exchange as a "Christmas gift" to New Yorkers. The city was so happy with this "gift" that it was permanently installed in Bowling Green. Since then the Charging Bull has become one of the most photographed artworks and one of the main tourist attractions in the Financial District.

Legend has it your finances will improve if you rub the bull's horns, nose and testicles. You can see why these parts of the statue are so shiny.

On 7 March 2017, another sculpture, called Fearless Girl, was placed in front of the bull. While the figurine caused quite a controversy, she is still facing down the raging bull at the time of publication. This sculpture was also a temporary installation, but will probably be given a permanent location over time.

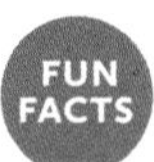

In 2004, the artist announced that the sculpture is for sale, on condition that the buyer does not move the bull from its current location.

The Bull is the second most-photographed sculpture in New York City after the Statue of Liberty.

INSTAGRAMMABLE PLACES IN THE NEIGHBORHOOD

COFFEE	Latte Art: 15 Stone Street (3 min. walk)
SEE	National Museum of the American Indian (2 min. walk)
	The Battery (2 min. walk)

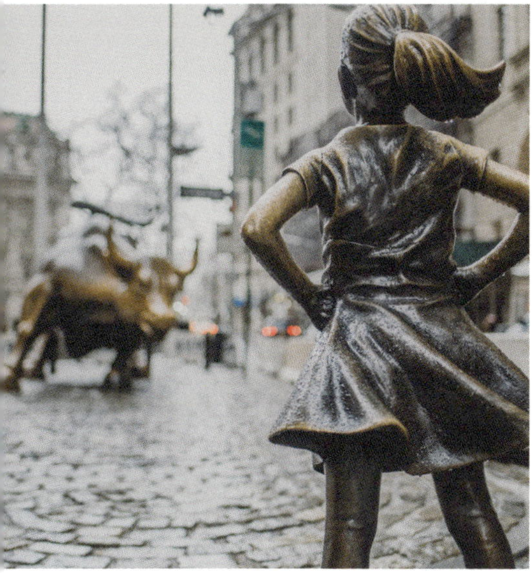

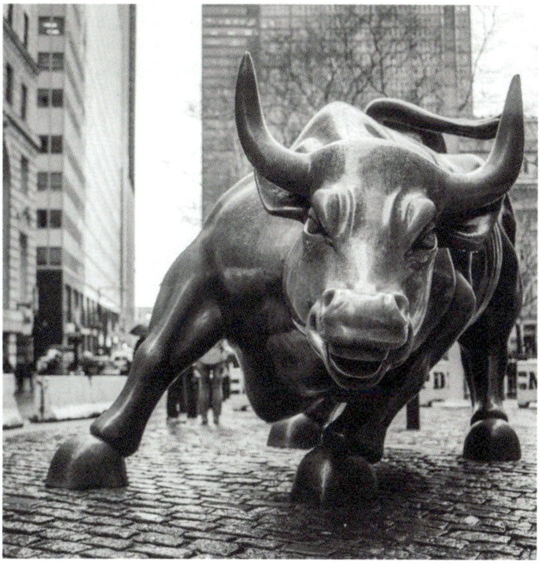

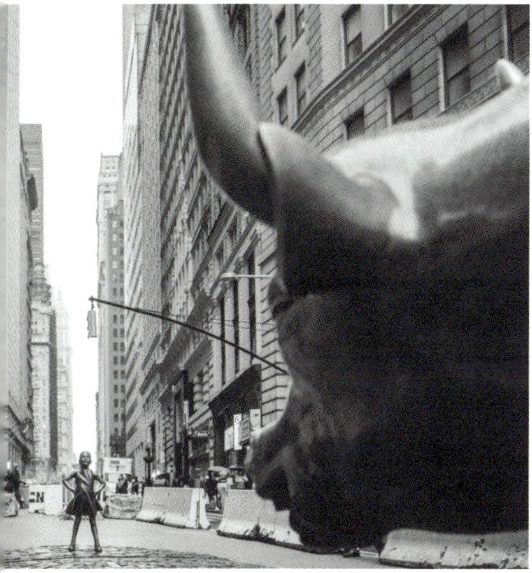

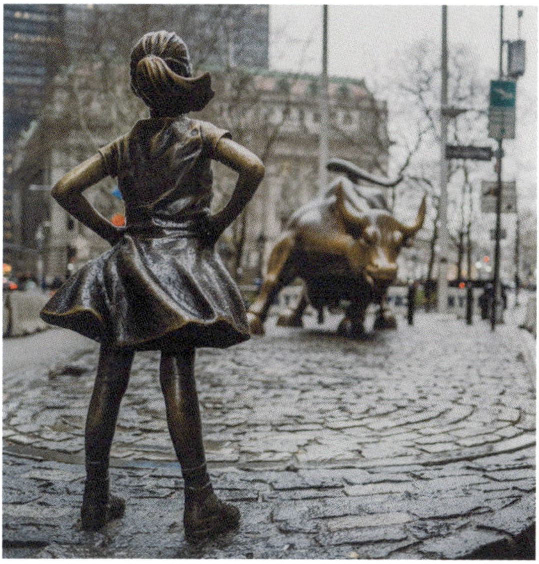

#wallstreetbull #chargingbull #fidi #downtown #lowermanhattan #wallstreet

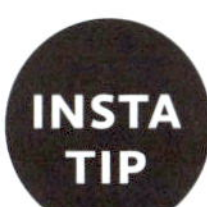

As one of the most touristic attractions in New York City, it is difficult to shoot the statue without troops of people around him. Early in the morning or on a rainy weekday, you have the best chance to catch to bull in private.

❻ BROOKFIELD PLACE

Brookfield Place
230 Vesey Street

HOW TO GET THERE
Subway 2 or 3 (red) or A (blue) to Chamber Street

Subway 4 or 5 (green) to Fulton Street

Subway E (blue) to Path Station World Trade Center

Brookfield Place is a high-end shopping mall, and the home of several international fashion brands including Gucci, Hermès, Michael Kors, Diane Von Furstenberg...

This retail hub is just gigantic! It has two floors with shops of some of the world's most renowned designers. The food hall offers amazing views of the Hudson River and Ellis Island. You can walk to the Oculus through an underground pedestrian pathway (under neath the WTC Complex). Brookfield is the place to go if you love designer clothes.

While it is the perfect place to indulge in some (window) shopping, it is also the only place in New York City that is dotted with palm trees. The large amphitheater-shaped hall makes you feel as if you're in LA, albeit with a view of the Hudson River. This large, open space, with its impressive glass dome, has the perfect light conditions for some unusual snapshots.

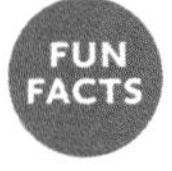

After 9/11 the mall sustained some heavy damage. The renovation to restore the complex's sleek and glitzy appearance costs 300 million dollars.

INSTAGRAMMABLE PLACES IN THE NEIGHBORHOOD

COFFEE AND FOOD	Le District is a 30.000 square French inspired market space inside Brookfield Place
SEE	World Trade Center (1 min. walk)
	The Irish Hunger Memorial (7 min. walk)

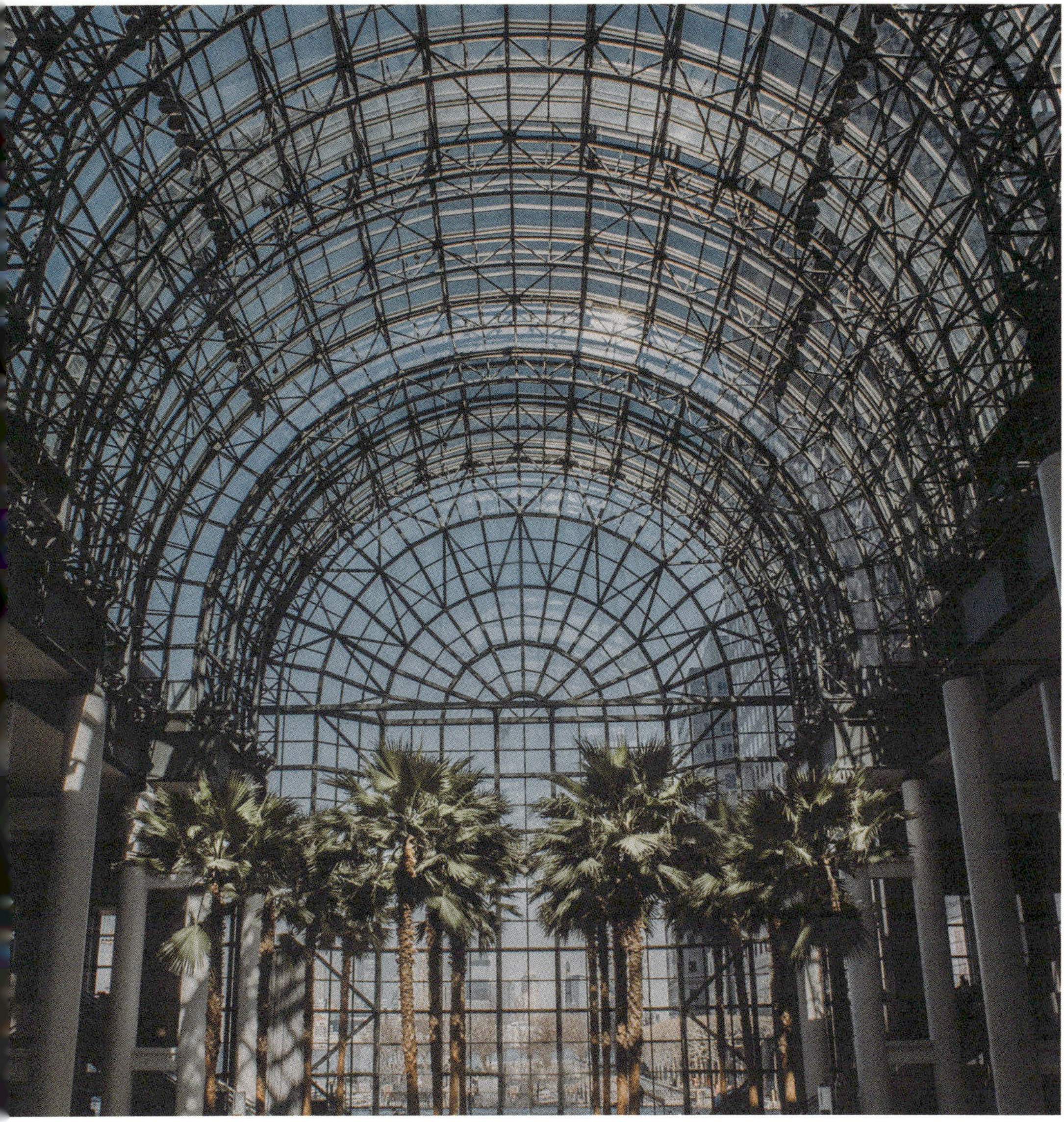

#brookfieldplace #brookfieldplaceny #downtown #downtowniswhatsup @brookfieldplace

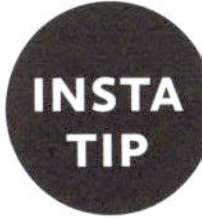

Standing on the stairs in the main hall gives you a beautiful view of the palm trees and the spectacular glass ceiling. When taking the picture, try to keep your image as symmetric as possible to create an attractive effect.

7 FREEDOM TOWER

Freedom Tower or One World Trade Center
285 Fulton Street

HOW TO GET THERE

Subway E (blue) to Path Station World Trade Center (4 min. walk)

Subway 2, 3 (red) or A (blue circle) to Chamber Street (7 min. walk)

Subway 4 or 5 (green) to Fulton Street (9 min. walk)

$

One World Trade Center, which is also called the Freedom Tower, has changed Manhattan's skyline.

After 9/11, the World Trade Center complex was rebuilt. It has several buildings of which the Freedom Tower is the main building.

The iconic Freedom Tower with its supertall antenna and stainless steel and glass façades, that reflect the light and the clouds, exudes confidence and faith in the future. The 541-metre tall building is once again New York's tallest building and the tallest building in the Western Hemisphere.

If you don't have a fear of heights, you can take the superfast elevator to floors 100 and 102. During your elevator ride, you can watch the history of New York City unfold on the elevator's walls and see how it has changed over the years in an immersive time-lapse. The observation deck is called the One World Observatory and the view and experience are both equally breathtaking.

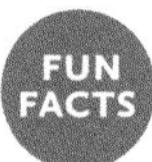

The building has 7 elevators, including 5 express elevators, which can attain a maximum speed of 35.5 km/hour!

In September 2013, three daredevils base-jumped from the Freedom Tower. Although they were arrested, you can still find the original footage of their adventure on YouTube.

INSTAGRAMMABLE PLACES IN THE NEIGHBORHOOD

COFFEE, FOOD AND SHOPPING	the shopping center at The Oculus (4 min. walk) the shopping center at Brookfield Place (4 min. walk)
SEE	The 9/11 memorial (1 min. walk). The Irish Hunger Memorial (8 min. walk).

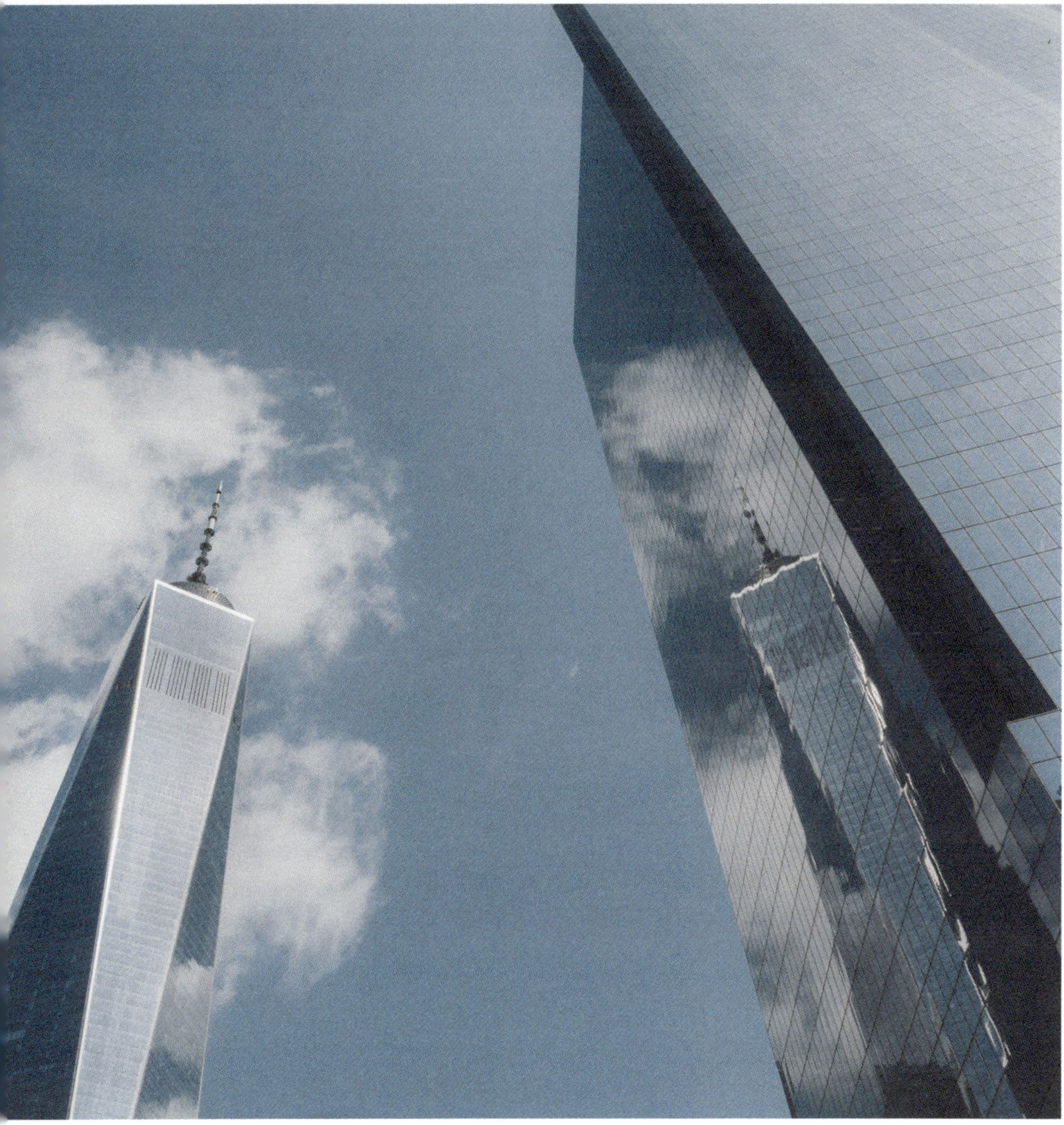

#OneWorldTradeCenter #OneWorldObservatory #Freedomtower #WTC #nycarchitecture

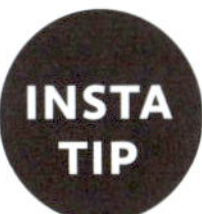

The Freedom tower is the perfect tower to play with reflection.

You can let the tower reflect in the surrounding buildings or you can let the clouds reflect on the tower. Special effects are guaranteed!

8 OCULUS

WTC Oculus
Church Street

HOW TO GET THERE
Subway 4 or 5 (green) to Fulton Street

Subway R W (yellow) to Cortland Street

Subway E (blue) to World Trade Center

The Oculus is a memorial, a transportation hub and a shopping mall all in one. The astonishing structure proved an immediate Instagram hit when it was inaugurated in 2016.

The Spanish architect Santiago Calatrava designed the Oculus as a symbol of a new beginning after the 9/11 attacks. The design was inspired by a bird's outspread wings just before taking off.

The massive white ribs and marble floor only add to the building's futuristic appearance, causing a sensation on social media when this amazing architectural feat was completed. The Oculus has since become the place to go to for a selfie in New York!

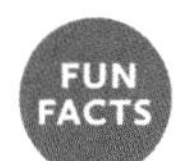

The Oculus cost more than 4 billion dollars to build, making it the world's most expensive train station.

The shape and dimension of the Oculus's steel ribs are so unique that there were only four companies around the world that could produce them.

INSTAGRAMMABLE PLACES IN THE NEIGHBORHOOD

COFFEE	*inside The Oculus*	Joe Coffee
FOOD	*inside The Oculus*	Sugerfina. Did you say champagne candy? Yes please!
SHOP	The Oculus is a shopping center, so knock yourself out!	
SEE	The 9/11 Memorial (1 min. walk)	
	St. Paul's Chapel of Trinity Church (1 min. walk)	
	The Freedom Tower (1 min. walk)	

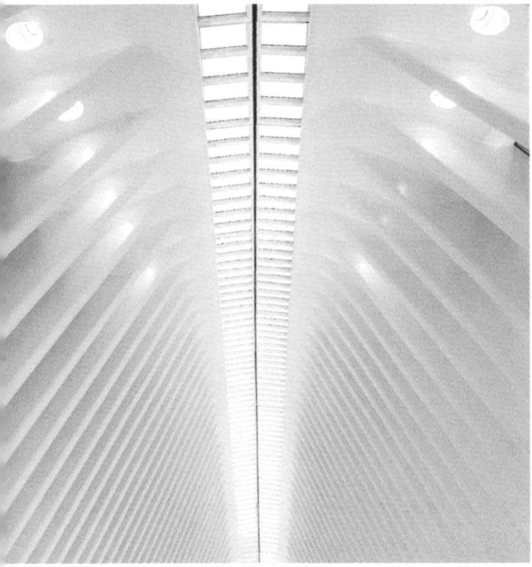

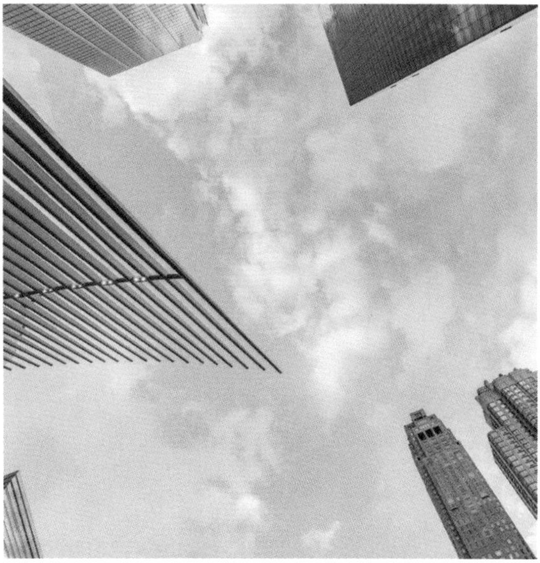

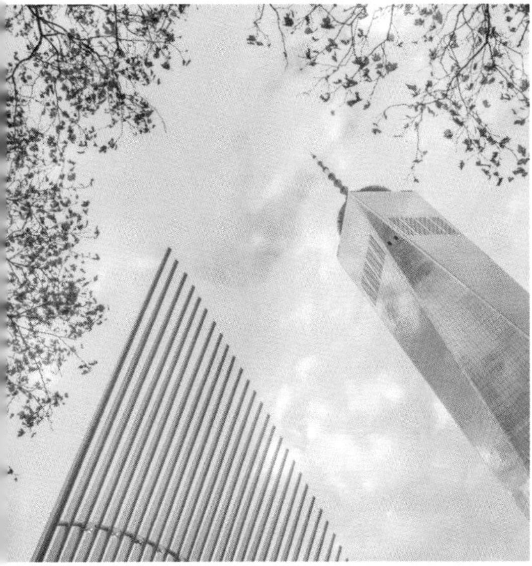

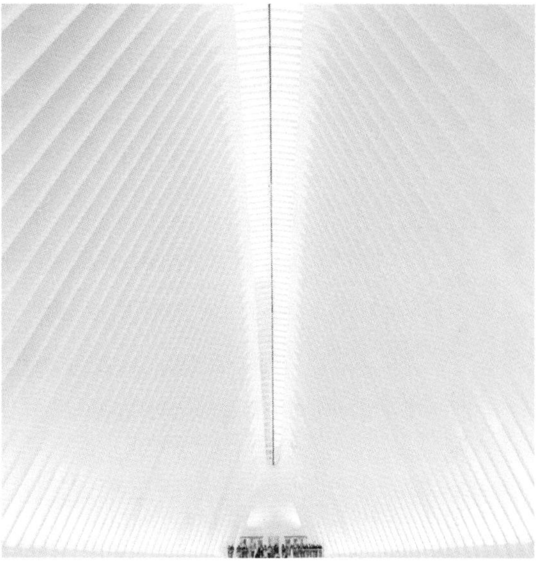

#oculus #oculus_ig #wtc #worldtradecenter #bellyofthewhale #nycarchitecture

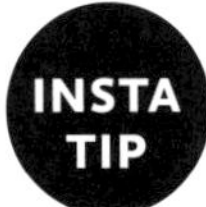

There are stairs on both sides inside the Oculus. Standing at the top of one set of stairs, right in the middle, will give you the epic view of the building. Either aim your camera up, to get a picture of the amazing ceiling, or aim it down a little bit, to snap some people looking like ants.

9 THE IRISH HUNGER MEMORIAL

The Irish Hunger Memorial

HOW TO GET THERE
Subway 2 or 3 (red circle) to Chambers Street

Subway E (blue circle) to Path Station World Trade Center

The Irish Hunger Memorial is a little piece of Ireland in the center of Manhattan. The memorial is dedicated to the Great Hunger, which killed over a million people in Ireland between 1845 and 1849. It also prompted the mass migration of Irish people to the United States, most of whom travelled through New York.

The monument is inspired by an Irish cottage and has several "layers":

The stones that were used were sourced from Ireland's 32 counties. In between the stones, you can find text fragments that make the sad story of the Great Irish Famine even more moving.

You enter the monument through a dark granite corridor, which is lit with wall engravings. In the corridor you hear a voice reading excerpts from poems, letters and parliamentary documents about this tragic event.

You can then walk down the pathway to a viewing point atop the "cottage". All the planting feature native Irish flora. The view of the Hudson River from the plinth is simply stunning.

The Irish Hunger Memorial is a unique and special place where the victims of this famine are commemorated.

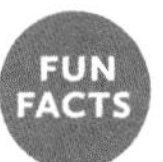

In 2017, the monument underwent a very costly, 4.5-million euro renovation, which is actually more than its original building cost. The renovation was prompted due to significant damage after water infiltration.

INSTAGRAMMABLE PLACES IN THE NEIGHBORHOOD

COFFEE, FOOD AND SHOPPING	the shopping center Brookfield place (4 min. walk)
SEE	The Teardrop Park with a lovely water playground (4 min. walk)
	World Trade Center (5 min. walk)

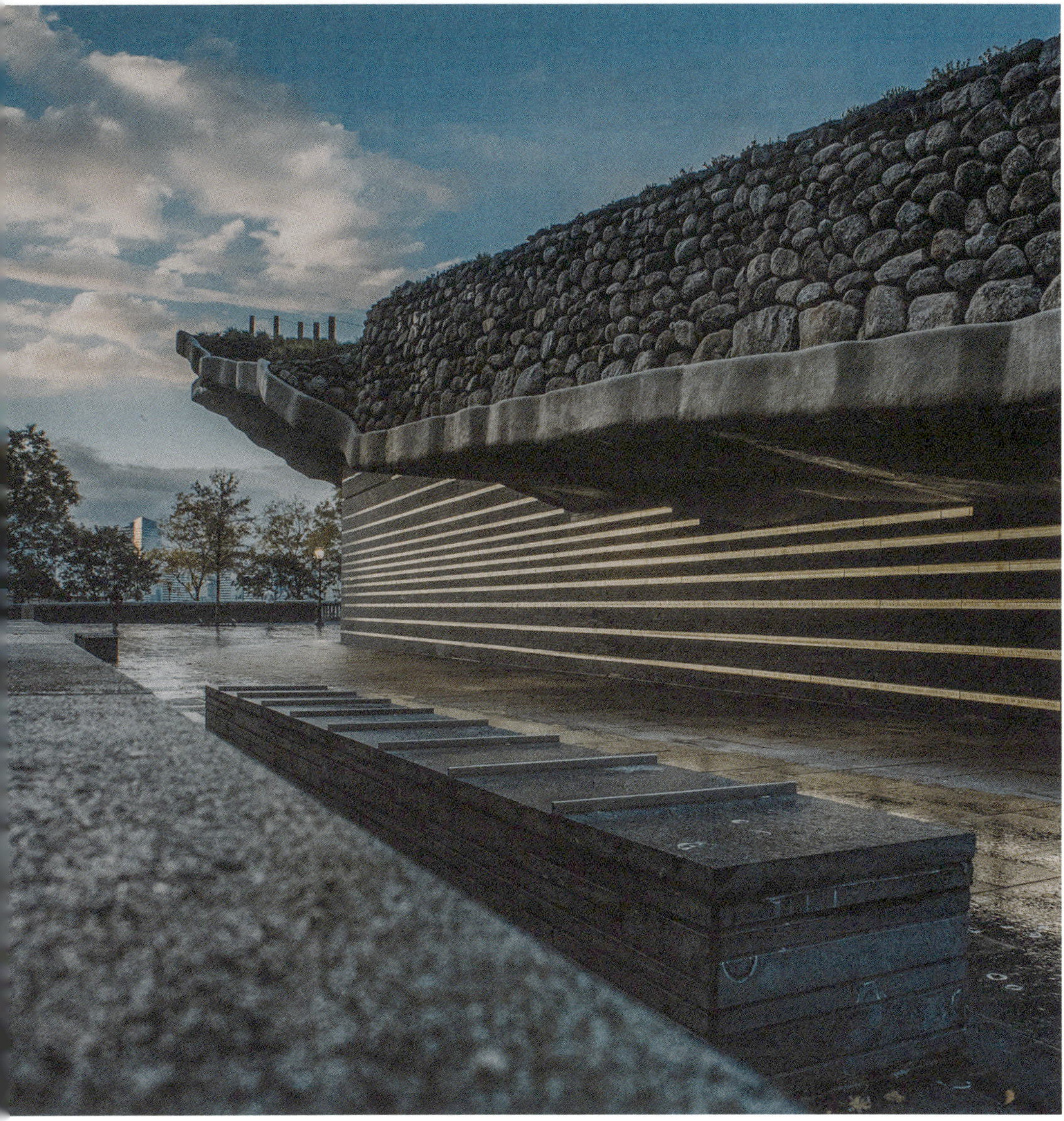

#irishhungermemorial #downtownnyc #batterypark #nycarchitecture

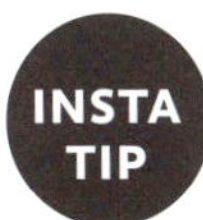

Use the lines with quotes as "leading lines". They can help to direct the attention of the viewer to the right place in the picture.

⑩ SOUTH STREET SEAPORT

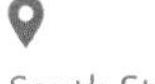

South Street Seaport

HOW TO GET THERE
Subway 2 or 3 (red) to Fulton Street

Subway 4 or 5 (green) to Fulton Street

The South Street Seaport is the historical area where you can really see and feel New York's amazing maritime history. The restored 19th century ship houses in the seaport have since been transformed into fashionable restaurants, coffee bars and shops that all exude that unique port culture and ambience.

Old New York largely owes its rapid (economic) growth to its port (which was one of the world's largest ports at the time). From 1822 until its move to the Bronx in 2005, the Fulton Fish Market, America's oldest fish market, was also located here.

The South Street Seaport is still recovering after the hit of Hurricane Sandy in 2012. Since then several ambitious projects have been launched to rebuild this area.

During the summer months, this neighborhood can be very lively because of its many outdoor bars, events and the nice terraces on the piers. The piers also offer stunning views of Manhattan, Brooklyn, the Brooklyn Bridge and the restored historical sailing ships that are docked here.

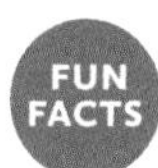

At one time, Water Street mainly had brothels, rum holdes and a lively rat population...

Godzilla first came ashore near the Fulton Fish Market.

INSTAGRAMMABLE PLACES IN THE NEIGHBORHOOD

COFFEE	Jack's Stir Brew Coffee: 222 Front Street
FOOD	El Luchador: Tacos vs Burritos! 87 South Street
SHOP	Bowne & Co. Stationers: 211 Water Street
SEE	Imagination Playground: Front Street

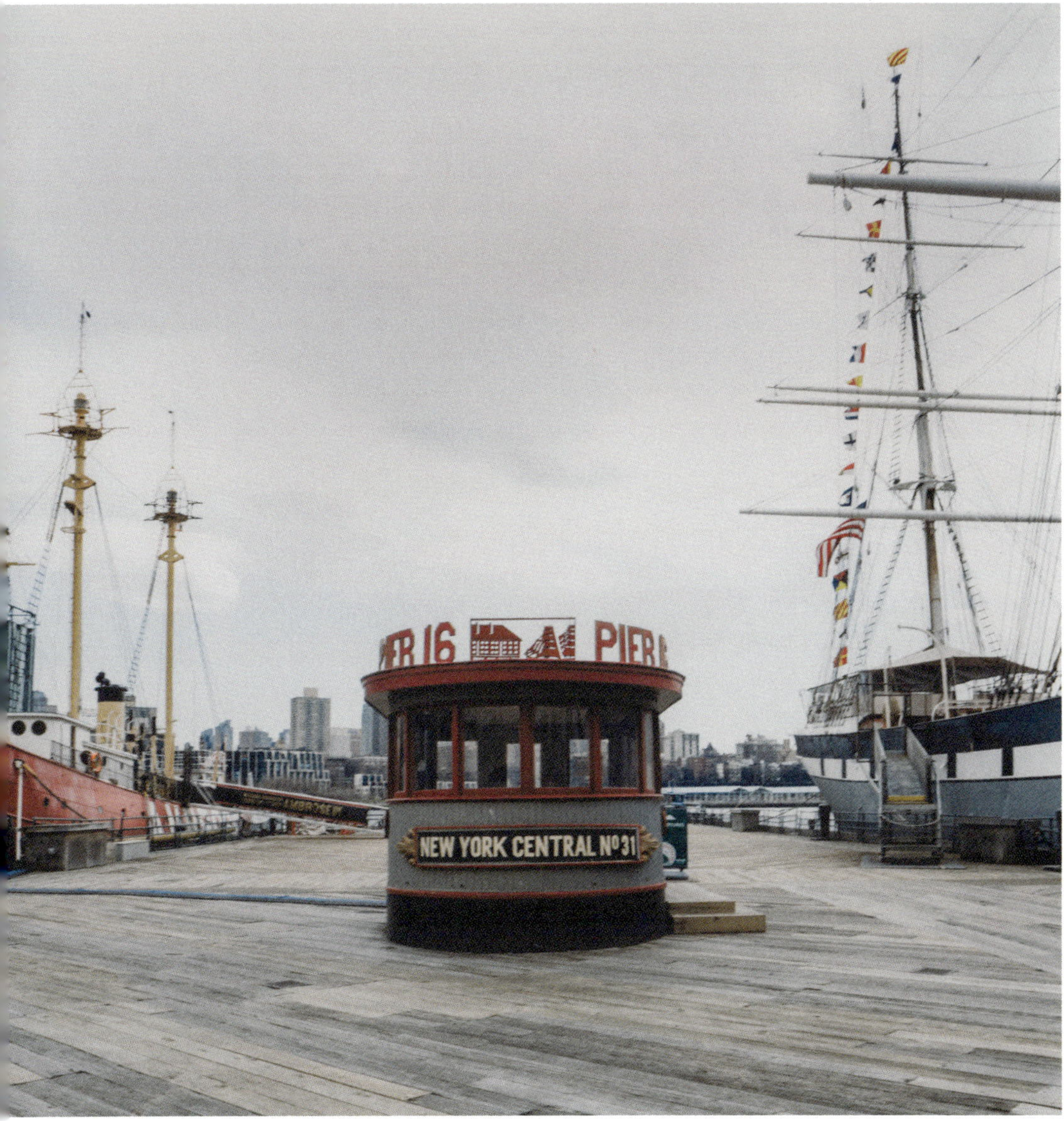

#southstreetseaport #seaportdistrict #seaportnyc #historicnyc

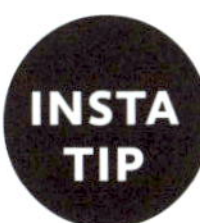

To capture the atmosphere of this neighborhood, make sure to include some "maritime objects". There are plenty of them and it's nice to play around with different angles, viewpoints and leading lines.

⓫ ECONOMY CANDY

Economy Candy
108 Rivington Street

HOW TO GET THERE
Subway M (orange) to Essex Street

Subway F or M (orange) to Delancey Street

Economy Candy originally began as a shoe and hat repair shop with a small push cart out front that sold candy to attract the attention of potential customers (the cart is still there).

When the Depression hit in the thirties, the candy cart became more profitable than the shoe shop, which is why the company changed its name to Economy Candy in 1937.

Nowadays this epic candy shops sells over 2,000 types of candy. The ceiling-high shelving units are stacked with vintage chocolate bars you can't find anywhere else and with sweets you never even surmised existed.

This definitely is a sweet trip down memory lane.

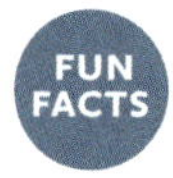

Economy Candy is New York's oldest candy shop and has been run by three generations of the same family since it was established.

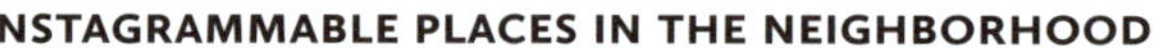

INSTAGRAMMABLE PLACES IN THE NEIGHBORHOOD

COFFEE	Ludlow Coffee Supply: 176 Ludlow Street (2 min. walk)
FOOD	The Meatball Shop: 84 Stanton Street (3 min. walk)
SEE	Tenement Museum: 103 Orchard Street (3 min. walk)
	Jump Into the Light VR Cinema: 180 Orchard Street (4 min. walk)

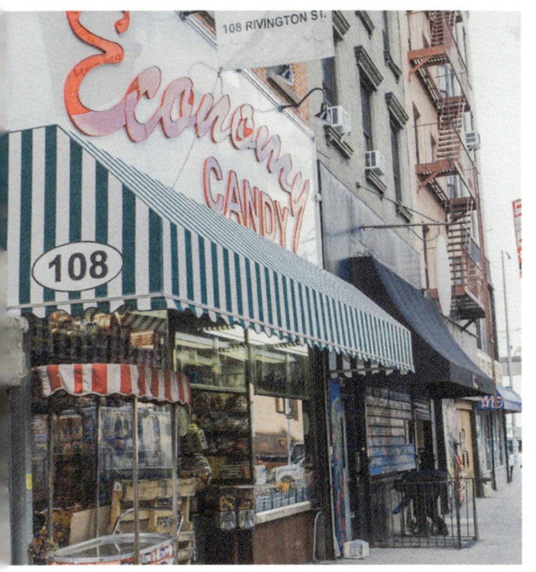

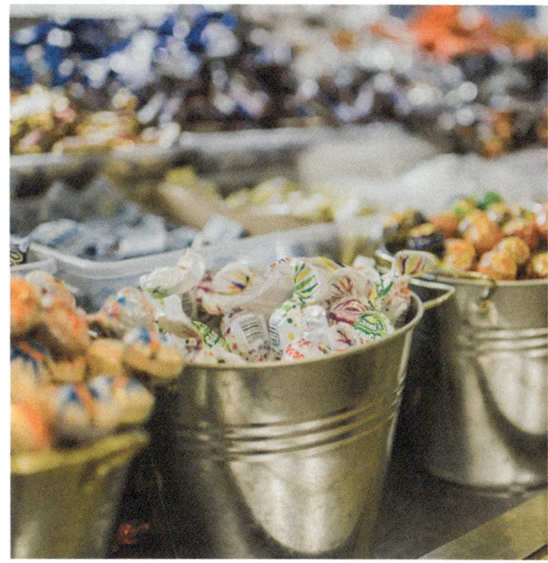

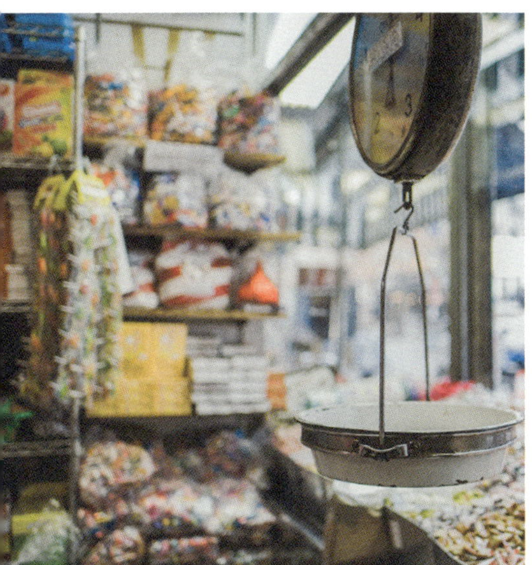

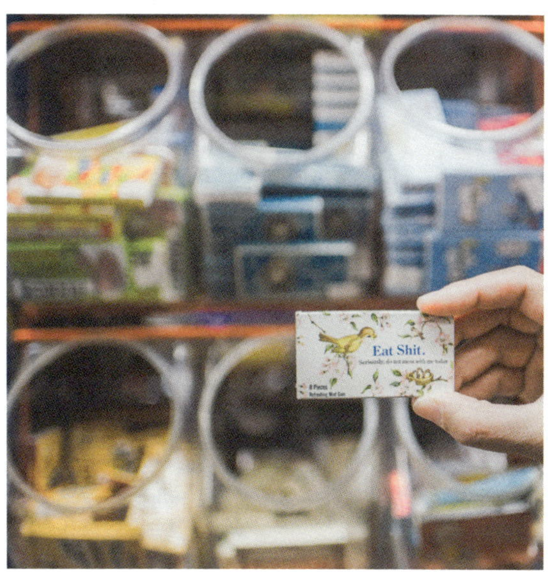

#EconomyCandy #vintagecandy #LowerEastSide #LES

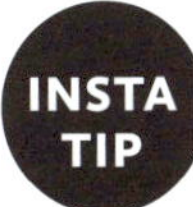

The inside of this shop can be overwhelming.

Try to focus on one product by placing it in front of a background of candy. The more space between your subject and the background, the more of a blurry background you can create.

12 METROGRAPH

Metrograph
7 Ludlow
Street

HOW TO GET THERE
Subway F (orange) to East Broadway

Subway B or D (orange) to Grand Street

Subway M (orange) to Essex Street

Metrograph is an arthouse cinema, which only screens archive-quality 35 mm prints. This movie theatre also programs new Indie films and New York classics, but is also a book shop, a candy shop, a lounge and a restaurant.

The building's stylish minimalist design is definitely worth admiring. The entire place exudes a certain twenties elegance, offsetting nostalgia with modern touches.

The small book shop has an amazing selection of books for literary cinema fans. Many of the books they sell here are very rare.

But the candy shop is the real Instagram hit. The sparkling white shelves are stacked with beautifully packaged film snacks, that have been carefully arranged as if the owners have arranged everything for you so you can take a great picture.

The balcony lounge and restaurant were inspired by a commissary or studio restaurant from the Golden Age of Hollywood. The perfect place to sip a cocktail or order something from the Writer's Menu.

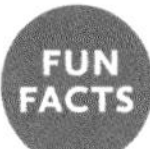

The Writer's Menu was created especially for writers, so they could eat and drink with one hand, while continuing to write with the other. How about some Apples & Cashew Butter, Fried Chickpeas & Popcorn, Bresaola... Are you hungry yet?

Famous stars like Patti Smith, Sienna Miller, Jake Perlin and David Cross attended The Metrograph Theater's anniversary party!

INSTAGRAMMABLE PLACES IN THE NEIGHBORHOOD

COFFEE AND FOOD	the Metrograph lounge or restaurant, *quoi*!
SEE	The Tenement museum (6 min. walk)
	Chinatown (10 min. walk)

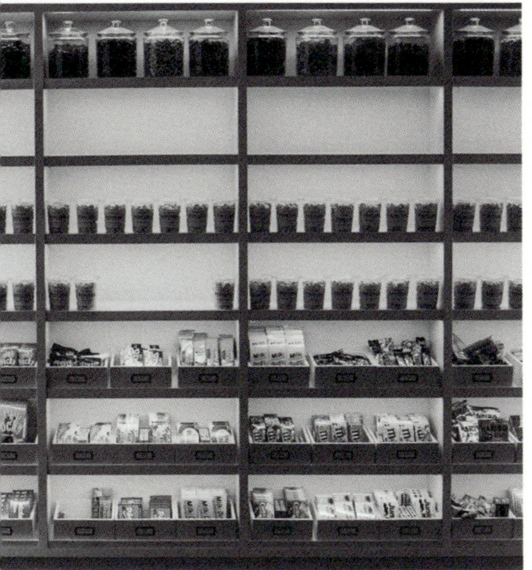

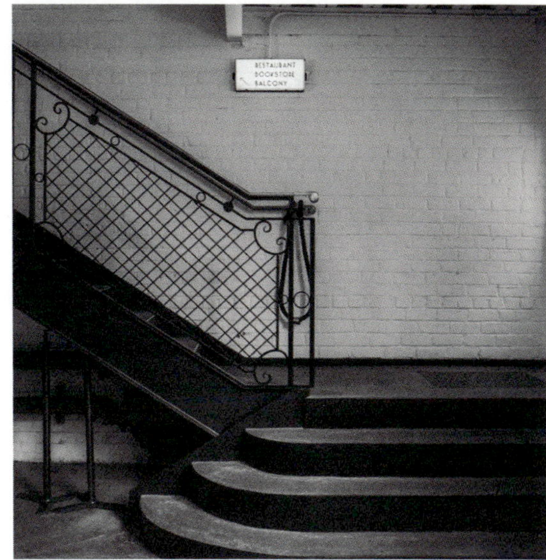

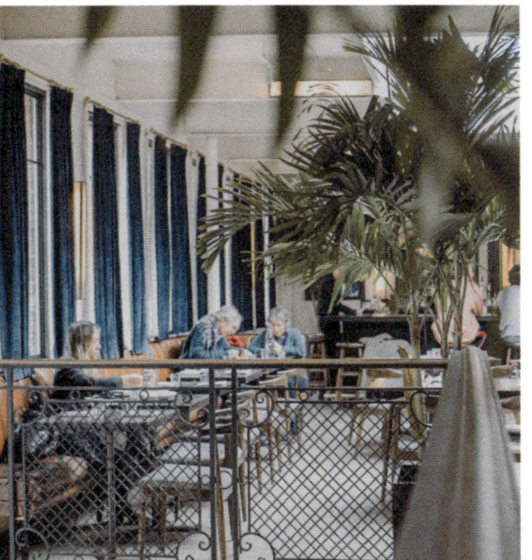

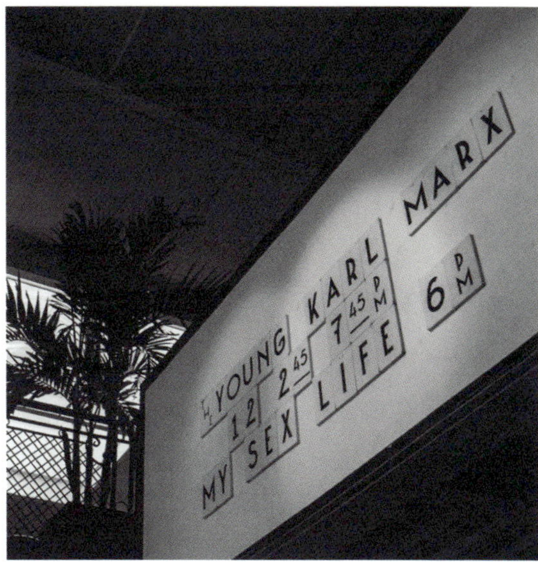

#metrograph #metrographnyc #LowerEastSide #LES
@metrographnyc

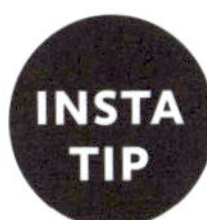

As this is an inside environment, there will not be a lot of light. Make sure to use all available light and look for the most lit spots.

13 TAIYAKI

Taiyaki NYC
119 Baxter
Street

HOW TO GET THERE
Subway 6 (green) to Canal Street

Subway N or Q (yellow) to Canal Street

Subway B or D (orange) to Grand Street

$

Taiyaki NYC is famous for its fish-shaped Japanese waffle that is chewy on the inside and crispy on the outside. It's absolutely delicious and blends perfectly with the glorious artisan flavors of their soft serve ice cream.

Taiyaki is usually a fish-shaped cake, made of batter that resembles waffle batter. This is then poured into a cast iron mould after which a filling is piped into it (e.g. red bean paste). The result is a warm cake cone that is filled with delicious ice cream flavors like matcha and/or black sesame!

These ice creams are so pretty that it is almost a pity to eat them. Do take some photos before they start to melt. There are different "models" available. This is the perfect place for foodstagrammers with a sweet tooth.

Order a Unicorn Taiyaki if you want to sample the most photogenic ice cream or one of their seasonal creations, which they add to their menu on Halloween, Christmas and Easter.

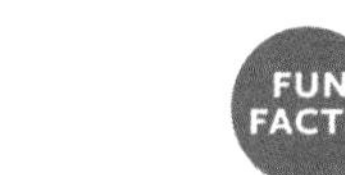

FUN FACTS The most literal translation of *Taiyaki* is fried fish! *Tai* is the king of Japanese fish, while *yak* can mean to deep-fry, fry or grill.

INSTAGRAMMABLE PLACES IN THE NEIGHBORHOOD

MATCHA AND SWEETS	Cha Cha Matcha: 373 Broome Street (5 min. walk)
SEE	Lady Liberty Mural: 105 Mulberry Street (2 min. walk)
	Little Italy Sign: 177 Hester Street (2 min. walk)

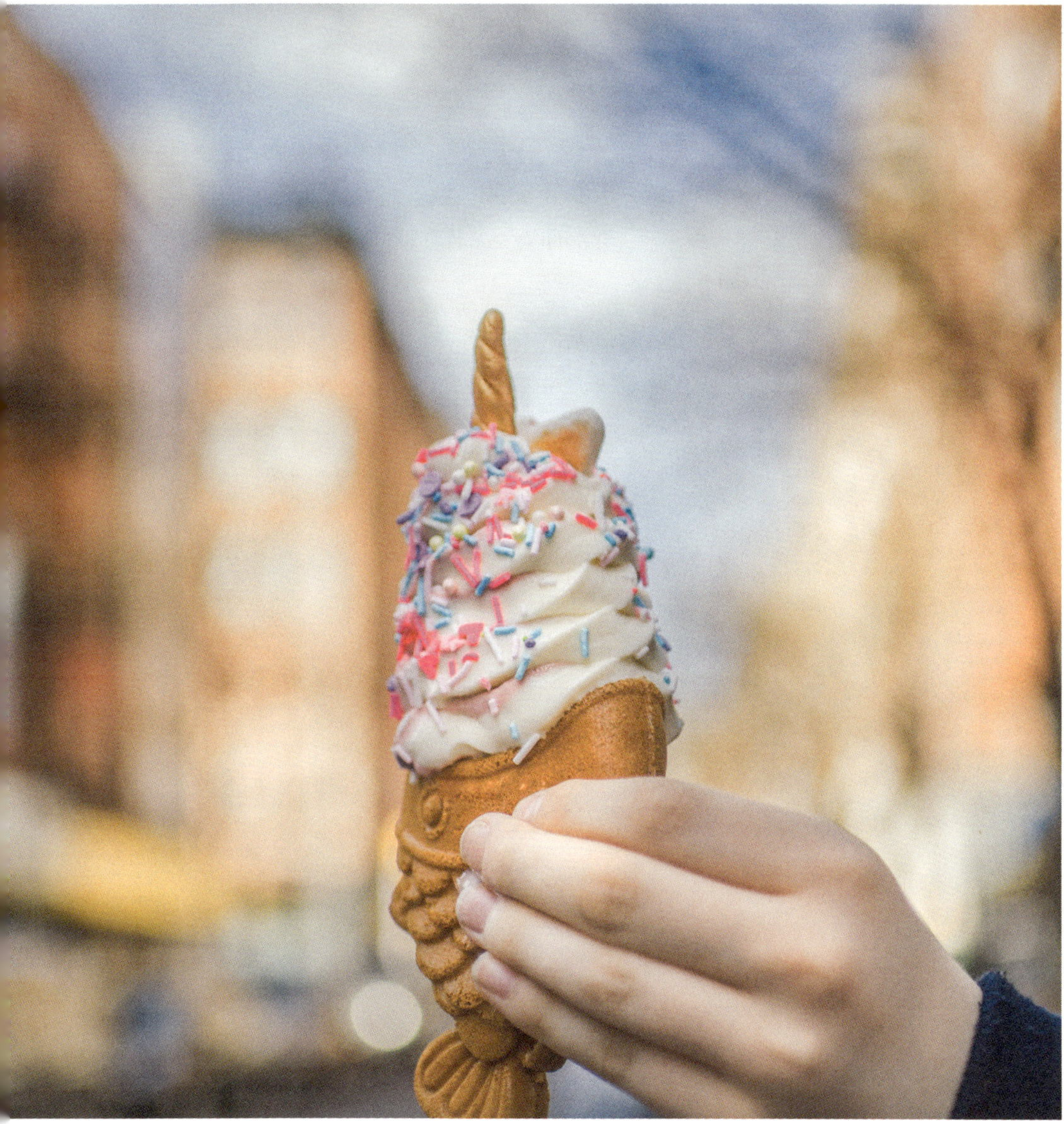

#TaiyakiNYC #LowerEastSide #LES #nycfood #nyceats
@taiyakinyc

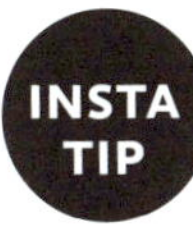

Hold your Teriyaki in front of the street. This way you create a distance between your subject (the ice cream) and the background, which results in a blurry background.

If you have enough patience and are feeling lucky, you can wait for the right colored cars to match your ice cream colors!

14 CHINATOWN

Chinatown

HOW TO GET THERE
Subway 6 (green) or the N or Q (yellow) to Canal Street

Subway 4 or 5 (green) to Brooklyn Bridge City Hall Station

Subway B or D (orange) to Grand Street

Chinatown is a veritable maze of tiny streets and alleys, with plenty of different scents, colors and flavors!

This famous neighborhood attracts visitors from around the world.

You won't know where to look first in Chinatown as there are such large quantities of (foreign) food ingredients everywhere: different types of fish and seafood, stalls with fresh herbs and vegetables and bins of mushrooms you may have never seen before.

Don't need any fresh produce but have a hankering? There are plenty of restaurants to choose from in this neighborhood. Ask a New Yorker for recommendations or check social media to find the best restaurants in Chinatown. Don't forget to try the dumplings!

There are countless souvenir shops in Chinatown where you can buy typical New York souvenirs. There are also plenty of creative, hand-made alternatives.

Chinatown is the perfect neighborhood for close-ups of interesting details or colorful street scenes.

FUN FACTS

New York has the largest Chinese population outside of Asia.

Some of New York City's few natural water sources were originally in the location where Chinatown is located today. To prevent contamination a canal was dug to the Hudson River in the early 19th century. The canal proved useless and was soon transformed into an open sewer. In 1819, it was filled and given a new lease on life as Chinatown's main street, Canal Street.

INSTAGRAMMABLE PLACES IN THE NEIGHBORHOOD

FOOD	Eggloo: 60 Mulberry Street
KIDS	Columbus Park: Mulberry Street & Baxter Street
SEE	Everything in this neighborhood!

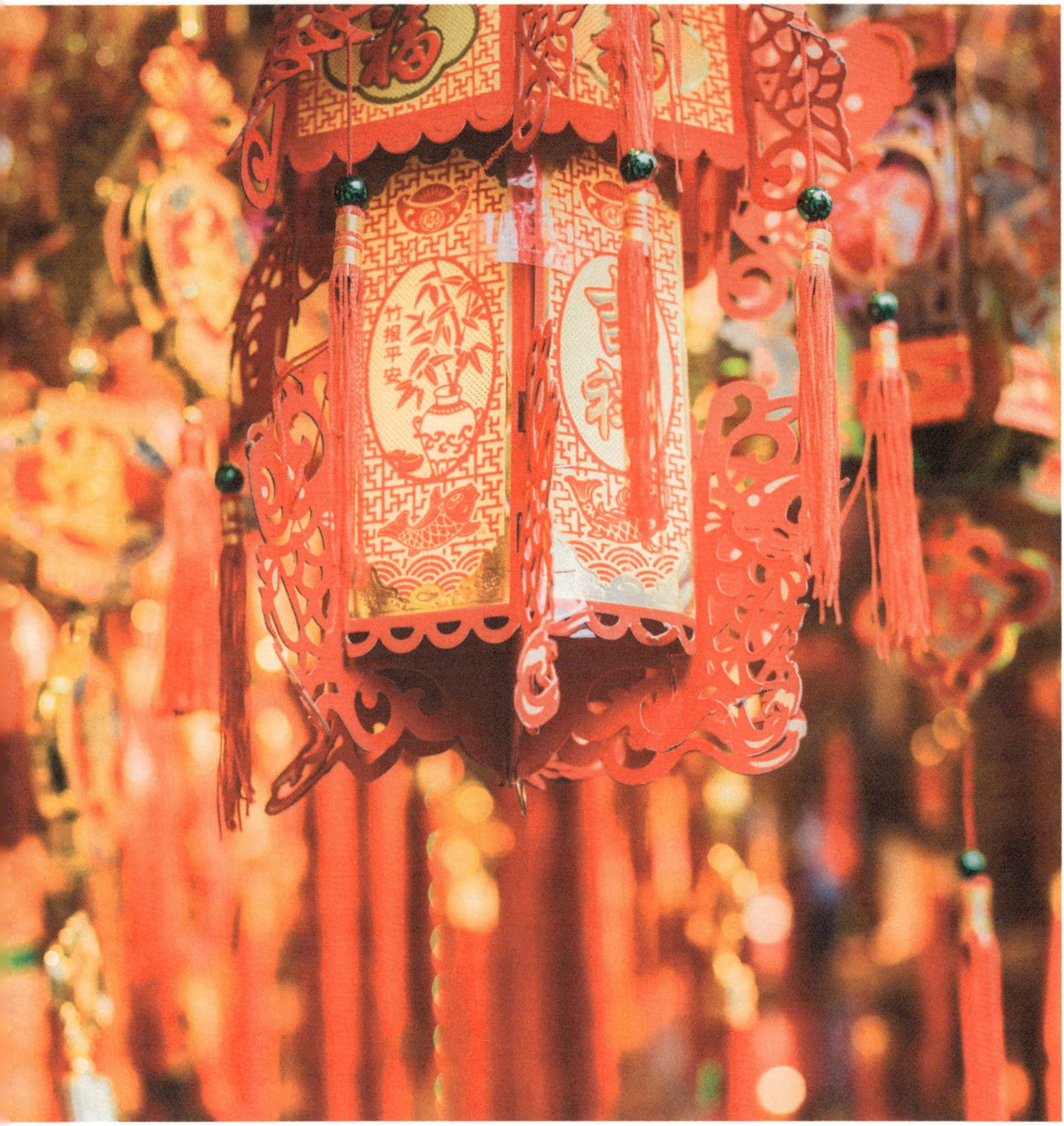

#chinatown #chinatownnyc #downtown #lowermanhattan

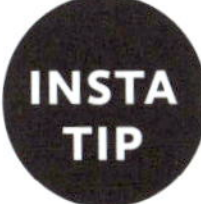

All the visuals in Chinatown can be overwhelming. Instead of making an overview you can also focus on one detail or one color to make your picture pop out on the Instagram feed. Consider visiting Chinatown after dark if you want to capture Chinatown's neon lights.

15 LITTLE ITALY

Little Italy

HOW TO GET THERE
Subway 6 (green) or the N or Q (yellow) to Canal Street

Subway 4 or 5 (green) to Brooklyn Bridge City Hall Station

Subway B or D (orange) to Grand Street

Little Italy's borders are gradually shrinking. This iconic neighborhood was once the lively center of Italian-American culture, spanning 50 city blocks in the old days!

Most of the Italian-American residents have since relocated to other (Italian) neighborhoods. On the south side, Chinatown is slowly encroaching on Little Italy while trendy NoLIta (deriving from North of Little Italy) is invading from the north.

Walk into Little Italy under the famous neon sign at the intersection of Hester and Mott Streets.

You can still get a real feel of Little Italy's distinctive and original character in the section of Mulberry Street between Canal and Broome. There are several restaurants here and Tristan Eaton's stunning mural of Audrey Hepburn.

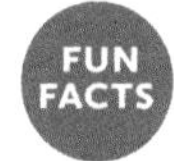

If you go to Italy, you will not find that dish we all love, i.e. spaghetti and meatballs, anywhere. It was actually invented in Little Italy by Italian immigrants.

Lombardi's Pizza in Spring Street is recognized as the first Stateside pizza by The Pizza Hall of Fame.

INSTAGRAMMABLE PLACES IN THE NEIGHBORHOOD

COFFEE AND FOOD	you are at the epicenter of Italian coffee and food!
SEE	Little Italy Sign: 177 Hester Street
	Audrey Hepburn Mural: 176 Mulberry Street

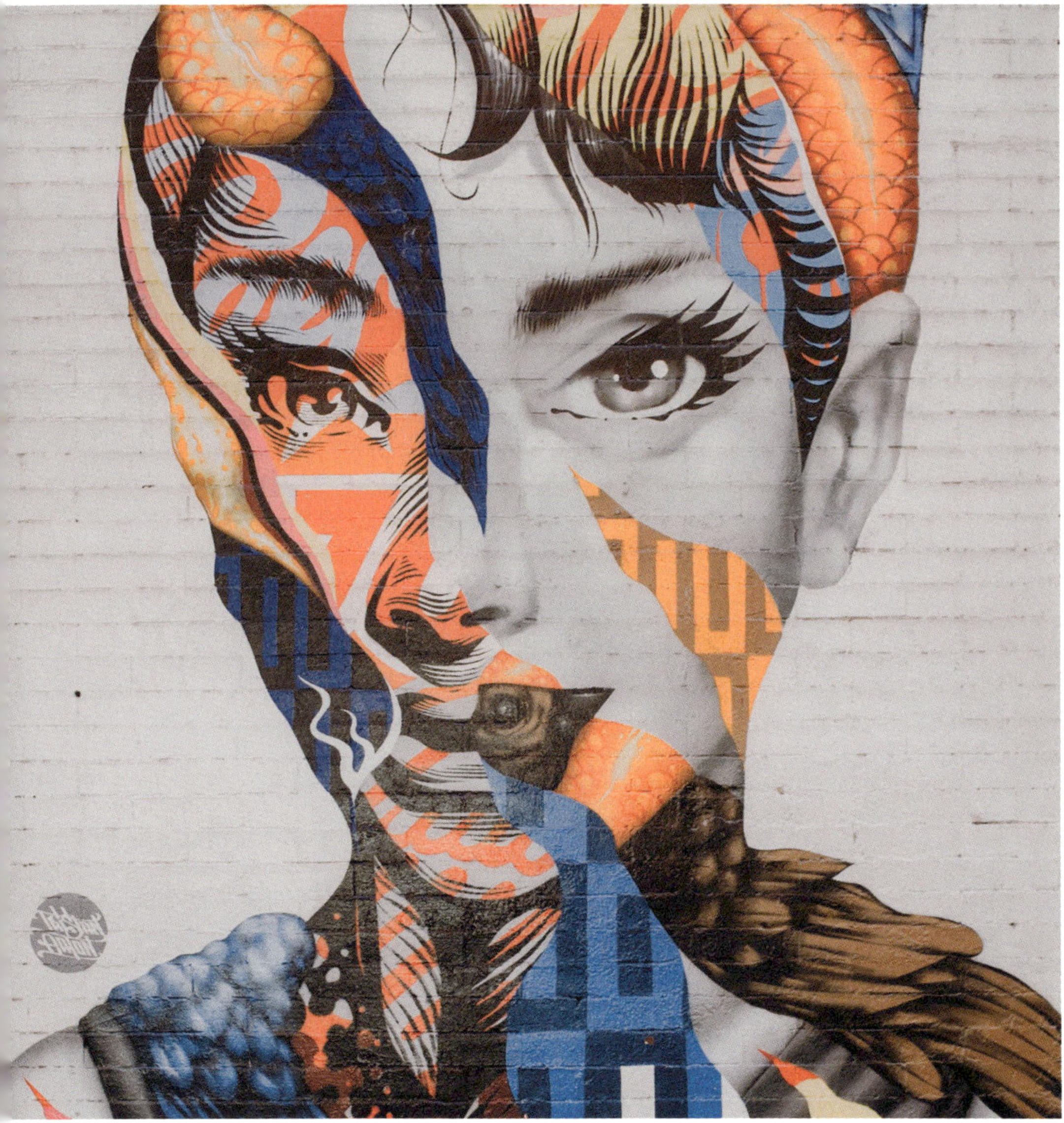

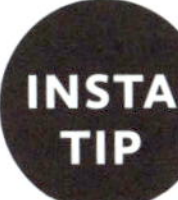

#littleitaly #littleitalynyc #downtown #audreyhepburnmural
@tristaneaton

INSTA TIP

A little patience ensures that no one stands in front of the artwork or, you can wait until someone passes by at the right time.

When posting a Mural on Instagram, always mention the artists name in a hashtag and/or link. They are mostly mentioned on the mural itself. The Audrey Hepburn mural is made by @tristaneaton.

The mural may not be the most typical view of Little Italy. It is definitely the most instagrammable one!

⓰ SOHO

Soho

HOW TO GET THERE
Subway 6 (green) to Spring Street

Subway B, D, F or M (orange) to Broadway - Lafayette Street

Subway W (yellow) to Prince Street

The name Soho refers to South of Houston Street.

In the seventies and eighties, Soho was very popular with artists. Nowadays this neighborhood is one of the city's best places to shop. Hipsters, trendwatchers and high-end fashion lovers can easily spend several days in Soho without ever being bored.

This hotspot also attracts trendy celebrities and hip models and is definitely the place to be for some good people watching.

You'll find plenty of unique shops, amazing restaurants, stunning (rooftop) bars, a lot of street art and many instagrammable spots along Soho's cobbled streets.

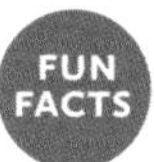

In the fifties, this neighborhood was called Hell's Hundred Acres, because of a series of fires in which several firemen were killed. The name reflects the atmosphere in this rundown neighborhood with its many small factories and sweatshops.

The Earth Room is located in a gallery on Wooster Street, Soho. A 22-inch-deep-layer of earth is spread across a 3,600-square-foot room. The artwork was created in 1977 and yes, they haven't changed the earth since then!

INSTAGRAMMABLE PLACES IN THE NEIGHBORHOOD

MATCHA Cha Cha Matcha: 373 Broome Street

FOOD Pietro Nolita: 174 Elizabeth Street
The Butcher's Daughter: 19 Kenmare Street

SHOP Sézane L'Appartement: 254 Elizabeth Street
Le Labo: 233 Elizabeth Street

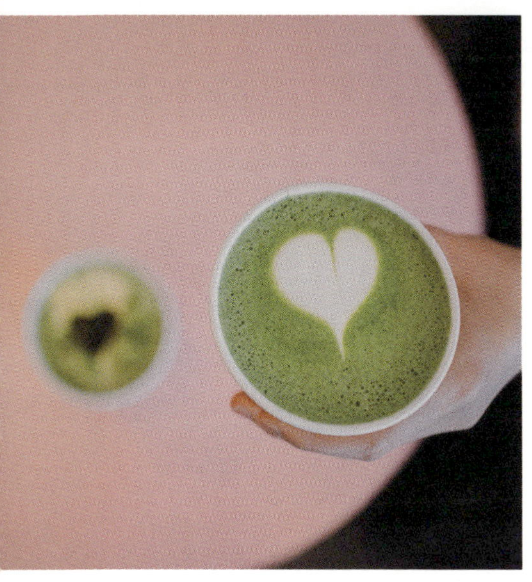

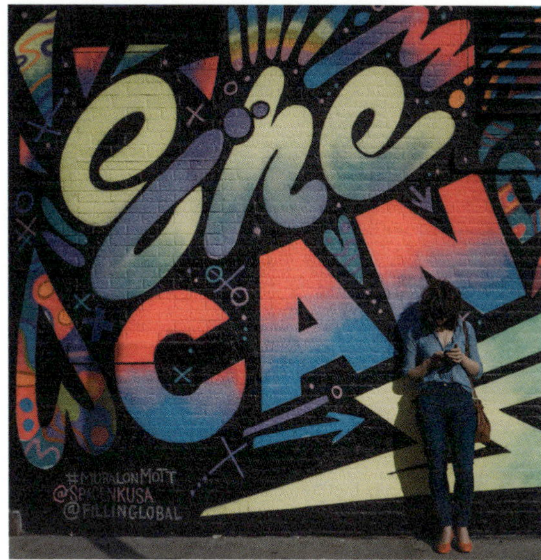

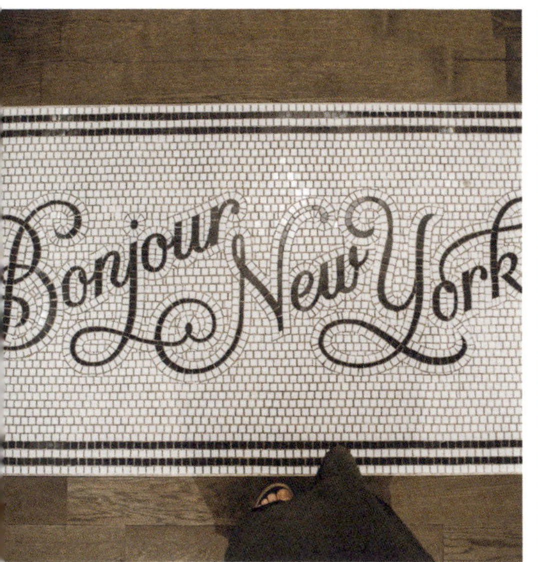

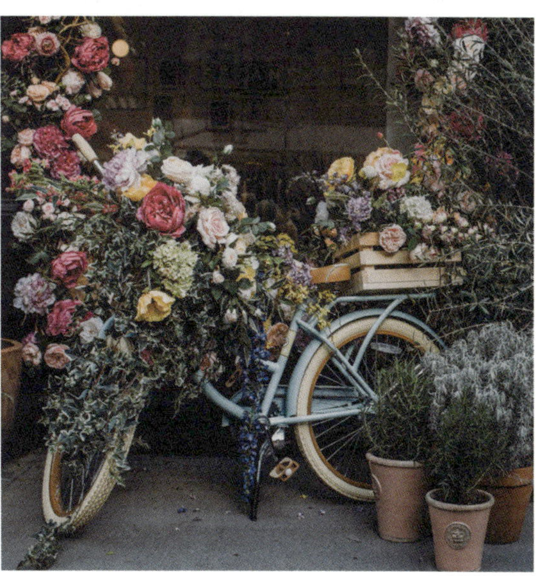

#soho #sohonyc #downtown #prettycitynewyork

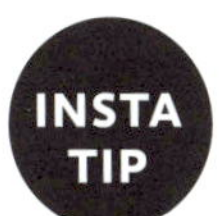

Soho is filled with instagrammable spots:

Top left: Cha Cha Matcha: the perfect place for pink and green combinations.

Top right: #themuralonmott by @jasonnaylor.

Bottom left and right: Sézane L'appartement: the perfect place to make Instagram hits!

17 WASHINGTON SQUARE PARK

Washington Square Park

HOW TO GET THERE
Subway 6 (green) to Astor Place

Subway B, D, F or M (orange) to West 4 Street - Washington Square

Subway R or W (yellow) to 8 Street

Washington Square Park is the beating heart of Greenwich Village. Many New Yorkers absolutely prefer this vibrant park over the city's many other parks.

Washington Square Park is not just a park but the place to be for aspiring artists, a meeting place for students, a popular place for protests and rallies, and the right spot for some daredevil events. The park has several playgrounds, both for children and dogs. The fountain is the park's epicenter and a great place to cool down sore feet during the hot summer months.

The park is well-known for its magnificent Washington Square Arch, honoring America's first president George Washington and a great backdrop for many special pop-up artworks or music concerts.

There's always something to see or do in this park, whether an epic pillow fight or a meeting of dachshunds and their owners. Take some time and allow yourself to be distracted or inspired by this unique place in New York City.

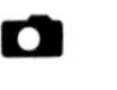

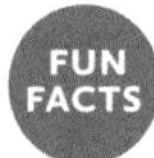

Manhattan's oldest tree lives in Washington Square Park: the Hangman's Elm is located in the park's northwest corner and is at least 330 years old.

In 1797, this park was used for public executions and as a public cemetery. More than 20,000 people are rumored to be buried under the park... *Brr...*

11 Washington Square Park North is the address of Robert Neville, the character played by Will Smith in the film *I am Legend*. The distinctive façade with its columns is easy to recognize.

INSTAGRAMMABLE PLACES IN THE NEIGHBORHOOD

FOOD AND DRINKS	MacDougal Street! One street, more than 40 restaurants and bars! (3 min. walk)
SWEETS	Dö, Cookie Dough Confections: 550 LaGuardia Pl (2 min. walk)
SHOP	The Evolution Store: 687 Broadway (5 min. walk)

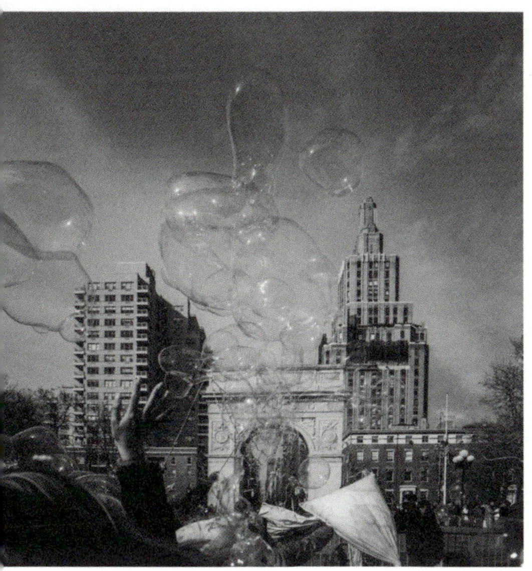
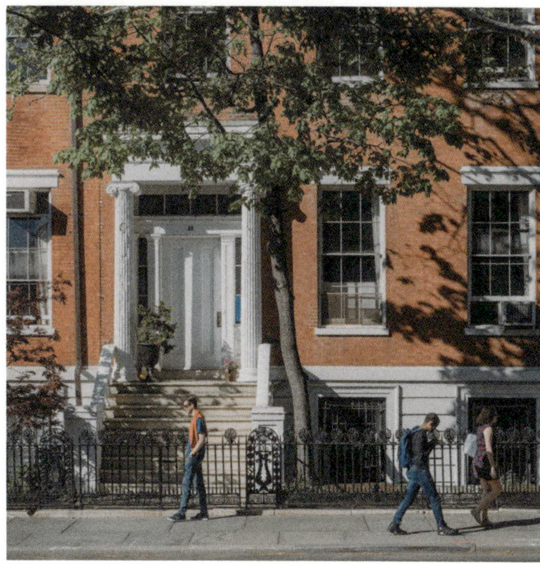
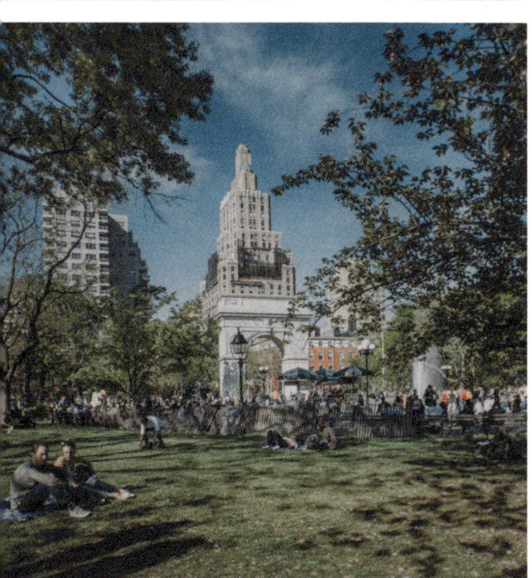
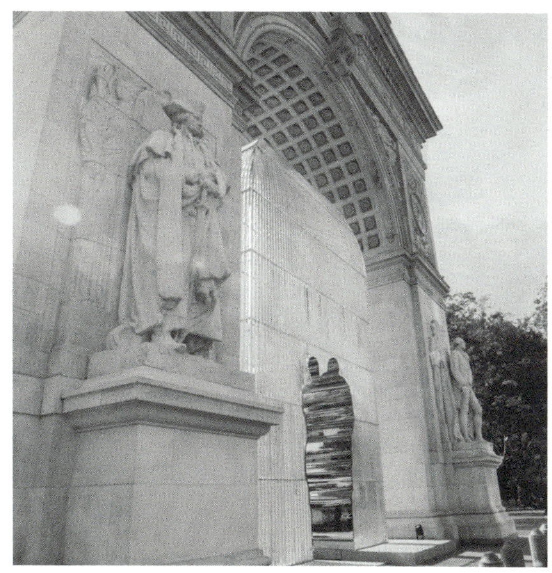

#washingtonsquarepark #washingtonsquare #greenwichvillage #thevillage #findyourpark

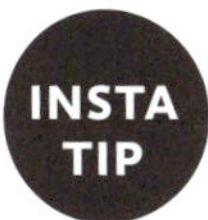

The Washington Square Arch is a magnificent monument, but it is also very large. So do take several steps back if you want to get a good picture of it.

Don't forget to have a look at the stunning houses around the park.

18 STRAND BOOKSTORE

Strand Bookstore
828 Broadway

HOW TO GET THERE
Subway 4 or 6 (green) or N (yellow) or L (grey) to 14 Street - Union Square Station

Have you ever wanted to know what 18 miles (29 km) of books look like? Then pop into the Strand Bookstore where you can take your pick from a collection of 2.5 million books!

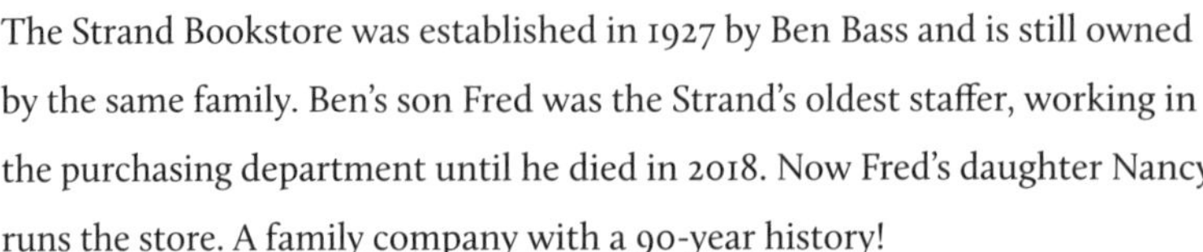

The Strand Bookstore was established in 1927 by Ben Bass and is still owned by the same family. Ben's son Fred was the Strand's oldest staffer, working in the purchasing department until he died in 2018. Now Fred's daughter Nancy runs the store. A family company with a 90-year history!

The bookshelves of this literary paradise are literally heaving under the weight of new, used and rare books, including a special edition of James Joyce's *Ulysses*, signed by the author himself and Matisse, who created the illustrations for this particular edition. It will set you back a mere 45,000 dollars...

Do you love a well-filled library? At the Strand you can also buy books by the foot. Are you looking for a book shelf with just red or yellow books or a book collection with backings in rainbow colors, or a collection of books with leather backings? They can provide you with a book selection to match any interior.

Three stories full of books and plenty of walls full of Instragrammable quotes. Heaven on earth for book lovers and photographers.

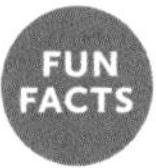

Patti Smith briefly worked at the Strand in the early seventies.

The Strand's most popular employee is Gizmo (or Gizzy to his friends). A dog! Gizmo is the merchandise director's dog. The store's resident canine visits the store now and then to promote books about animals. She also has her own Instagram account @NewYorkDog.

INSTAGRAMMABLE PLACES IN THE NEIGHBORHOOD

COFFEE AND FOOD	Breads Bakery: 18 E 16th Street (6 min. walk)
SHOP	if you want sneakers instead of books, Flight Club: 812 Broadway (1 min. walk)
SEE	Union Square Park (3 min. walk)

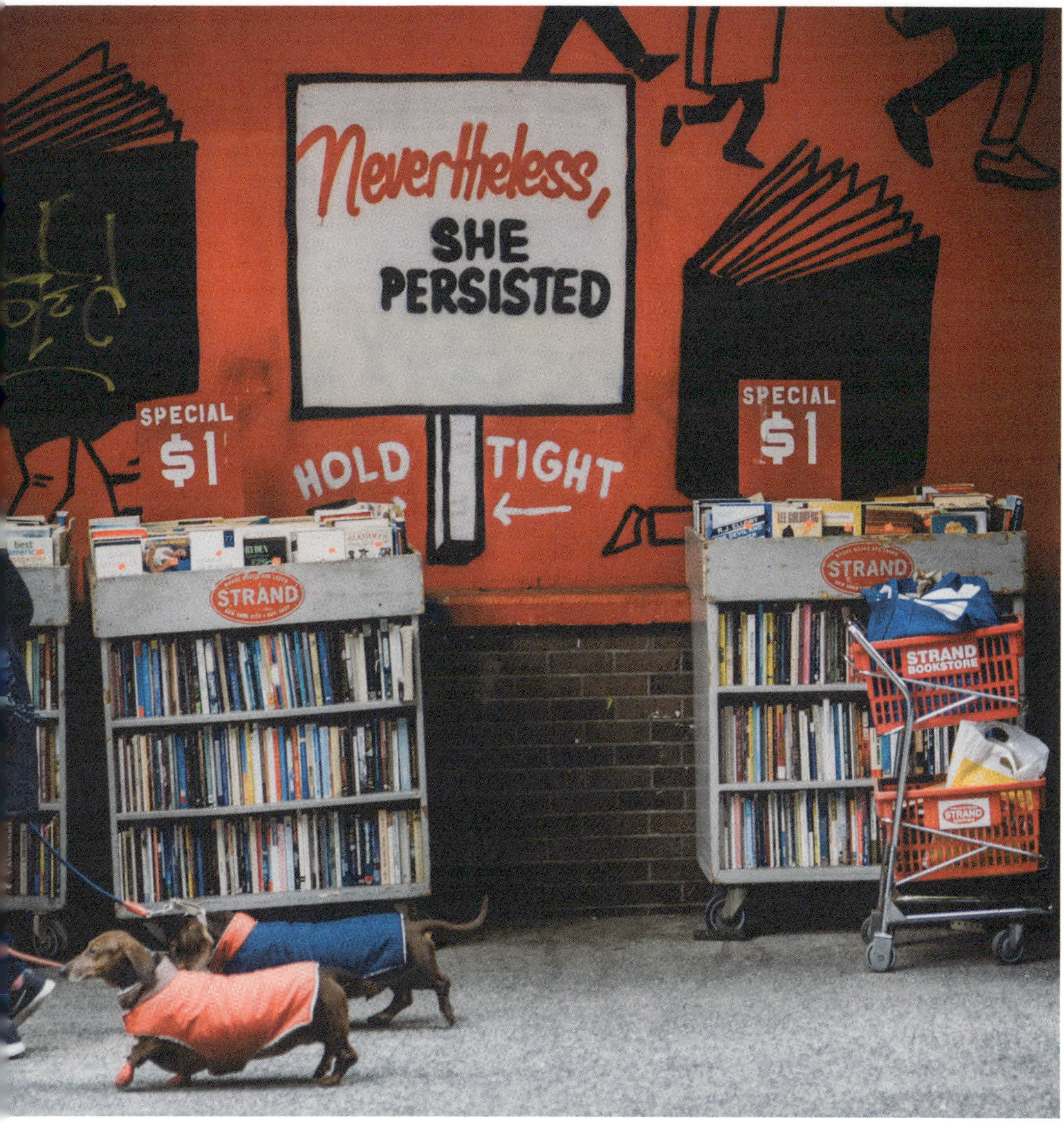

#strandbookstore #18milesofbooks #bookstagram #nycbookstore #strandbookstore

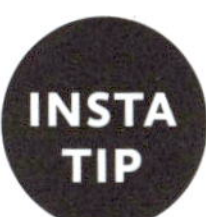

The Strand Bookstore is instagrammable on the inside and on the outside!

The color red plays an important role in the store. You can make use of this by looking for a composition with different red accents.

⓳ THE BOWERY MURAL

The Bowery Mural
76 E Houston Street

HOW TO GET THERE
Subway 6 (green) to Bleecker Street

Subway B, D, F or M (orange) to Broadway - Lafayette Street

You'll stumble upon the Bowery Mural wall on the corner of Houston Street and the Bowery. This rotating canvas for street art is managed by the real estate developers who have owned this wall since the eighties. Its owner Tony Goldman wants to provide a platform for contemporary street artists to showcase their art.

The Bowery Mural has already been used as a canvas by some of the world's leading street artists including Keith Haring, David Choe, Os Gêmeos, Banksy and many others for their powerful and controversial works.

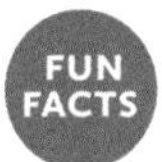

Bowery is the English version of *bouwerij*, an old Dutch word for farm or *boerderij*. In the 17th century, this area connected the farmland with the city's fringe.

In September 2017, Lakwena created a kaleidoscopic mural on the Bowery Wall, featuring the inscription Lift You Higher, as part of a collaboration with Instagram for their #kindcomments campaign.

INSTAGRAMMABLE PLACES IN THE NEIGHBORHOOD

COFFEE Bluestone Lane: 35 Spring Street (6 min. walk)

FOOD Tacombi Fonda Lolita: 267 Elizabeth Street (1 min. walk)

SHOP Sézane: 254 Elizabeth Street (2 min. walk)

SEE International Center of Photography Museum: 250 Bowery (2 min. walk)
The Debbie Harry Mural: 2 Bleecker Street (2 min. walk)
The Mickey Mural: corner Mott Street and E Houston Street (2 min. walk)

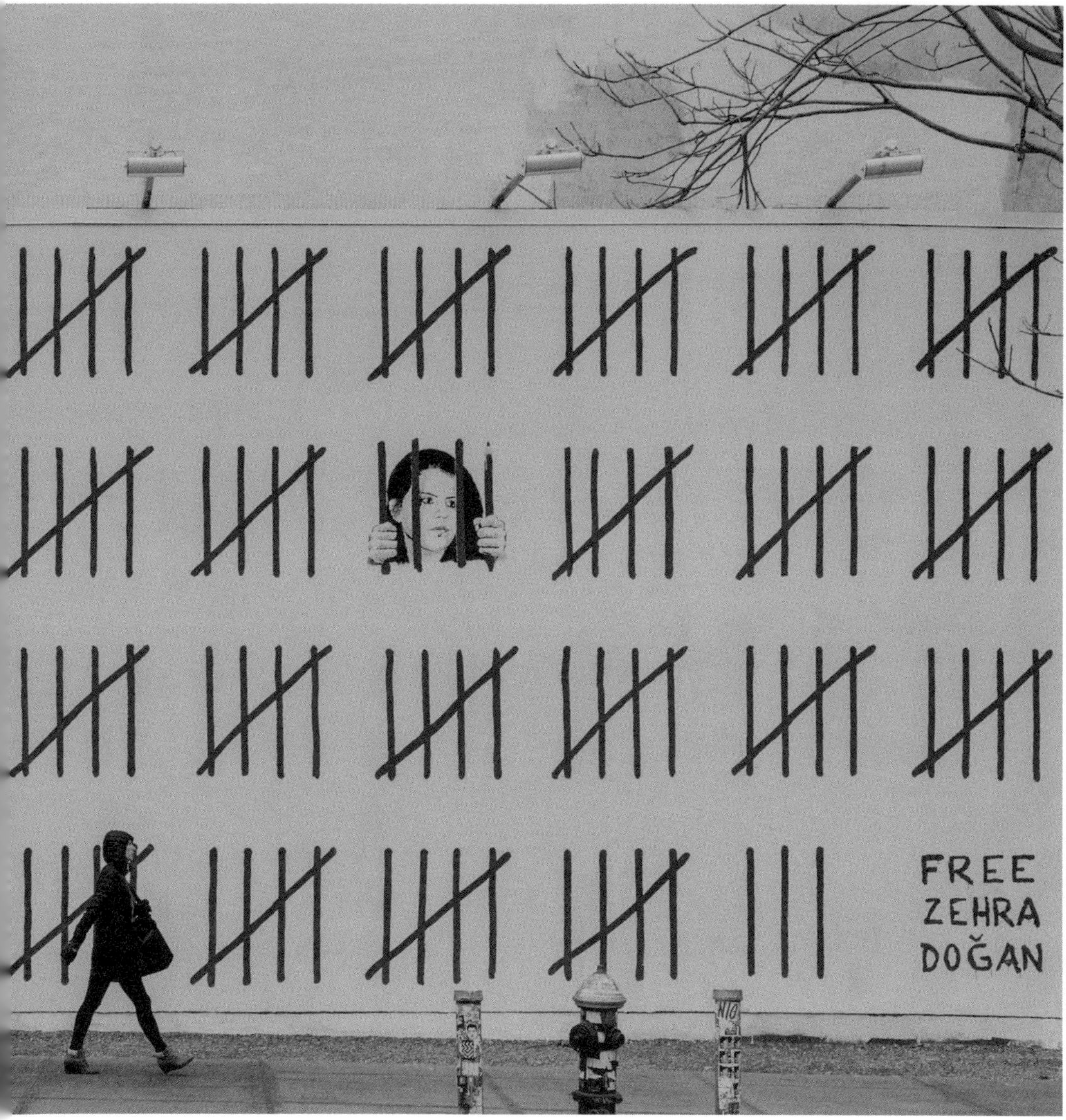

#bowerymural #bowery #nycstreetart #streetarteverywere #banksy
@banksy

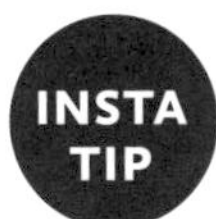

To highlight the dimensions of a mural, it is a good idea to photograph a person with it. Make sure the model fits in the composition without distracting the attention from the subject.

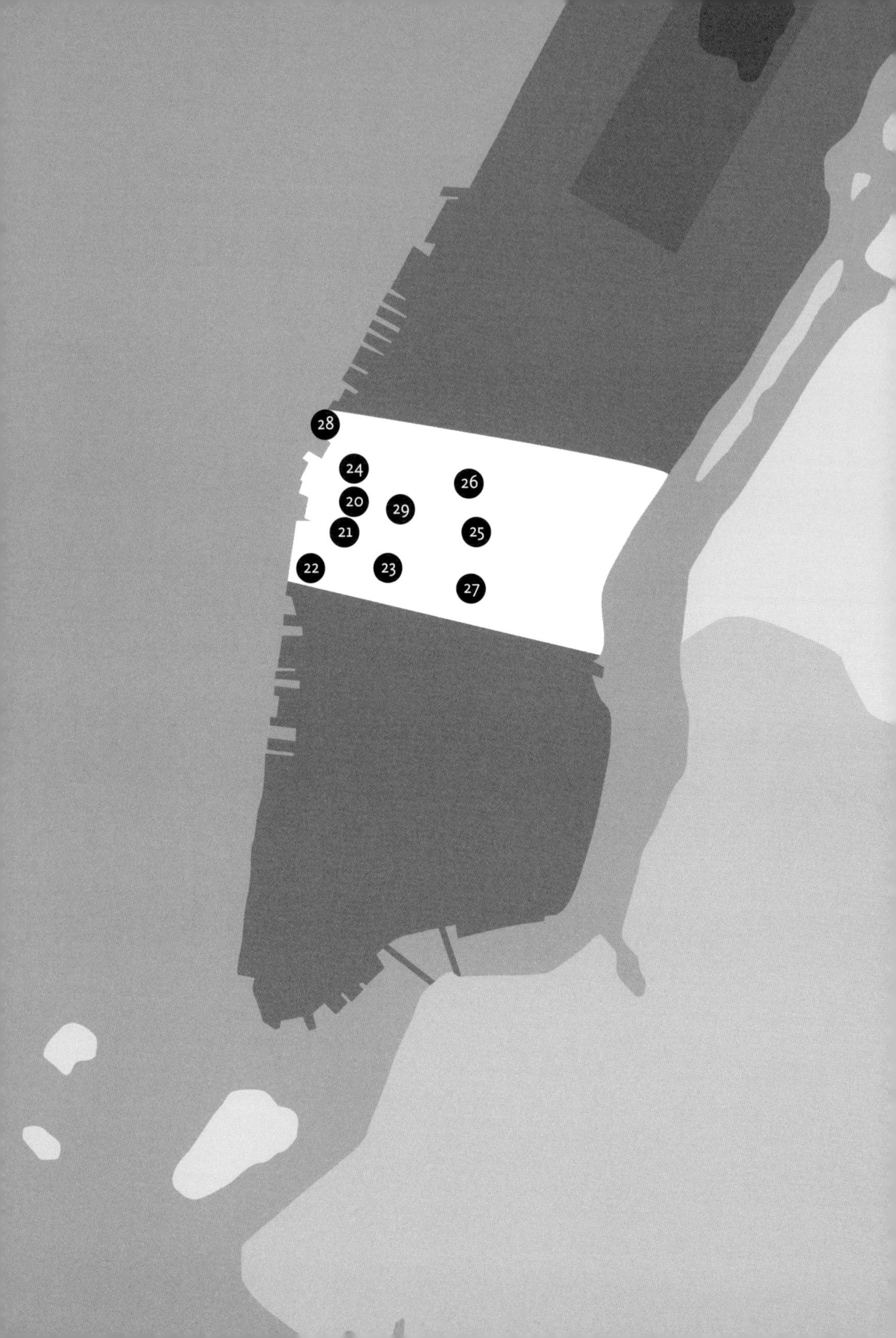
28
24
26
20
29
21
25
22
23
27

BETWEEN DOWNTOWN & MIDTOWN

 CHELSEA

Chelsea

HOW TO GET THERE
Subway 1 (red circle) or C or E (blue circle) to 23 Street

Chelsea connects Downtown with Midtown on the west side of Manhattan.

This neighborhood is bursting with innovation and art. It's the nucleus of the global art market and home to progressive galleries, imaginative street art, innovative projects and statement architecture. You name it, this neighborhood has it.

The High Line is an artwork in itself. The former railway line which was transformed into a park now connects Chelsea with the Meatpacking District. When you walk along the High Line, you'll find yourself literally strolling among new and eye-catching skyscrapers.

Chelsea has the highest concentration of art galleries in the world, most of which are located between 11th and 12 Ave, between W 21th Street and W 27th Street. They are famous for the experimental and progressive art they show, but you can also find something here if you're into more conventional art.

Do stop by the iconic Chelsea Hotel where famous artists like Jimi Hendrix, Bob Dylan, Robert Mapplethorpe and Patti Smith lived. Leonard Cohen and Janis Joplin spent many romantic nights here, Dylan Thomas drank himself to death in the hotel and Sid Vicious killed his girlfriend and later died here from an overdose in one of its rooms. Can you see why this hotel is so iconic?

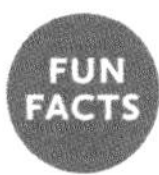

The *Titanic* was on its way to Chelsea Piers before it hit an iceberg.

The Movie *2001: A Space Odyssey* has been written by writer Arthur C. Clarke in his room at The Chelsea Hotel.

INSTAGRAMMABLE PLACES IN THE NEIGHBORHOOD

COFFEE Café Grumpy: 224 W 20th Street.
FOOD Billy's Bakery: 184 9th Avenue.
SHOP Comme Des Garçons Boutique: 520 W 22nd Street.
SEE Hotel Chelsea: 222 W 23rd Street.
The High Line

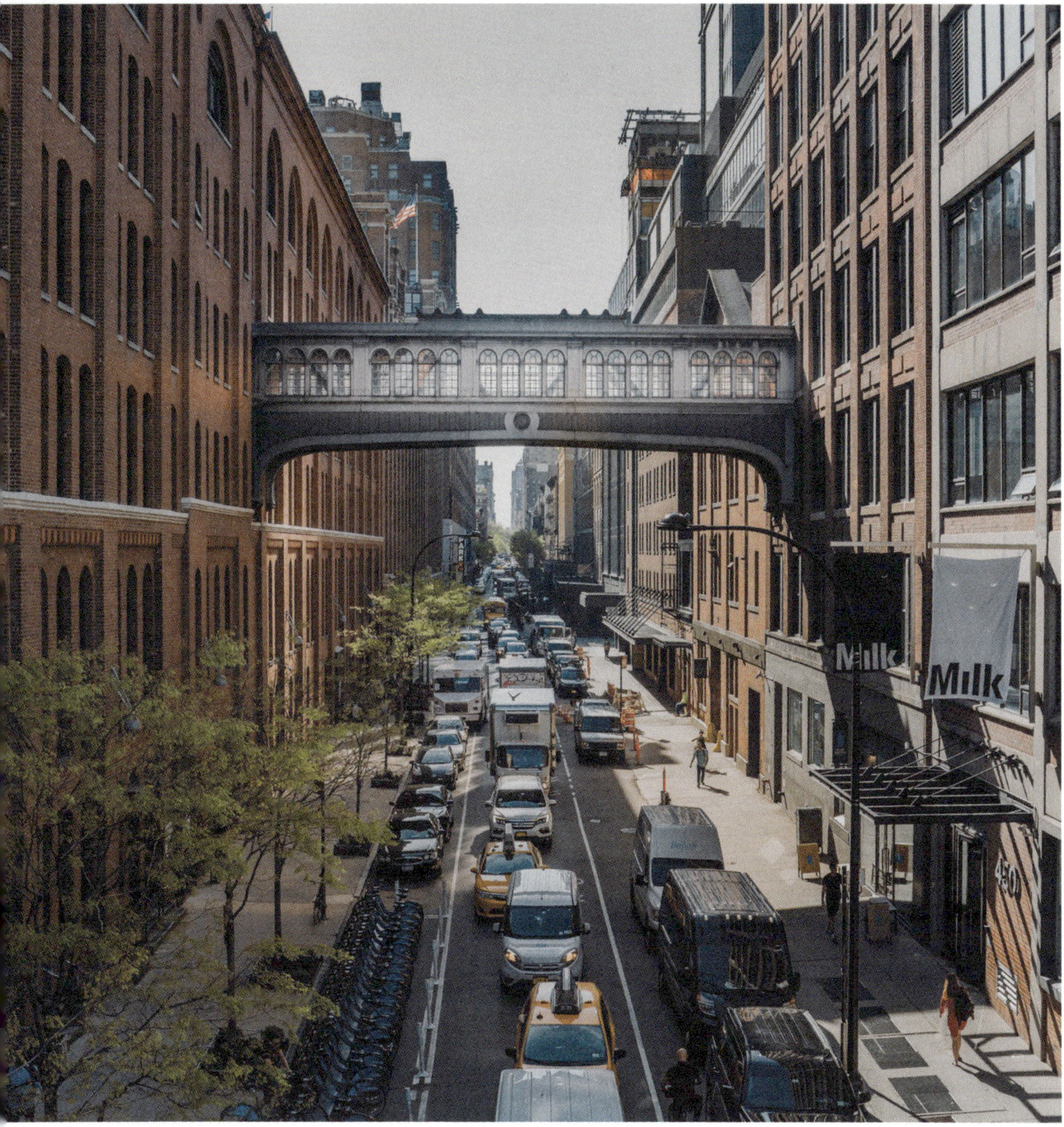

#chelsea #chelseanyc #chelseastreetart #nycstreetart #nycgallery

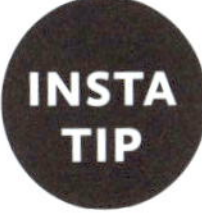

The Chelsea High Line is a prime vantage point for an overview of the streets of Chelsea. The High Line at W 15th Street is a very popular spot for Instagrammers because from there you can take a picture of the footbridge that connects the former cookie factory (now the Chelsea Market) with the former administrative buildings on the other side of the road.

21 CHELSEA MARKET

Chelsea Market 75 9th Avenue

HOW TO GET THERE
Subway 1 (red) or C or E (blue) to 23 Street

Chelsea Market is an enclosed food court and shopping mall and covers an entire block in the Meatpacking District.

Traditionally food has always been bought and sold in this neighborhood. Native Americans traded their grain on the banks of the Hudson River, butchers used ice blocks from the Hudson to keep their meat cool and the National Biscuit Company (Nabisco) had a factory in the building where the market is now located. Many of the factory building's authentic elements have been preserved, adding to the indoor market's unique character.

Check out the 40 (!) food stalls where they serve sushi, pizza, noodles, nuts, cheesecake, wine, beef jerky spices, cupcakes... if you can't find it here, you won't find it anywhere!

But there's more. Several local artists, creative entrepreneurs and artisan companies have set up shop here, selling their products in the Artists and Fleas shop (or the "collective retail experience" as they like to call it).

With over 9 million visitors a year, Chelsea Market is one of New York City's most popular attractions. It can get very busy here, especially on the weekend.

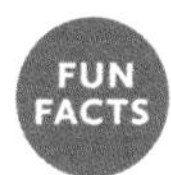

The famous Oreo cookie was invented in 1912 by Nabisco in the building where Chelsea Market is now located. You can find a few references to the factory and the Oreo cookie inside.

YouTube has a film studio on one of the floors above Chelsea Market. You can rent it for free, and use all the equipment, if you have a YouTube channel with more than 10,000 subscribers!

INSTAGRAMMABLE PLACES IN THE NEIGHBORHOOD

COFFEE, FOOD, SHOP	there are so much coffee, food and shops you could stay here a whole day without getting bored or hungry!
SEE	The High Line (1 min. walk)
	The Whitney Museum of American Art (6 min. walk)

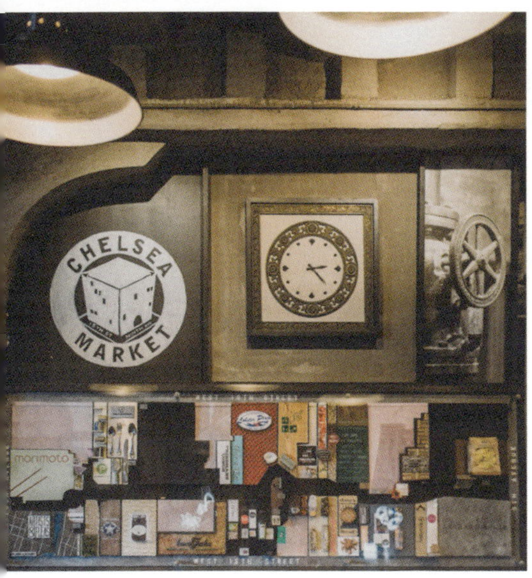

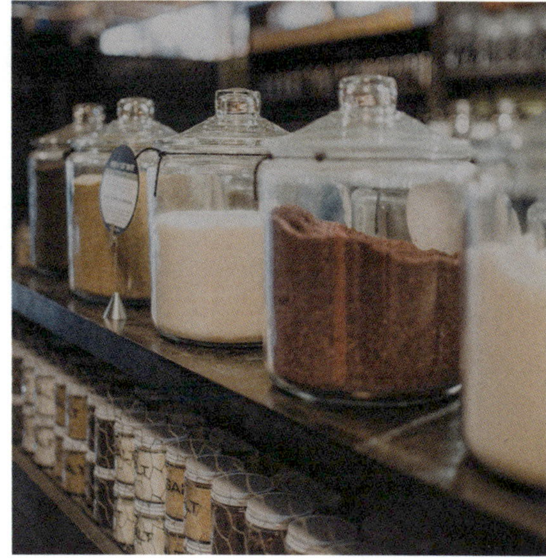

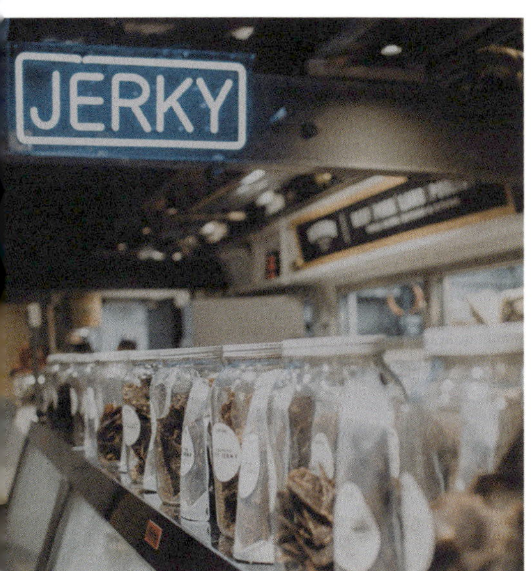

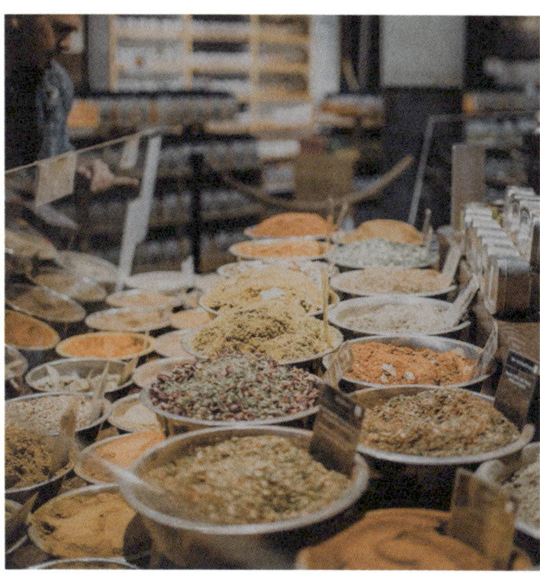

#chelseamarket #chelseanyc #spicemarket #nyceats
@chelseamarketny

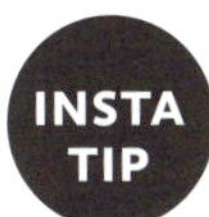

Chelsea Market is an inside market, so there is no natural light. Look for the available artificial light and use it as much as possible when taking pictures.

22 WHITNEY MUSEUM OF AMERICAN ART

Whitney Museum of American Art
99 Gansevoort Street

HOW TO GET THERE
Subway A or C (blue) o L (grey) to 14 Street/ Avenue

Subway 1, 2 or 3 (red) to 14 Street

$

The Whitney Museum is located in the Meatpacking district in a distinctive building that was designed by Renzo Piano. The museum has 8 stories, including a theatre, a library, a reading room, a café on the top floor and various observation decks that look out onto the High Line, Greenwich Village and the Hudson River. What a view!

The museum's collection includes a wide range of contemporary American artworks, with an emphasis on works by living artists where possible. Consequently the museum has always purchased works in the year in which they were created, often well before the artist became famous. Cindy Sherman, Andy Warhol, Alexander Calder, Sally Mann... are just a few of the 3,400 artists whose works you can see here.

Many tourists will have never heard of the Whitney, but if you like contemporary art this is definitely a must-see.

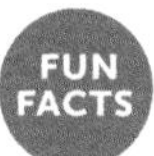

In 1976, the Whitney hosted an exhibition about the body as art. One of the bodybuilders on display was Arnold Schwarzenegger.

In 2014, the Whitney loaned two paintings by Edward Hopper to the White House where President Obama hung them in his Oval Office.

INSTAGRAMMABLE PLACES IN THE NEIGHBORHOOD

FOOD — The cafe on the 8th floor offers toasts, soups and salads and above all an amazing view. On Fridays and Saturdays you can also sip a cocktail!

SHOP — Chelsea Market: 75 9th Avenue (5 min. walk)

SEE — The High Line (1 min. walk)

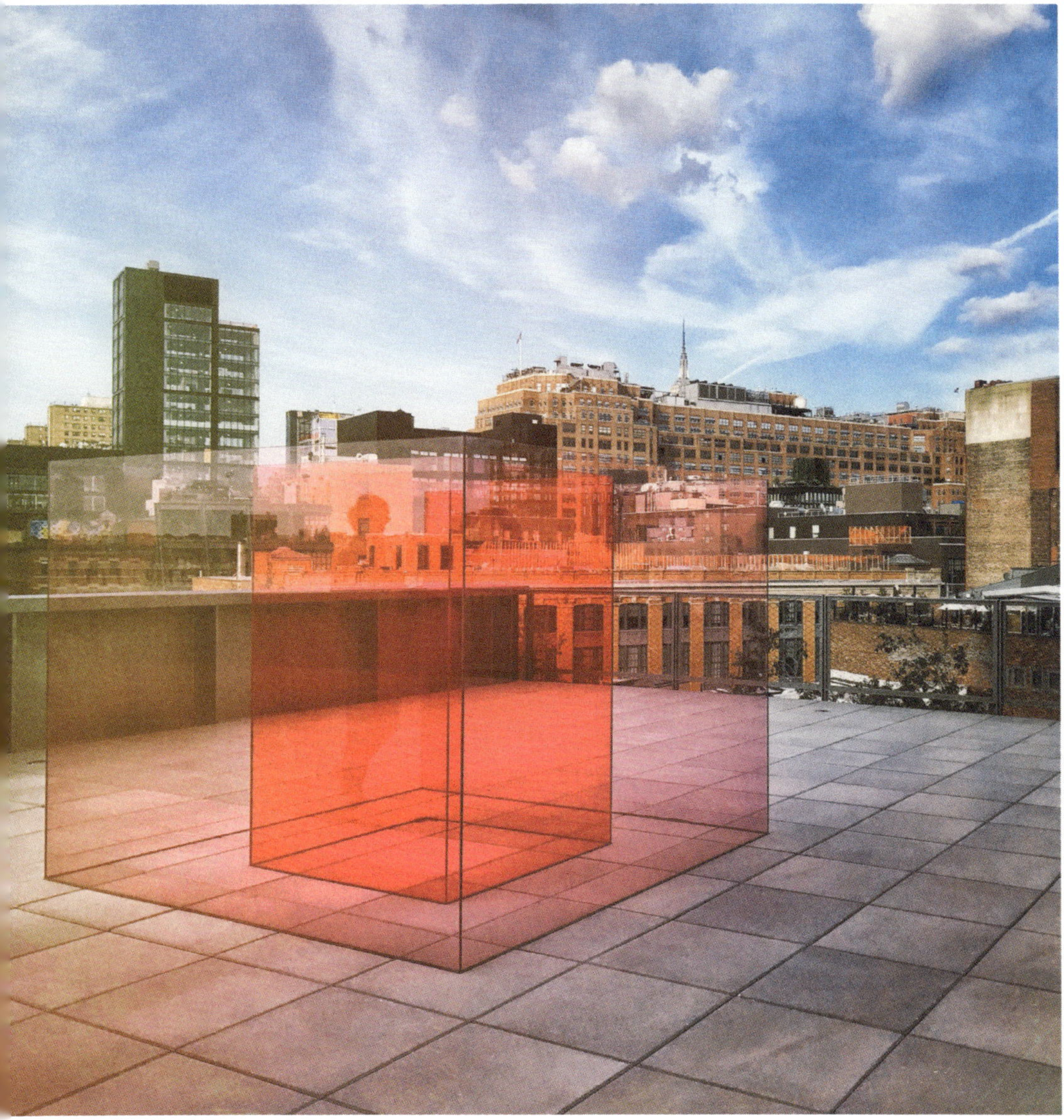

#whitneymuseum #whitneycollection #americanart #nycmuseums #meatpackingdistrict @whitneymuseum

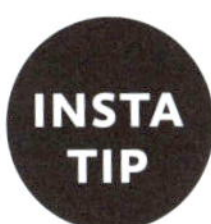

The observation decks also feature wonderful pieces of art. When taking pictures here, you can combine the art with the New York skyline. Double beauty!

On this picture: Installation view Pacific Red (I-V), (detail) 2017 by Larry Bell © Larry Bell

㉓ LIFE UNDERGROUND

Life Underground 14th Street/ 8 Avenue Subway Station

HOW TO GET THERE
Subway A, C, E (blue) or L (grey) to 14 Street/ 8 Avenue

If you happen to end up in this subway station, you'll might think there's nothing special about it at first glance. But once you notice the tiny figures, you'll be tempted to seek them all out. Don't forget to look up or down now and then...

The designer of these tiny figures is Tom Otterness. He was inspired by the construction of the subway station, which explains why so many of the sculptures carry large tools. Another source of inspiration was the class struggle and corruption, as you can see in the figure of the working woman, who is reading a book while sitting on a dead businessman who is laying on a pile of money.

Life underground is not the only place where you can see work by Tom Otterness:

You can find a giant sculpture in a playground at 42nd Street, between 11th Ave and 12th Ave. You can climb through its arms and slide back through its legs.

You can find The Real World, a mix of fun characters in a fairy-tale world, that you can walk in between, under and over, in Rockefeller Park.

"A lot of work is about class and money and crazy surrealist images that don't make any sense but it just sort of fits," according to Tom Otterness.

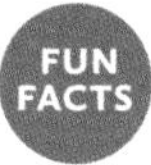

It took ten years to complete the installation in the 14th Street/ 8th Ave subway station.

Every New York subway station is different and most have some sort of art installation. You can see works by several prominent contemporary artists when taking the subway including Roy Lichtenstein (42nd Street-Times Square), Vik Muniz (2nd Ave - 72nd St), Chuck Close (2nd Ave - 86th St) and many more!

INSTAGRAMMABLE PLACES IN THE NEIGHBORHOOD

MATCHA MatchaBar Chelsea: 256 W 15th Street (1 min. walk)
FOOD Insomnia Cookies: 304 W 14th Street (1 min. walk)
SEE Whitney Museum of American Art: 99 Gansevoort Street (8 min. walk)

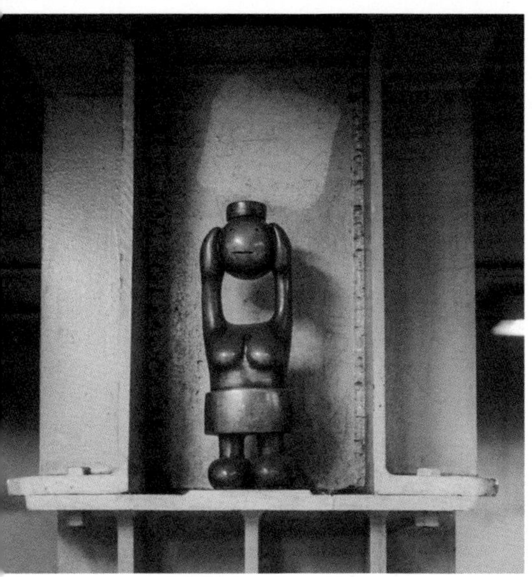

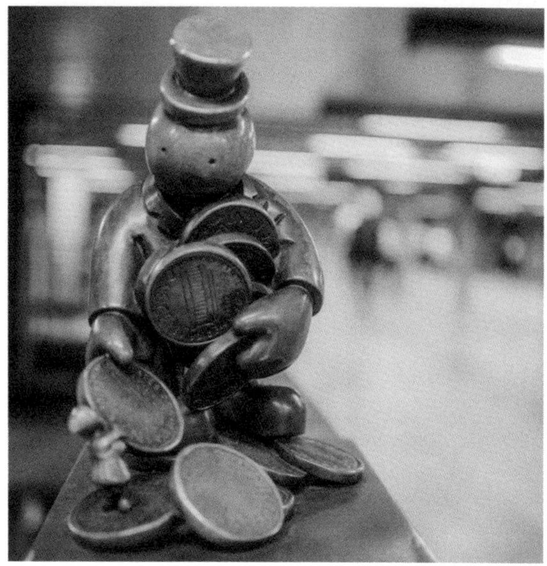

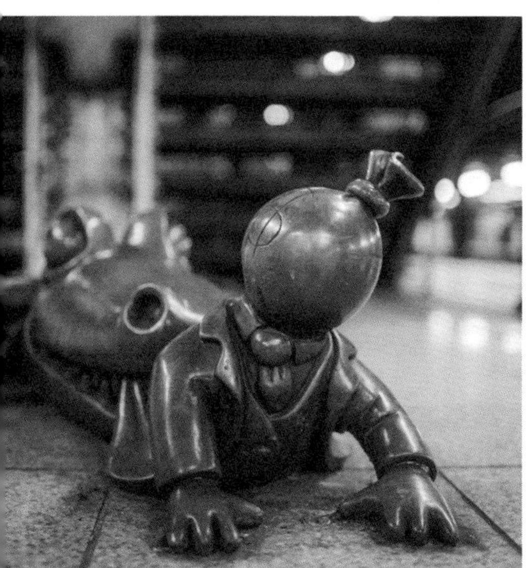

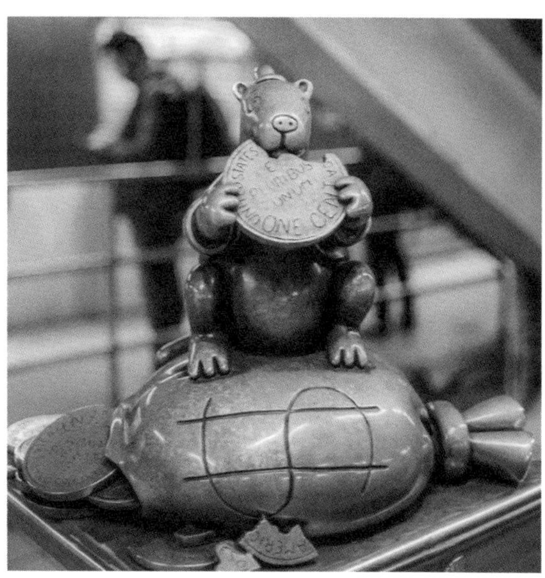

#tomotterness #subwayart #publicart #lifeunderground
@tomotterness

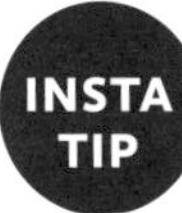

The more you look around, the more figurines you will see appearing.

You can use the many subway constructions as leading lines in your composition.

Go down or put you camera on the floor to to get the perfect picture of the creatures on the ground.

㉔ THE HIGH LINE

The High Line

HOW TO GET THERE
Subway 7 (purple) to 34th Street - Hudson Yards

Start or end at The Whitney: 99 Gansevoort Street.
Or start or end at West 34th Street, between 11th Avenue and 12th Avenue.

The High Line is a railway line that runs 30 feet (9 meters) above ground, above the streets. It was built in 1934 and last used as a railway in 1980.

Since then the railway tracks have been transformed into a 1.5 mile (2.4 km) long public park, that was inaugurated in 2009. The High Line is a green oasis among the imposing skyscrapers and above the never-ending traffic in the city.

The High Line's architecture and plantings are quite unique. The plants are the same plants that used to grow on the disused railway tracks and are alternated with unique artworks and exhibitions, creating a unique combo of nature and the urban landscape.

Welcome to wonderland.

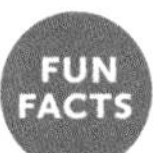

The High Line is regularly featured in movies, as a background in Pat Benatar's *Love is a Battlefield* music video, in the opening scene of Woody Allen's *Manhattan* and in *Taxi Driver* in which we join Robert De Niro in Hectors Diner, just under the High Line.

Because the High Line is such a special place, couples regularly choose it for their wedding proposal. If you do have romantic intentions, then do try to keep your trembling hands under control. High Line staff have regularly had to assist nervous men with engagement rings that fell down the cracks between the wooden walkways.

The High Line has not yet been completed. Once the last section is finished it will have a Bird's Nest Forest and several of the nearby skyscrapers will have entrances that lead directly onto the High Line.

INSTAGRAMMABLE PLACES IN THE NEIGHBORHOOD

COFFEE AND FOOD	Friedman's: 450 10th Avenue (5 min. walk from the High Line starting point at 34th Street)
COFFEE, FOOD AND SHOP	Chelsea Market: 75 9th Avenue (at the side of the High Line, 26 min. from the starting point or 6 min. if you start from the Whitney)
SEE	Plants! Artwork! Views!

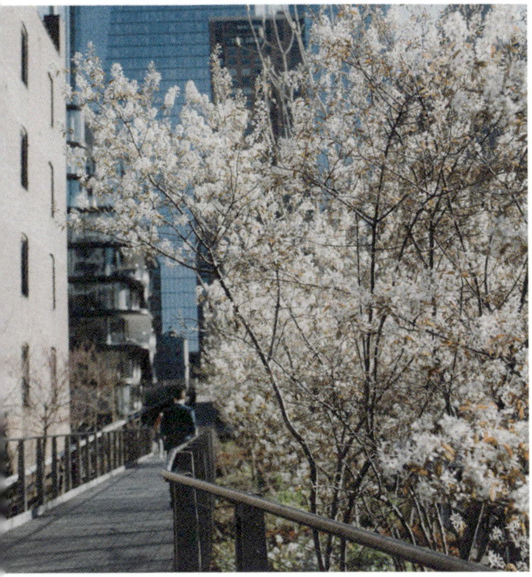

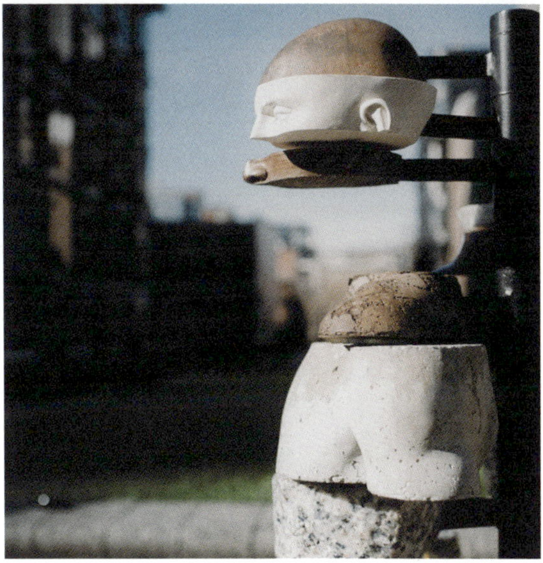

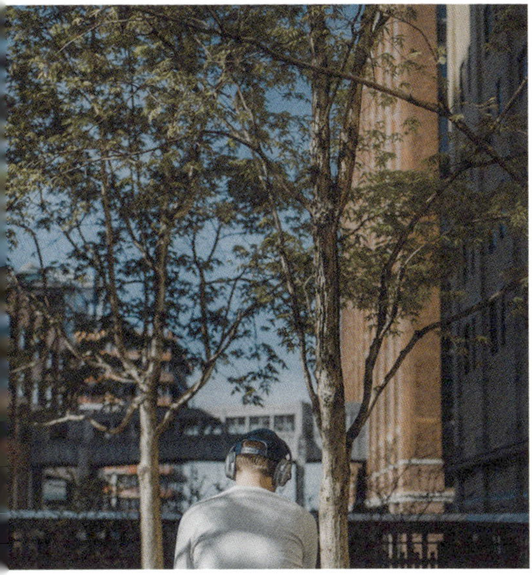

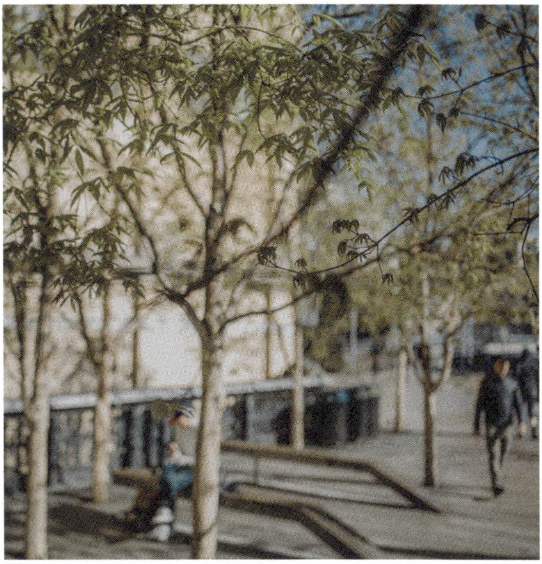

#thehighlinenyc #highlinepark #highlineartnyc #gardeninginthesky
@thehighlinenyc @highlineartnyc

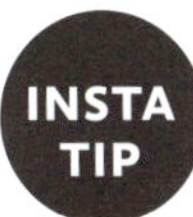

The High Line can be very crowded during summer: more than 20,000 visitors per weekend! To have the best High Line experience and to make the best pictures, you'd better get here before 9am. The early bird catches the best views (and pics)!

❷⁵ FLATIRON BUILDING

The Flatiron Building
175 5th Avenue

HOW TO GET THERE
Subway 6 (green circle) E (blue circle) F or M (orange circle) to 23rd Street

Subway R or W (yellow circle) to East 23rd Street

The Flatiron Building is one of New York's best known and quintessential icons. In fact, the building is so popular that the entire neighborhood is named after it, i.e. the Flatiron District.

Not everyone loved it initially. When the building was built in 1902, many crticis were convinced that a slender building like this one, which is just 6.46 feet (1.95 meters) at its narrowest point, would never survive a strong gust of wind. The design was also deemed less than convincing. The New York Tribune even called it "a stingy piece of pie."

You only notice the building's unique shape when you are standing in front of it. Depending on the direction from which you are coming, you might actually walk past it without noticing anything in particular about this building. Once you have seen the building in all its glory, you will probably notice its unusual shape as well as the many stunning details in the masonry.

The interior is not open to the public. The ground floor corner is entirely made of glass. The Flatiron Art Space in the building's prow is used for art installations.

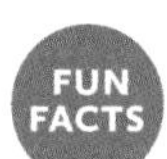

The building's official name is the Fuller Building (after the architect George A. Fuller) but its nickname stuck.

You can find mosaics of flying hats on the walls of the subway station under the Flatiron Building. These refer to the hats that were swept off people's heads (and the women's skirts that were lifted) by the gusts of wind when people walked past the Flatiron Building near 23rd St and 5th Ave.

INSTAGRAMMABLE PLACES IN THE NEIGHBORHOOD

COFFEE, GELATO, FOOD AND SHOP	Eataly NYC: 200 5th Avenue (1 min. walk)
SHOP	The Lego Store: 200 5th Avenue (1 min. walk)
SEE	Momath: 11 E 26th Street (4 min. walk)
	Sony Square NYC: 25 Madison Avenue (3 min. walk)

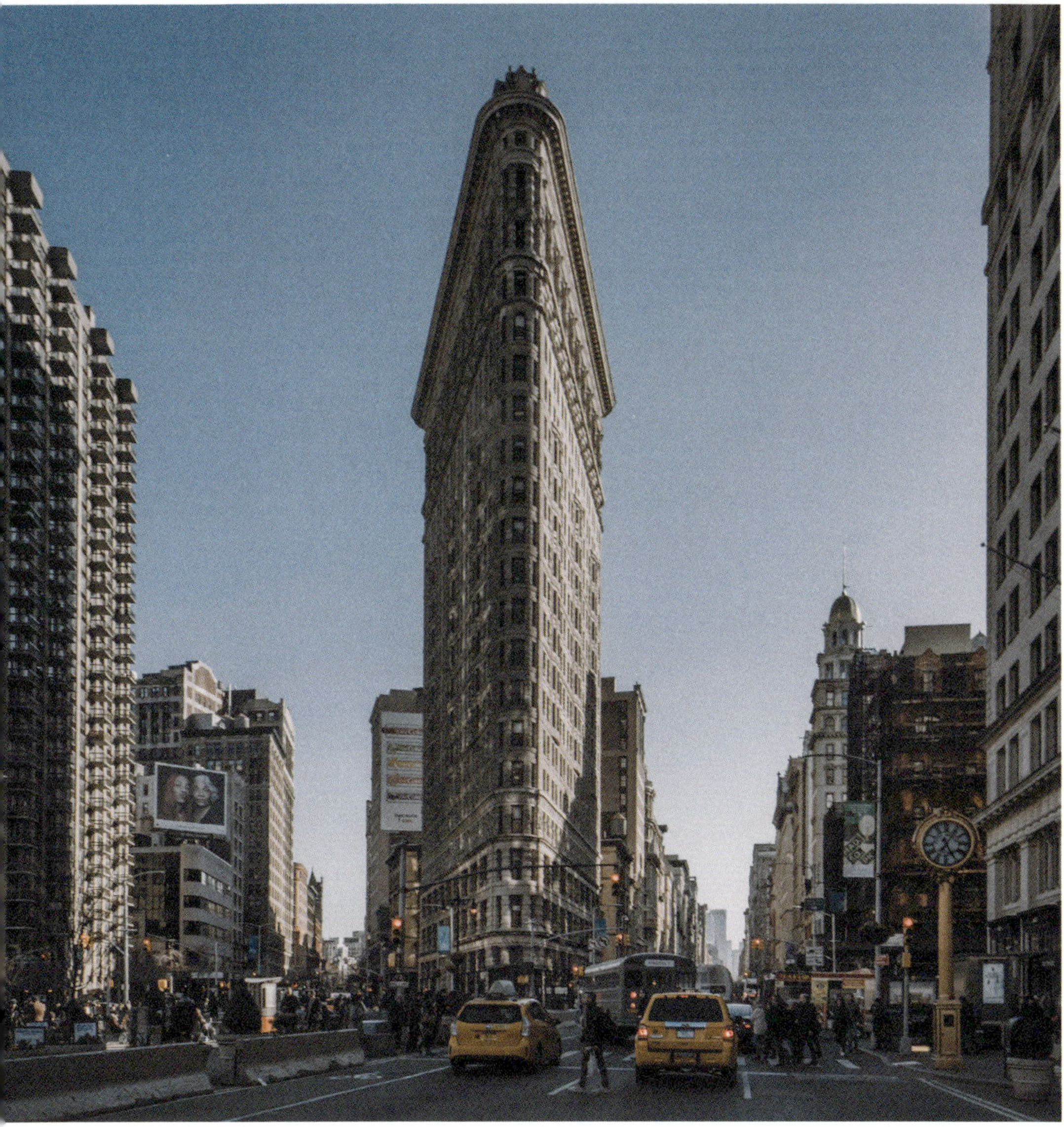

#flatiron #flatironbuilding #discoverflatiron #madisonsquarepark
@flatironny @madsqparknyc

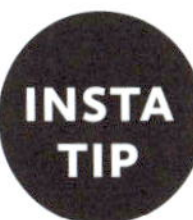

Standing on the corner of 24th Street and 5th Avenue gives you the most iconic view of the building. Make sure to wait until some yellow cabs pass by, to complete the image.

26 FLATIRON ROOM

The Flatiron Room
37 West
26th Street

HOW TO GET THERE
Subway N, Q, R, W (yellow circle) or 6 (green circle) to 28 Street

Subway F (orange circle) to 23 Street

Enter the Flatiron Room and you will love its stylish, intimate, shady allure, which is reminiscent of a twenties jazz spot or a speakeasy.

The Flatiron Room is famous for its whiskeys, with a list of 1,000 different ones to choose from. Fortunately they also have friendly whiskey guides who will help you pick one. Do you want to learn more about whiskey? Then why not enroll in their whiskey school which organizes courses for all levels?

Not a whiskey fan? No problem. They also have a really good selection of delicious cocktails and wines. Ask the barmen about the most instagrammable cocktail and they will gladly advise you. The live jazz music in the background is a nice touch!

The Flatiron District has plenty of good bars and restaurants but the Flatiron Room is definitely unique!

$

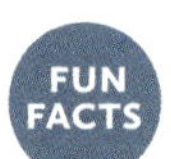

Upon entering, you'll immediately notice the mantelpiece, with a painting of a small dog with a crown on its head. Shortie used to live in an adjoining house and spent his whole day hanging around the neighborhood. The staff became so attached to the dog that it became their mascot and got its own painting.

The bar has a Bottle Keep program. You can buy your favourite bottle, drink as much as you want of it, and if the bottle is not empty, they will label it and store it for you in their bottle keep until your next visit.

INSTAGRAMMABLE PLACES IN THE NEIGHBORHOOD

FOOD AND BEER	Belgian Beer Cafe NoMad: 220 5th Avenue (2 min. walk)
FOOD AND DRINKS	Rooftop Bar NYC: 230 5th Avenue (3 min. walk)
SEE	Flatiron Building: 175 5th Avenue (6 min. walk)

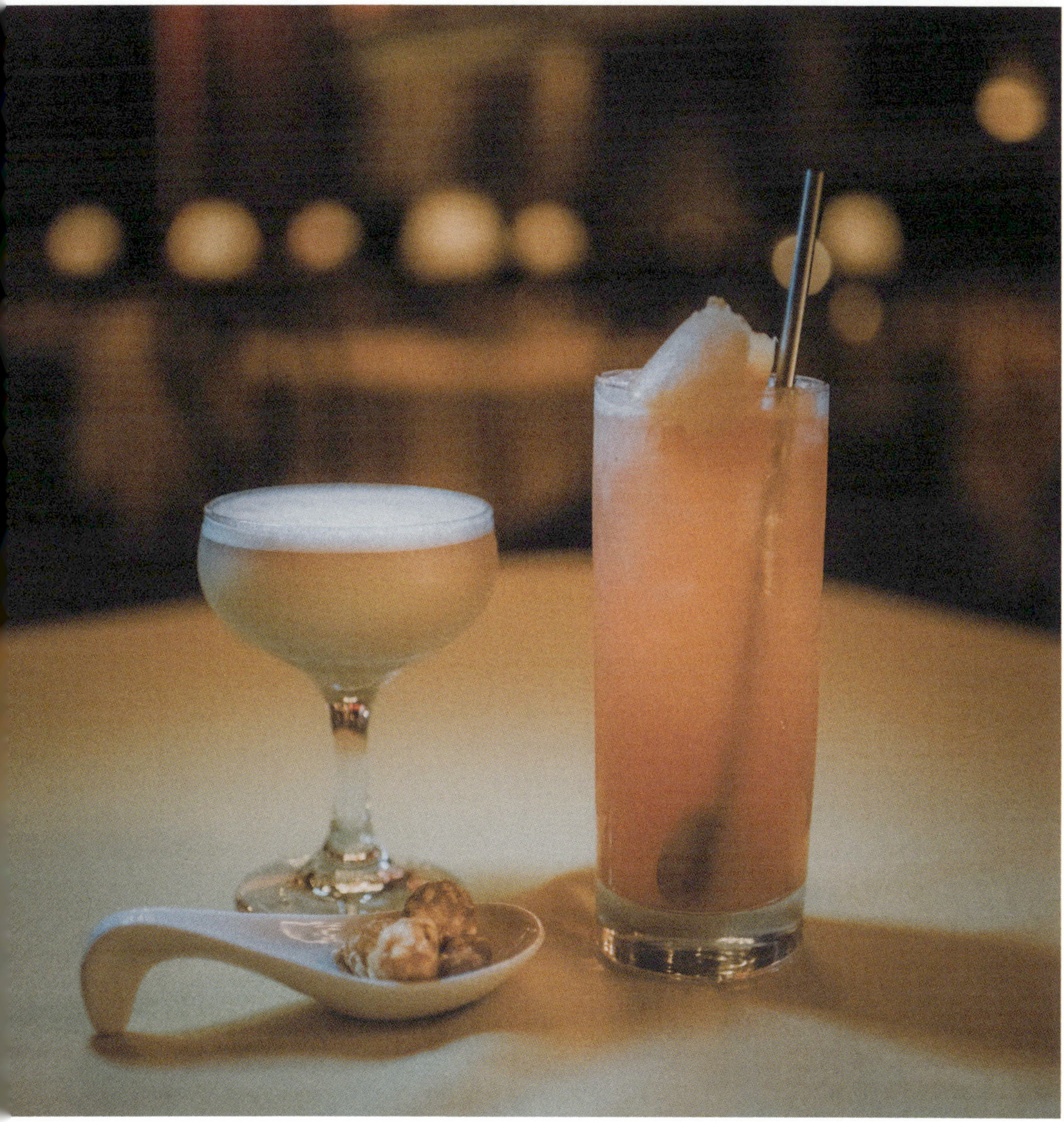

#theflatironroom #cocktailbar #mixology #flatirondistrict @theflatironroom

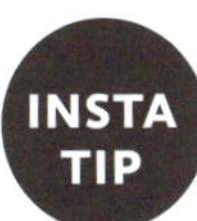

The bar has very cosy lighting, so you can use some extra light when making a picture of your beautiful cocktail. You can use another phone to light the cocktail from the side. Just make sure the light is not to harsh to keep a natural effect.

27 UNION SQUARE

Union Square

HOW TO GET THERE
Subway 4, 5 or 6 (green circle) or L (grey circle) or N, Q, R, W (yellow circle) to 14 Street Union Square Station

Union Square is located at the intersection of various neighborhoods (Greenwich Village, Chelsea, East Village) and is the preferred meeting place of breakdancers, readers, dog lovers, chess players and activists. It is famous for its Union Square Greenmarket (@unsqgreenmarket), or Farmer's market, which is organized on Monday, Wednesday, Friday and Saturday.

The imposing monument of George Washington on horseback, the magnificent statue of Abraham Lincoln and the idyllic corner with Mahatma Gandhi's statue are all popular places with all kinds of activities. This park has a long-standing tradition of protests and rallies, which started in September 1992 when more than 10,000 laborers convened in Union Square for America's first Labor Day.

These days it's a very vibrant park, where there's always something to see, do, smell or taste. Union Square really is an excellent location for some great snapshots.

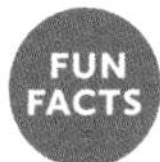

In the 18th century, Union Square used to be a cemetery for poor New Yorkers.

The very first Sherlock Holmes movie was filmed in Union Square in 1900.

INSTAGRAMMABLE PLACES IN THE NEIGHBORHOOD

COFFEE AND FOOD	Breads Bakery: 18 E 16th Street (3 min. walk)
FOOD	Kellogg's NYC: 31 E 17th Street, 1st floor (1 min. walk)
	Chloe's Soft Serve Fruit: 25 E 17th Street (1 min. walk)
SHOP	Barnes & Noble: 33 E 17th Street (1 min. walk)
	Strand Bookstore: 828 Broadway (4 min. walk)
	Flight Club: 812 Broadway (5 min. walk)

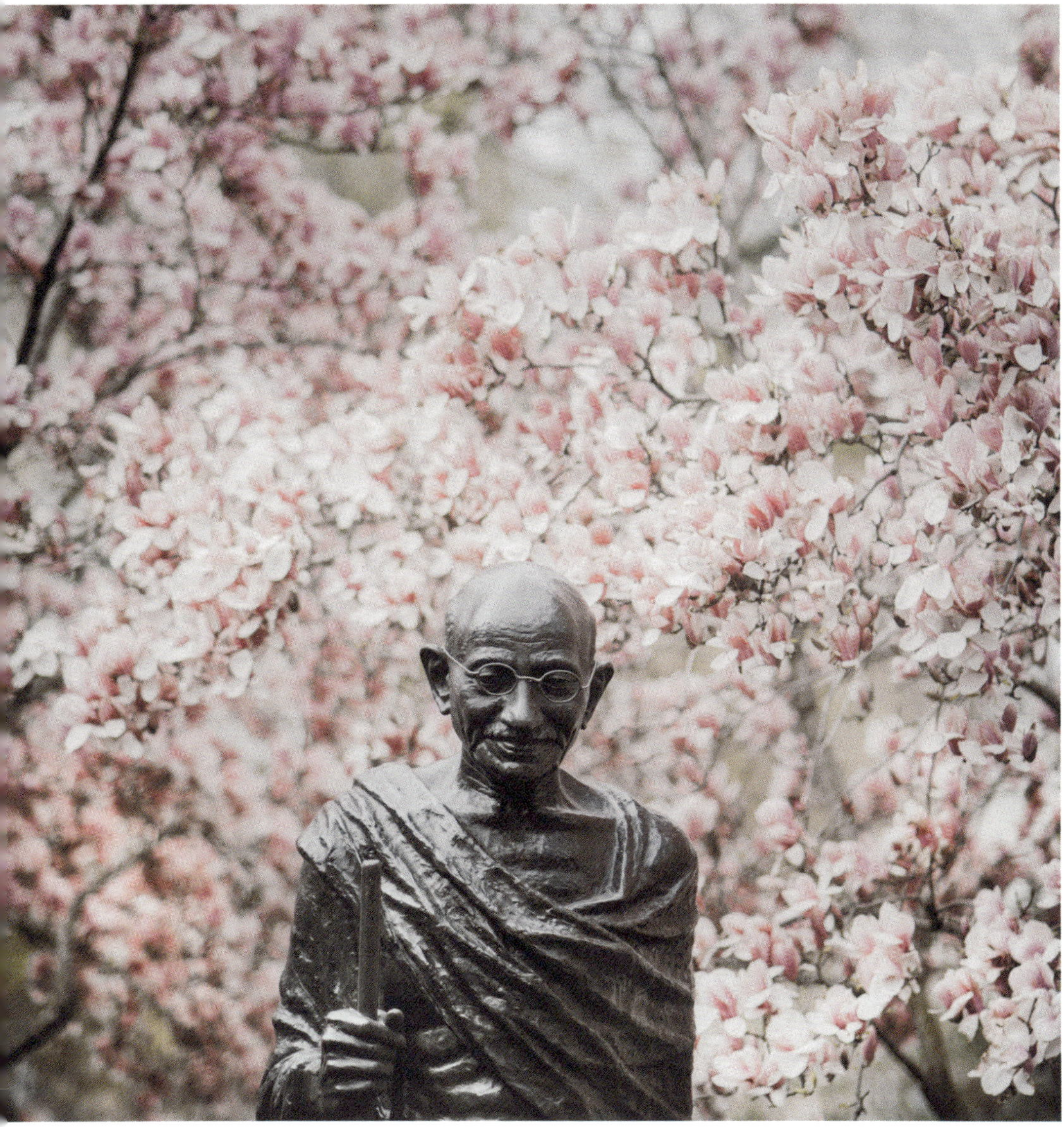

#unionsquare #unionsquarenyc #unionsquaregreenmarket #nycparks
@unsqgreenmarket @unionsquareny

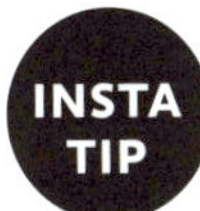

The Mahatma Gandhi Statue is hidden in a little green corner on the South-West-corner of the park.

You can take beautiful seasonal pictures from the statue covered with snow or surrounded by blooming magnolias or fresh green leaves. Even when standing in the rain Gandhi remains fierce!

㉘ THE FRYING PAN

Frying Pan
207 12th
Avenue

HOW TO GET THERE
Subway 7 (purple circle) to 34th Street - Hudson Yards

The Frying Pan is a historical ship which is permanently docked at Pier 66, on the Hudson River.

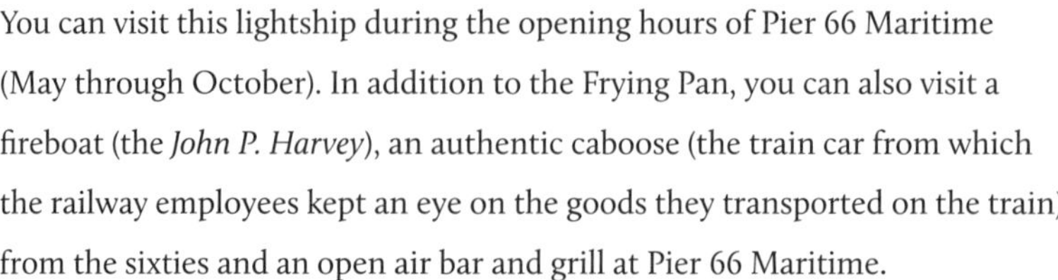

You can visit this lightship during the opening hours of Pier 66 Maritime (May through October). In addition to the Frying Pan, you can also visit a fireboat (the *John P. Harvey*), an authentic caboose (the train car from which the railway employees kept an eye on the goods they transported on the train) from the sixties and an open air bar and grill at Pier 66 Maritime.

The open air bar is a hotpot for after-work drinks and dinners. It can get quite busy here. It's a nice place to kick back with a craft beer, a cocktail or some good seafood.

The gentle swaying motion and the historic artefacts combine to create a unique experience but the real highlight is the stunning view. If you only come for the view, then head straight to the observation deck. By day you can wave at the Statue of Liberty and at sunset you can take in the incredible views of the skylines of New York City and New Jersey.

The location, the view and the food are all highly instagrammable.

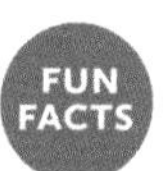

The Frying Pan languished underwater for three years. After she was raised, the outside of the ship was restored, but the inside remained as it is, in a tribute to the Frying Pan's adventurous past.

INSTAGRAMMABLE PLACES IN THE NEIGHBORHOOD

COFFEE	La Colombe Coffee Roasters: 601 W 27th Street (5 min. walk)
SHOP	Printed Matter, Inc: 213 11th Avenue (5 min. walk)
SEE	The Hudson River Park (1 min. walk)
	The High Line: enter at 526 W 26th Street (8 min. walk)

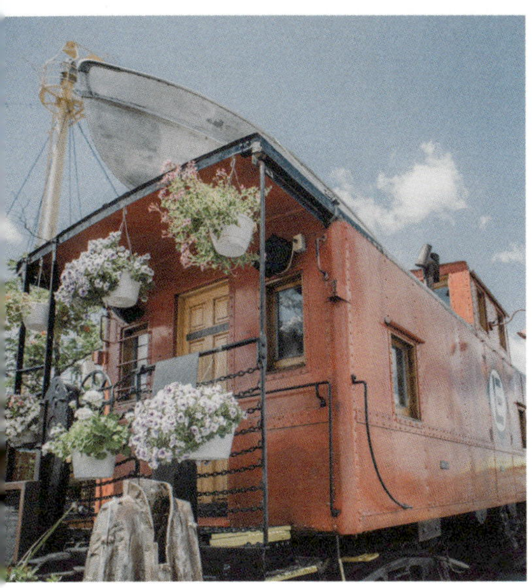

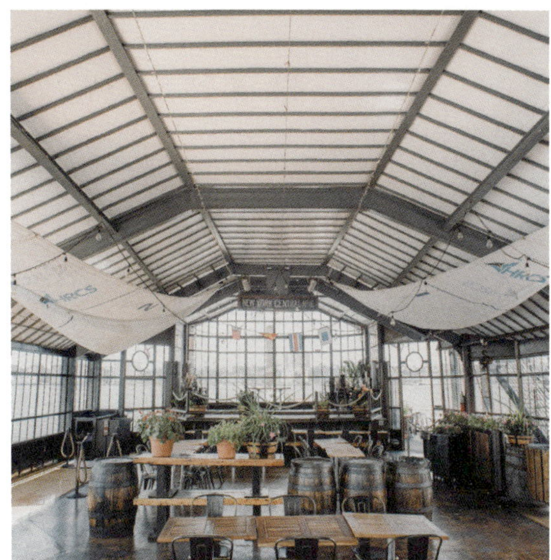

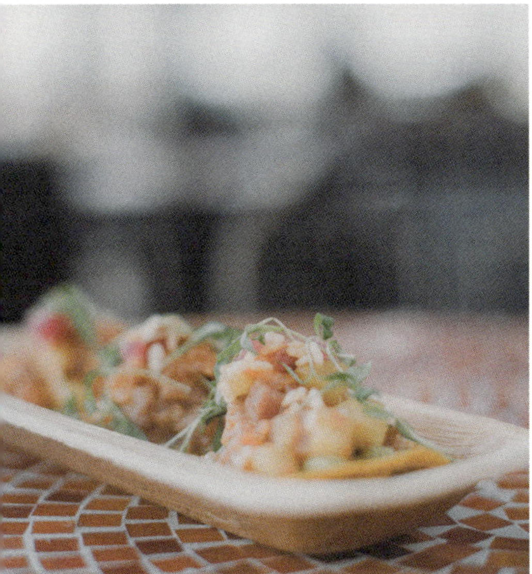

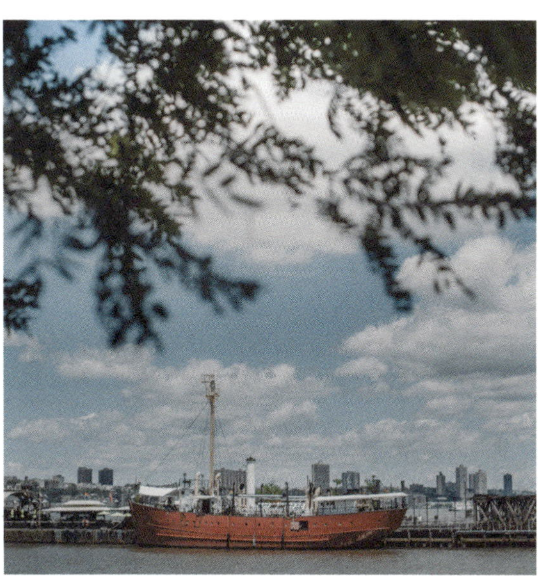

#fryingpannyc #nyceats #nycfood #hudsonriver
@fryingpannyc

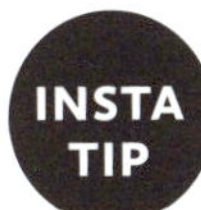

The Frying Pan has many Instagrammable corners, as well from the inside as from the outside.

29 BILLY'S BAKERY

Billy's Bakery
184
9th Avenue

HOW TO GET THERE
Subway C or E (blue) to 23th Street

$

Enter Billy's Bakery and you'll feel like you've just walked into a family kitchen from the forties. The sweet smells, the soft pastel hues and the retro charm make you feel as if you are visiting your grandmother just as she's baking a cake.

Some say that Billy bakes the best cupcakes in NYC. They are freshly baked on the spot every day, from the pastry down to the icing and the decoration. They have an amazing selection of flavors, with seasonal additions. The icing is either vanilla and/or chocolate.

But there's more! Have a look at their other sweets and pastries. Taste their Ice Box Cake, their cheesecake, their scones, cookies and tarts. Everything looks and tastes like a childhood memory here.

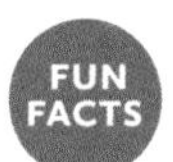

Billy's Bakery is named after its founder Billy Reece. He worked for the Magnolia Bakery for two years before opening Billy's Bakery with two of his former roommates.

Cupcakes are named thus because of the basic recipe, which is expressed in cup measurements: 1 cup of butter, 2 cups of sugar, 3 cups of flour and 4 eggs.

INSTAGRAMMABLE PLACES IN THE NEIGHBORHOOD

FOOD Milk Bar: 220 8th Avenue (4 min. walk)
SHOP Chelsea Market: 75 9th Avenue (8 min. walk)
SEE The High Line: enter at 500 W 20th Street (6 min. walk)

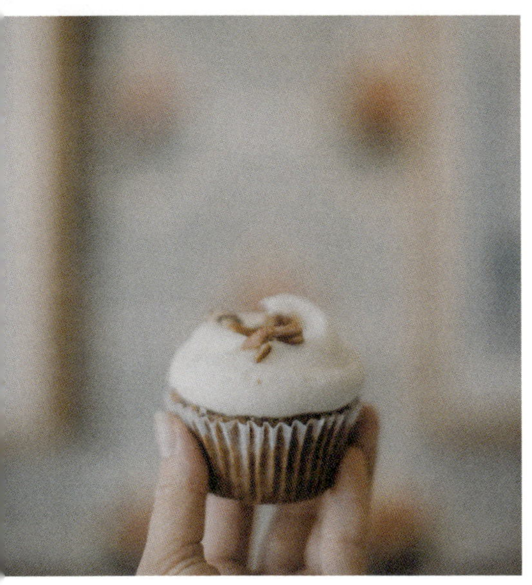
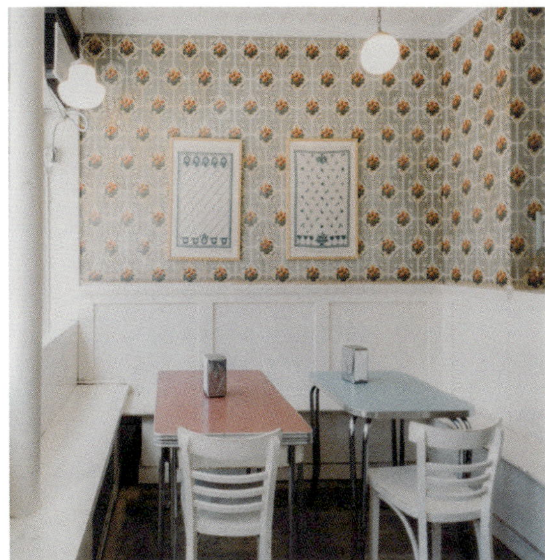
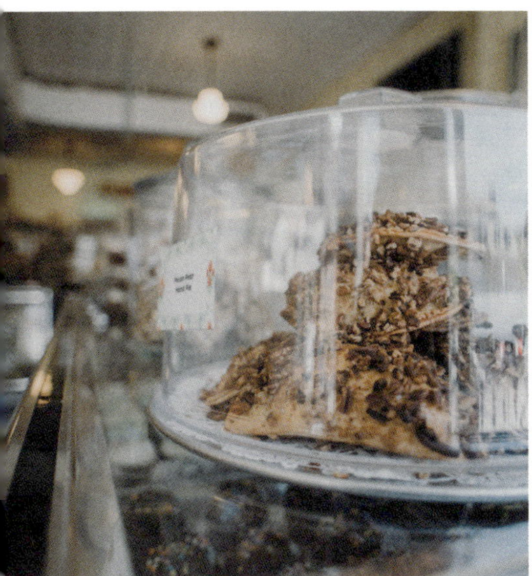
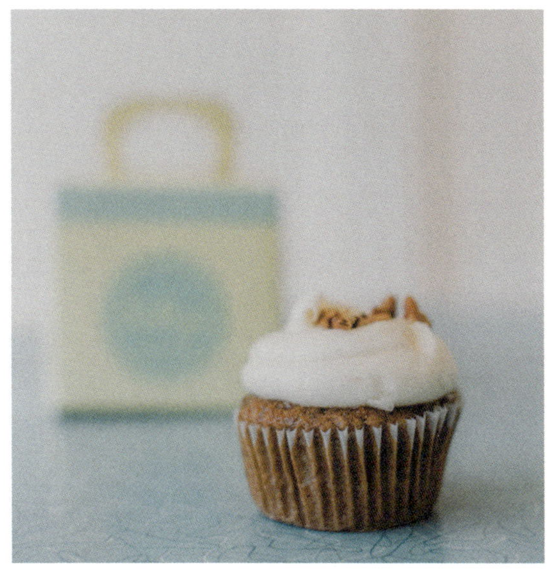

#billysbakerynyc #billyscupcakes #eatfamous #nyceats
@billysbakerynyc

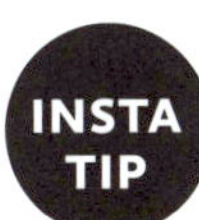

Use the nostalgic wallpaper as a backdrop for your cupcake.

The further away you are from your background, the more blurry it will get.

Make sure to stay as close to the windows as you can, to benefit from the window light.

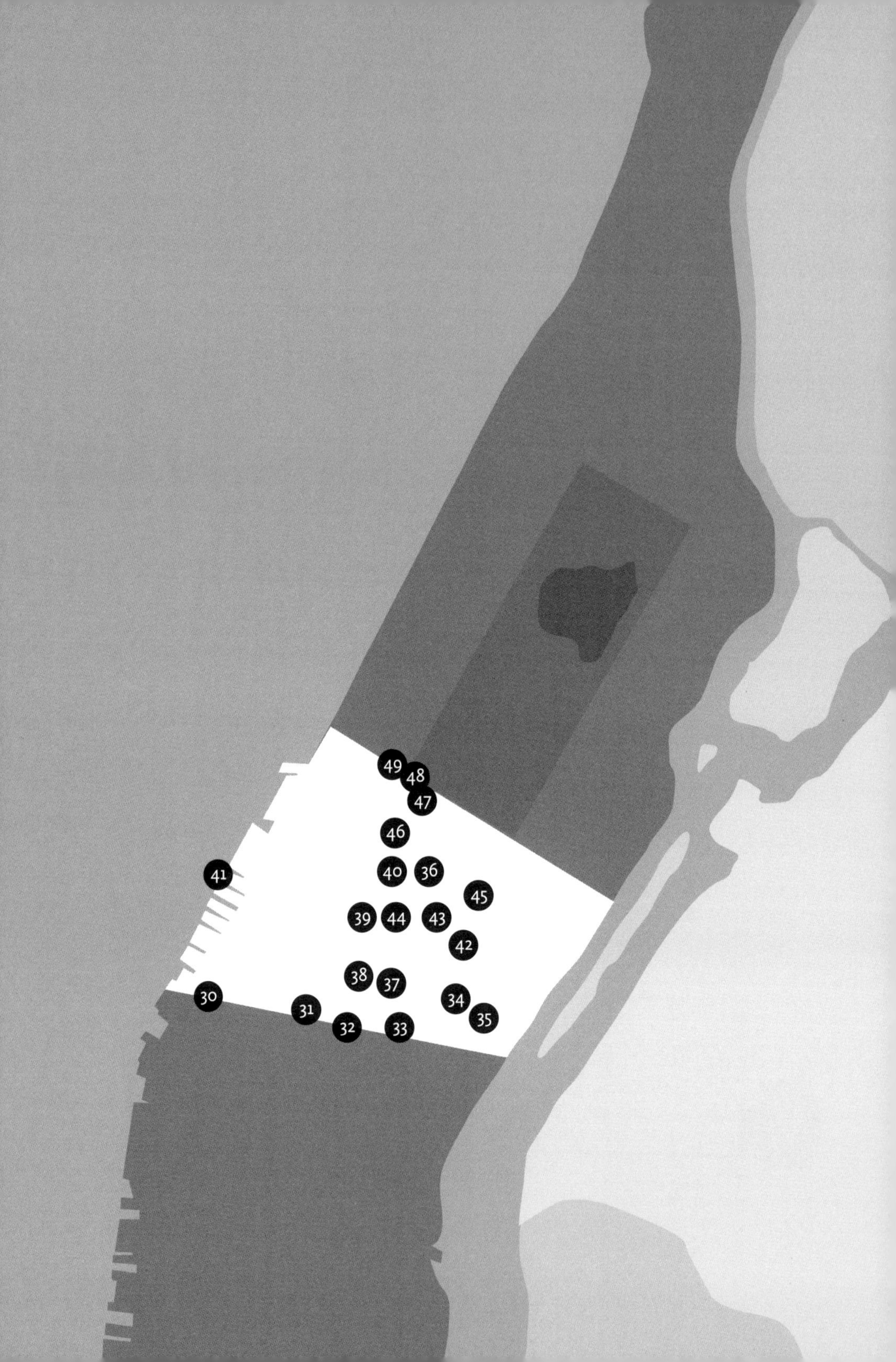
49
48
47
46
41
40
36
45
39
44
43
42
38
37
30
34
31
35
32
33

MIDTOWN

❸⓪ HUDSON YARDS & THE VESSEL

Hudson Yards & The Vessel

HOW TO GET THERE
Subway F (purple) to Hudson Yards Station

Hudson Yards is still under development. This completely new neighborhood will have an impressive collection of tall, taller and tallest buildings, with 30 Hudson Yards (the highest outdoor observation deck in the Western Hemisphere) as its main eyecatcher.

The Vessel is also nearing completion and is already shaping up to be a New York landmark. This unique structure was inspired by Indian stairwells and is reminiscent of M.C. Escher's work. The 154 staircases of this honeycomb, with 2,500 individual steps and 80 landings, will offer impressive views of New York and the brand-new Hudson Yards development.

The Vessel is the centerpiece of The Public Square and Gardens in Hudson Yards and will connect with the High Line. The park and The Vessel are scheduled to open in the spring of 2019.

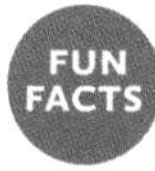

Sections of Vessel were produced in Italy and transferred to New York on 6 cargo ships.

INSTAGRAMMABLE PLACES IN THE NEIGHBORHOOD

COFFEE	Think Coffee: 500 W 30th Street (5 min. walk)
COFFEE AND FOOD	Bluestone Lane: 435 W 31st Street (5 min. walk)
FOOD	Friedman's: 450 10th Avenue (5 min. walk)
SEE	The High Line is connected to the Vessel
	The Hudson Yards Gardens are connected to the Vessel
	Jacob K. Javits Center: 655 W 34th Street (5 min. walk)

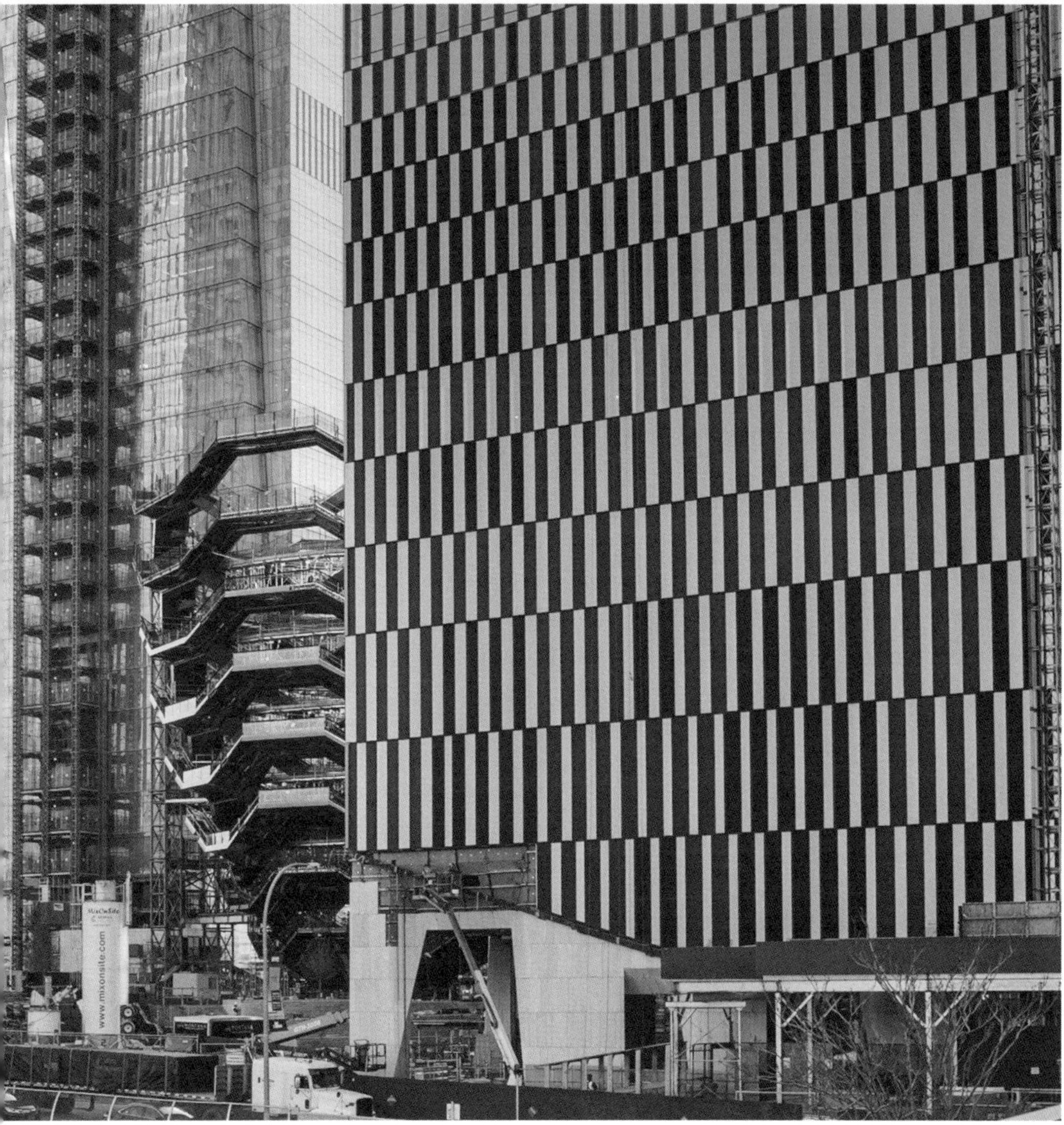

#thevesselnyc #thevessel #hudsonyards #hellohudsonyards #nycarchitecture @thevesselnyc @_hudsonyardsnyc

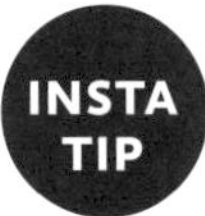

The Vessel is a huge structure among even taller structures. Move further away to get the full picture. The High Line is the perfect place to take a snapshot of this development.

31 MACY'S

Macy's
151 W 34th
Street

HOW TO GET THERE
Subway 7 (purple) to Hudson Yards Station

Subway D, F, M (orange) or E (blue) to 34 Street - Harold Square Station

Macy's is an American department store chain. Its flagship and most famous store is in Herald Square and was The World's Largest Store until 2009, occupying an entire block (6th and 7th Avenues and 34th and 35th Streets). Just under 2.5 million square feet (232,258 square metres) of retail space to browse: a shopper's delight!

Macy's Herald Square was one of the first stores in the US with a modern-day escalator. Some of these old wooden escalators are still in operation, adding to the nostalgic feel of this immense store (you can't miss the magnificent, Insta-worthy escalators when you go to the upper floors). It was also the first store to have an In-Store Santa Claus in 1870. Since then, Macy's has always been the place to go for a magical meet and greet with Santa.

Every year, Macy's organizes its spectacular Thanksgiving Day Parade to welcome Santa Claus to the city. The parade, with its gigantic balloons, attracts 3.8 million people and is always a good opportunity to take some great pictures.

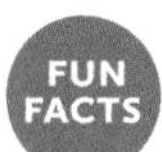

Macy's and its Thanksgiving Day Parade are the stars in *Miracle on 34th Street*, a classic Christmas movie from 1947.

Some of the helium-filled balloons in the parade are so large that they need more than 90 balloon handlers to safely navigate the 4-mile route.

INSTAGRAMMABLE PLACES IN THE NEIGHBORHOOD

COFFEE	Skylight Diner: 402 W 34th Street (9 min. walk)
FOOD	Nap York: 480 7th Avenue (3 min. walk)
SEE	The Empire State Building: 350 5th Avenue (6 min. walk)
	Fashion Institute of Technology (F.I.T.): 227 W 27th Street (7 min. walk)
SHOP	ThinkGeek: 1282 Broadway (3 min. walk)

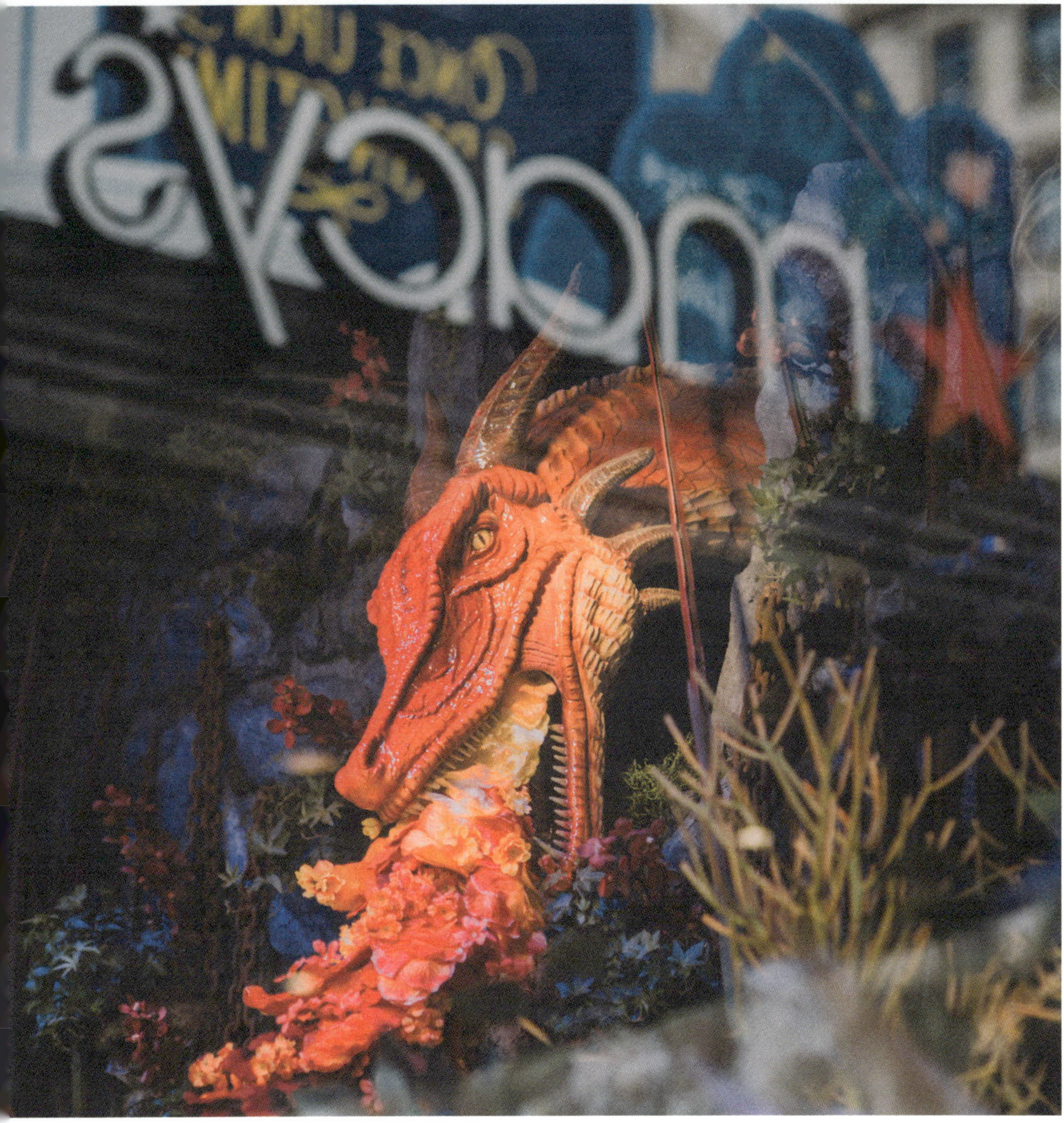

#macysnyc #macyslove #heraldsquare #shoppingfun @macys

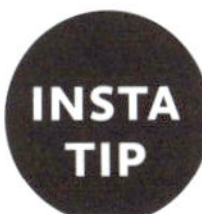

Macy's holiday displays on special occasions (Christmas, Flower Show...) are always impressive. Don't worry about the reflections when taking photos of the shop windows, just include them in your photo and/or composition.

32 EMPIRE STATE BUILDING

Empire State Building
350 5th Avenue

HOW TO GET THERE

Subway 6 (green) to 33 Street Station

Subway Q, R, W (yellow) or E (blue) or F, M (orange) to 34 Street - Herald Square Station

No visit to Manhattan is complete without a stop at the Empire State Building. The 102-story skyscraper, with a roof height of 1,250 feet (381 metres), can be seen from every part of New York City. This also explains why it held the title of Tallest Building in the World for forty years (1931-1972).

The airship mast that was added to the top, to ensure it would be taller than the Chrysler Building, is mainly there for decorative purposes. The colors and lights are adapted to the season and for special events (Christmas, Valentine's Day, Independence Day, St. Patrick's Day...)

It was the first building ever to exceed 100 floors (it has a total of 102). The observation deck on the 102nd floor offers some breath-taking views. Because the building is so centrally located in Manhattan, you have a 360-degree view of all the city's other iconic buildings. A standard ticket will take you to the 86th floor. Tickets to the observation deck are slightly more expensive but you won't regret paying more once you see the spectacular views.

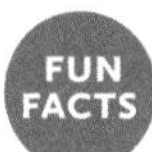

The Empire State Building organizes an annual Building Run-up, challenging runners from around the world to race to the 86th floor! This means running up 86 flights, or 1,576 steps. Seasoned runners pull of this feat in just 10 minutes!

In 1945, the pilot of a B-25 Mitchell bomber became disoriented because of the thick fog on his way to La Guardia. He successfully dodged various skyscrapers but ended up crashing into the north side of the Empire State Building, between the 78th and 79th floors, causing a huge explosion. The pilot and two crew members as well as 11 people in the building died.

INSTAGRAMMABLE PLACES IN THE NEIGHBORHOOD

COFFEE Stumptown Coffee Roasters: 18 W 29th Street (6 min. walk)

FOOD Korea Town: W 32nd Street, between Broadway and 5th Avenue (5 min. walk)

SHOP Macy's: 151 W 34th Street (5 min. walk)
The Complete Strategist: 11 E 33rd Street (1 min. walk)

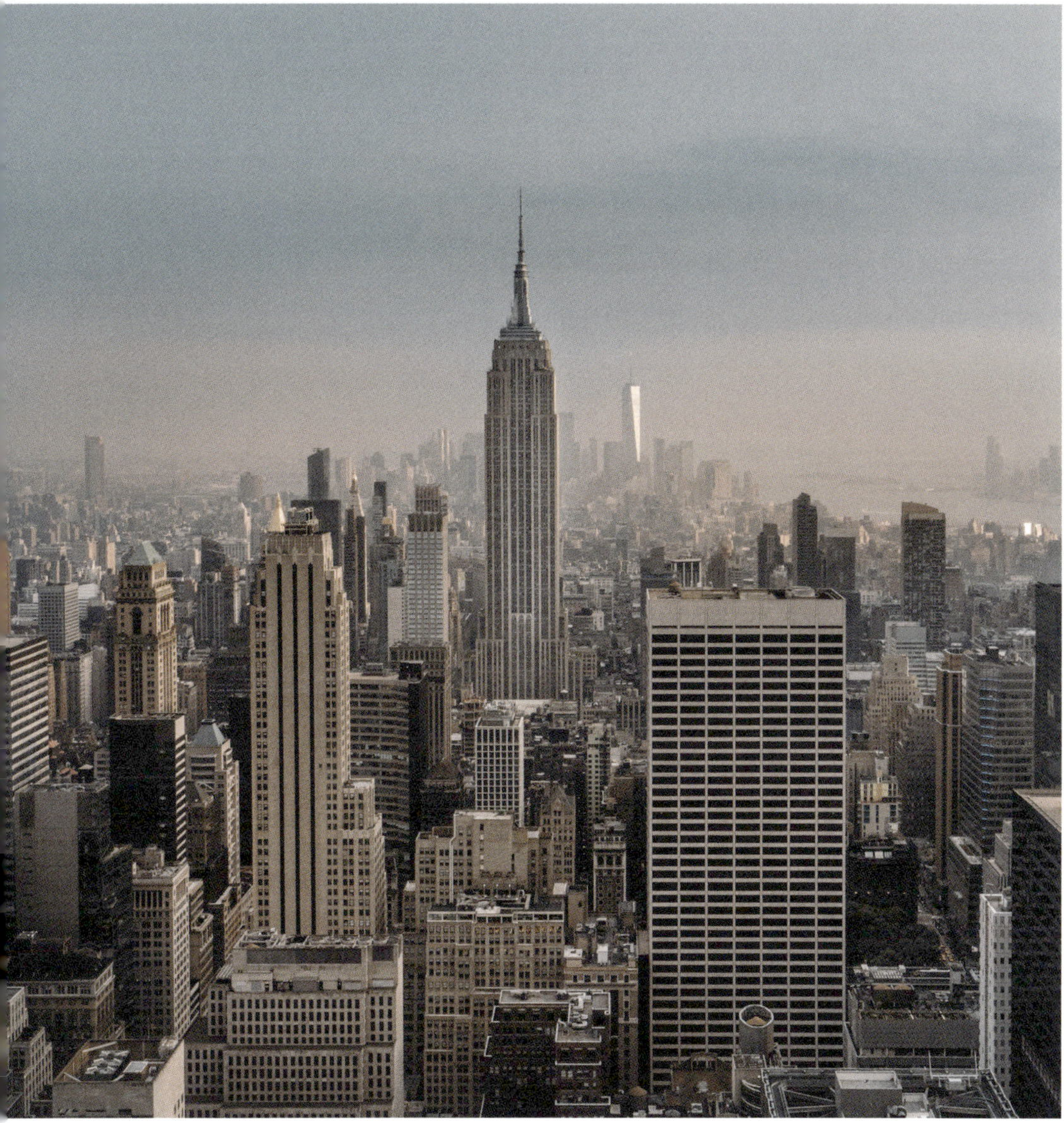

#empirestatebuilding #empirestateofmind #empirestateview #nycarchitecture @empirestatebldg

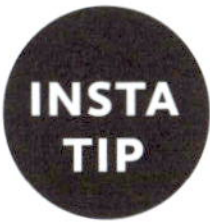

The perfect spot to take a picture of the Empire State Building in all its glory is from the Top of the Rock! The observation deck on top of the Rockefeller Center offers a phenomenal view of the Empire State building and its surrounding buildings in all seasons and weather circumstances.

㉝ THE MORGAN LIBRARY AND MUSEUM

The Morgan Library and Museum
225 Madison Avenue

HOW TO GET THERE
Subway 6 (green) to 33 Street

Subway 4, 5, 6 (green) or 7 (purple) to Grand Central

$

The Morgan Library, completed in 1906, was built to house the private library of the financier and art collector John Pierpont Morgan. The architect Charles McKim was tasked with building a library worthy of its contents, and the intimate renaissance-style palazzo he designed is considered by many to be McKim's masterpiece.

J.P. Morgan died in 1913 and in 1924 his son donated the library to the public. Here you can see one of the world's most impressive collections of rare books and manuscripts, including a manuscript of Charles Dickens's *A Christmas Carol* with edits and a markup by the author, original drawings by William Blake, letters from Vincent Van Gogh and George Washington, and the scraps of paper on which Bob Dylan jotted down *Blowin' in the Wind*. The library reopened in 2006 after a multi-year renovation by Renzo Piano (who co-designed the Centre Pompidou), which added 75,000 square feet and doubled the exhibition space.

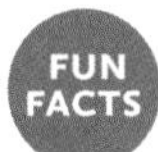

The entrance is guarded by two lionesses, which were sculpted by Edward Clark Potter. He also produced the two lions at the main entrance of the New York Public Library. The library has a life mask of the first president of the United States, George Washington. The French sculptor Jean-Antoine Houdon made a plaster cast of his face in 1785. The house was one of the first private residences in New York to have electric lighting.

INSTAGRAMMABLE PLACES IN THE NEIGHBORHOOD

COFFEE Gregory's Coffee: 20 E 40th Street (3 min. walk)
FOOD Bareburger: 514 3rd Avenue (9 min. walk)
SEE The Empire State Building: 350 5th Avenue (5 min. walk)
Grand Central: 89 E 42nd Street (6 min. walk)
New York Public Library: 476 5th Avenue (6 min. walk)

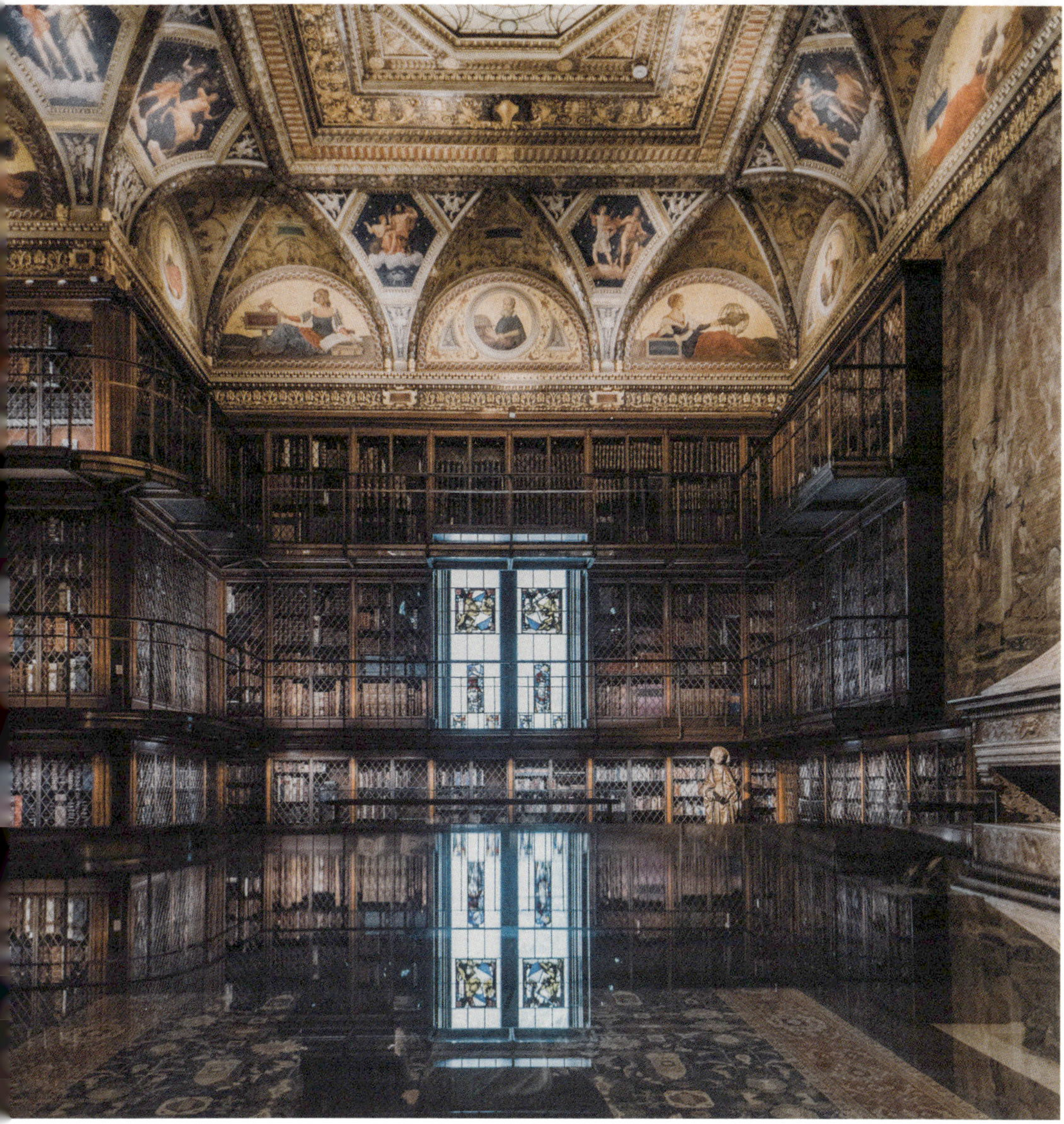

#morganlibrary #themorganlibrary #themorgan #nycmuseums #libraryofinstagram @themorganlibrary

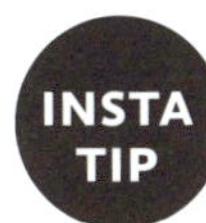

At the library there are a couple of glass display cabinets that you can use to create reflections of the impressive bookshelves.

34 GRAND CENTRAL

Grand Central
89 E 42nd Street

HOW TO GET THERE
Subway 4, 5, 6 (green) or 7 (purple) or S (grey) to Grand Central Terminal

Grand Central Terminal covers 48 acres (19.5 hectares), making it the world's largest train station. Every day, more than 750,000 people walk through the magnificent station hall.

The main information booth in the center of the concourse is the most popular place to meet for New Yorkers. What's more, you can always check whether you are on time on the brass clock above the kiosk. Each of the four faces is made of opalescent or milk glass, and their value has been estimated to be 10 million dollars.

Is your date late? No need to worry. Just look up at the astronomical ceiling, with the signs of the Zodiac and 2,500 stars. It's a great way to pass time. The stunning Vanderbilt Hall, Grand Central Market, the Great Northern Food Hall and the many events that are organized here make Grand Central Terminal one of the most visited venues in New York City.

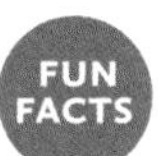

The large chandeliers in Vanderbilt Hall weigh 2,500 lbs (1,100 kilos) each! Let's hope they're properly attached...

In 1990, they cleaned the entire ceiling, except for one little section. Can you spot the tiny black square, if you follow the line from the lobster's leg to the corner? That's what the ceiling looked like before it was cleaned.

There is a hidden platform under Grand Central Terminal with a special elevator into the Waldorf-Astoria Hotel above it. It was used by President Roosevelt to enter the hotel, and to avoid people seeing him being wheeled into the hotel in his wheelchair (the president had polio but wanted to hide this fact).

INSTAGRAMMABLE PLACES IN THE NEIGHBORHOOD

COFFEE AND FOOD	You can find at least 20 different dining-options at the Lower Level Dining Concourse
FOOD	Grand Central Oyster Bar & Restaurant
SEE	The Whispering Gallery in front of the Oyster Bar
	The Vanderbilt Tennis Club at the Court Floor

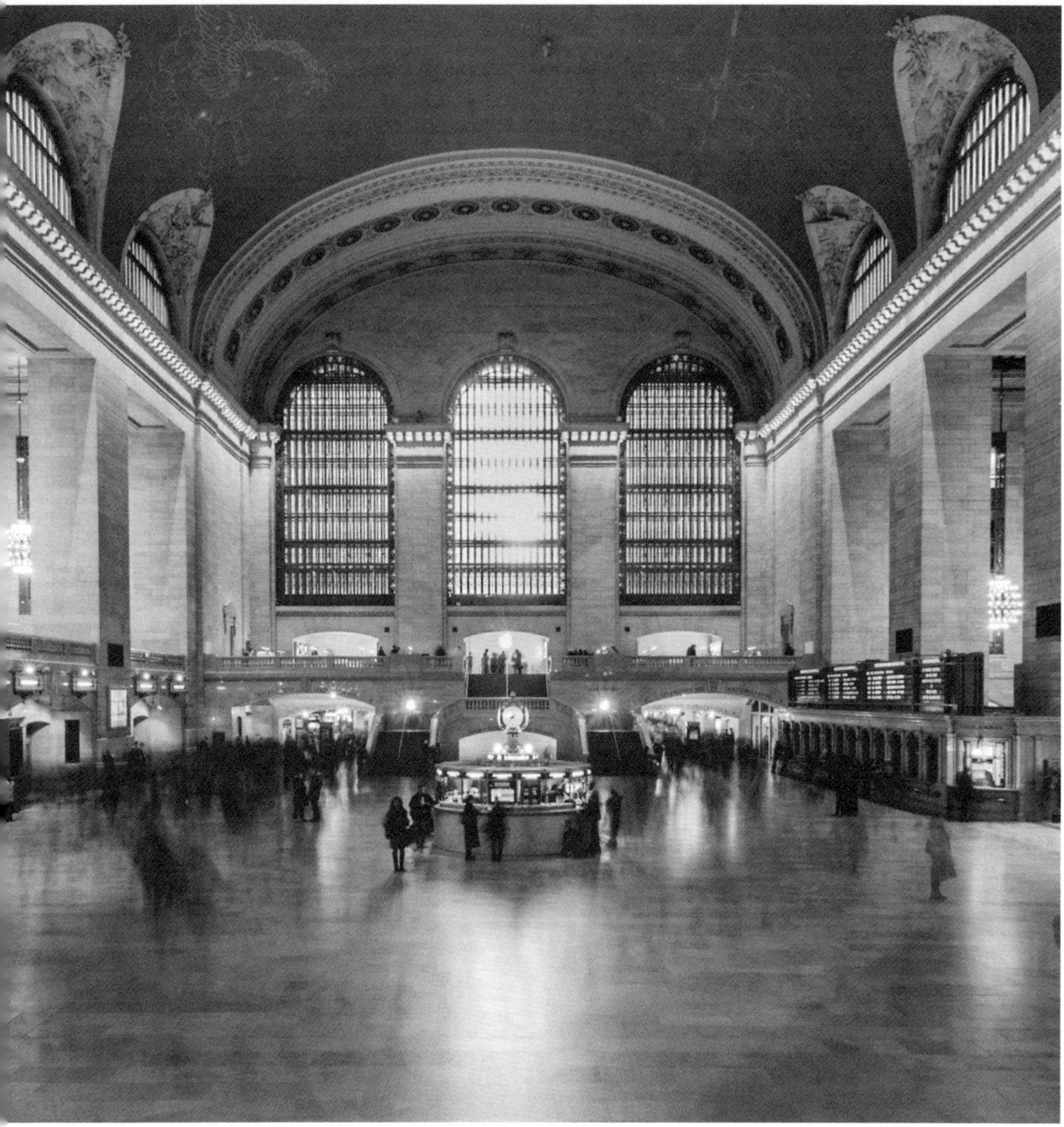

#grandcentralnyc #grandcentralterminal #sharegct @grandcentralnyc

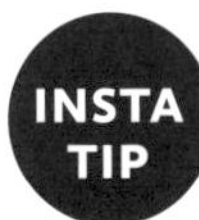

You're never alone in Grand Central. It is the perfect place for some spooky photos with a slow shutter speed. A slow shutter speed ensures that everything that moves comes out blurry whereas stationary objects are in focus. Rest your camera on the balustrade of one of the two large staircases to avoid camera shake. If you position it in the center you will have a great view of the entire terminal.

35 CHRYSLER BUILDING

Chrysler Building
405 Lexington Avenue

HOW TO GET THERE

Subway 4, 5, 6 (green) or 7 (purple) or S (grey) to Grand Central Terminal

Many people agree that the Chrysler Building is the most beautiful skyscraper of New York and perhaps the entire United States. The design of this Art Deco-style skyscraper is simply unrivalled.

In the race for the title of the Tallest Building in the World, the Chrysler Building was the first building to exceed 1,000 feet (304 meters). It was the tallest building for about 11 months, standing at 1,050 feet (320 meters) until the Empire State Building came along.

The building was constructed by Walter Chrysler as a tribute to The Golden Age of the Motorcar. Its design was inspired by the radiator caps and the ornament on the hood of the 1929 Chrysler Plymouth.

You cannot visit or tour the Chrysler Building. The lobby with its stunning Art Deco murals and interior is open to the public.

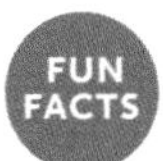

When the Chrysler Building opened in 1931, there was an observation deck on the 71st floor. It closed in 1945 and never reopened.

The magnificent lobby was originally intended as a showroom for Chrysler cars.

INSTAGRAMMABLE PLACES IN THE NEIGHBORHOOD

COFFEE Pennylane Coffee: 305 E 45th Street (8 min. walk)

FOOD Urbanspace Vanderbilt: corner of E 45th Street and Vanderbilt Avenue (6 min. walk)

SEE The United Nations Headquarters: corner of United Nations Plaza and 42nd Street (10 min. walk)

The Ford Foundation Atrium: 1440 Broadway (6 min. walk)

Table of Love: 237 Park Avenue (5 min. walk)

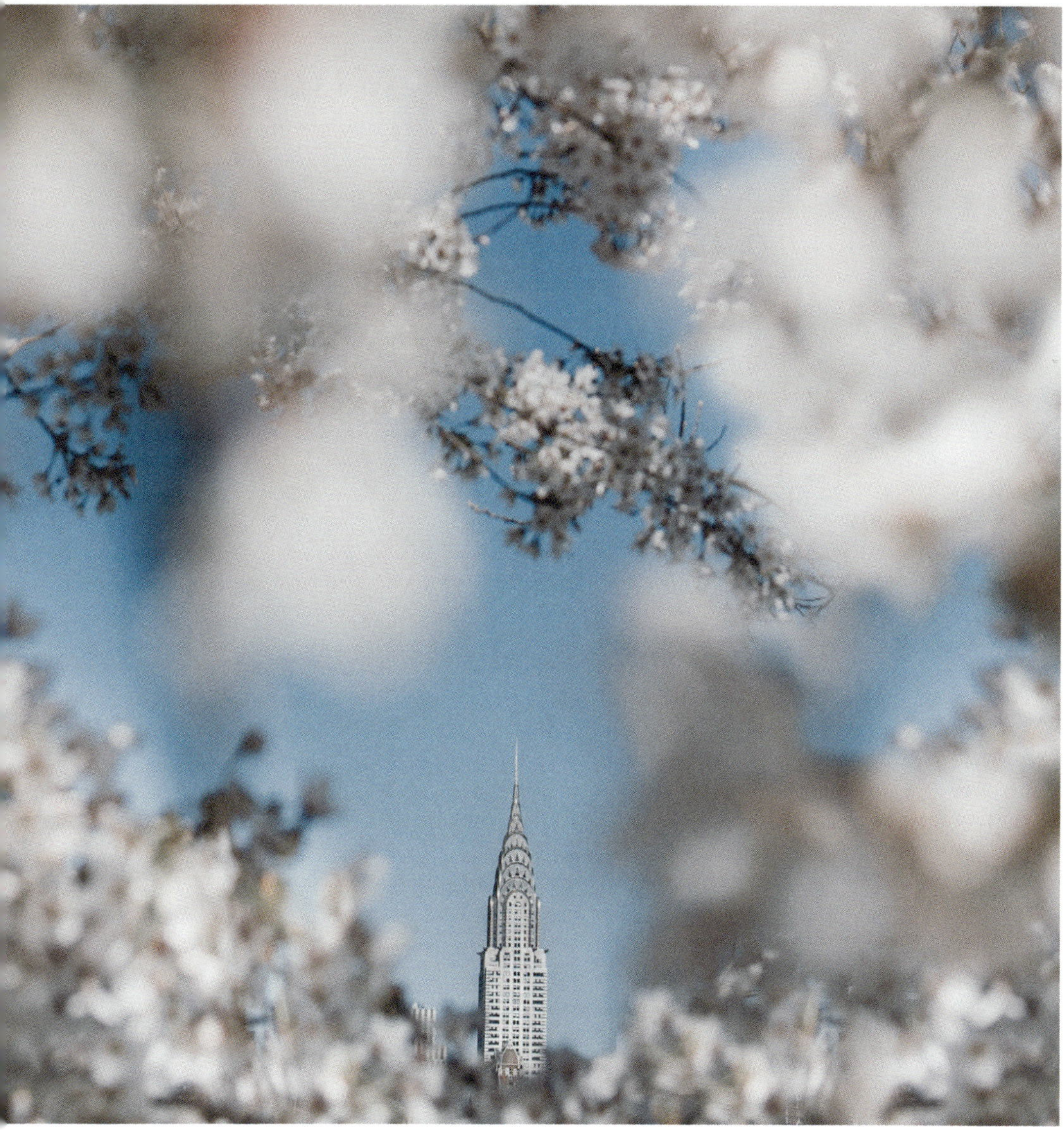

#chryslerbuilding #chryslerbuildingnyc #nycarchitecture #artdeco #nycskyscrapers

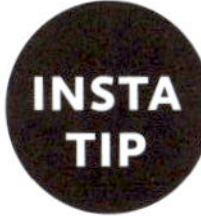

The Chrysler Building is tall but it is surrounded by even taller buildings, making it difficult to photograph from close up. Walk a few blocks and take a photo from the Tudor City Overpass (intersection of 42nd Street and Tudor City Place).

You can also choose to go even a little bit further: this photo was taken from Long Island City, on the other side of the East River.

36 LOVE & HOPE SCULPTURE

Love & Hope Sculpture
Hope: 200 W 53rd Street
Love: W 55th Street & 6th Avenue

HOW TO GET THERE
Subway F (purple) to Hudson Yards Station

The Love and Hope sculptures were created by the pop art artist Robert Indiana. This sculptor/ painter/ poet was one of the founders of the pop art movement in the sixties. He often includes language in his artworks, choosing to describe them as "sculptural poems".

The Love image was designed in the sixties for the MoMa's Christmas card. In the seventies, the image graced a US postage stamp. The first actual Love sculpture was produced in 1970 for the Indianapolis Museum of Art. Since then, various different Love sculptures have popped up in the US, Europe and Asia. It has become a symbol of a positive worldview and optimism.

The Hope sculpture was produced in 2008, to support Barack Obama's presidential campaign. Since then, many more Hope sculptures were produced in various formats, which can be found all over the world.

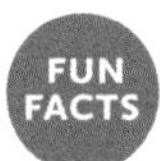

Spanish, Italian, Hebrew and Chinese versions of the Love sculpture exist.

If you like Robert Indiana's art, you may want to visit the Whitney Museum of American Art to see some more of his work.

INSTAGRAMMABLE PLACES IN THE NEIGHBORHOOD

COFFEE Blue Bottle Coffee: 10 E 53rd Street (8 min. walk)
FOOD Burger Joint at the Parker Meridian: 119 W 56th Street (5 min. walk)
SEE The Moma: 11 W 53rd Street. (5 min. walk)
Rockefeller Center: Rockefeller Plaza (4 min. walk)
Times Square (4 min. walk)

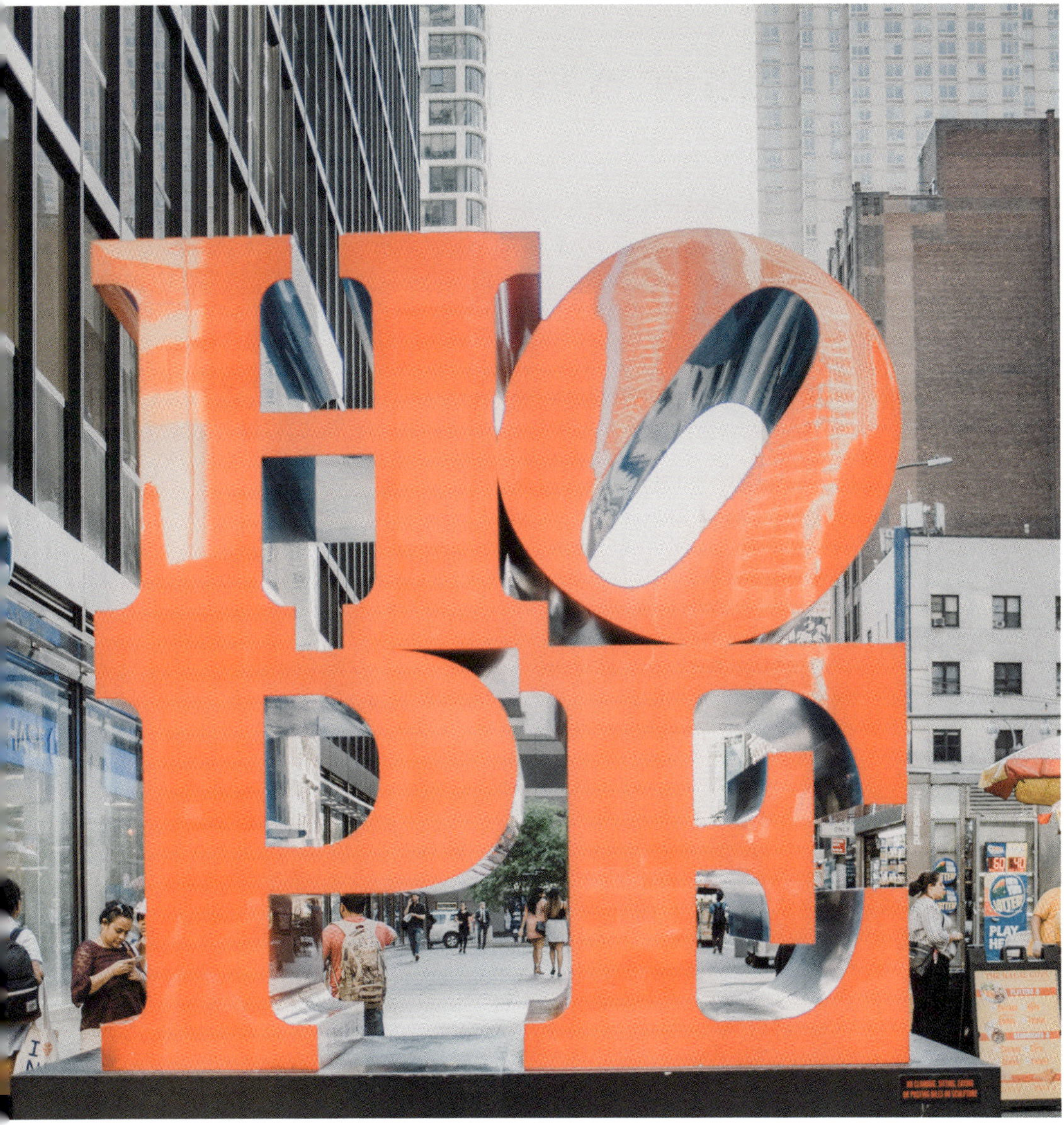

#hopesculpture #lovesculpture #robertindiana #publicart #midtown

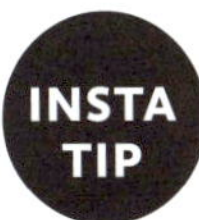

On weekend days, the area around the Love sculpture can get quite busy. There's often a line of people waiting to take a picture of the statue. The Hope sculpture is easier to photograph.

37 NEW YORK PUBLIC LIBRARY

New York Public Library 476 5th Avenue

HOW TO GET THERE

Subway F (purple) to 5 Avenue - Bryant Park Station

Subway E (blue) or B, D, F, M (orange) to 42 Street - Bryant Park Station

The New York Library has more than 90 neighborhood branches all over New York City. The largest and best-known branch is the Public Library in the Stephen A. Schwarzman building on 5th Avenue.

The library opened in 1911, after the merger of the collections of two private libraries of considerable importance, i.e. the Astor Library and the Lennox Library. Two lions welcome you at the entrance. They were originally named after the founders, Leo Astor and Leo Lennox, but have since been renamed Patience and Fortitude.

The main attraction is the magnificent Rose Main Reading Room on the third floor. The 300-foot (91 meter) expanse is home to a collection of over 30,000 books. Sit down at one of the tables, which have been occupied by countless writers and researchers over the years, and look around at the many bookcases that line the walls and up at the breath-taking ceiling painting.

The main reading room as well as the many other smaller reading and research rooms are all impressive. Every year, the library's magnificent spaces, unique collections and fascinating exhibitions attract millions of visitors.

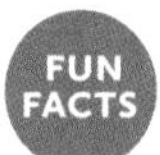

Want to meet a film star? Well, you can! Head to the Children's Center (ground floor) where you can find the one and only Winnie The Pooh and his friends (Kanga, Piglet, Eeyore and Tigger).

One of the two lions comes to life in the movie *The Wiz* (1978), joining Dorothy and Toto on their adventure to Oz.

INSTAGRAMMABLE PLACES IN THE NEIGHBORHOOD

COFFEE Gregory's Coffee: 20 E 40th Street (2 min. walk)

COCKTAIL The Algonquin Lounge: 59 W 44th Street (8 min. walk)

FOOD Urbanspace Vanderbilt: corner E 45th Street @ Vanderbilt Avenue (8 min. walk)

SEE Bryant Park (2 min. walk)

The Library Walk on the sidewalk on E 41st Street, between Park Avenue and Fifth Avenue

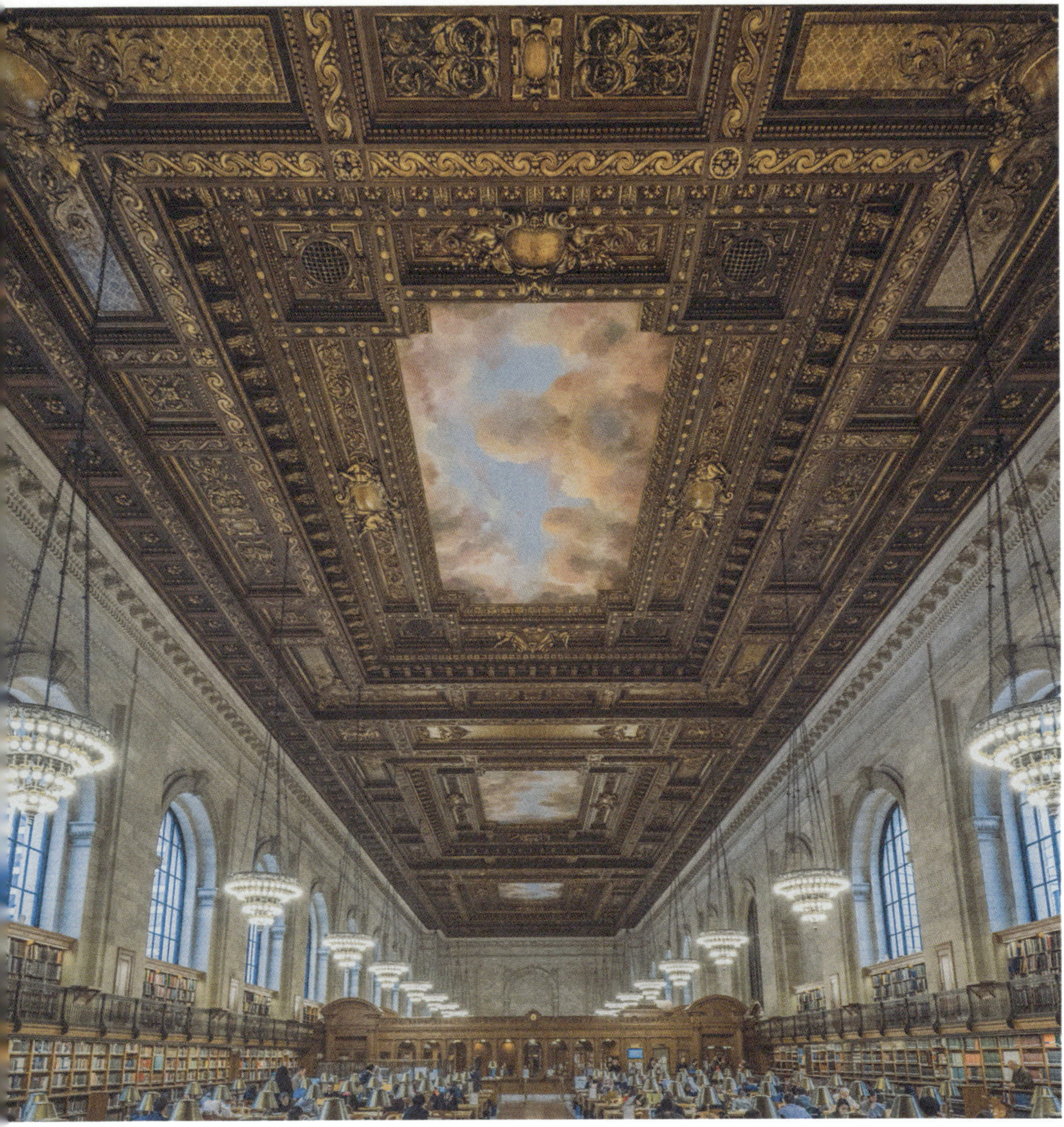

#nypubliclabrary #nypl #newyorkpubliclibrary #libraryofinstagram #midtown @nypl

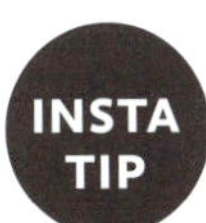

The main reading room is open to the public. To get a good shot of this column-free expanse, you should move to the far side, for a full view of the reading room.

Make sure to position yourself exactly in the middle of the room for a nice, symmetrical image. If possible, use your camera's grid lines to line up your composition.

❸❽ BRYANT PARK

Bryant Park

HOW TO GET THERE
Subway F (purple) to Hudson Yards Station

Bryant Park is a lively park with an interesting history. It was a Potter's Field (a cemetery for the poor) in 1823, a water reservoir in 1840, home to The Chrystal Palace (an exhibition building) in 1853 and a camp for the Union Army Troops in 1860. In 1884, it was named Bryant Park, after the poet William Cullen Bryant.

Nowadays this busy park in the center of Manhattan attracts locals and tourists alike with its many leisure facilities. They include chess, board games, the reading room, *boules* and pingpong, as well as daily (free) workshops (Tai Chi, juggling, knitting and fencing) and weekly events (movie screenings, opera, dance or music performances, the Winter Village with an ice skating rink).

The colorful tables and chairs and the huge lawn are the perfect place for a picnic and a great place to stop and be overwhelmed by all the goings-on in the park and the amazing buildings that line the park.

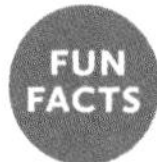

The Gertrude Stein statue was installed in 1902 in Bryant Park and was the first statue of an American woman to be placed in a New York City park.

The library's cellars extend under Bryant Park and are home to 37 miles (60 km) of bookcases.

New York City's most luxurious public restroom is located in Bryant Park. In spite of the long lines, it is the best place in New York for a pit stop, with a 280,000 dollar upgrade, fresh cut flowers daily, an adapted playlist with classical music, air conditioning and full-time staff.

INSTAGRAMMABLE PLACES IN THE NEIGHBORHOOD

COFFEE	La Colombe Coffee Roasters: 1045 6th Avenue (2 min. walk)
FOOD	Take-away from the Whole Foods Market (1095 6th Avenue) and eat it at Bryant Park.
SHOP	Kinokuniya New York bookstore: 1073 6th Avenue (1 min. walk)
SEE	New York Public Library: 476 5th Avenue (2 min. walk)

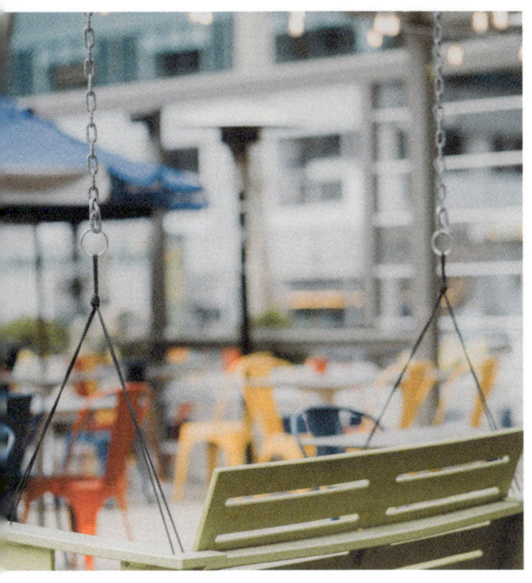
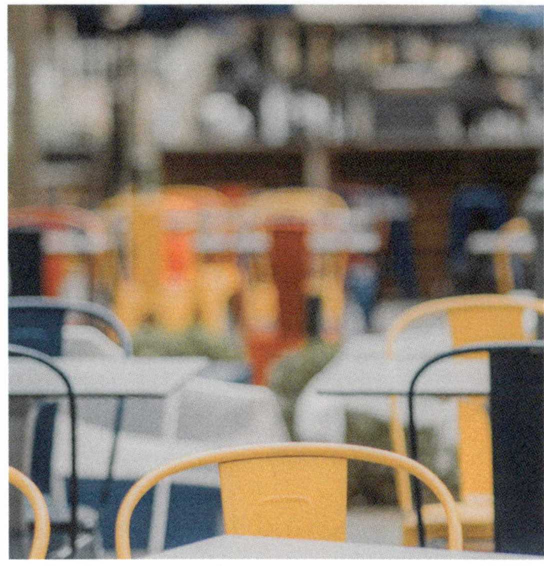
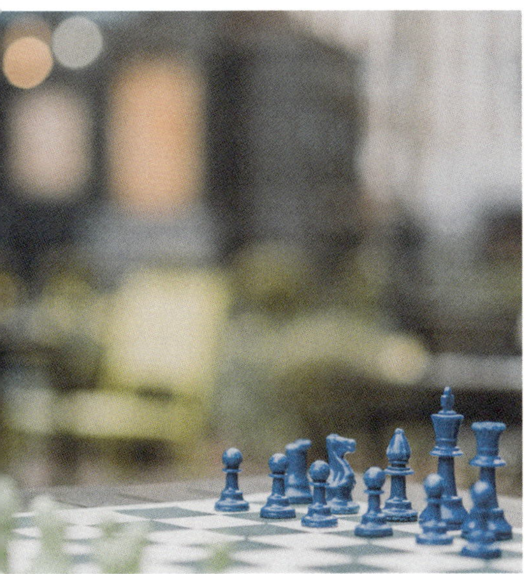
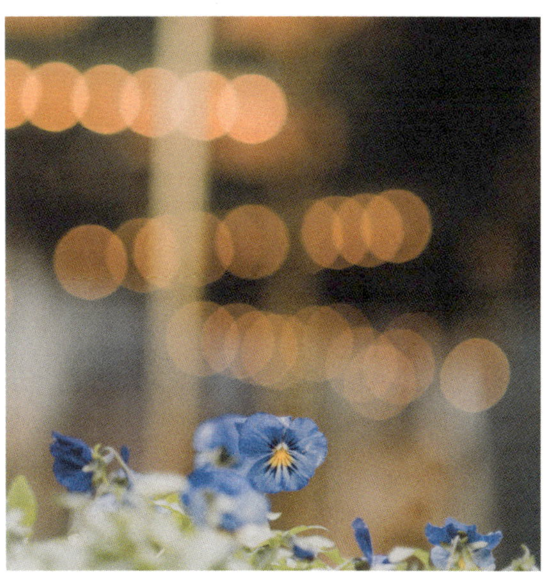

#bryantpark #bryantparknyc #bryantparkwintervillage #bryantparkfountain #nycparks @bryantparknyc

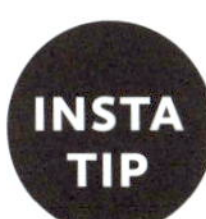

INSTA TIP

There is so much to see and do in Bryant Park. Zoom in on some of the details to capture the park's colorful and upbeat atmosphere.

39 TIMES SQUARE

Times Square

HOW TO GET THERE
Subway A, E (blue), N, Q, R (yellow), 1, 2, 3 (red) or 7 (purple) to 42 Street - Times Square Station

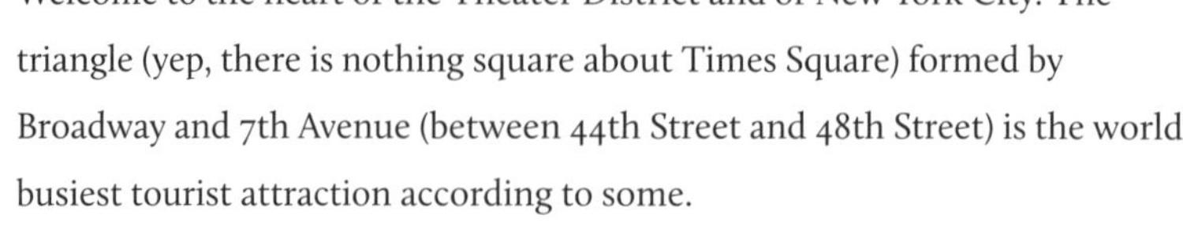

Welcome to the heart of the Theater District and of New York City. The triangle (yep, there is nothing square about Times Square) formed by Broadway and 7th Avenue (between 44th Street and 48th Street) is the world's busiest tourist attraction according to some.

As Alicia Keys famously sang: "Big Lights Will Inspire You", and this is definitely the case when you're standing in the center of this fascinating square, which has the world's largest concentration of billboards. It is said you can even see the light from space.

On New Year's Eve, you can watch the world-famous Dropping of the Ball here, along with 2 million other revelers. A spectacular event that is watched by another 10 million viewers on TV. But there's always something equally spectacular going on here, on the 364 other days of the year.

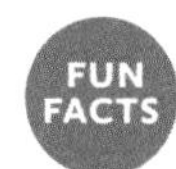

Times Square was only given its name in 1904, when the New York Times moved its headquarters to the new intersection. It was previously known as Longacre Square. The New York Times also organized the first New Years Eve Party in Times Square, which has since become a tradition.

Listen to the permanent sound installation by the artist Max Neuhaus under the subway ventilation grate between 45th and 46th Street.
It is nicknamed The hum and you can only hear it when you stand on the grate.

Want to promote your company? A LED billboard at Times Square costs anything between 1 million and 4 million dollar a year.

INSTAGRAMMABLE PLACES IN THE NEIGHBORHOOD

COFFEE	Bibble & Sip: 253 W 51st Street (5 min. walk)
FOOD	Los Tacos No. 1: 229 W 43rd Street (1 min. walk)
SEE	Midtown Comics Times Square: 200 W 40th Street (4 min. walk)

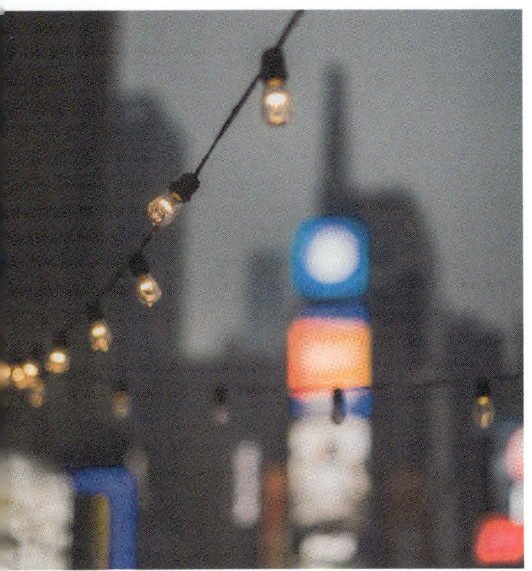

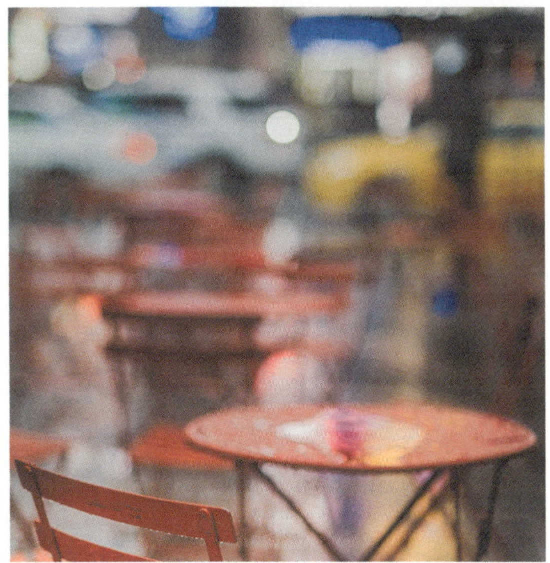

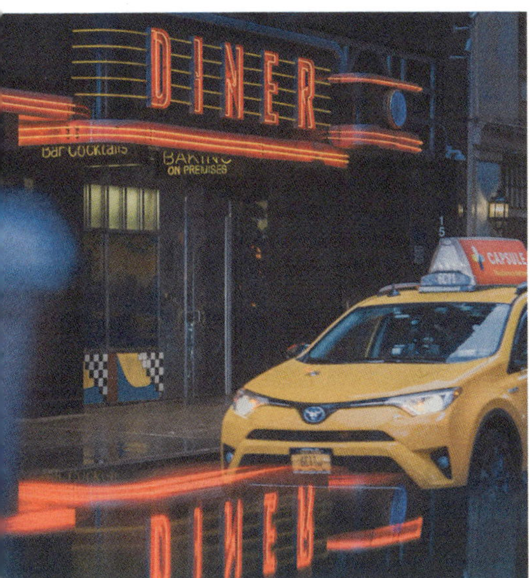

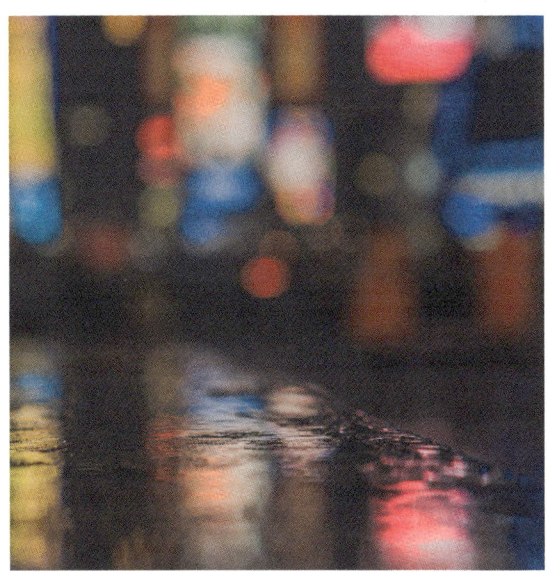

#timesquare #timesquarenyc #timesquarenewyork #midtown #empirestateofmind

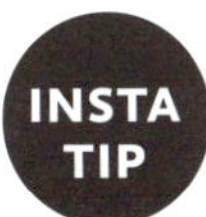

Rainy days are the perfect time to visit Times Square. The crowds are thinner and you can also use the water puddles, which magically reflect the colourful lights of the many billboards.

⓸⓪ BROADWAY

Broadway & The Theater District

HOW TO GET THERE
Subway N, Q, R, W (yellow) to 49 Street Station

Subway 1, 2 (red) to 50 Street Station

Follow the twinkling lights from Times Square along Broadway to walk to the Theater District. Broadway theater refers to the theatrical performances in the 41 Broadway theaters currently in operation. Only four of these theaters are actually located on Broadway. To be eligible for the title of Broadway Theater, a production must be in a house with at least 500 seats (100-499 is called "off Broadway" and under 100 seats "off off Broadway"). In recent years, Broadway shows have experienced a huge revival among New Yorkers. While tickets can be quite expensive, attending a real Broadway show while in New York is a fun experience.

If you want to understand the meaning of "Bright lights, big city", then take a walk around this neighbourhood where even the subway station and the hamburger joints have illuminated signs!

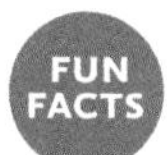

Broadway owes its nickname, The Great White Way, to the many electric signs, that dazzle visitors. In 1880, it was one of the first streets in the US to have electric lights.

The church bells of St Malachi's, The Actor's Chapel (W 49th Street, between Broadway and 8th Avenue) play *There's No Business Like Show Business* on Wednesdays and Saturdays.

Phantom of The Opera premiered in 1988 in The Majestic Theater, where it is still performed today, making it the longest-running Broadway show to date.

INSTAGRAMMABLE PLACES IN THE NEIGHBORHOOD

COFFEE	Simon Sips: 1185 6th Avenue
FOOD	Bea: 403 W 43rd Street
SEE	The Lyceum Theatre: 149 W 45th Street
	The Majestic Theatre: 245 W 44th Street

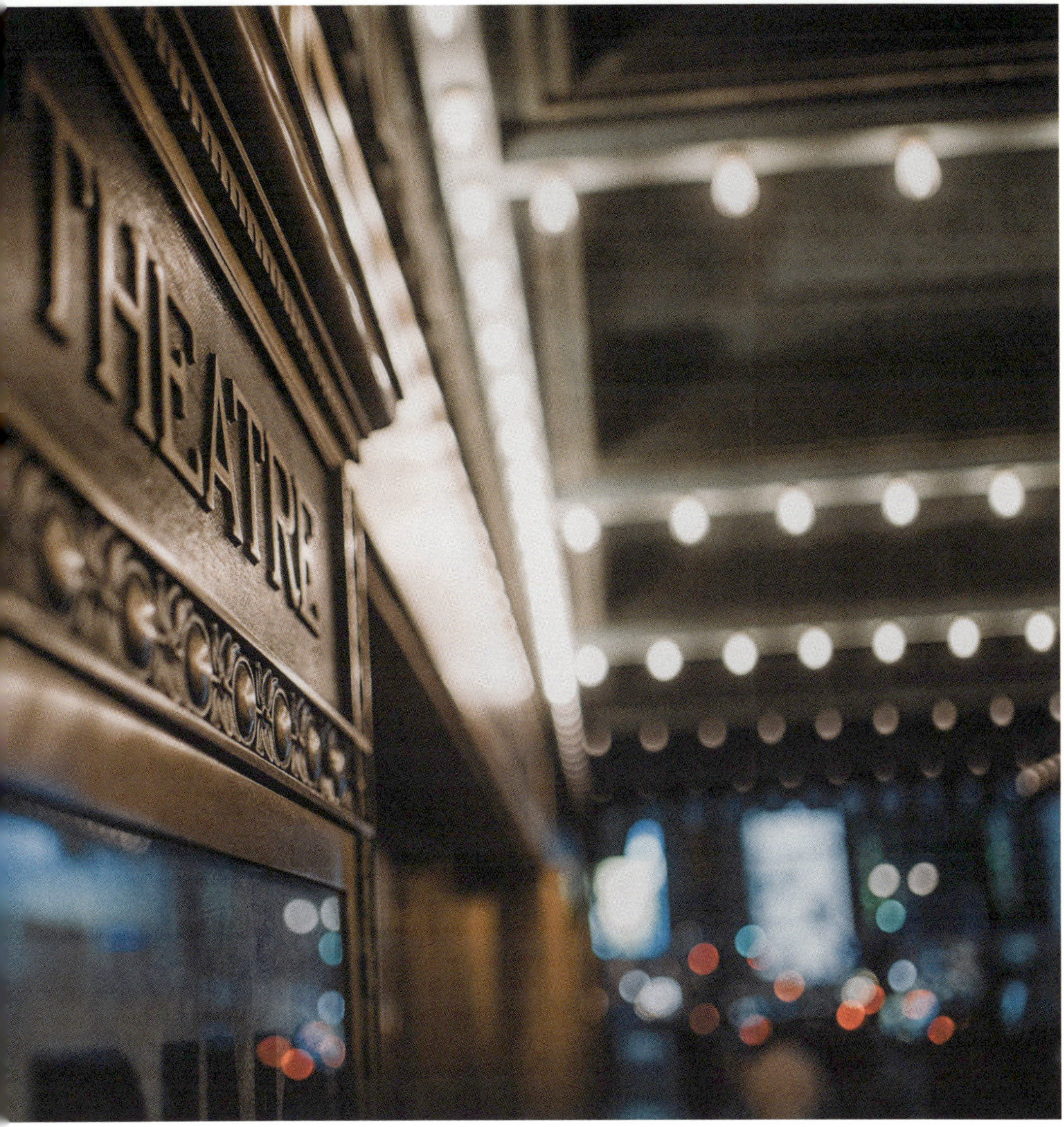

#broadway #broadwaytheater #theaterdistrict #midtown #brightlightsbigcity

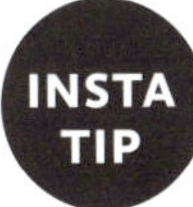

"Light" is the theme of this neighborhood! At night especially, you can enjoy the typical electric signs of Broadway's theaters. It's really worth waiting for darkness to fall if you want to take the most amazing Insta-pics.

41 HUDSON RIVER PARK

Hudson River Park – Pier 84
555 12th Avenue

HOW TO GET THERE
Subway 7 (purple) to Hudson Yards Station

Hudson River Park is America's largest riverside park, covering a surface area of 550 acres (2.2 km^2). If you want to explore the whole park, you'll have to walk 4.5 miles (7.2 km) from Battery Place to W 59th Street.

The park consists of bicycle and pedestrian paths, through beautiful landscaped gardens, various idyllic spots for a picnic, playgrounds and a dog run, tennis and soccer fields and more than 1,700 trees.

The park also has several piers, some of which are still used as a mooring for (tourist) boats like the Circle Line at Pier 83. Others were converted into recreational zones, with additional facilities. You can rent a kayak or a bicycle at Pier 84 for example. If you prefer to kick back, then head to the grassy area where you can tan and cool off in the dancing fountains. They also regularly organize Tai Chi classes here, as well as jazz concerts.

The park is definitely worth a visit for its stunning view of the majestic Hudson River and its impressive boats and ships.

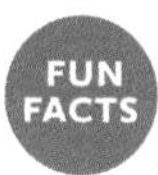

The Hudson River is an estuary, mixing freshwater and salty seawater, with freshwater from New York City to Poughkeepsie and salty water flowing from Poughkeepsie to Lake Tear of the Clouds.

Native Americans used to call the Hudson River the river that flows in two directions because it's a tidal river.

INSTAGRAMMABLE PLACES IN THE NEIGHBORHOOD

COFFEE — Think Coffee: 620 W 42nd Street (5 min. walk)

FOOD — Gotham West Market: 600 11th Avenue (5 min. walk)

SEE — Pier 83, Beast Speedboat Ride: W 42nd Street and 12th Avenue (2 min. walk)

Pier 86, Intrepid Sea Museum: W 46th Street and 12th Avenue (2 min. walk)

Pier 66, Pier 66 Maritime and the Frying Pan: W 26th Street and 12th Avenue (17 min. walk)

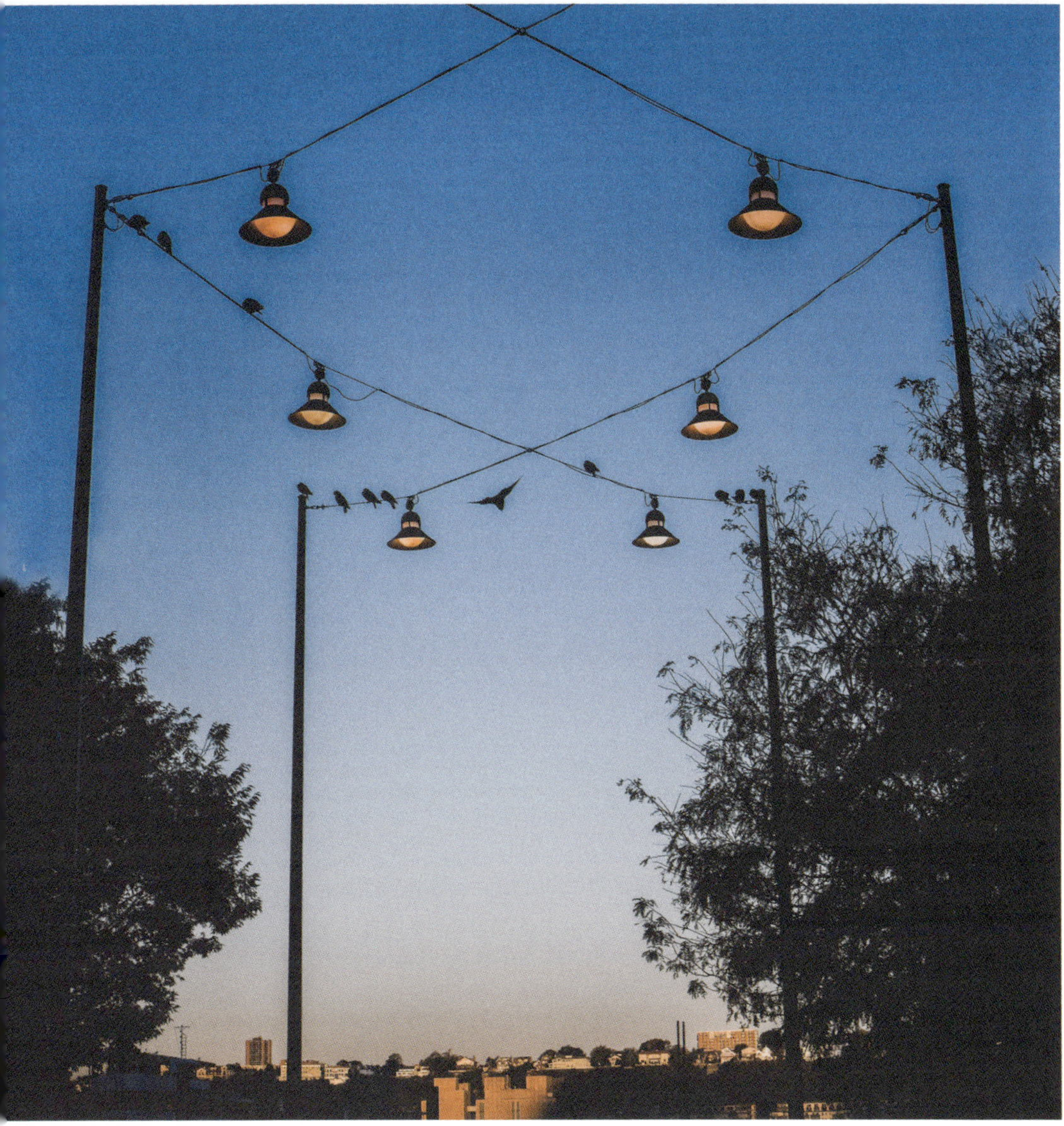

#pier84 #hudsonriverpark #hrpk #nycwaterfront #hellskitchen @hudsonriverpark

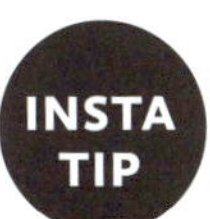

The Hudson River flows along the west side of Manhattan. As a result, the New Jersey skyline is beautifully illuminated by the rising sun and you can enjoy a spectacular sunset here in the evening.

Keep your camera ready for the Golden Hours, just after sunrise and just before sunset.

42 ROCKEFELLER CENTER

Rockefeller Center

HOW TO GET THERE
Subway E (blue) or B, D, F, M to 47-50 Streets - Rockefeller Center Station

The Rockefeller Center calls itself A City Within A City. This impressive complex is located in the center of Midtown Manhattan.

The Rockefeller Center comprises 19 buildings on different blocks, between 5th Avenue and 6th Avenue and 48th Street and 51st Street.

The main building is 30 Rock, an Art Deco skyscraper, which was inaugurated in 1930. The Top of the Rock is the observation deck on the 70th floor, which has a spectacular view of Central Park and the Empire State Building.

The Rockefeller Center is also known for its famous ice-skating rink and monumental Christmas tree. On average the spruce stands 80 feet tall (24 meters) and is decorated with more than 50,000 LED lights. Thousands of New Yorkers and tourists attend the annual Tree Lighting Ceremony.

There are more than 100 artworks in and around the Rockefeller Center. The golden statue of Prometheus is said to be the most photographed sculpture.

$

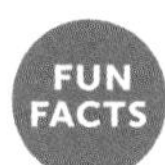

Charles E. Ebbets's famous photo called *Lunch Atop a Skyscraper* was taken during the construction of 30 Rock.

You can see a breath-taking Lego replica of the Rockefeller Center in the Lego Store in Rockefeller Plaza.

The Christmas tree is always recycled after the holidays and the timber is donated to charity. It has been used among others to rebuild houses in the aftermath of Hurricane Katrina.

INSTAGRAMMABLE PLACES IN THE NEIGHBORHOOD

COFFEE Irving Farm Coffee Roasters: 135 E 50th Street (7 min. walk)
FOOD Chloe: 1 Rockefeller Plaza (1 min. walk)
SEE Radio City Music Hall: 1260 6th Avenue (3 min. walk)
Saint Patrick's Cathedral: 5th Avenue, between E 50th and 51st Street (2 min. walk)

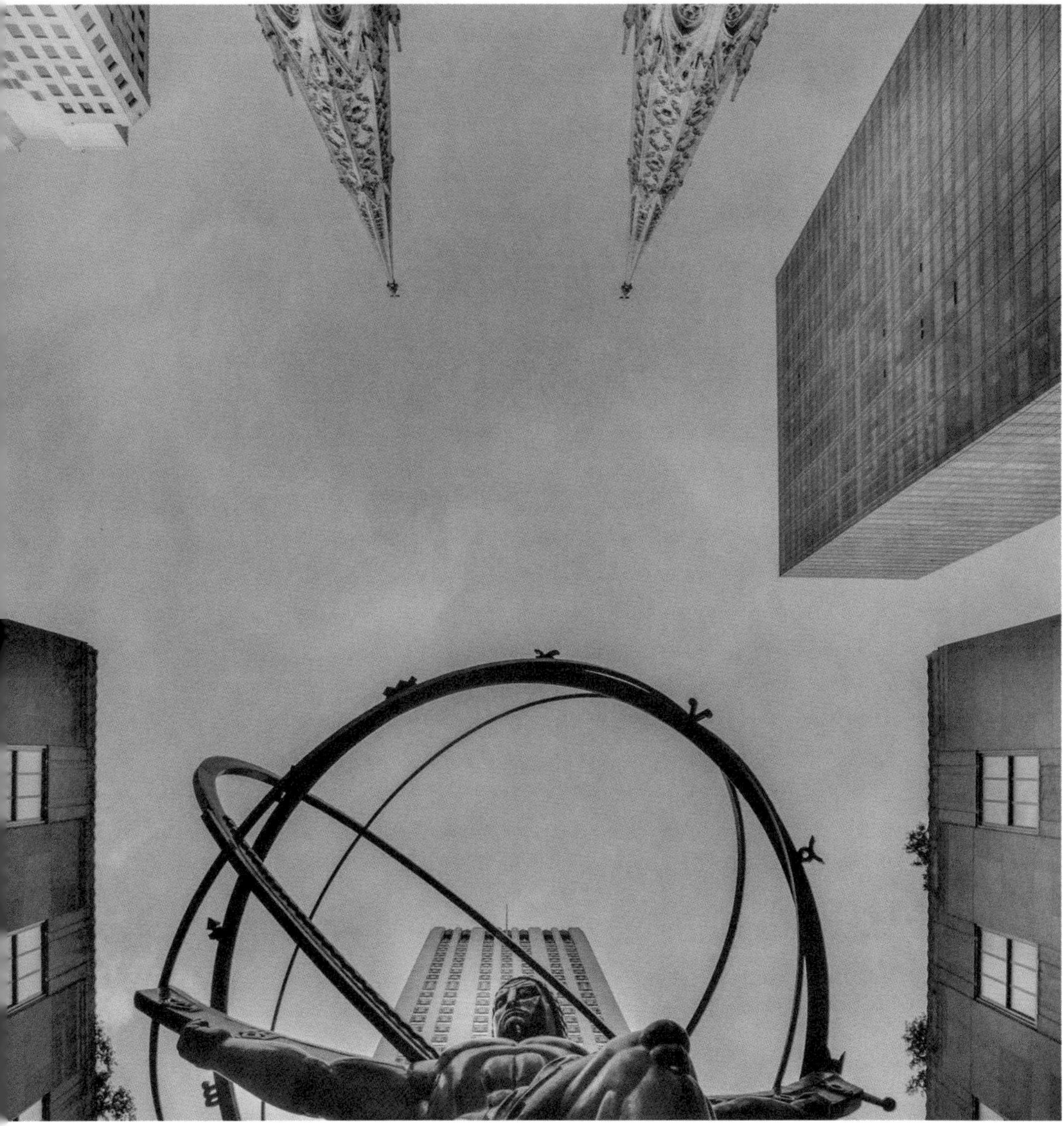

#rockefeller #rockcenternyc #rockcenter #topoftherock #rockcenterplaza
@rockcenternyc

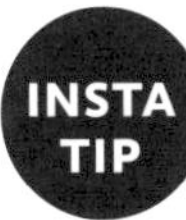

The Atlas sculpture is one of the many artworks in and around Rockefeller Center. You can find it at 45 Rockefeller Plaza, opposite St. Patrick's Cathedral.

When standing under the sculpture, tip your camera and look straight up. You will be able to fit the cathedral's towers and the sculpture in your composition. Try to hold your camera as low as possible to get as much as possible in the frame.

43 RADIO CITY MUSIC HALL

Radio City Music Hall
1260 6th Avenue

HOW TO GET THERE
Subway E (blue) or B, D, F, M to 47-50 Streets - Rockefeller Center Station

$

Radio City Music Hall is an Art Deco style musical hall and is part of the Rockefeller Center. It was the first part of the complex to open and is named after its first tenant, The Radio Corporation of America (RCA).

When the 6,000-seat music hall opened in 1932, it was the world's largest theatre, earning it the nickname of Showplace of the Nation. The Rockettes were one of the opening acts and have since become a Radio City Music Hall icon.

The Radio City Christmas Spectacular starring the world-famous Rockettes is an annual tradition since 1933, attracting over a million spectators every year.

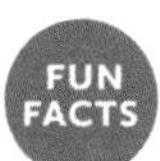

The two large Wurlitzer organs on stage are the largest ever such organs to be built.

A secret tunnel connects Radio City Music Hall and The Rockefeller Center. Artists use it to dodge the paparazzi.

The Rockettes wear wireless microphones in their shoes to amplify the sound of their tap dancing. Watch your step, ladies!

INSTAGRAMMABLE PLACES IN THE NEIGHBORHOOD

SHAKES AND BURGERS	Black Tap: 136 W 55th Street (7 min. walk)
FOOD	The Little Beet: 135 W 50th Street (2 min. walk)
SEE	Waterfall Tunnel: 142 W 49th Street (3 min. walk)
	Moma: 11 W 53rd Street (5 min. walk)
	Hope Sculpture: 200 W 53rd Street (6 min. walk)
	Love Sculpture: Corner W 55th Street and 6th Avenue (4 min. walk)

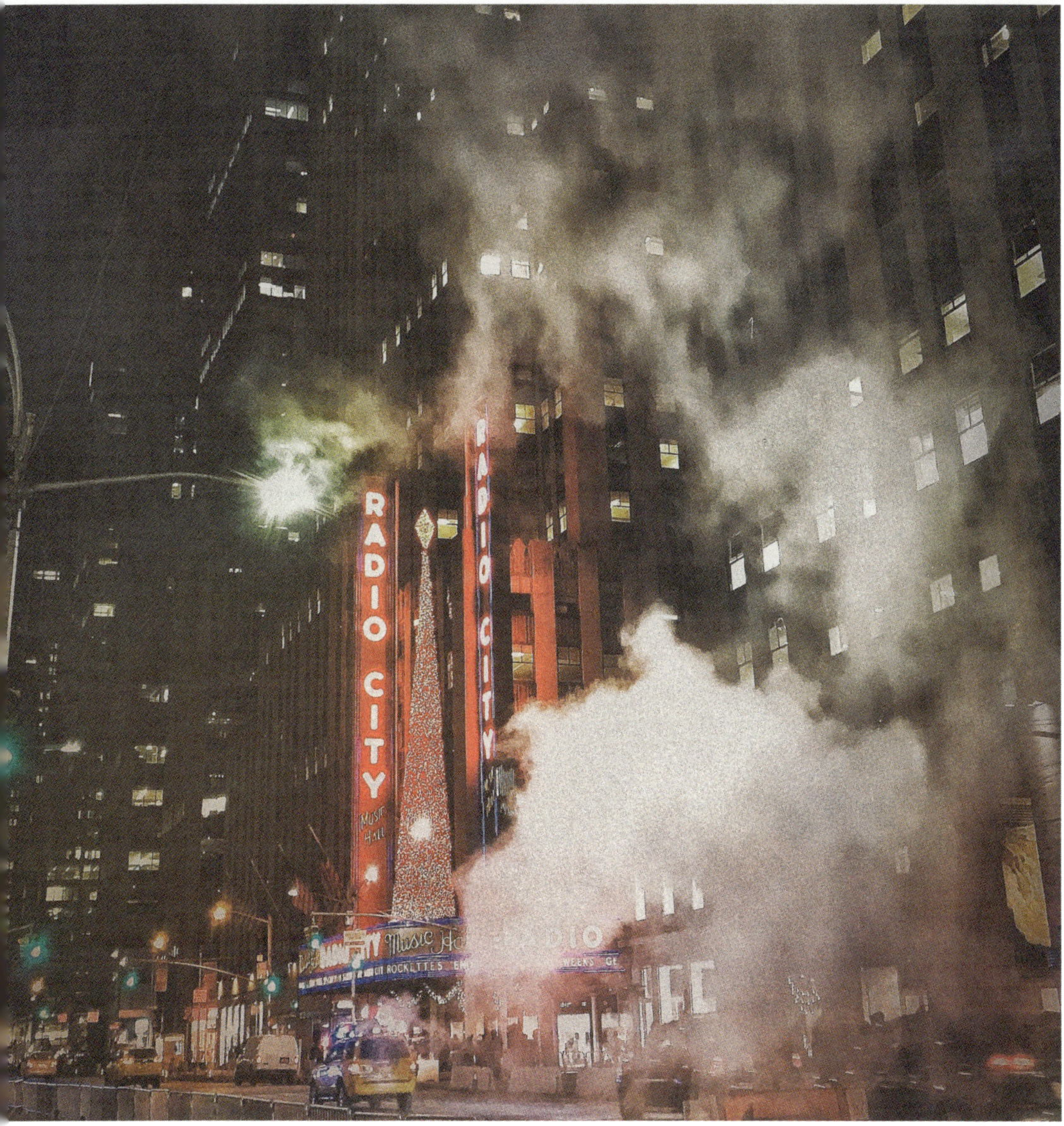

#radiocitymusichall #radiocity #rockcenter #midtown @radiocitymusichall

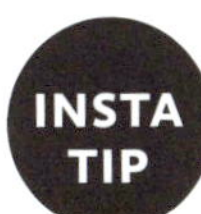

Radio City Music Hall has some stunning electric signs, which look amazing in night-time photos. You can often spot steam rising out of the manholes on 6th Avenue, which only add to the atmosphere of your evening and night-time shots.

❹❹ WATERFALL TUNNEL

Waterfall Tunnel McGraw Hill Park, 142 W 49th Street

HOW TO GET THERE
Subway E (blue) or B, D, F, M to 47-50 Streets - Rockefeller Center Station

Subway N, R, W (yellow) to 49 Street Station

A mini park is tucked away in between the skyscrapers on the west side of the McGraw-Hill Building. The pocket-sized park connects 48th and 49th Street and has a waterfall/ fountain. The waterfall is 40 feet (12 meters) wide and 20 feet (5 meters) tall and has a Plexiglas tunnel you can walk through.

This mini park is a picturesque place to relax in busy Manhattan and a popular lunchtime spot with New Yorkers who work nearby.

You can also regularly see pop-up artworks here. Recent installations include Playlab's *Grown Up Flowers* and Gillie & Marc's *Paparazzi Dogman & Paparazzi Rabbitgirl.*

You can only walk through the serene waterfall tunnel during daytime. The park is closed at night, with a gate. On weekdays it is open from 9 am till 6 pm and on weekends from 9 am till 3 pm.

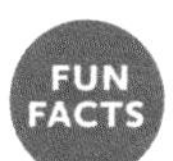

There are approximately 520 P.O.P.S. (privately owned public spaces) in Manhattan. Passers-by rarely notice these small "parks" among the tall buildings. Each park has its own personality and story.

The rock band Kiss once posed for a photo shoot at the Waterfall Tunnel.

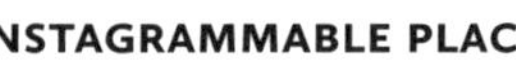

INSTAGRAMMABLE PLACES IN THE NEIGHBORHOOD

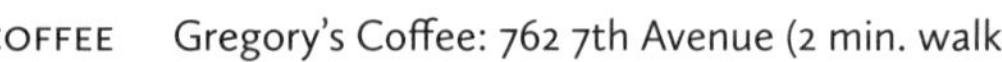

COFFEE	Gregory's Coffee: 762 7th Avenue (2 min. walk)
FOOD	The Little Beet: 135 W 50th Street (2 min. walk)
SEE	Radio City Music Hall: 1260 6th Avenue (3 min. walk)
	Moma: 11 W 53rd Street (8 min. walk)

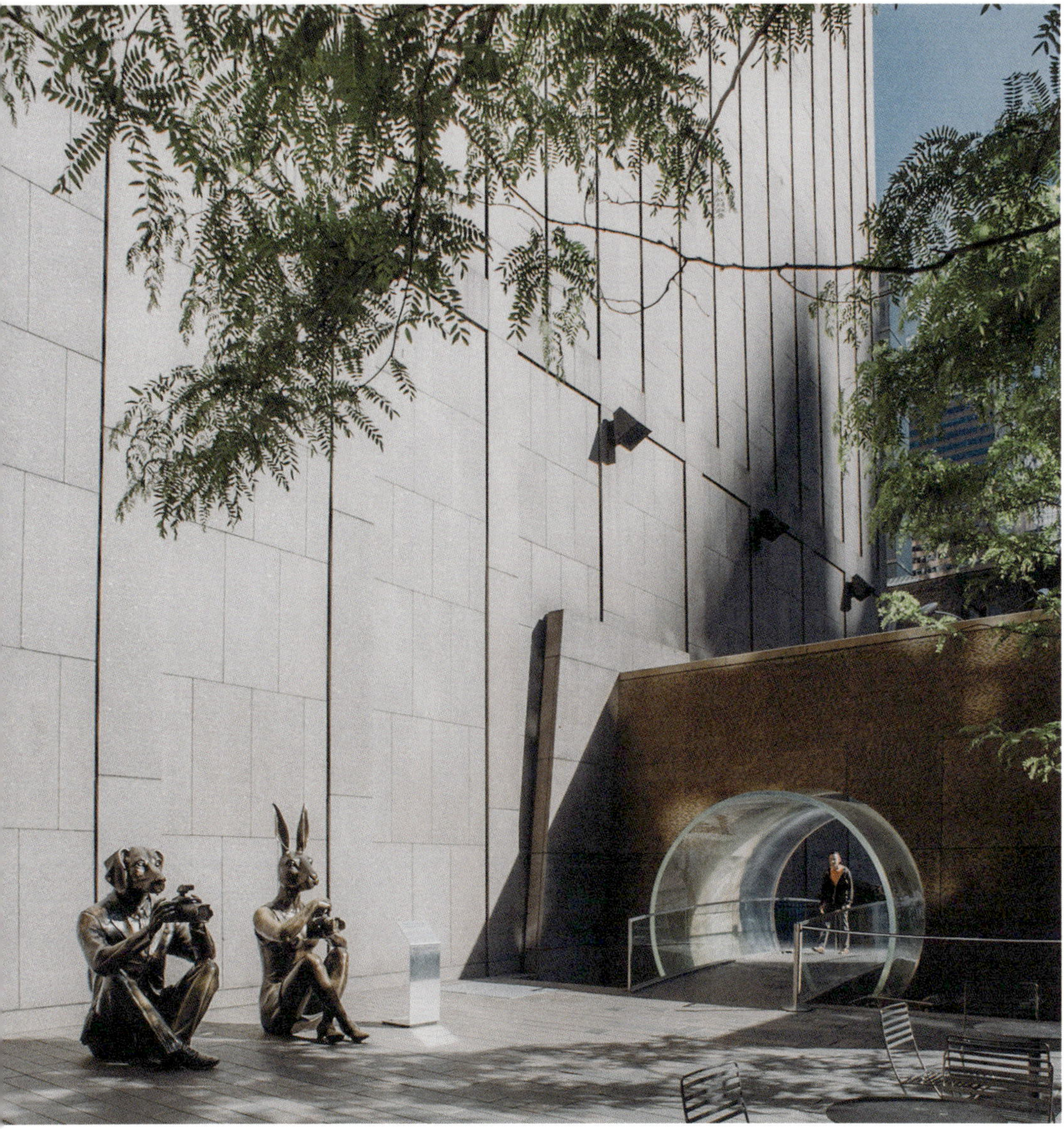

#waterfalltunnel #nycsecrets #nychiddengems #midtown #pocketparks

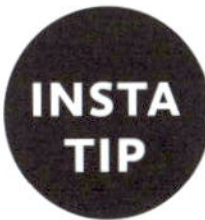

The tunnel and park are pocket sized and are surrounded by tall buildings. Take a photo of a passer-by to illustrate its size. You can ask one of your travel companions to pose or wait for someone to walk through the tunnel.

45 MOMA

Moma
(The Museum of Modern Art)
11 W 53rd Street

HOW TO GET THERE
Subway E (blue) or M (orange) to 5 Avenue / 53 Street Station

$

Art is everywhere in New York, and you can find public art or a museum on almost every street corner.

One of the most prominent and best-known museums of New York (and the world) is The Museum of Modern Art, which is better known as MoMA.

Here you can see art by some of the world's most famous modern and contemporary artists, including Pablo Picasso's *Les Demoiselles D'Avignon*, Vincent Van Gogh's *The 'Starry Night*, Andy Warhol's *Campbell's Soup Cans*, and more than 150,000 other artworks, many of which you will probably recognize from your school books.

MoMA PS1, debuted in Long Island City (Queens), in 2000, after being initially founded in 1976 as the P.S. 1 Contemporary Art Center.

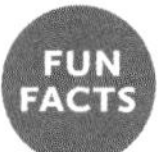

One of The MoMA's founders was Abby Aldrich Rockefeller, the wife of John D. Rockefeller, who built the Rockefeller Center. As her husband disliked modern art, she was unable to count on his financial support. The first artworks were acquired thanks to donations and her solicitation of the public and corporations for funding.

The iconic Love sculpture on 55th Street is inspired by an original image for a MoMA Christmas card in 1964.

INSTAGRAMMABLE PLACES IN THE NEIGHBORHOOD

MILKSHAKES	Black Tap: 136 W 55th Street (4 min. walk)
FOOD	Burger Joint at the Parker Meridian: 119 W 56th Street (4 min. walk)
SEE	Hope Sculpture: 200 W 53rd Street (2 min. walk)
	Love Sculpture: Corner W 55th Street and 6th Avenue (6 min. walk)

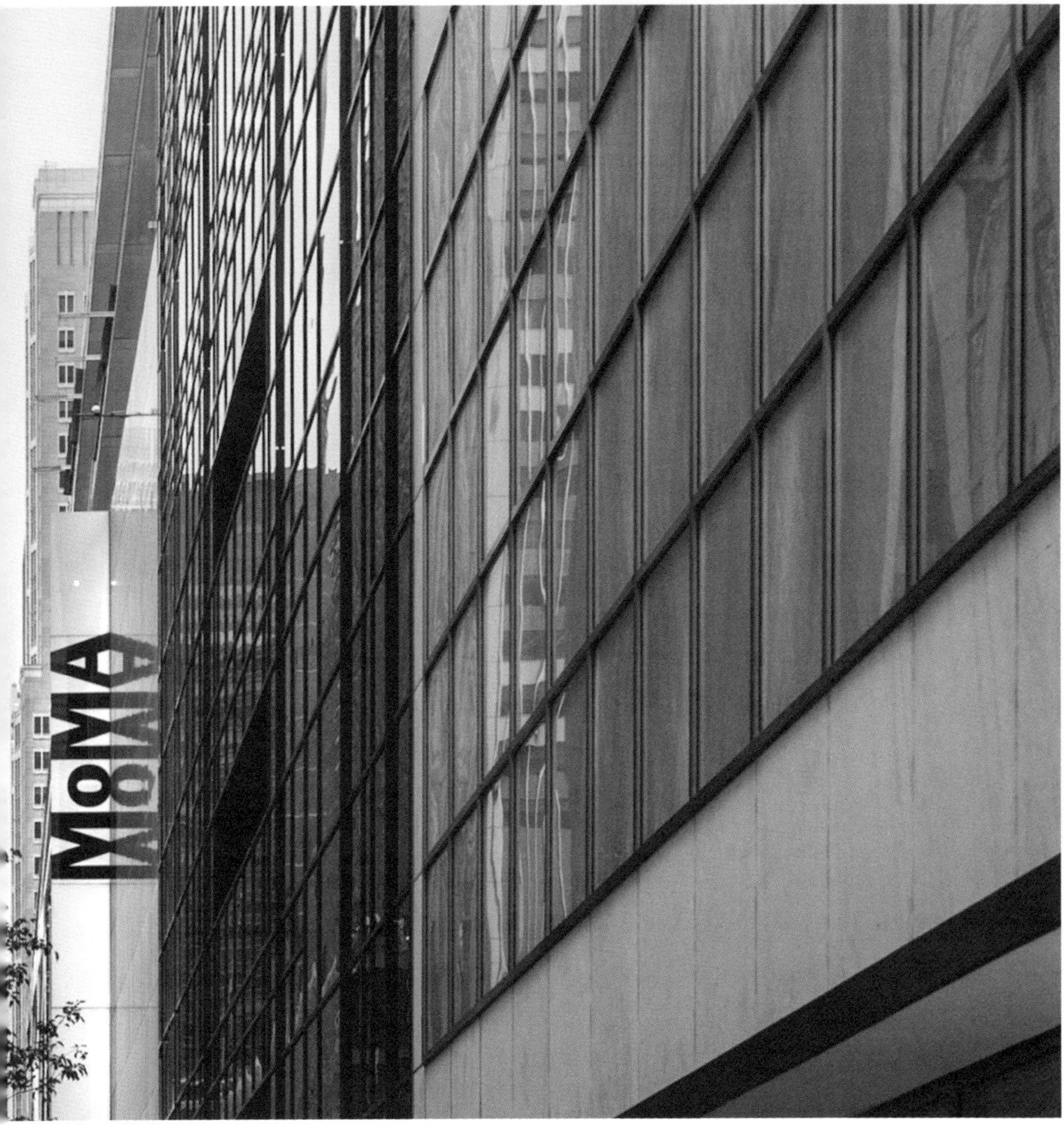

#moma #momanyc #themuseumofmodernart #nycmuseums @themuseumofmodernart

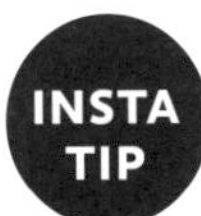

Even the font of MoMA has an iconic look & feel. You can capture it at the entrance while it reflects in the glass building.

46 SPYSCAPE

Spyscape
928 8th
Avenue

HOW TO GET THERE
Subway
1 (red) to
59 Street -
Columbus
Circle Station

Subway N
(yellow) or F
(orange) to 57
Street

Subway E
(blue) to 50th
Street

Spyscape is an interactive spy museum, that was created with the assistance of former directors of intelligence services. During this immersive experience, you become a spy in training, who must complete various challenges.
On entry, you are handed a digital wristband, which stores your personal information and results and you are guided to a gigantic elevator where you are briefed.

Every gallery features an interesting combination of historical objects, fascinating stories and fun challenges. You can complete your training by decoding texts and dodging lasers (which makes for some fun photos).

At the end of your training a digital mirror reveals which spy job is best suited to you. Head to the bar for a Martini afterwards. "Shaken, not stirred" of course.

FUN FACTS

There's a huge display case filled with Guy Fawkes masks and some of them are signed by the actual members of the Anonymous hacker collective.

Spyscape also has a book shop on the ground floor. The collection, which was curated by hackers, features over 700 rare and first edition espionage books.

INSTAGRAMMABLE PLACES IN THE NEIGHBORHOOD

COCKTAIL Tanner Smith's: 204 W 55th Street (3 min. walk)
FOOD Bareburger: 313 W 57th Street (3 min. walk)
SEE Museum of Arts and Design (MAD): 2 Columbus Circle (4 min. walk)
Time Warner Center: 10 Columbus Circle (5 min. walk)

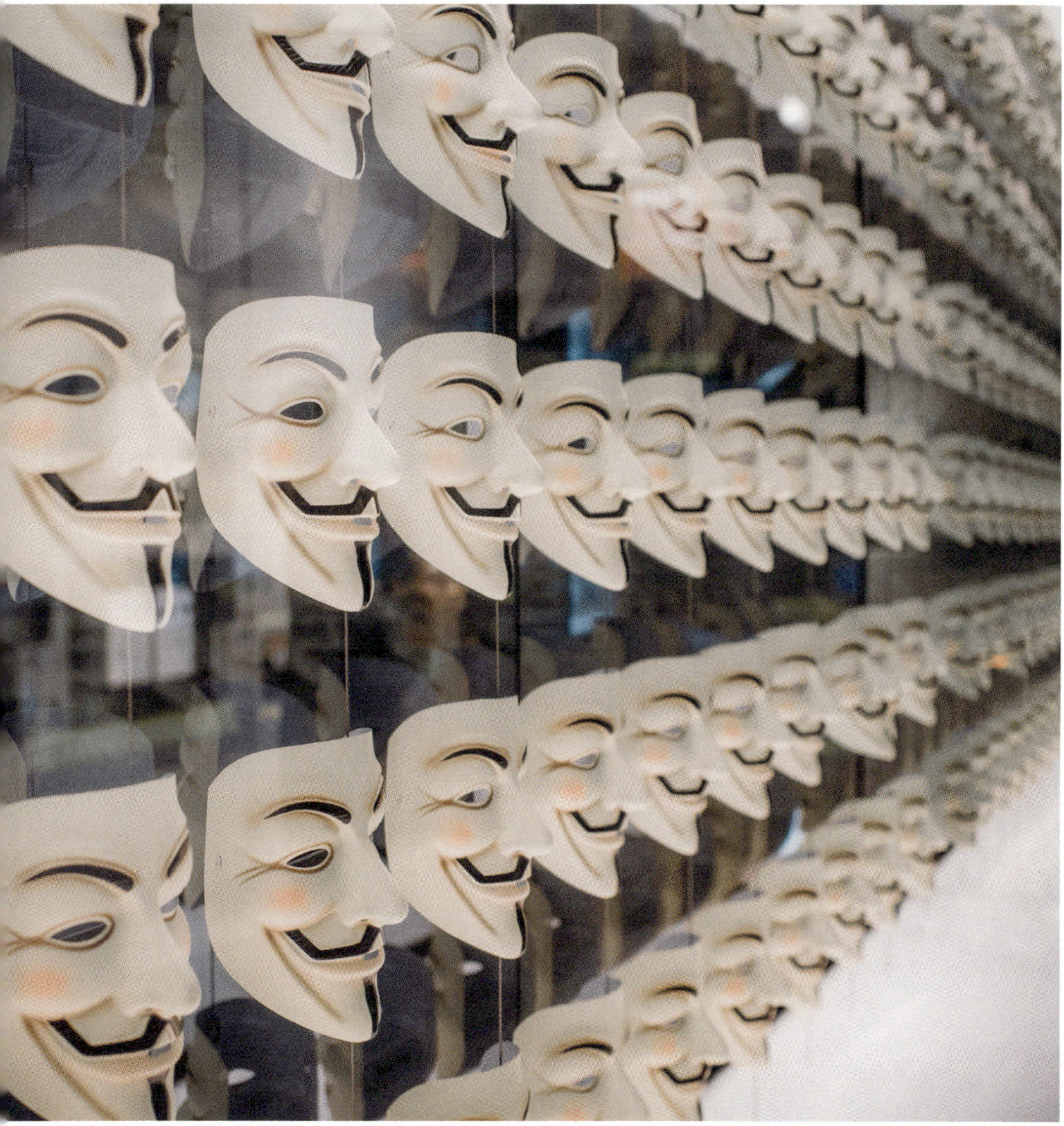

#spyscape #spyscapenyc #quetioneverything #ispyny @spyscape

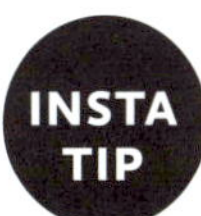

The display case with the Guy Fawkes (Anonymous) has a mirror on the side, so you can achieve an infinite effect.

47 MUSEUM OF ARTS AND DESIGN (MAD)

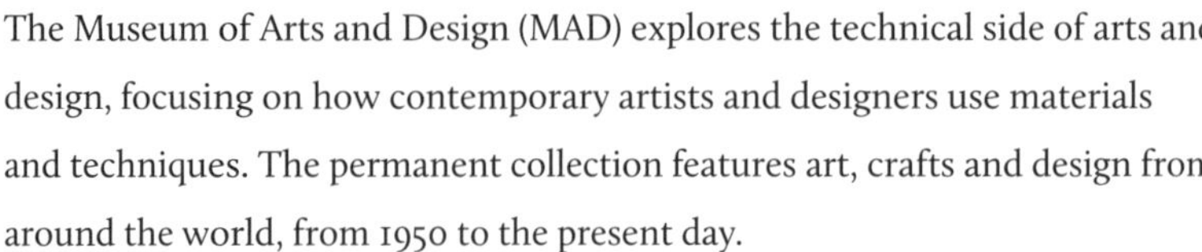

Museum of Arts and Design
2 Columbus Circle

HOW TO GET THERE
Subway 1, 2 (red) or A (blue) or D (orange) to 59 Street - Columbus Circle

The Museum of Arts and Design (MAD) explores the technical side of arts and design, focusing on how contemporary artists and designers use materials and techniques. The permanent collection features art, crafts and design from around the world, from 1950 to the present day.

The museum mainly wants to educate visitors, which is why it has three open artist studios where artists in residence offer a hands-on experience, teaching visitors about the creative production process and allowing them to test their skills. You can visit the studios and the artists daily, from 10 am until 5 pm.

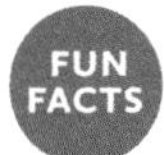

FUN FACTS

You can also visit the Tiffany & Co Foundation Gallery in the MAD, where you can see contemporary jewelry in study drawers.

Restaurant Robert is located on the museum's top floor. This classic restaurant offers impressive views of Columbus Circle and Central Park.

INSTAGRAMMABLE PLACES IN THE NEIGHBORHOOD

COFFEE AND FOOD	Turnstyle Underground Market (foodhall): Located beneath 8th Avenue, between 57th and 58th, at the 59th St - Columbus Circle station (no Metro Card required). Here you can find: 16 Handles x Mochidoki, Chick 'n Cone, Doughnuttery, Panda Bubble Tea...
COFFEE	Birch Coffee: 884 9th Avenue (4 min. walk)
FOOD	Bareburger: 313 W 57th Street (2 min. walk)
SEE	The Lincoln Center: 10 Lincoln Center Plaza (8 min. walk)
	Wollman Rink: 830 5th Avenue (9 min. walk)

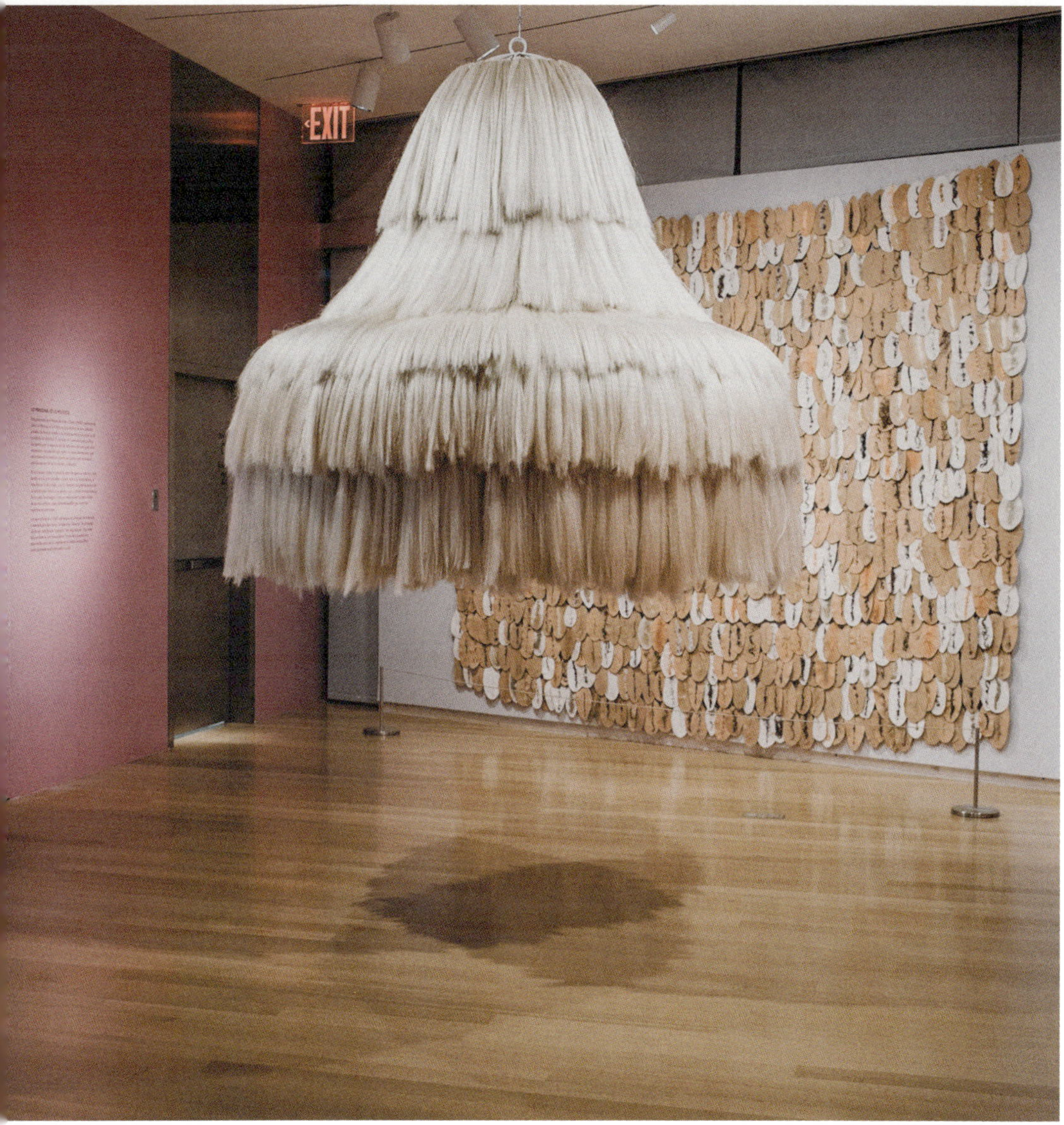

#madmuseum #madnyc #nycmuseums #artsanddesign @madmuseum

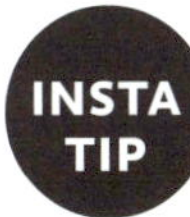

The MAD museum specializes in materials and techniques and both are interesting photo subjects. You can try to combine two different works in one shot to draw attention to the materials' texture.

On this picture:Tanya Aguiñiga, Palapa, 2017, Tanya Aguiñiga: Craft & Care.

⓸⓼ COLUMBUS CIRCLE

Columbus Circle 848 Columbus Circle

HOW TO GET THERE

Subway 1, 2 (red) or A (blue) or D (orange) to 59 Street - Columbus Circle

Columbus Circle marks the boundary between Midtown and the Upper West Side and is located at the intersection of Broadway, 8th Avenue, 59th Street and Central Park. This is one of the few circles in Manhattan, which is laid out in a grid pattern.

Columbus Circle became known as such in 1892, on the 400th anniversary of the discovery of America by Christopher Colombus. The 76-foot (23 metre) monument at the center of the circle features a marble statue of the intrepid explorer, who looks out over the city. This monument is the city's geographic center and the point from which official highway distances to and from New York City are measured.

When you exit the 59th St - Columbus Circle (NE corner) subway station, you'll see the large Globe Sculpture rise up in front of you as you walk up. This large globe (30 feet/ 9 metres) is a tribute to the even larger Unisphere (120 feet/ 36 metres) in Corona park in Queens.

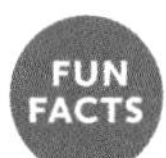

The Stay Puft Marshmallow Man crashes through Columbus Circle in the Ghostbusters movie.

The Columbus statue was donated to the City of New York by the Italian-American community. The funds for the sculpture were raised by the Italian newspaper Il Progresso.

INSTAGRAMMABLE PLACES IN THE NEIGHBORHOOD

COFFEE AND FOOD	Turnstyle Underground Market (foodhall): Located beneath 8th Avenue, between 57th and 58th, at the 59th St - Columbus Circle station (no Metro Card required). Here you can find: 16 Handles x Mochidoki, Chick 'n Cone, Doughnuttery, Panda Bubble Tea...
SEE	Lincoln Center: 10 Lincoln Center Plaza (7 min. walk)
	The Museum of Art & Design (MAD): 2 Columbus Circle (1 min. walk)
	Time Warner Center: 10 Columbus Circle (1 min. walk)

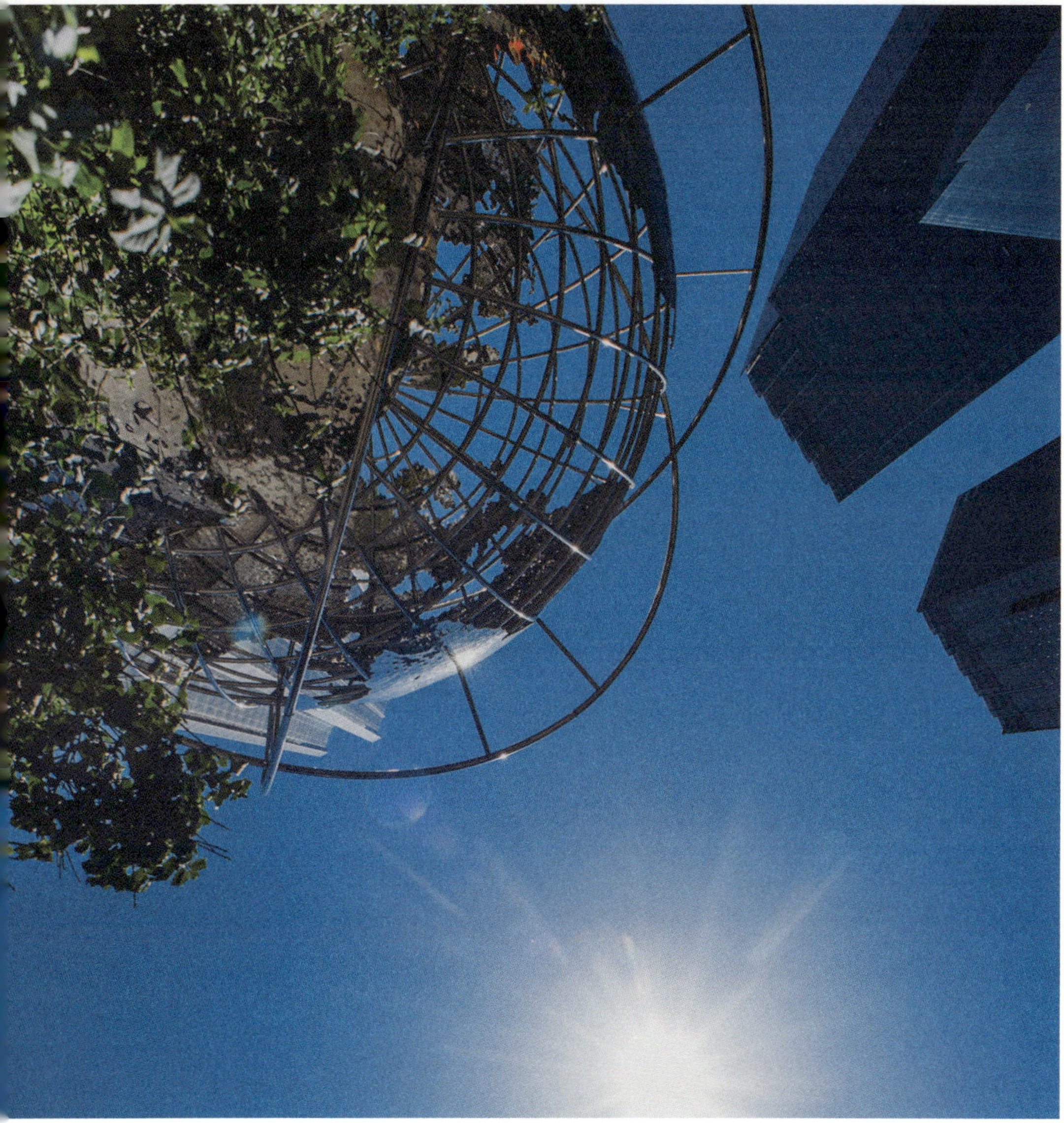

#columbuscircle #columbuscirclenyc #columbuscircleglobe #manhattanstreets #nycstreets

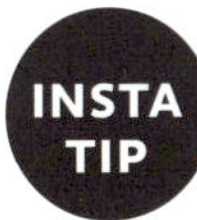

The Globe sculpture is a perfect artwork for a photo from a frog's eye perspective.

Take a photo from the entrance of the subway station next to the sculpture to fit as much as of the globe as possible in your frame. The result is an unusual composition combining the globe's rounded shape and the Time Warner Center's towers.

49 TIME WARNER CENTER

Time Warner Center 10 Columbus Circle

HOW TO GET THERE
Subway 1, 2 (red) or A (blue) or D (orange) to 59 Street - Columbus Circle

This building's architecture is quite unique. Sometimes the two glass towers literally disappear before your eyes because of the reflection of the sky and the clouds while the curved façade seems to trace the outline of Columbus Circle. The building thus becomes the outer circle of the actual circle.

The center was designed as a city in a building, and has a mall and offices, a (five star) hotel and various award-winning restaurants. You can also rent luxury residences in the building, which is also occupied by the CNN studios and the concert venues of Jazz @ Lincoln.

Even if you're not up for some shopping or aren't hungry, it's always worth your while to take a walk around the Center. The view of Columbus Circle from the second floor is always amazing, making it the perfect spot for a photo.

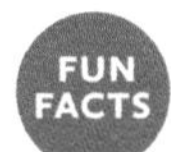

The Time Warner Center has its own subway entrance to 59th St - Columbus Circle Station.

The axis of 59th Street runs through the center, and the architects have indicated this by cleaving the structure into two towers and creating a space in between them.

INSTAGRAMMABLE PLACES IN THE NEIGHBORHOOD

COFFEE AND FOOD	Whole Foods Market at the basement floor
COFFEE AND PASTRY	Bouchan Bakery at the 3rd floor
FOOD	Momofuko at the 3rd floor
SHOP	Sugerfina at the atrium
SEE	The view at the 2nd floor

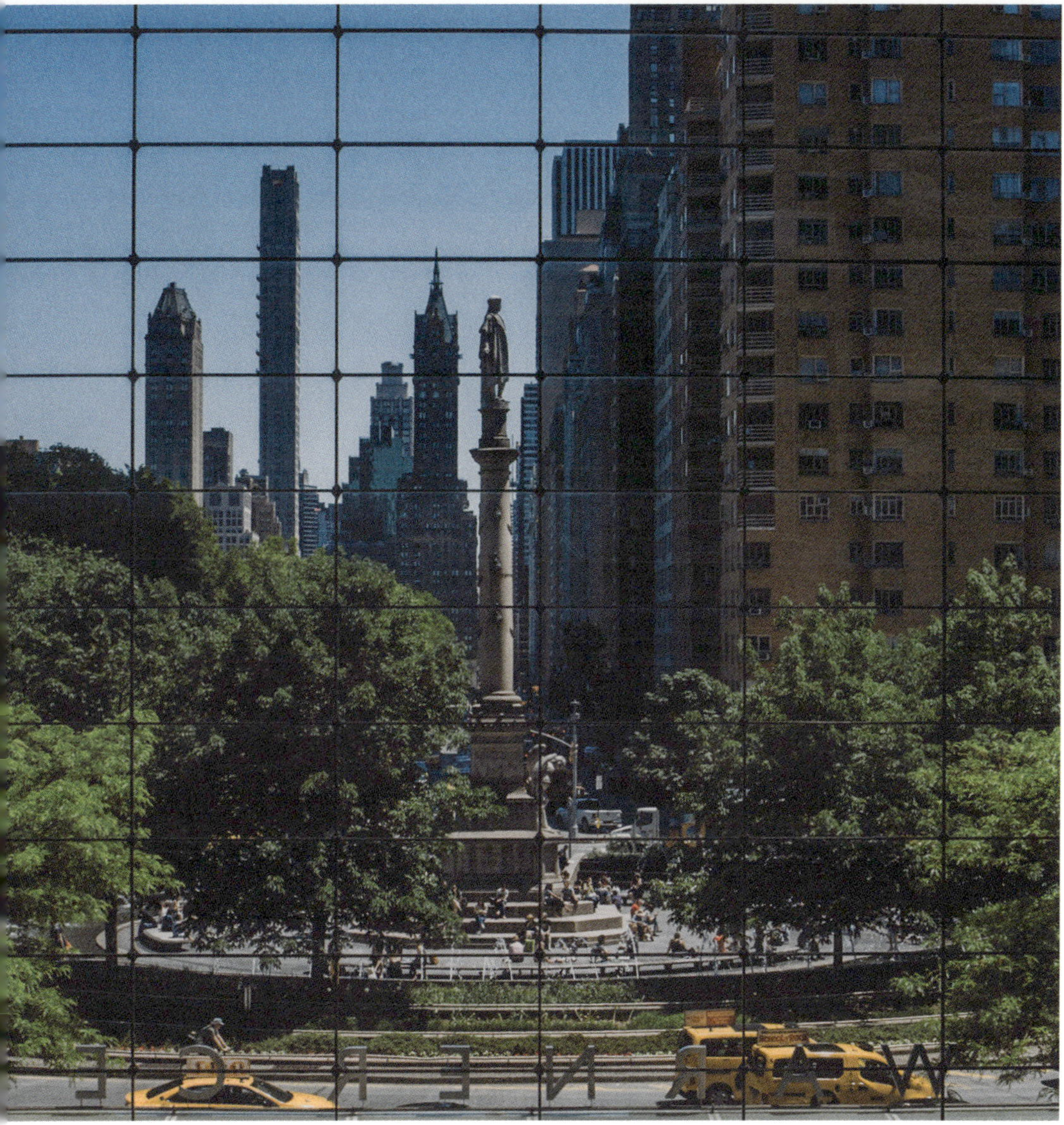

#timewarnercenter #timewarner #columbuscirclemall #columbuscircleshopping
@theshopsatcolumbuscircle

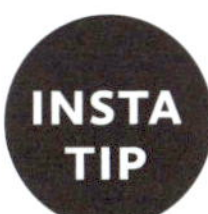

The second-floor terrace offers amazing views of Columbus Circle. You almost come eye to eye with Columbus here. Turn on the camera grid lines to ensure that all the horizontals and verticals in your photo are straight.

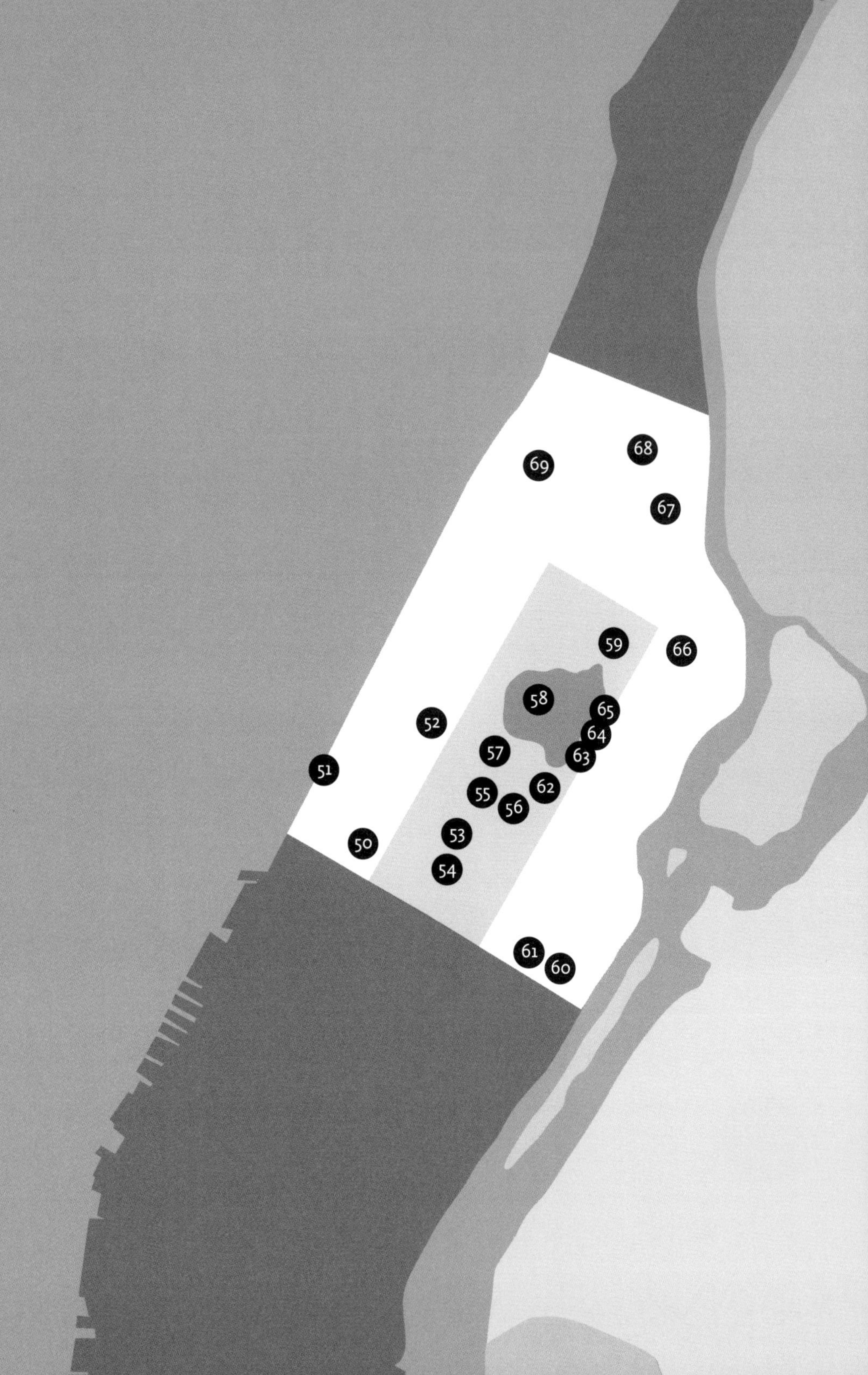

68
69
67
59
66
58
65
52
64
57
63
51
62
55
56
53
50
54
61
60

UPPER WEST
CENTRAL PARK
UPPER EAST
HARLEM

50 LINCOLN CENTER

Lincoln Center of Performing Arts Columbus Avenue, between W 62nd Street and W 65th Street.

HOW TO GET THERE
Subway 1, 2 (red) or A (blue) or D (orange) to 59 Street - Columbus Circle

Lincoln Center is the home of several world-famous cultural organizations, including the New York Philharmonic, the New York City Ballet and the New York City Opera.

It is also the place to go if you love culture. And even if you don't plan on attending a performance, then do visit this amazing center. There are magnificent parks in between the theatres where you can often see dancers and musicians of the Juilliard School of Performing Arts practicing. Take a walk through Hearst Plaza. This square has a large grassy area, which floats over W 65th Street and is reflected in a large rectangular water feature, resembling the set of a futuristic movie. Damrosch Park is just as magnificent, albeit perhaps not as green and can seat 3,000 spectators during open-air performances.

The main eye-catcher is the Revson Fountain. Definitely worth a visit (and a photo) after sunset.

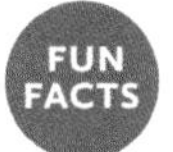

The beaded curtain that covers the glass windows of the New York State Theater consists of 8 million gold-coloured balls: one for every citizen of New York in 1964, when the theater opened.

The David Rubenstein Atrium (on Broadway between 62nd and 63rd Street) is the hidden gem of Lincoln Center. Here you can buy tickets and get information, but it is also a beautifully designed public space (vertical gardens on the walls!) with a coffee bar. This lively meeting place for locals and visitors also hosts free weekly performances.

The Revson Fountain has wind sensors that adjust water, pressure, height and volume so the magnificent water show always looks the same regardless of the weather.

INSTAGRAMMABLE PLACES IN THE NEIGHBORHOOD

COFFEE David Geffen Hall Café: 10 Lincoln Center Plaza
Lincoln Center Public Plaza and Cafe: 61 W 62nd Street

SEE The Revson Fountain: at the center of the Josie Robertson Plaza
Hearst Plaza: 30 Lincoln Center Plaza
Damrosch Park: 60 Lincoln Center Plaza

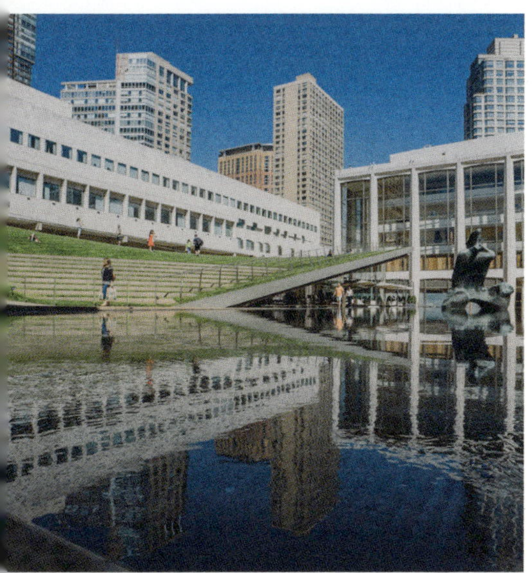

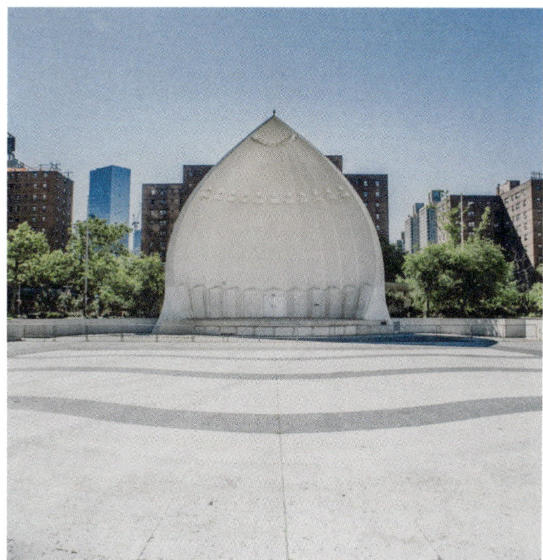

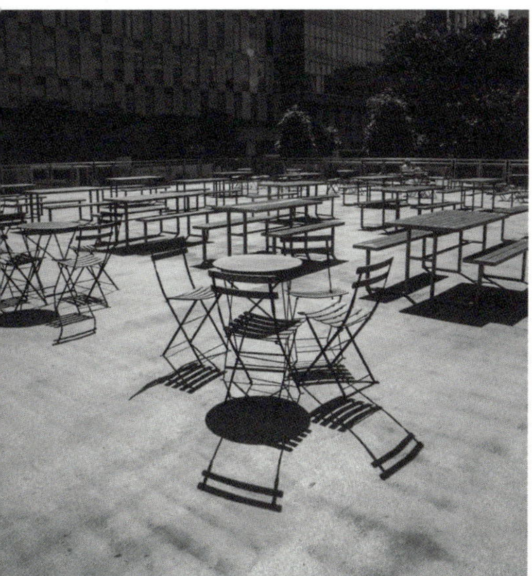

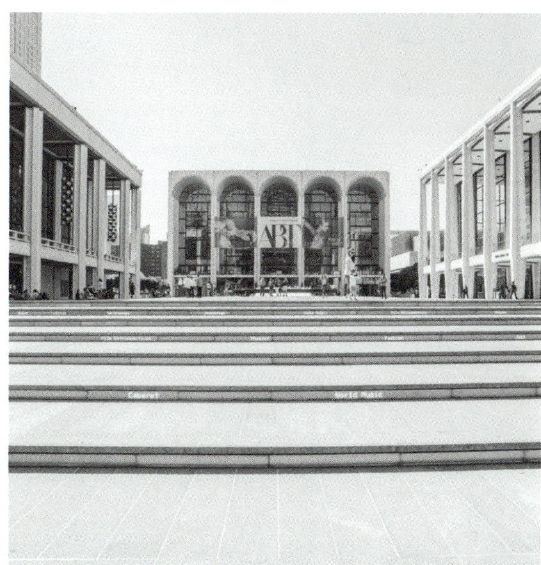

#lincolncenter #lincolncenternyc #lincolncenterplaza @lincolncenter

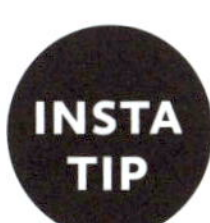

When you explore this site, you'll soon notice the many lines. Focus on this to add a new, original perspective to a location that has already been photographed many times before.

51 PIER I CAFE

Pier i cafe
500 W 70th Street

HOW TO GET THERE
Subway 1, 2 or 3 (red) to 72 Street - Broadway Station

The Pier i café is an outdoor terrace on the Hudson River, near Pier I, where you can enjoy a casual lunch or dinner with a stunning view.

The café is situated in the relatively new Riverside Park South (the first part opened in 2001, the last section is scheduled to open in 2019). This site was a former location of the New York Central Railroad. The dock was used for the transfer of railroad cars from the rail line to car floats, to and from the hinterland. In 1920, New York's population depended on this dock for its supplies, which is why it was nicknamed New York's lifeline.

The designers of Riverside Park chose to retain several industrial elements and incorporate in the green park. The result is a success, as you can tell from the many locals who can be found jogging, playing and walking in the park every weekend.

Pier I is the last pier in this area on which you can still walk. All that remains of Piers B, D, E, F and G are a few posts in the water. Pier I is currently being restored and is now used by fishermen, joggers and for public activities and events in the summertime.

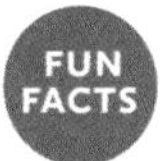

Riverside Park has a number of quiet zones. No radios, team sports or dogs are allowed here.

The Hudson River Greenway bike path is New York City's longest cycling route, connecting Battery Park in the south with Dyckman Street in the north of the city, cutting through Hudson River Park and Riverside Park.

INSTAGRAMMABLE PLACES IN THE NEIGHBORHOOD

FOOD & DRINKS — Pier i Café!

SEE — The Sanctuary: open air public art: 9a Hudson River Greenway (7 min. walk)

The Eleanor Roosevelt Memorial: W 72nd Street (3 min. walk)

The Seventy-ninth Street Boat Basin: W 79th Street (12 min. walk)

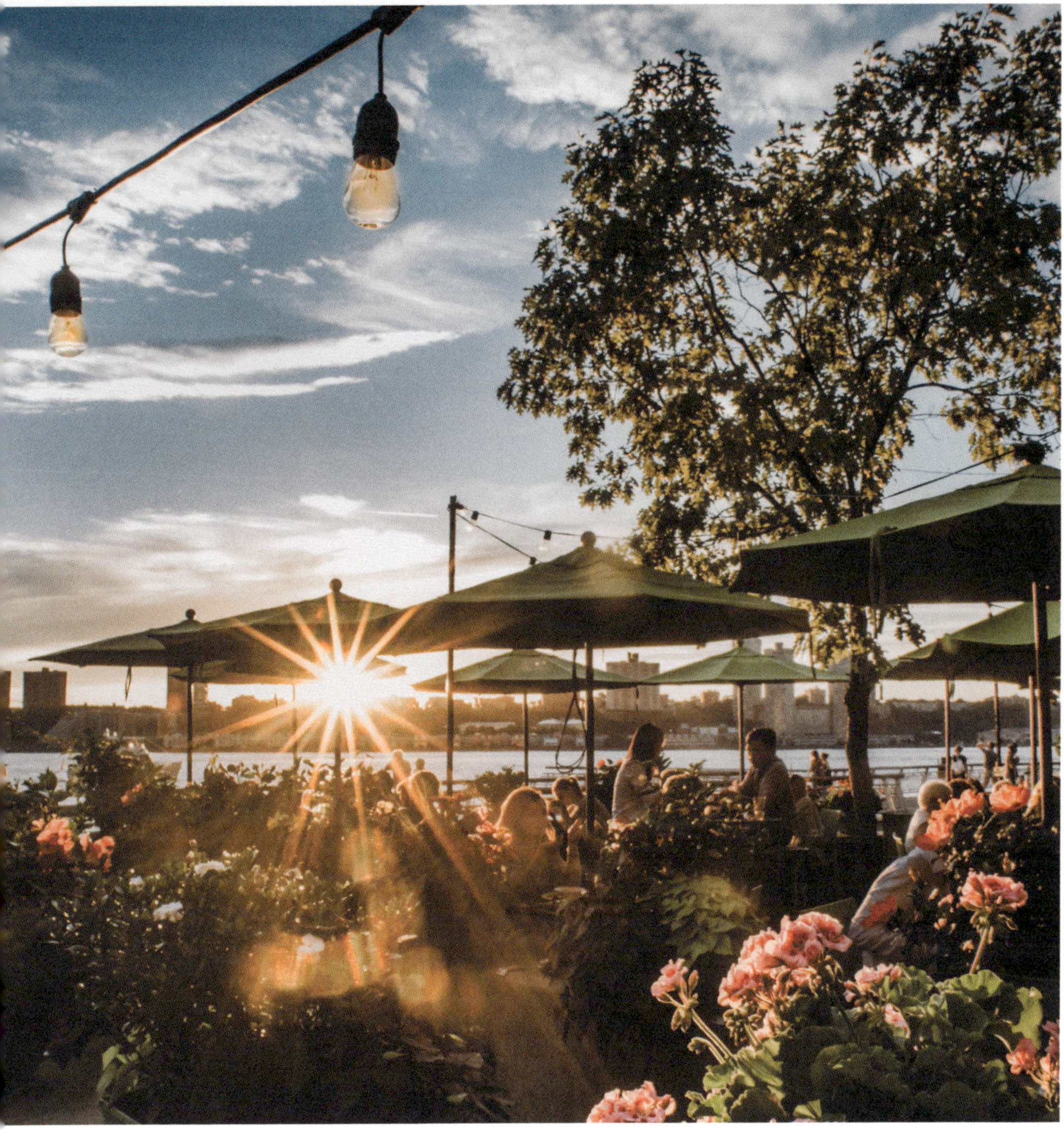

#piericafe #outdoorcafe #escapethecity #hudsonriver #riverparksouth
@piericafe

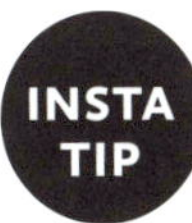

The Pier-i-cafe is the perfect spot for a dinner at sunset. Dinnertime is also an excellent time to capture the sun as it sets over the Hudson River. The cafe's flowers, the lights and the parasols combine to create the perfect frame for your picture.

52 AMERICAN MUSEUM OF NATIONAL HISTORY

American Museum of National History Central Park West & 79th Street

HOW TO GET THERE
Subway C (blue) or B (orange) to 81 Street - Museum of Natural History Station

The American Museum of National History is the world's most famous and largest museum of natural history. Fans of *Night at the Museum* think this is the coolest museum ever.

After the museum's original location in Central Park became too small, a larger building was constructed in 1874 for the more than 32 million artefacts that you can see in the current location next to Central Park. The museum has the largest collection of dinosaur bones, which have been combined into 600 complete and almost complete displays of dinosaur skeletons on the fourth floor.

In 1999, the museum was expanded with the magnificent Rose Center for Earth and Space. At night, the gigantic globe is beautifully lit, adding to the view from Roosevelt Park next to the museum.

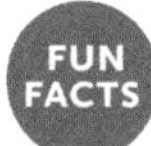

The large T-Rex is composed almost entirely of real fossil bones, from two different dinosaurs however.

You can sit next to an impressive group of elephants in the center of the Akeley Hall of African Mammals. One of the elephants was donated to the museum by president Theodore Roosevelt. He shot it himself in 1909.

There is a time capsule at the entrance in Columbus Avenue. It contains typical objects from the second millennium and was sealed in the year 2000. It will only be reopened on January 1st of the year 3000. A bit of a wait, in other words.

INSTAGRAMMABLE PLACES IN THE NEIGHBORHOOD

COFFEE	Parliament: 170 Central Park West (1 min. walk)
FOOD	Chopt Creative Salad: 341 Amsterdam Avenue (9 min. walk)
SEE	The Arthur Ross Terrace: 200 Central Park West (1 min. walk)
	The Swedish Cottage Marionette Theatre: W 79th Street at Central Park (4 min. walk)

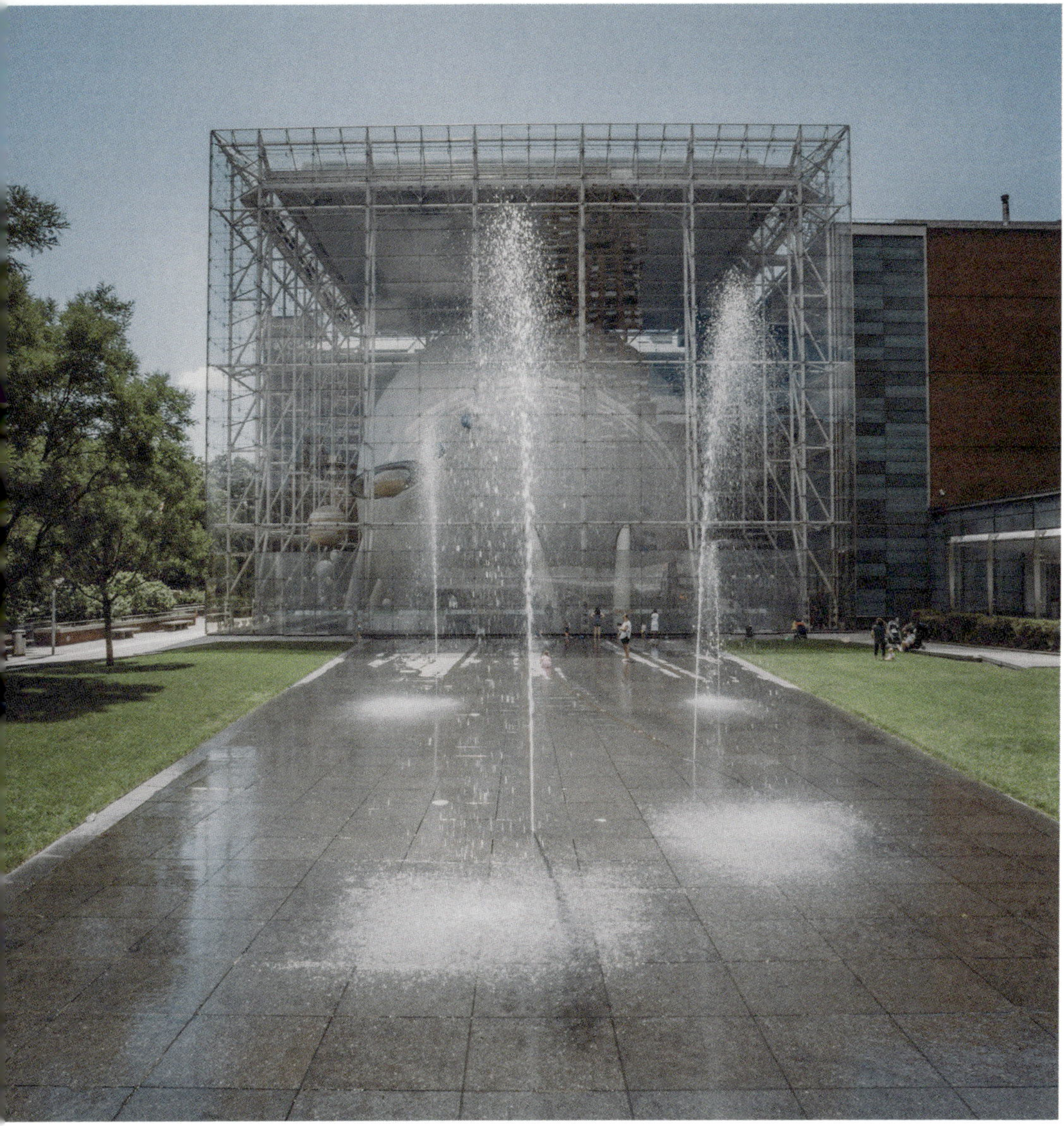

#americanmuseumofnaturalhistory #amnh #naturalhistory #nycmuseums @amnh

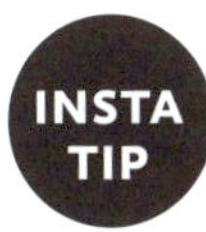

From the Arthur Ross Terrace you have a beautiful view on the Rose Center for Earth and Space.

53 BETHESDA FOUNTAIN

Bethesda Fountain & Terrace

HOW TO GET THERE
Subway C (*blue circle*) or B (*orange circle*) to E 72 Street and then a 10 min. walk through the park

Subway 4 6 (green circles) to W 77 Street and then a 14 min. walk through the park

The Bethesda Fountain is the stunning focal point of the Bethesda Terrace and one of the largest and most magnificent fountains in New York.

The water sculpture is a bronze angel, which has been nicknamed Angel of the Waters. She/ he (for angels have no gender after all) is surrounded by four small cherubs, symbolizing health, purity, moderation and peace.

The fountain is situated on the lower level of the Bethesda Terrace. You have a view of Central Park Lake from the upper level. This is often regarded as the park's center. If you think this is a stunning view, then check out the hall underneath the terrace however. It's as if you've stepped into a ballroom in a castle, where a fairy-tale prince or princess will walk down the staircase any minute. The stunning wood carvings on the terrace depict the four seasons and the times of the day and is beautifully lit at night.

From the fountain you can walk to The Mall, a lovely promenade among tall elms.

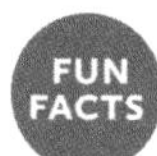

The quote of Matthew Perry's character Alex Whitman in the movie *Fools Rush In* (1997) still rings very true: "There's a spot in Central Park, the Bethesda Fountain, where, if you sit there long enough the entire city walks by."

Over the years, Bethesda Terrace has welcomed various "cultures". There was an outdoor restaurant here in the late sixties, after which it became the meeting place of the Hair-generation. In the seventies, it was the place to be for drug dealers.

INSTAGRAMMABLE PLACES IN THE NEIGHBORHOOD

COFFEE The Loeb Boathouse Express Cafe (4 min. walk)
FOOD The Loeb Boathouse Lakeside Restaurant (4 min. walk)
SEE The Mall and Literary Walk (1 min. walk)
The Umpire Rock at Central Park (8 min. walk)
The Wollman Rink at Central Park (6 min. walk)

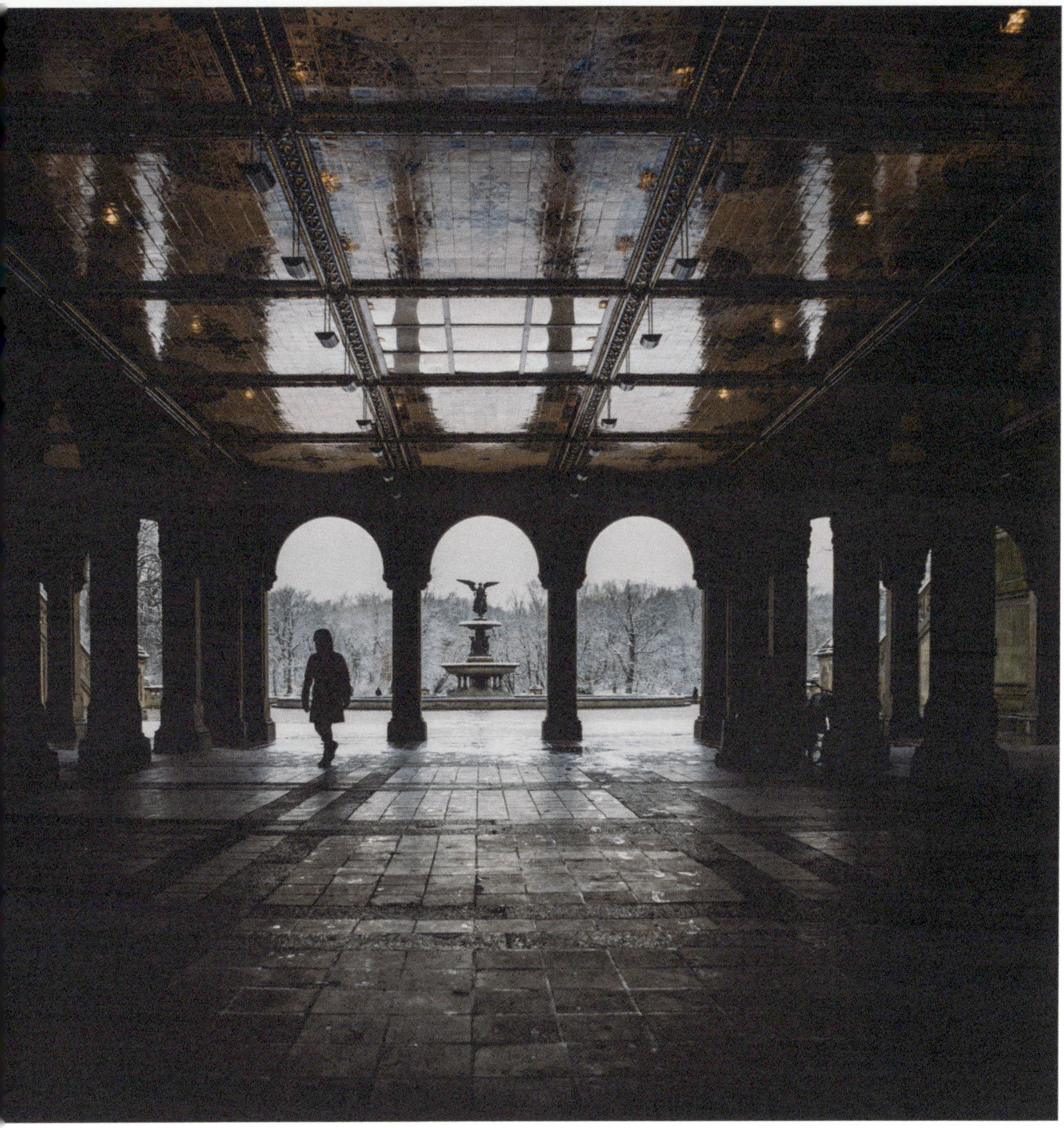

#bethesdafountain #bethasdaterrace #angelofthewaters #centralparknyc #centralparkmoments

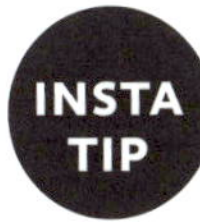

When standing on the terrace, you have a unique view of the fountain and the magnificent ceiling.

If you position the fountain in the center of the arch, then you can create an outline of a random passer-by or a friend who agrees to pose for you in the left and/or right arch.

 THE MALL & LITERARY WALK

The Mall & Literary Walk Between 66th Street and 72nd Street

HOW TO GET THERE
Subway 4 or 6 (green) to 68 Street Station

Subway 1, 2 or 3 (red) to 72 Street - Broadway Station

The inspiration for the Mall, a promenade, came from the promenades of Versailles. It is the only straight line in Central Park, leading to The Bethesda Terrace in the north and The Olmsted Flower Bed in the south.

The Mall is one of the most photographed features of Central Park, partly because of the amazing rows of American Elm Trees, which form a cathedral-like canopy over the path. They are one of the last remaining stands of American Elms in North America, which is why the Central Park Conservancy works so hard to protect them.

The southern part of The Mall is also called The Literary Walk. Here you can take a stroll among the statues of several prominent writers, including Fitz-Greene Halleck, Robert Burns, Sir Walter Scott and William Shakespeare. The fifth statue, of Christopher Columbus, is the odd man out.

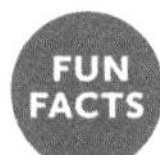

There are 29 statues in Central Park, five of which are on Literary Walk. The most popular statues are those of Alice in Wonderland, Balto the sled dog and Duke Ellington.

Central Park has a total of 58 miles (93 km) of pedestrian paths. The Mall is only a quarter of a mile long, so there are plenty of other paths to explore.

INSTAGRAMMABLE PLACES IN THE NEIGHBORHOOD

COFFEE	Le Pain Quotidien: E 72nd St & 5th Ave (6 min. walk)
FOOD	The Loeb Boathouse: E 72nd St & Park Drive North (5 min. walk)
SEE	The Bethesda Terrace and Fountain: Terrace Drive (1 min. walk)
	The Balto Statue: East Drive (2 min. walk)

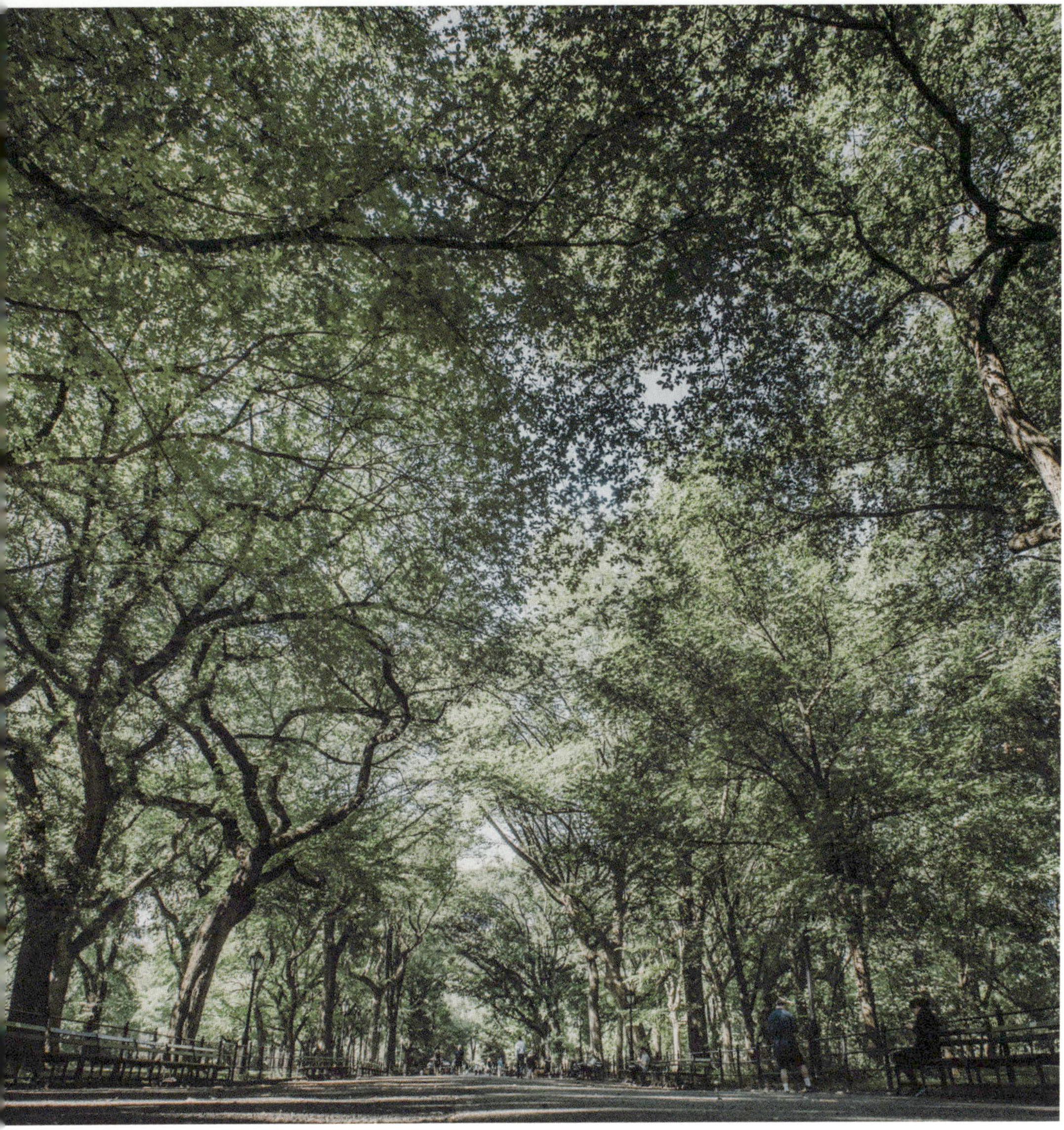

#literarywalk #centralparknyc #centralparkmoments #nycparks @centralparknyc

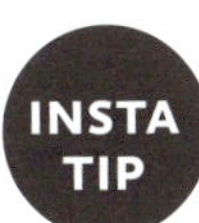

To capture the majestic natural roof above the promenade, I would advise to keep your camera as close to the ground as possible (if possible, just position it on the surface).

55 LOEB BOATHOUSE

Loeb Boathouse E 72nd Street & Park Drive North

HOW TO GET THERE
Subway 1, 2 (red) or A (blue) or D (orange) to 59 Street - Columbus Circle

Do you want to dine on the banks of the famous Central Park Lake? Fancy a row boat? Or do you prefer to leave this arduous job to a gondolier who will take you on a tour of the lake with his Venetian gondola? The Loeb Boathouse has all the ingredients for a romantic day in the park!

You can rent a rowboat for 30 minutes. You'll need some muscle power but the view and the photo opps are well worth it. You have a view of Bethesda Fountain and Terrace and can distinguish the New York City skyline above the park's greenery.

Do you tend to get sea sick easily? Don't worry. The Conservatory Water is just a 3-minute walk to the east of the boat house. Here you can sail model boats, which is a favorite pastime of many New Yorkers (of all ages) during the summer months (April to October).

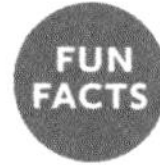

The Loeb Boathouse is the unofficial headquarters of the Central Park birdwatchers. They keep a log in the boathouse, recording all the birds they spotted.

There are seven water features in Central Park, occupying a total surface area of 370 acres (150 hectares). The park's total surface area is 843 acres (341 hectares), or eight times the size of Vatican City.

INSTAGRAMMABLE PLACES IN THE NEIGHBORHOOD

FOOD AND DRINKS	at the Loab Boathouse, The Lakeside Restaurant or The Outside Bar or The Express Cafe
COFFEE	Le Pain Quotidien: 72nd St and 5th Avenue (4 min. walk)
SEE	Conservatory Water: 72nd Street (3 min. walk)
	Hans Christian Andersen statue: E 74th Street (2 min. walk)
	Alice in Wonderland statue: E 74th Street (2 min. walk)

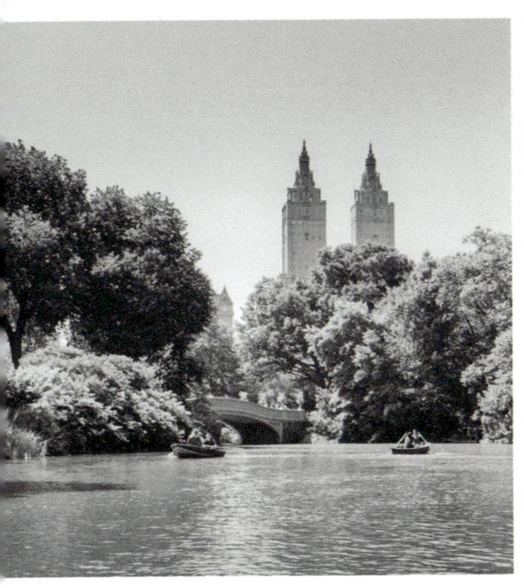

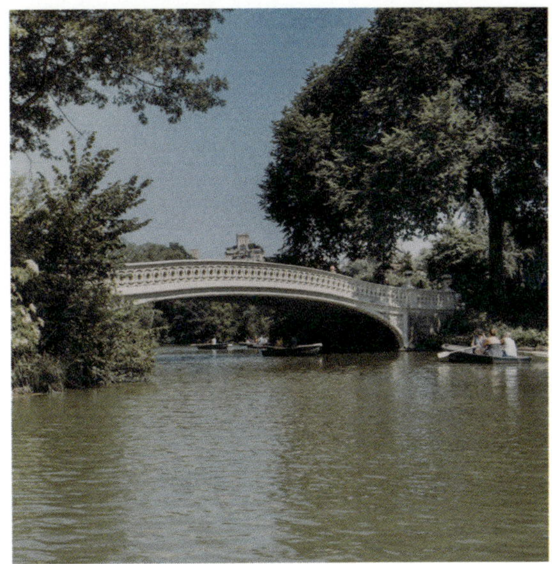

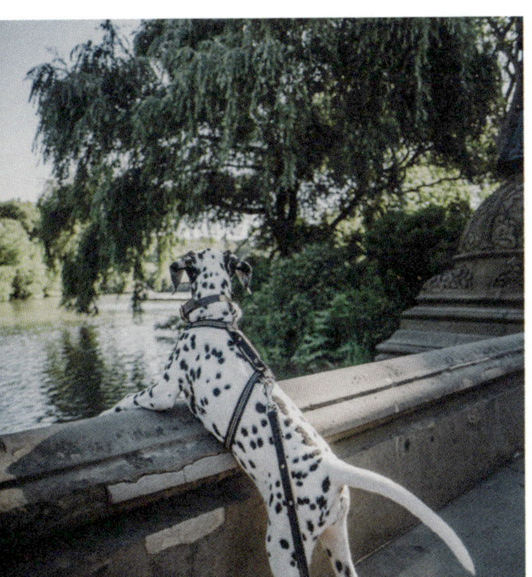

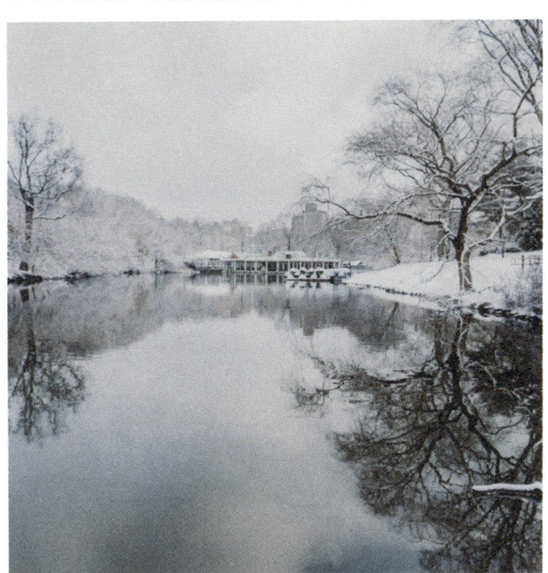

#loebboathouse #theloebboathouse #loebboathousecentralpark #centralparknyc #centralparkmoments

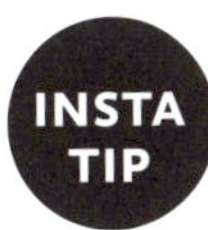

There are various spots from where you can see the Loeb Boathouse and the rowboats. In summertime, you can take pictures from your own rowboat. But the Loeb Boathouse is equally beautiful in wintertime.

56 ALICE IN WONDERLAND STATUE

Alice in
Wonderland
E 74th Street

HOW TO GET THERE
Subway 6 (green) to 77 Street Station

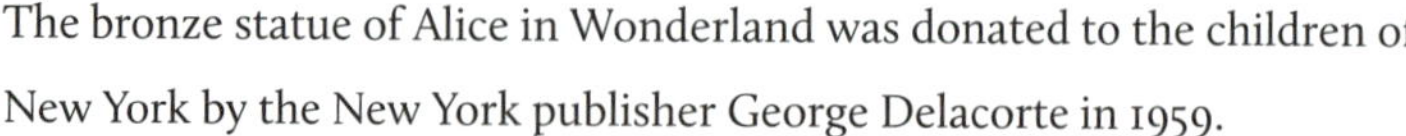

The bronze statue of Alice in Wonderland was donated to the children of New York by the New York publisher George Delacorte in 1959.

The sculpture of Alice and her friends features some amazing details and children (and adults) like to climb, touch and crawl all over Alice. In fact, the many thousands of hands and feet have polished and smoothed over the bronze over the decades. You can recognize where children like to sit and hide because of the shiny parts.

Not far from Alice you'll find another reference to fairy-tales. You can sit on the lap of Hans Christian Andersen while he is reading the story of *The Ugly Duckling*. This is the meeting point for the storytelling events of the Hans Christian Andersen Storytelling Center every Saturday morning during the summer months.

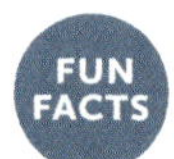

It is said that The Mad Hatter of the Alice in Wonderland statue is a caricature of George Delacorte.

George Delacorte did not just donate the Alice statue. He also paid for the musical Delacorte Clock near the Central Park Zoo and the magnificent Delacorte Theater, where you can enjoy the free open-air performances of Shakespeare in the Park.

INSTAGRAMMABLE PLACES IN THE NEIGHBORHOOD

COFFEE	Le Pain Quotidien: E 72nd Street and 5th Avenue (1 min. walk)
FOOD	Pick A Bagel: 1101 Lexington Avenue (9 min. walk)
SEE	The Hans Christian Andersen Statue (1 min. walk)
	The Metropolitan Museum of Art: 1000 5th Avenue (6 min. walk)

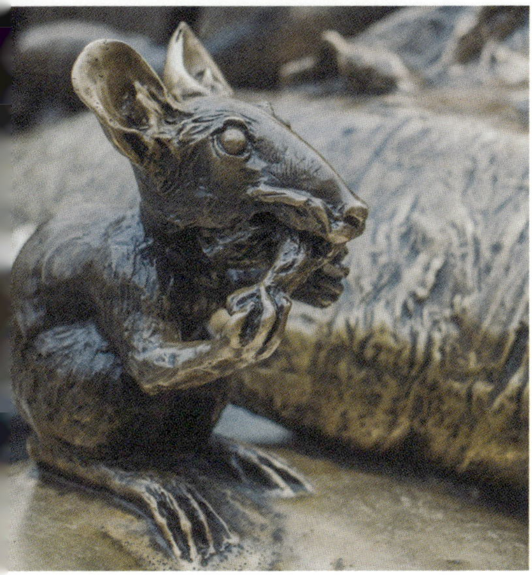

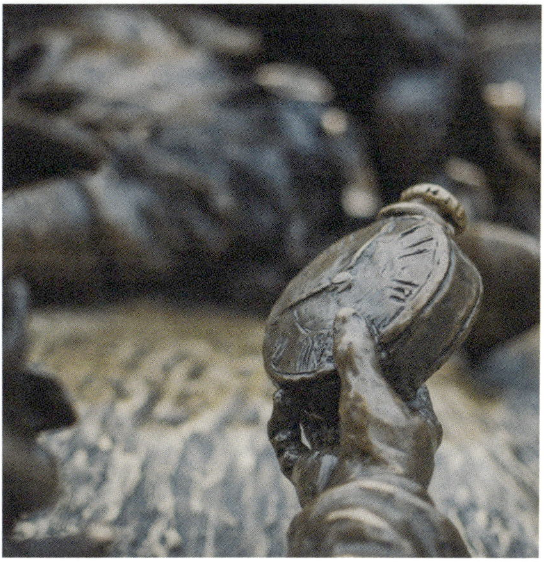

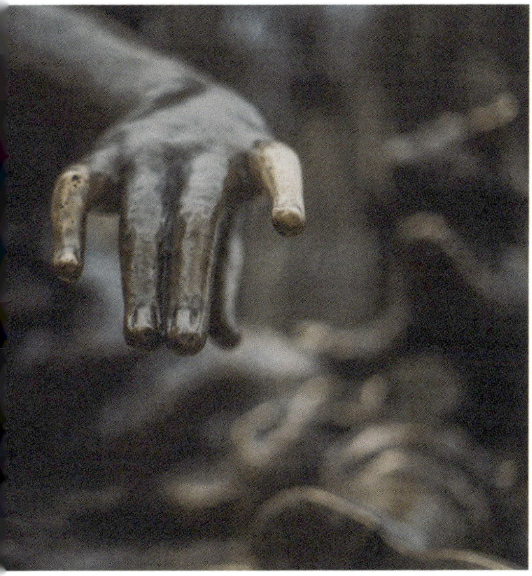

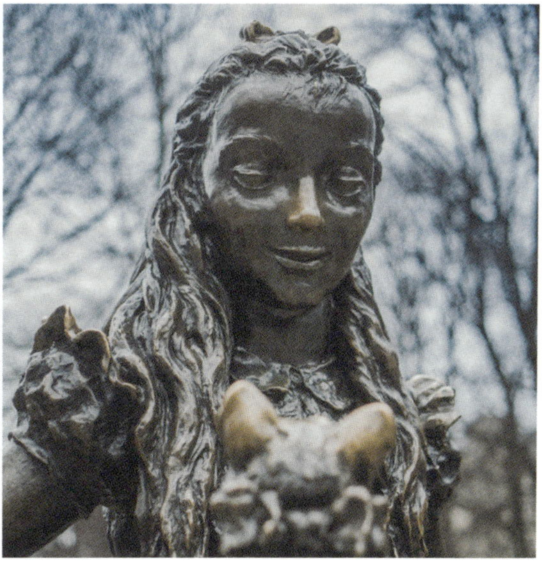

#aliceinwonderlandstatue #aliceincentralpark #madhatter#jabberwocky #centralparkmoments

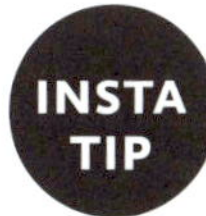

There is usually a crowd around the statue. Come early if you prefer a private audience with Alice and her friends.

If there are too many people, then focus on the amazing details rather than on the statue as a whole.

57 BELVEDERE CASTLE

Belvedere Castle
79th Street

HOW TO GET THERE
Subway C (blue) or B (orange) to 81 Street - Museum of Natural History Station

Subway 6 (green) to 77 Street Station

Belvedere Castle is a folly in Central Park, which was built in 1869 as a lookout. Named for the Italian *Belvedere*, meaning beautiful view, the castle's two balconies offer exactly what its name implies, i.e. sweeping views of The Great Lawn, the Delacorte Theater, The Ramble and New York's skyline. This is Central Park's highest point.

The castle also provides a fairy-tale backdrop for the Turtle Pond, which is located at the foot of Belvedere Castle. It owes its name to the fact that several New Yorkers rehomed their pets in the pond in the eighties. Since then, their population has exploded and the pond is now home to five different species of turtles, which you can spot swimming around the pond or sunbathing.

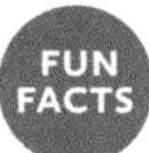

In the 1960s, the National Weather Service used the castle as a place for meteorological measurements. The temperature, wind speed and direction were recorded here and shared with the weather service's forecast office. You can still see some of the measuring instruments in the castle.

Gargamel used Belvedere Castle as his headquarters in the film *The Smurfs* (2011) and it is also the home of the Count von Count, a Sesame Street character.

INSTAGRAMMABLE PLACES IN THE NEIGHBORHOOD

COFFEE — Parliament: 170 Central Park West (7 min. walk)

FOOD — The Loeb Boathouse: E 72nd Street & Park Drive North (6 min. walk)

SEE — The Swedish Cottage Marionette Theatre: W 79th Street in Central Park (2 min. walk)

The American Museum of Natural History: Central Park West & 79th Street (6 min. walk)

The Metropolitan Museum of Art: 1000 5th Avenue (8 min. walk)

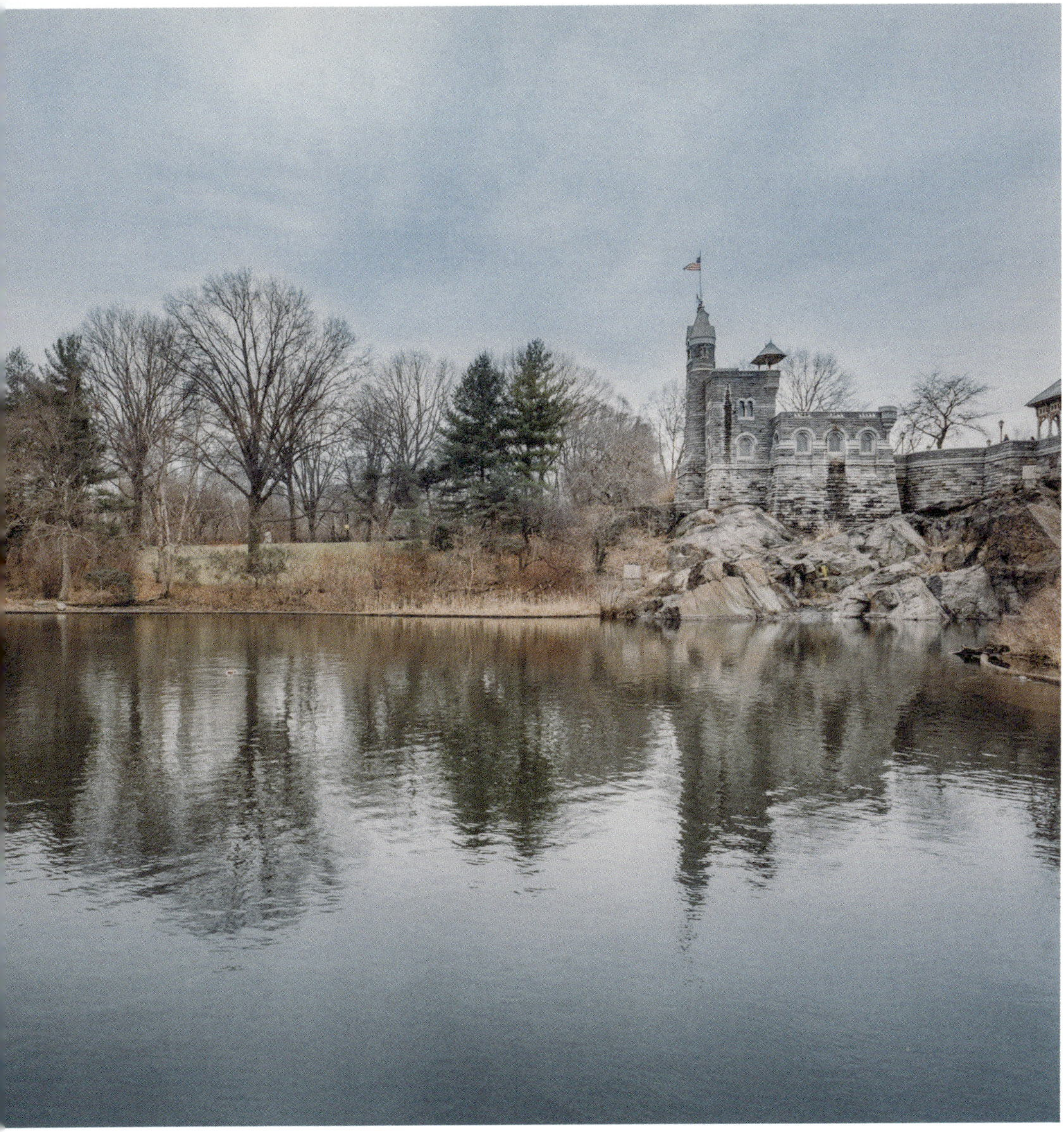

#belvederecastle #belvederecastlenyc #centralparkmoments #turtlepond

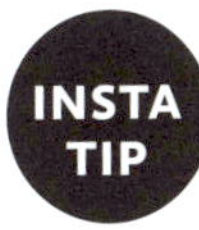

From the banks of Turtle Pond, you have a great view of the Belvedere Castle. Try to capture the castle with its reflection for a beautiful, romantic image.

58 J. KENNEDY ONASSIS RESERVOIR

Jacqueline Kennedy Onassis Reservoir

HOW TO GET THERE
Subway 4 or 6 (green) to 86 Street - Lexington Avenue Station or to 96 Street Station

The Jacqueline Kennedy Onassis Reservoir is an excellent location to shoot some nice photos. The greenery of Central Park is reflected in the water, as well as some of the more prominent buildings on the city's skyline. It covers a surface area of approximately 106 acres (43 hectares) and contains more than a million gallons of water.

The Central Park reservoir was built in the 1860s and has since been decommissioned. It does supply water to the other ponds and lakes in Central Park and has become an important nature reserve, housing many different species of waterbirds.

In 1994, the Central Park Reservoir was renamed the Jacqueline Kennedy Onassis Reservoir, after the former First Lady who lived near the reservoir and liked to go jogging around it. The trail around the reservoir is 1.58 miles (2.54 km) long (attention: one-way only) and popular with many famous people. You may even spot Bill Clinton or Madonna here.

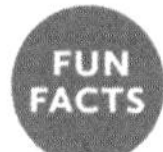

The one billion gallons of water in the reservoir were sufficient to supply New York with water for two weeks in the 1860s. Nowadays, the city would be able to survive for just four hours on this.

Are you lost? The 1,600 lantern posts in the park help you find your way. Each post has four numbers embossed onto it. The first two indicate the nearest street and the last two tell you whether you are on the East or West side: even numbers are East, uneven are West.

INSTAGRAMMABLE PLACES IN THE NEIGHBORHOOD

COFFEE Bluestone Lane at the Church of the Heavenly Rest: 1085 5th Avenue
FOOD Gina Mexicana: 1288 Madison Avenue
SEE Guggenheim Museum: 1071 5th Avenue
Cooper-Hewitt Design Museum: 2 E 91st Street
The Gothic Bridge at the Bridle Path

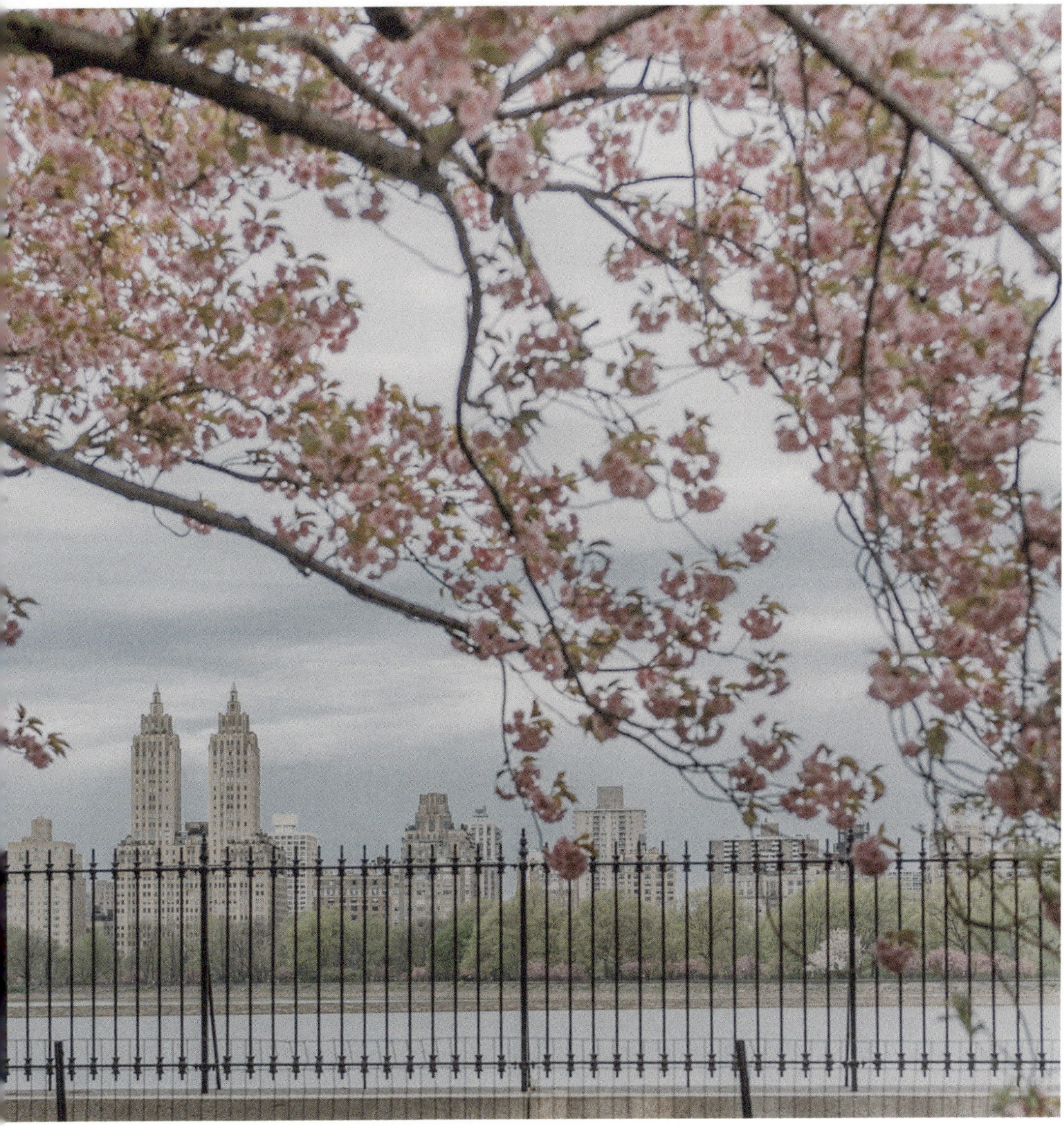

#centralparkreservoir #jackieonassisreservoir #sanremobuilding #centralpark #centralparkmoments

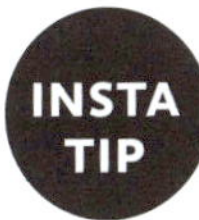

When standing on the eastern side of the reservoir, you have a view of the San Remo building, an apartment building with two towers that overlooks Central Park. The towers have become a typical backdrop for many photos of Central Park. You can use them as part of your composition and incorporate them in your photo.

59 THE CONSERVATORY GARDEN

Conservatory Garden
402 5th Avenue

HOW TO GET THERE
Subway 1, 2 (red) or A (blue) or D (orange) to 59 Street - Columbus Circle

Contrary to its name, the Conservatory Garden is not a garden in or near a conservancy. Nor is there a conservancy in the garden. The garden owes its name to the fact that this is where the greenhouses of Central Park's gardeners used to be (until the 1930s). The main entrance on Fifth Avenue is closed in the morning and evening by the magnificent iron Vanderbilt Gate, through which you can access this hidden garden. The park is divided into three smaller gardens, each with their own distinctive style.

The northern French-style garden includes the picturesque fountain of the Three Dancing Maidens. In spring, it is surrounded by a sea of colourful tulips, while Korean *chrysanthemums* create a colourful display in autumn. The Italian garden is located in the center, where you can't fail to notice the 12-foot high fountain. A dreamy walkway leads to a lovely pergola, which is a very popular venue for wedding ceremonies and romantic photo shoots. The intimate English-style garden is located to the south and resembles a cottage garden. A sculpture of two children playing stands in the lily pond. It is a tribute to Frances Hodgson Burnett's book *The Secret Garden*.

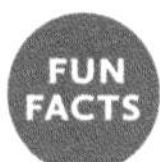

Central Park Conservancy has a free app, with a handy map, an events calendar and a Central Park Audio Guide in which 40 famous New Yorkers discuss 40 special places in the park. Listen to Candice Bergen as she tells you more about the Conservatory Garden. Are you curious about the favourite spots of Whoopi Goldberg, Glenn Close, Alec Baldwin, Sarah Jessica Parker and others? Then do check this fun app!

INSTAGRAMMABLE PLACES IN THE NEIGHBORHOOD

SEE
Museum of the City of New York: 1220 5th Avenue (3 min. walk)
Lasker Rink (winter) or Pool (summer): 110 Lenox Avenue (6 min. walk)
The Ravine: E 103rd Street (6 min. walk)
The Graffiti Hall of Fame: 106th Street en Park Avenue (5 min. walk)

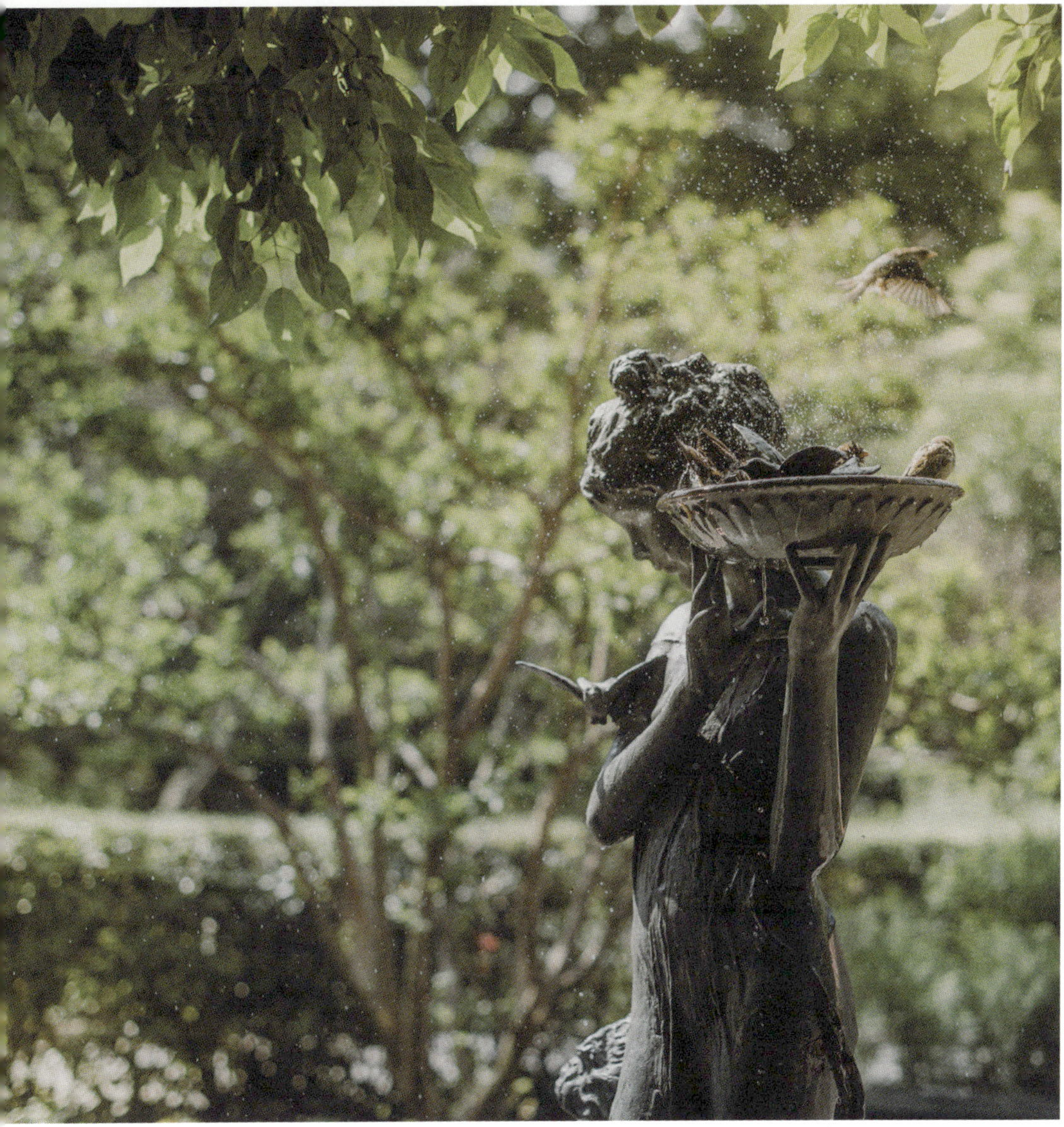

#conservatorygarden #conservatorygardencentralpark #centralparkgarden #centralparkmoments

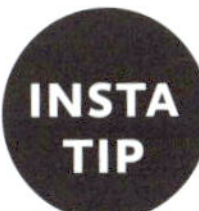

The sculpture of a girl in the English garden carries a water bowl with birds in it. In the early morning, a lot of real birds like to take a bath in the bowl, making it seem as if part of the statue has come to life.

60 DYLAN'S CANDY BAR

Dylan's
Candy Bar
1011 3rd
Avenue

HOW TO GET THERE
Subway E (blue) or B, D, F, M to 47-50 Streets - Rockefeller Center Station

Subway N, R or W (yellow) to 49 Street Station

Dylan's Candy Bar is a chain of boutique candy shops, with many locations all over the United States. The flagship store in New York has transformed the concept of a candy shop into a sweet shopping experience.

As you walk into the shop, all of your senses are immediately awakened by the intense candy smells and the vibrant colors. Take the – candy, of course – staircase to the basement where your senses will be stimulated even more by the giant lollipop tree, the mesmerizing candy wallpaper and displays with dazzling arrays of all kinds of different sweets. A playlist with "candy music" provides a backdrop for your visit, making you wonder whether you've just stepped into a modern-day version of Willy Wonka's magical factory.

The range of 7,000 types of candy, the 3D gummy machine, the ice cream bar and the darling restaurant on the top floor all contribute to making your visit an unforgettable experience. No wonder that Dylan's Candy Bar on 3rd Avenue has become such a popular tourist attraction, with its lashings of Instagrammable sweetness!

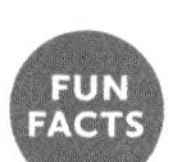

Don't forget to check out the display of the favorite candy (and autographs) of some famous candy fans on the ground floor. The Famous Favorites Wall features the selections of Kim Kardashian, Steven Spielberg, Nicki Minaj, Al Pacino and Bill Clinton among others.

The shop was founded by Dylan Lauren, Ralph Lauren's daughter, who has clearly inherited her father's flair for design and fashion. The shop's creative design and branding are absolutely fabulous. You can find her candy portrait near the check-out.

INSTAGRAMMABLE PLACES IN THE NEIGHBORHOOD

COFFEE Serendipity 3: 225 E 60th Street (1 min. walk)

FOOD Jackson Hole: 232 E 64th Street (5 min. walk)

SEE The Roosevelt Island Tramway: corner E 59th Street and 2nd Avenue (3 min. walk)

Bloomingdale's: 1000 Third Avenue (3 min. walk)

Sprinkles Cupcake ATM: 780 Lexington Avenue (3 min. walk)

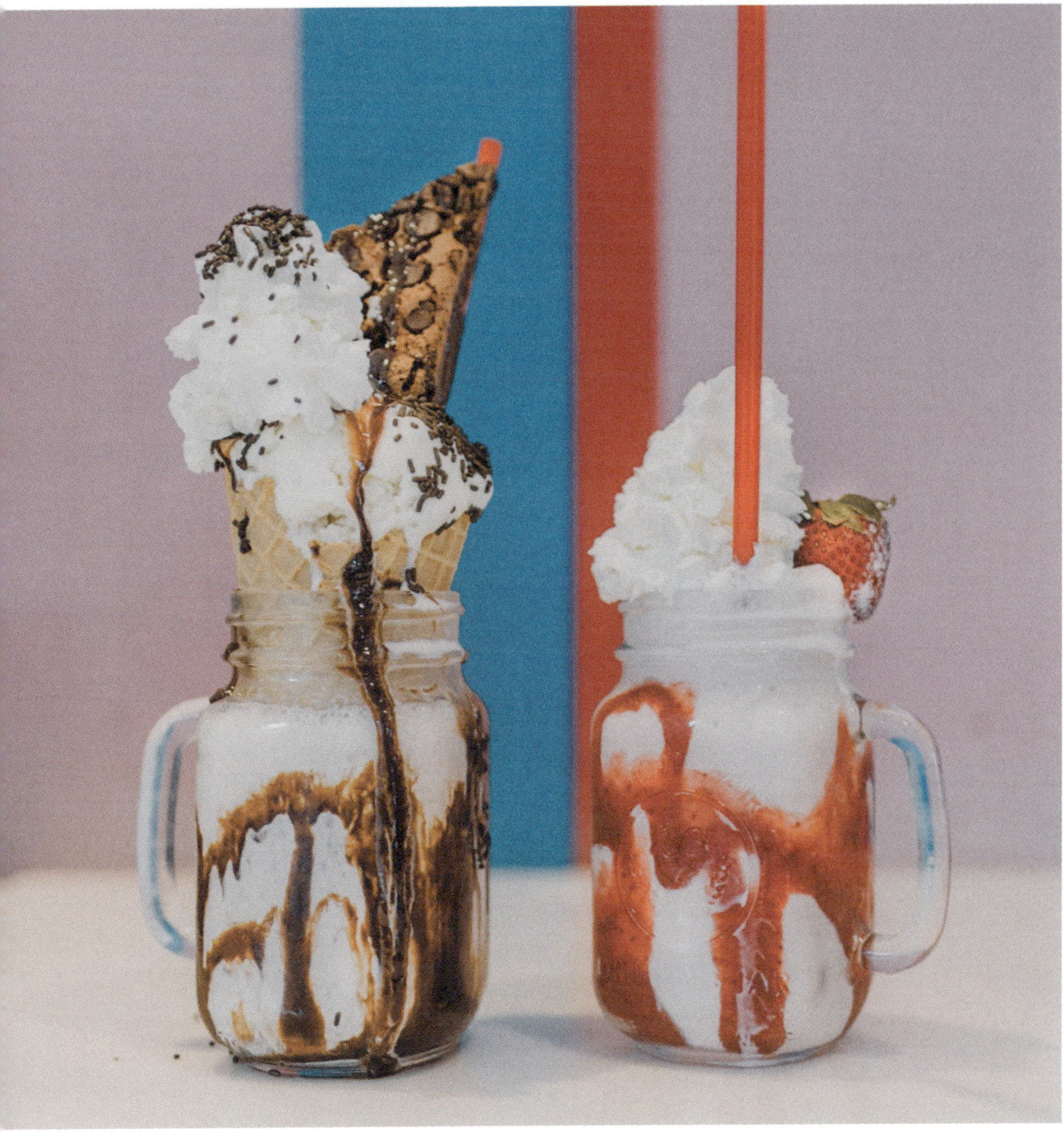

#dylanscandybar #dylanscandy #nyceats #nycsweets #candyshop @dylanscandybar

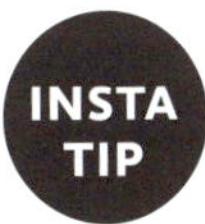

Have a look at the menu of the second-floor restaurant to see which milkshakes are super photogenic! If possible, request a table by the window so you can use natural light for your photo.

 SPRINKLES CUPCAKE ATM

Sprinkles Cupcakes ATM
780 Lexington Avenue

HOW TO GET THERE
Subway E (blue) or B, D, F, M to 47-50 Streets - Rockefeller Center Station

Subway N, R or W (yellow) to 49 Street Station

Have you ever been overcome by an overwhelming desire for a cupcake at 4am in the morning? Well, there is no need to worry because this is New York after all, where you can score a freshly-baked cupcake 24/7 at the Sprinkles ATM.

The principle is very similar to that of an ATM. The screen lists the cupcakes and cookies that were baked that day and that are still available. Once you have selected the cupcake you crave, you can watch onscreen how a giant robotic arm ingeniously transfers the pretty box to the ATM dropbox (without dropping it though!). All you have to do is take it out of the window. Food and entertainment all in one!

Sprinkles now has cupcake vending machines in several major American cities. Every vending machine goes through 700 to 1,000 cupcakes a day. The Cupcake ATM on Lexington Ave is located between the Sprinkles Cupcakes shop and the Sprinkles Ice Cream Shop. While these shops are also worth visiting, they are not open 24/7 obviously.

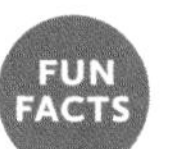

When one of the founders of Sprinkles was pregnant, she came up with the concept of the cupcake vending machine. She woke up with a craving for a cupcake in the middle of the night, but even though she had her own cupcake shop she was unable to get her hands on one when she needed it the most.

The cupcake shop (and sometimes also the vending machine) stocks cupcakes for dogs on occasion. So pay attention when selecting your cupcake!

INSTAGRAMMABLE PLACES IN THE NEIGHBORHOOD

COFFEE	Birch Coffee: 134 1/2 E 62nd Street (2 min. walk)
FOOD	Sprinkles Cupcakes (on the left side of the ATM) and Sprinkles Ice Cream (on the right side of the ATM)
SHOP	Bloomingdale's: 1000 Third Avenue (2 min. walk)
	Dylan's Candy Bar: 1011 3rd Avenue (3 min. walk)
SEE	The Plaza Hotel: 768 5th Avenue (9 min. walk)

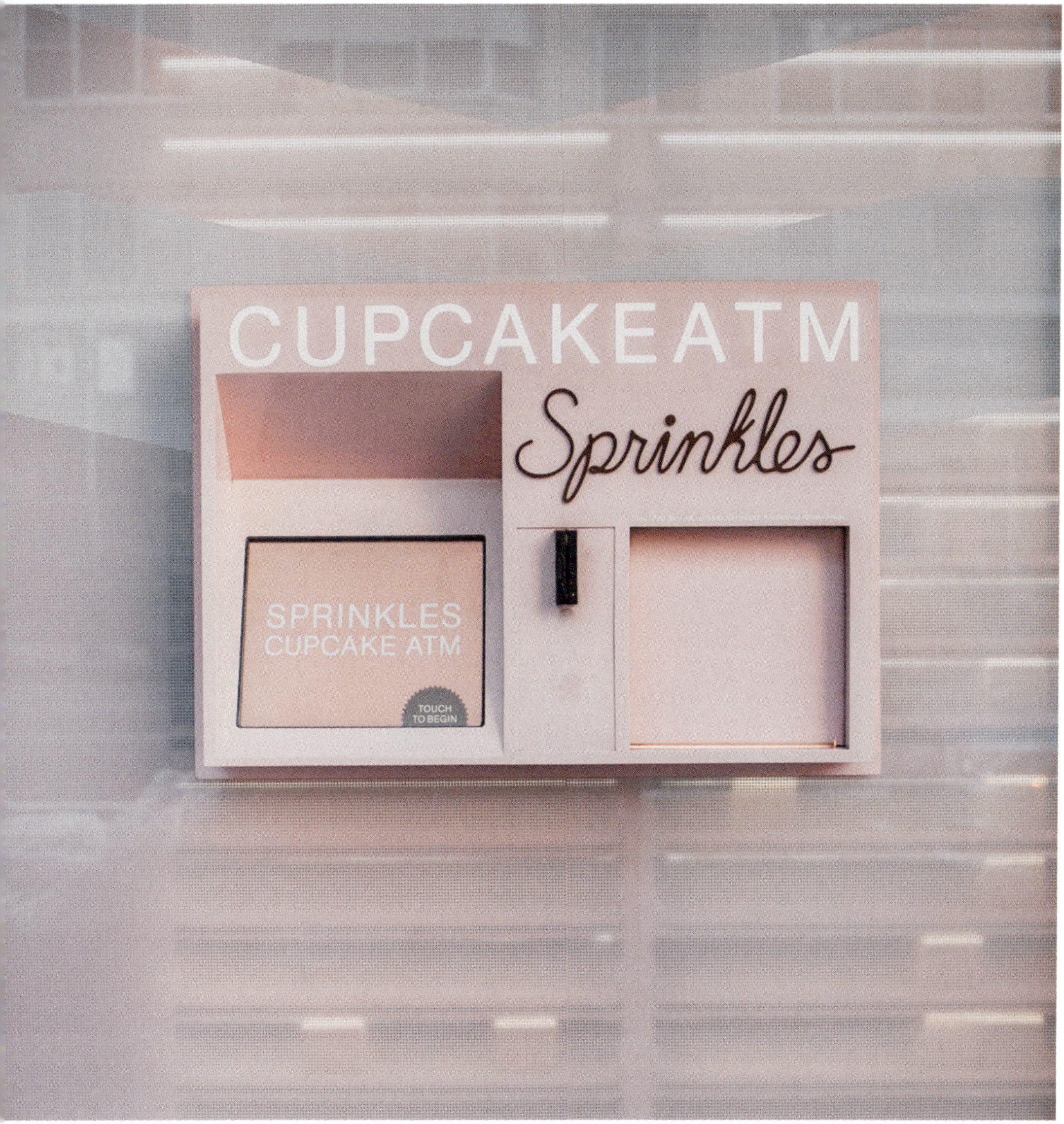

#sprinklesatm #sprinklesmoment #sprinklescupcakes #cupcakecraving #sprinkles @sprinklescupcakes

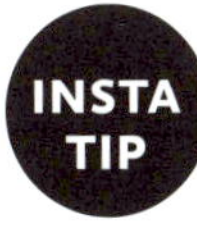

In the evening, when the shop is closed, there's often a line of people waiting patiently at the ATM. You can take a photo more easily during daytime.

The screen changes color every few seconds. If you wait for the pink screen, you can shoot a really pink picture.

62 THE METROPOLITAN MUSEUM OF ART

Metropolitan Museum of Art 1000 5th Avenue

HOW TO GET THERE
Subway 4, 5 or 6 (green) to 86 Street Lexington Avenue Station

The Metropolitan Museum of Art, which is also known as The Met, is one of the world's largest museums, covering a surface area of just under 2 million square feet (190,000 square meters). It's easy to get lost among the 2 million artworks on display.

Taking in all the galleries and all the works in the museum's collection in one visit is simply impossible. Make a list of what you want to see before visiting. Some photo faves:

- The wing with Greek sculptures to the left of the main entrance: a gallery of Greek models who manage to stand perfectly still while posing.
- The Egyptian Temple of Dendur in the Sackler Wing: the water beautifully reflects the temple and the floor to ceiling window with a view of Central Park.
- The Chinese courtyard in the Asian galleries on the second floor: the glass roof illuminates this serene place in the most sublime way.
- The sculpture garden on the fifth-floor roof terrace where you can admire a changing collection of sculptures, against the backdrop of New York's skyline.

The Met is the starting point of the Museum Mile. There are nine museums in the section of 5th Avenue, from 82nd Street to 105th Street on the Upper East Side.

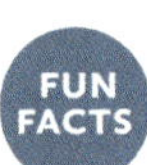

The Met has its own florist. Remco van Vliet creates stunning new floral arrangements for The Great Hall every week. His arrangements often are more than 10 feet (3 meters) tall and are real artworks.

Fashionistas also flock to this museum as The Costume Institute has a collection of more than 35,000 historical and contemporary items of clothing and accessories.

INSTAGRAMMABLE PLACES IN THE NEIGHBORHOOD

COFFEE	Irving Farm Coffee Roasters: 1424 3rd Avenue (8 min. walk)
FOOD	Pizza Beach: 1426 3rd Avenue (8 min. walk)
	The Penrose: 1590 2nd Avenue (11 min. walk)
SEE	Obelisk Cleopatra's Needle at Central Park: E 81st Street (8 min. walk)
	Guggenheim Museum: 1071 5th Avenue (7 min. walk)

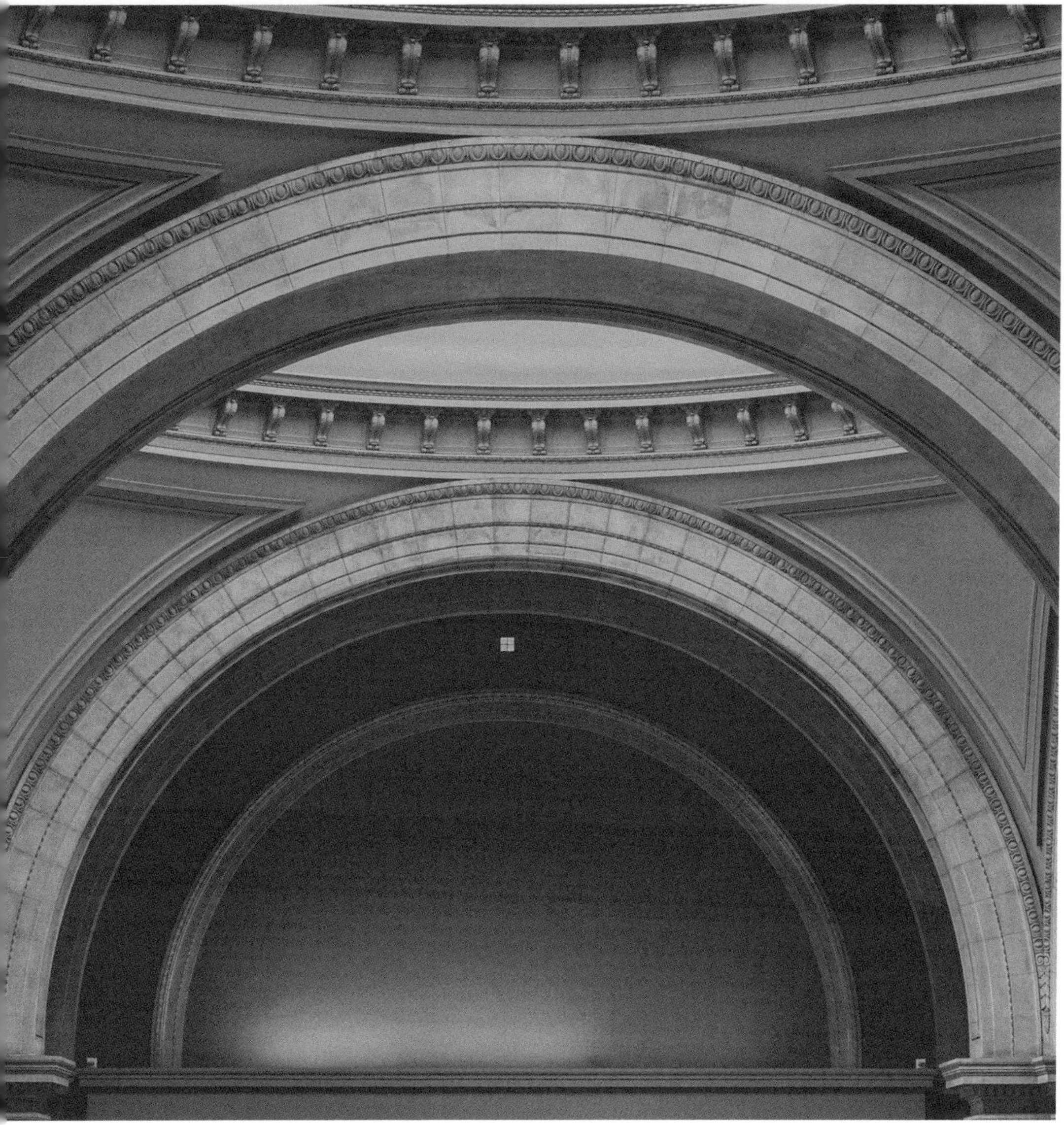

#themet #themetmuseum #metmuseum #nycmuseums @metmuseum

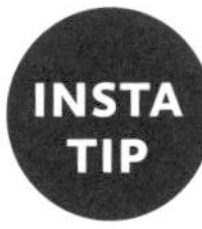

The Met does not only have beautiful works of art, but also has a wonderful architecture with is definitely worth capturing.

63 GUGGENHEIM MUSEUM

Guggenheim Museum
1071
5th Avenue

HOW TO GET THERE
Subway 4, 5 or 6 (green) to 86 Street Lexington Avenue Station

The Guggenheim Museum was inaugurated in 1959 and has since become one of the city's most controversial (the building's design and collection have prompted many discussions over the decades) and most impressive landmarks. Frank Lloyd Wright designed the building for the art collector Solomon R. Guggenheim.

The building is so unique that it is an artwork in its own right, which is why many visitors visit it for the art and/or the architecture. It was inspired by the ancient ziggurats of Babylon, but Wright chose to invert the temple structure. The museum is conceived as one large, airy, open space. The spiral staircase is reminiscent of a nautilus shell, guiding you past artworks and exhibitions to the top of the building and back down. The building is quite extraordinary, whether you are looking from the top or bottom or from the inside or outside. The open layout provides a large indoor exhibition space, which many artists use to create spectacular artworks.

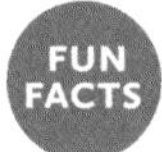

The architect Frank Lloyd Wright originally had a carmine red exterior in mind but his clients Guggenheim and Rabay did not agree with his proposal. They requested that he used concrete instead of red brick.

Neither Guggenheim, nor Wright ever saw the completed museum as Guggenheim died ten years before the opening and Wright just 6 months before the inauguration.

INSTAGRAMMABLE PLACES IN THE NEIGHBORHOOD

COFFEE Bluestone Lane at the Church of the Heavenly Rest: 1085 5th Avenue (1 min. walk)

FOOD Gina Mexicana: 1288 Madison Avenue (5 min. walk)

SEE Cooper-Hewitt Design Museum: 2 E 91st Street (2 min. walk)

The Metropolitan Museum of Art: 1000 5th Avenue (7 min. walk)

Jacqueline Kennedy Onassis Reservoir: other side of the road (1 min. walk)

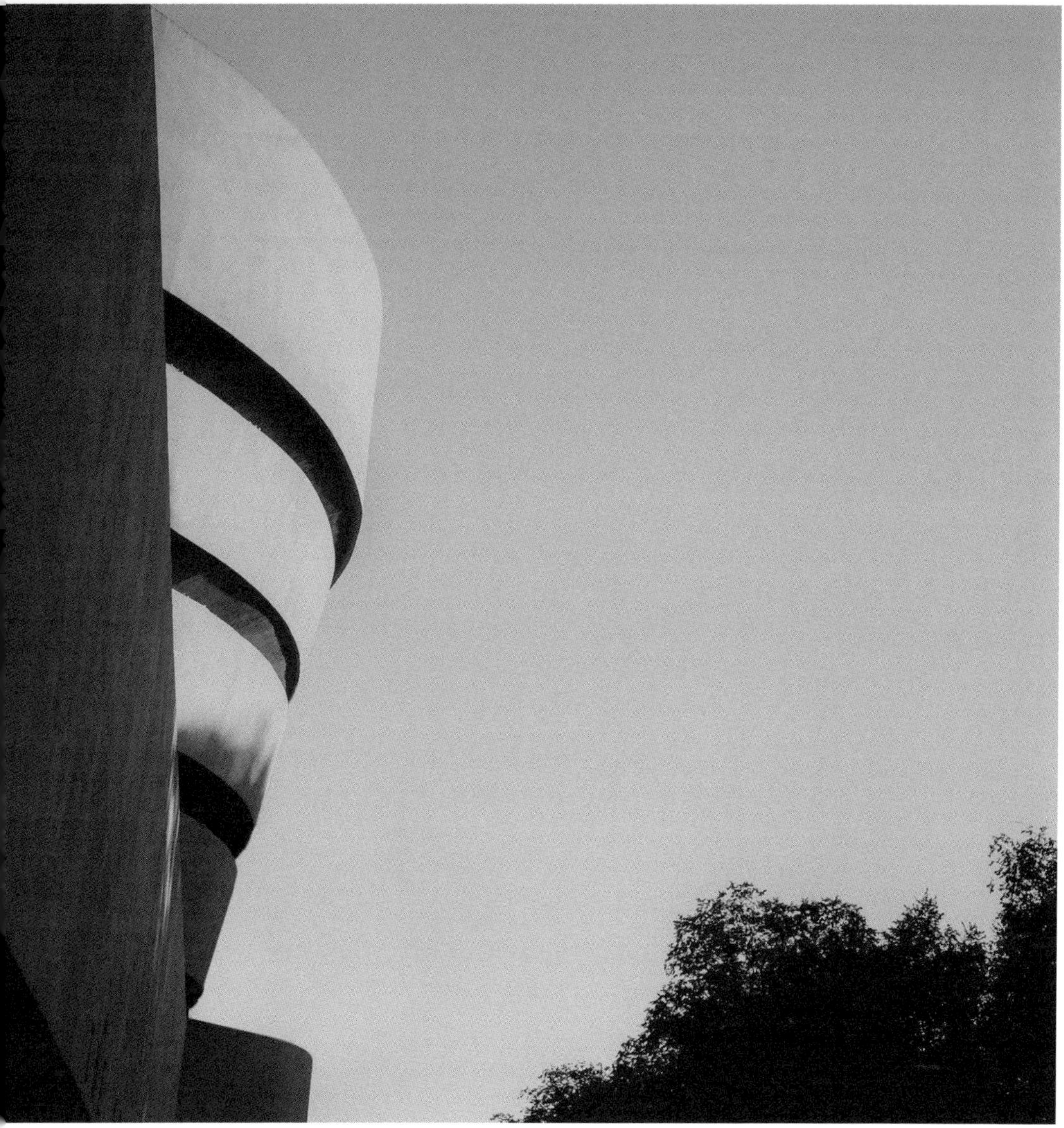

#guggenheim #guggenheimmuseum #guggenheimcollection #guggenheimnyc #franklloydwright @guggenheim

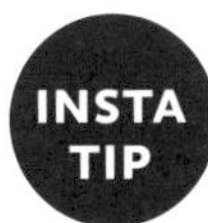

The Guggenheim Museum's shape and lines are so iconic that all you need to do is include just a tiny part of the building in your photo for people to recognize it. Apply the rule of thirds and the principle of chiaroscuro for an interesting photo.

64 BLUESTONE LANE AT THE CHURCH OF THE HEAVENLY REST

Bluestone Lane at the Church of the Heavenly Rest
1085 5th Avenue

HOW TO GET THERE
Subway 4, 5 or 6 (green) to 86 Street Lexington Avenue Station

Bluestone Lane has various popular coffee shops around New York City but the location next to the Church of the Heavenly Rest is without a doubt the most unique coffee shop you'll ever visit!

Since 2009, the Heavenly Rest Stop has been an integral part of the Church of the Heavenly Rest's seven-days-a-week open door policy. The church's former side chapel and library have been transformed into a lovely coffee bar where the arches and white sandstone walls make you feel as if you are sitting in a chapel. Stroll into the lively café through the entrance next to the main entrance of the large Art Deco church.

The café is the perfect stop for coffee and architecture lovers, or for anyone who likes the idea of a heavenly brunch or lunch. The shop is located along Museum Mile, in between the Guggenheim Museum and the Cooper Hewitt Museum, opposite the Engineers' Gate (the impressive entrance to the jogging track around the Jacqueline Kennedy Onassis Reservoir)!

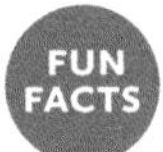

A scene in *The Devil's Advocate* (1997) starring Keanu Reeves and Charlize Theron was filmed in the church.

Seminarists often jokingly refer to the church as The Church Of The Celestial Snooze.

INSTAGRAMMABLE PLACES IN THE NEIGHBORHOOD

COFFEE AND FOOD	Divine coffee and blissfull dishes, they have it all!
SEE	Cooper-Hewitt Design Museum: 2 E 91st Street (2 min. walk)
	The Metropolitan Museum of Art: 1000 5th Avenue (7 min. walk)
	Jacqueline Kennedy Onassis Reservoir: other side of the road (1 min. walk)

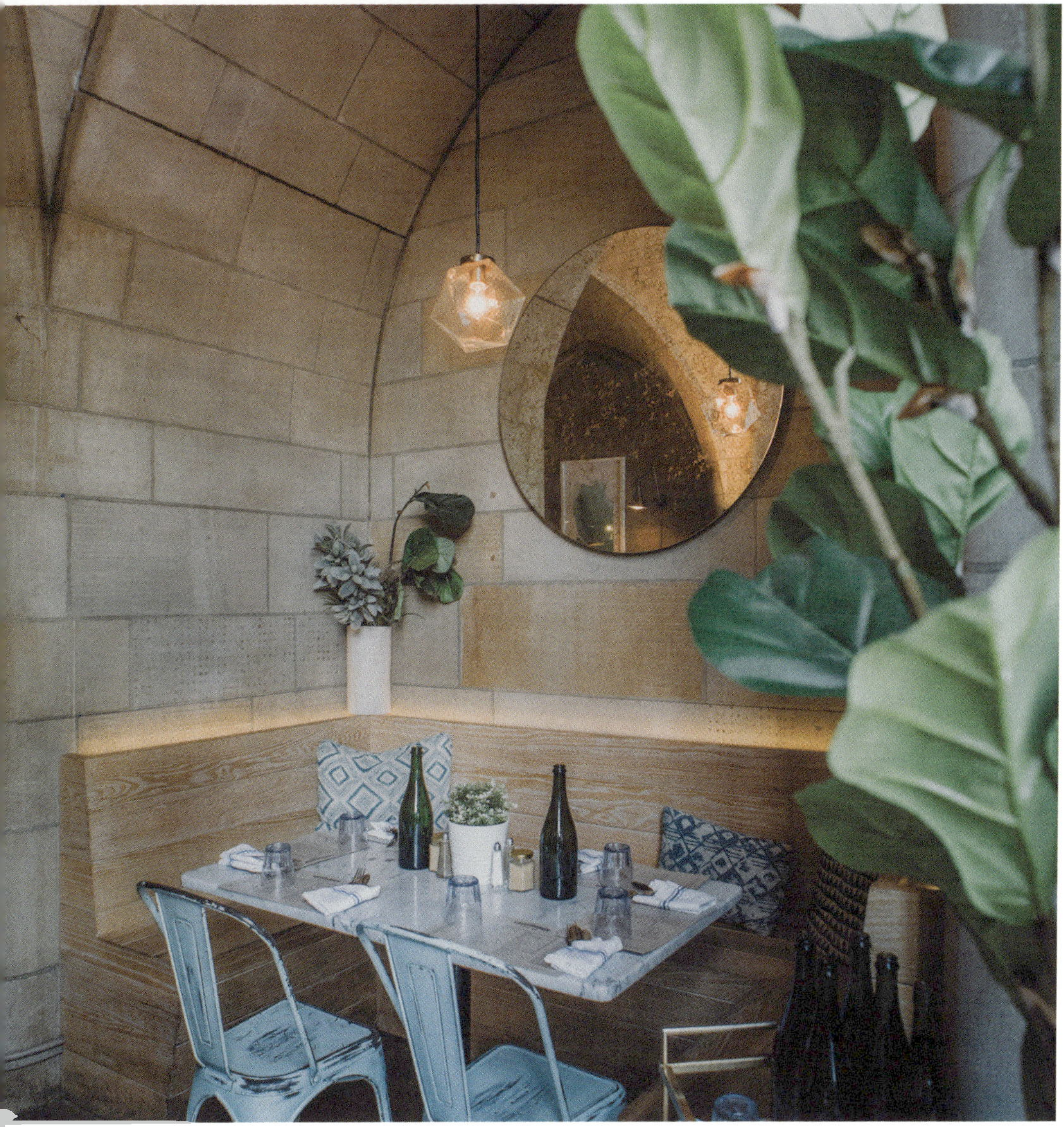

#heavenlyreststop #bluestonelane #churchoftheheavenlyrest #heavenlycoffee @bluestonelanecoffee

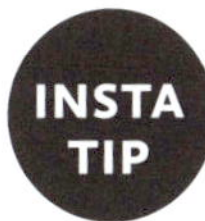

Choose the first table near the entrance for the nicest light. Natural light falls in through the large entrance and usually works better. If you prefer to take a photo inside the chapel, the lighting will bring out the orange in your picture. You can modulate cool down the image afterwards.

65 COOPER HEWITT DESIGN MUSEUM

Cooper Hewitt, Smithsonian Design Museum
2 E 91st Street

HOW TO GET THERE
Subway 4, 5 or 6 (green) to 86 Street Lexington Avenue Station

Carnegie Mansion, home of Cooper Hewitt, was built between 1899-1902. Cooper Hewitt donated the mansion to the Smithsonian Institution (1972) and in 1976 the museum opened to the public. The impressive museum's collection, older than the building itself, dates back to the mid-nineteenth century.

The museum aims to offer an interactive and personal visitor experience. You will be handed The Pen when you buy a ticket and can use it at the interactive tables where you can design your own furniture or utensil and/or save museum items that interest or inspire you. After your visit, you can visualize all your own designs and your saved items at home and check the corresponding information on the museum's website.

The mansion and garden are also worth a visit, in addition to the museum collection. You can enter the garden for free during the museum's opening hours and enjoy a coffee or a cake from the museum's bar there.

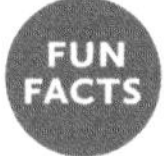

Because the museum's collection is so comprehensive, it is impossible to exhibit all the items simultaneously. Thanks to the interactive drawing tables and The Pen, visitors can digitally admire every item in the collection.

One of the museum's coolest galleries is the Immersion Room where you can scroll through the thousands of wallcoverings in the museum's collection on the interactive table and project the wallcovering of your choice on the room's walls and on your travel companions. The place to go for trippy pictures. You can also design your own wallcovering and save it in your pen.

INSTAGRAMMABLE PLACES IN THE NEIGHBORHOOD

COFFEE	Bluestone Lane at the Church of the Heavenly Rest: 1085 5th Avenue (1 min. walk)
FOOD	Gina Mexicana: 1288 Madison Avenue (5 min. walk)
SEE	The Guggenheim Museum (2 min. walk)
	Jacqueline Kennedy Onassis Reservoir: other side of the road (1 min. walk)

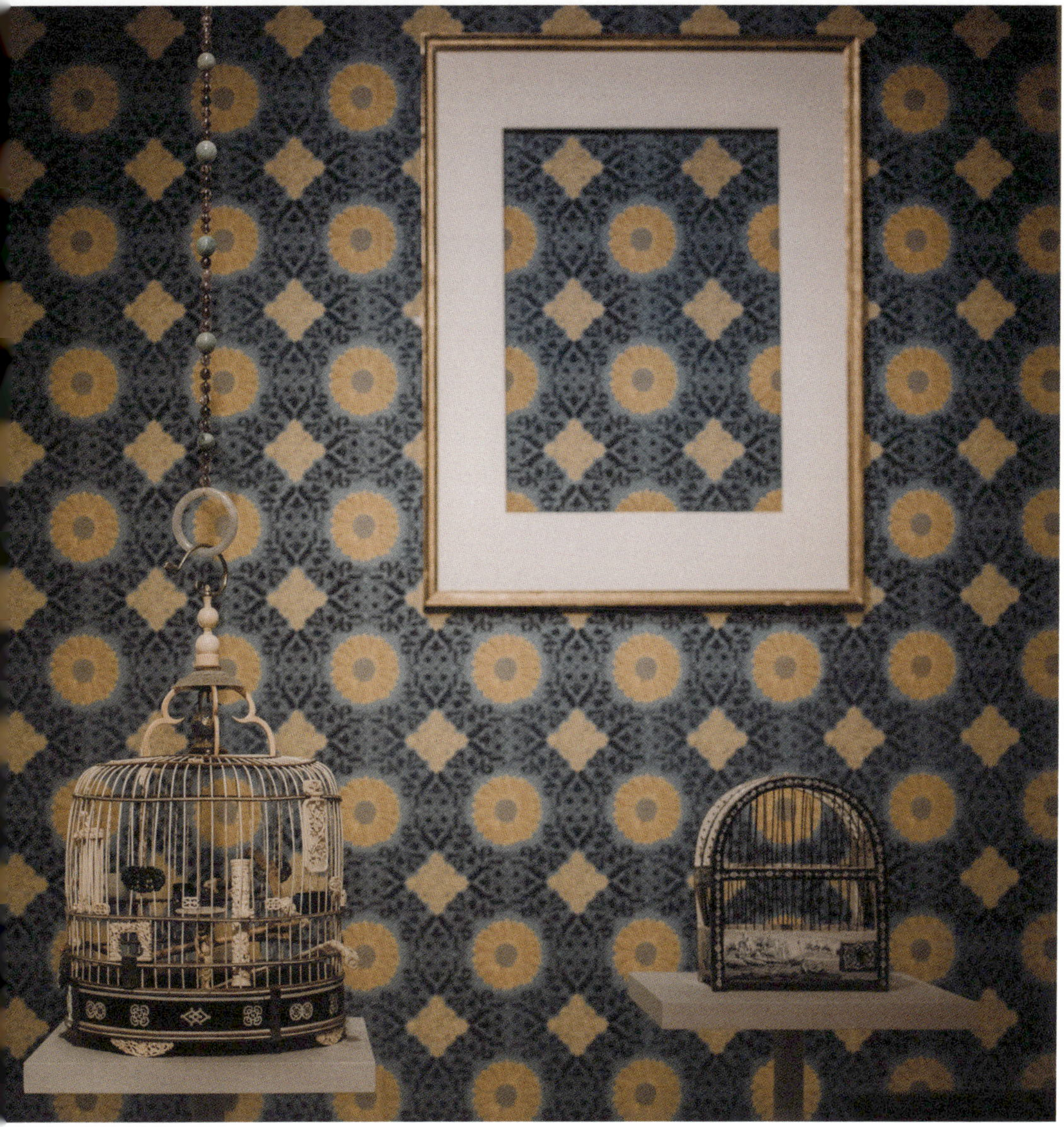

#cooperhewitt #cooperhewittmuseum #designmuseum #designinspiration #nycmuseums
@cooperhewitt

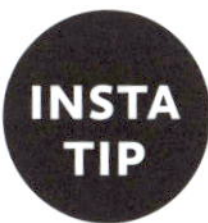

You can make your photo more interesting by combining several items in one image. The museum has plenty of places where the museum's collection is presented in such a way that all you need to do is point and shoot.

66 GRAFFITI HALL OF FAME

Graffiti Hall of Fame
Corner Park Avenue and E 106th Street

HOW TO GET THERE
Subway 4 or 6 (green) to 103 Street Station

The Graffiti Hall of Fame was founded in 1980 by community leader "Sting Ray" Rodriguez as a place to preserve and encourage graffiti as an art form. The concrete schoolyard walls of the Jackie Robins Educational Complex have become a place where graf artists can safely practice their skills with spray paint.

Since then, the Graffiti Hall of Fame's motto has changed to "Strictly Kings or Better" and the walls are covered with the work of some of the world's best professional street artists.

You can see the works through the iron fence around the schoolyard. On weekends, the yard is open from 8.30 am until 4 pm so you can see them up close. The work on the school's exterior wall is on the street side (on the corner of Park Ave and E 106th Street). No need to wait until the weekend to catch some superb street art in other words.

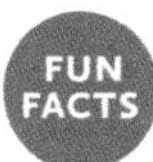

Whereas graffiti in New York City was mainly considered illegal in the eighties and manifested itself in and around the city's subways, there are now plenty of places in the city where graffiti artists receive a warm welcome and are given a canvas to exhibit their street art. Thanks to initiatives such as The Bushwick Collective in Brooklyn and The Welling Court Mural Project in Queens you can now find plenty of street art in the city.

INSTAGRAMMABLE PLACES IN THE NEIGHBORHOOD

COFFEE
- Dear Mama Coffee: 308 E 109th Street (11 min. walk)
- Little Bean Coffee: 111 Central Park North (12 min. walk)

SEE
- Museum of the City of New York: 1220 5th Avenue & 103rd Street (6 min. walk)
- Conservatory Garden: 402 5th Avenue (4 min. walk)
- The Duke Ellington Statue: corner 5th Avenue and 110th Street (8 min. walk)

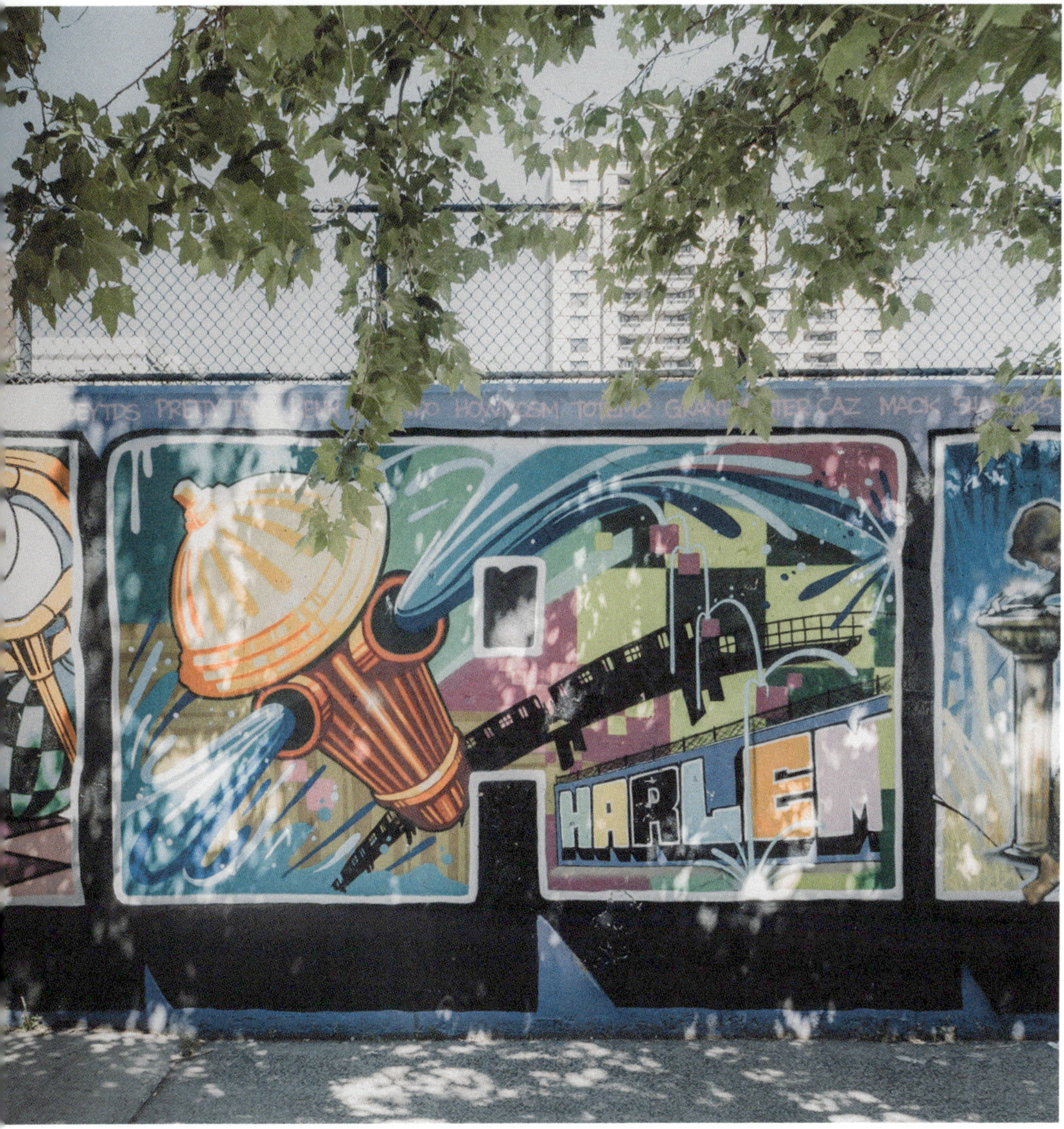

#graffitihalloffame #nycstreetart #streetartnewyork #streetartharlem #harlem

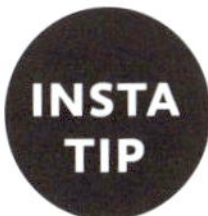

When you take a picture of the murals, it's often a good idea to include part of the surroundings. A building, a tree or a section of street gives the spectator a better idea of the mural's actual size.

67 RED ROOSTER

Red Rooster
310 Lenox
Avenue

HOW TO GET THERE
Subway A, C (blue) or B, D (orange) or 2, 3 (red) to 125 Street Station

Soul food spot Red Rooster was named after the legendary Harlem speakeasy, during the Prohibition in the United States in the twenties and thirties. These (often underground) bars served alcohol without a license. Which is why you had to speak quietly about such a place or when inside of it.

The restaurant is situated in the heart of Harlem and the chef believes in being part of the community. All the employees live locally, the restaurant sources its ingredients from local suppliers and they also offer cooking classes to the locals.

The restaurant's bar has a bustling, upbeat feel to it, with an elegant dining room and open kitchen behind it. You can admire unique artworks by local artists, both in the bar and the dining room.

Ginny's Supper Club is located one floor lower. This retro club pairs delicious food with live music. Gospel brunch or legendary soul music... on some days it feels like you've stepped back in time.

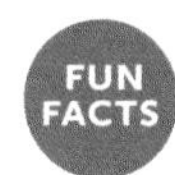

In 2009, Chef Samuelsson was invited to cook President Barack Obama's first state dinner.

INSTAGRAMMABLE PLACES IN THE NEIGHBORHOOD

COFFEE & FOOD	You are at the right place!
SEE	The Apollo Theater: 253 W 125th Street (7 min. walk)
	The Marcus Garvey Park: 6316 Mt Morris Park W (4 min. walk)
	Malcolm Shabazz Harlem Market: 52 W 116th Street (11 min. walk)
	The Crack is Wack Mural: 2nd Avenue and 128th Street (17 min. walk)

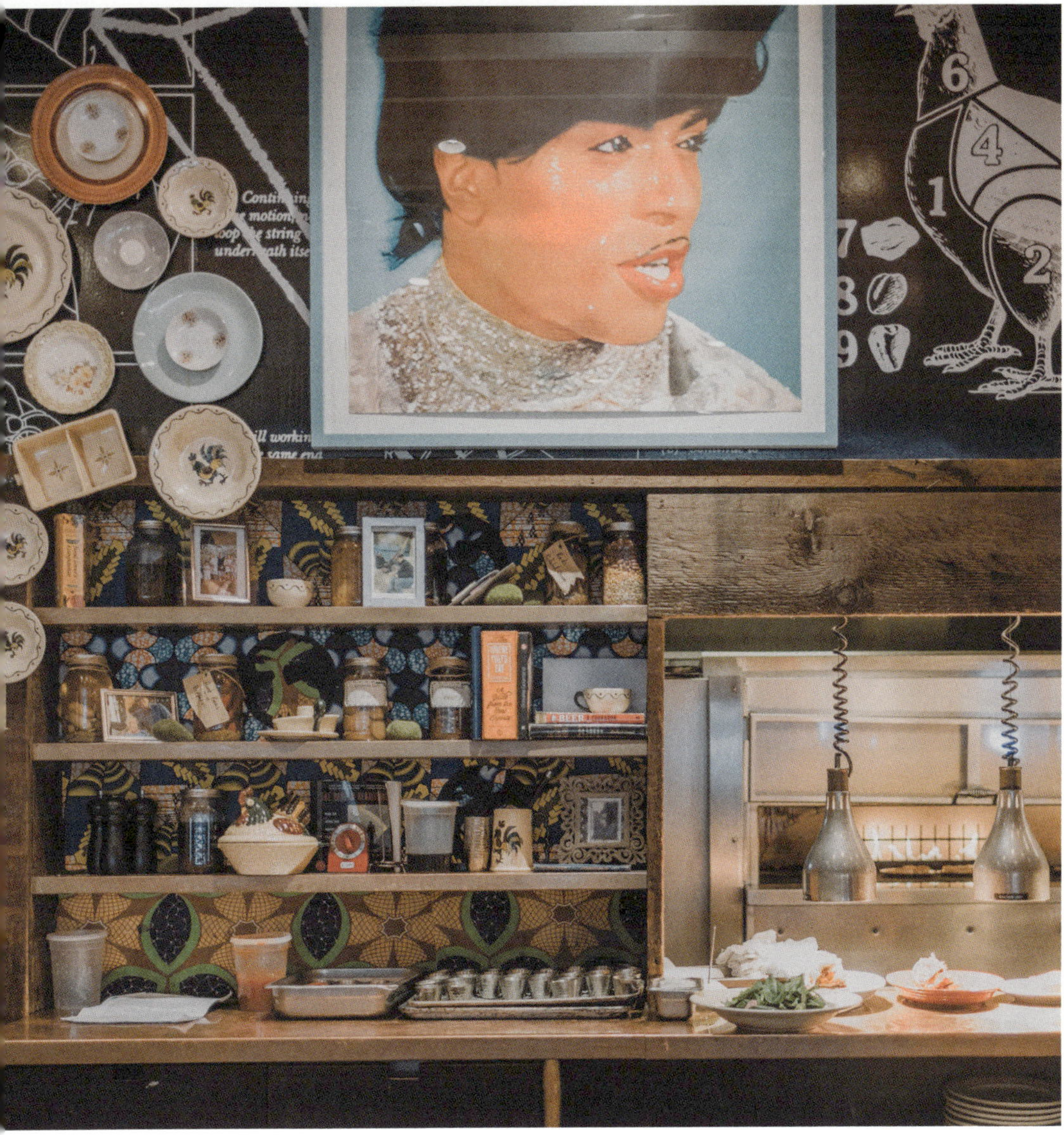

#redroosterharlem #redrooster #roosterharlem #soulfood #harlem @roosterharlem

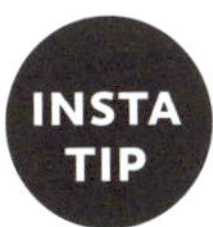

There's a lot to take in in this colorful, photogenic restaurant. When taking a photo of a restaurant interior, it's always fun if there's a reference to the restaurant in your shot. A plate with food, part of the kitchen, or some of the ingredients ensure your photo tells a story.

⑥⑧ APOLLO THEATER

Apollo Theater
253 W 125th Street

HOW TO GET THERE
Subway A, C (blue) or B, D (orange) or 2, 3 (red) to 125 Street Station

Once a burlesque theater, this theater rose to prominence since 1934, becoming a place "where stars are born and legends are made".

The Apollo Theater mainly owes its iconic status to all the stars that were discovered here during the Amateur Nights. Debuting musicians, singers, comics or dancers have just 90 seconds to convince the audience that they are the next Apollo legend. The audience decides who gets to stay, and who will literally be swept off the stage by the "Executioner".

Ella Fitzgerald won the first Amateur Night in 1934. She had originally intended to go on stage and dance but decided to sing instead at the last minute. A decision that would make her world famous. The careers of other stars such as Jimi Hendrix, Michael Jackson and the Jackson Five, Stevie Wonder, Aretha Franklin, Lauren Hill and many others also started at The Apollo.

The Apollo's interior and exterior have a New York City Landmark status. It has also been added to the National Register of Historic Places.

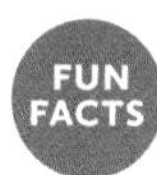

The "Godfather of Soul", James Brown, also participated in an Amateur Night one year. When he died in 2006, the first and only memorial service ever was held in the Apollo, giving thousands of grieving fans an opportunity for a public viewing.

A log, called the Good Luck Stump, sits atop a gold pillar in the wings of the right stage. Artists briefly touch the log before going on stage.

INSTAGRAMMABLE PLACES IN THE NEIGHBORHOOD

COFFEE Double Dutch Espresso: 2194 Frederick Douglass Blvd (8 min. walk)

FOOD Red Rooster: 310 Lenox Avenue (7 min. walk)

SEE Adam Clayton Powell Monument: corner Frederick Douglass Blvd and 125th Street (3 min. walk)

Harriet Tubman Memorial: Frederick Douglass Blvd and 122nd Street (4 min. walk)

Minton's Playhouse: 206 W 118th Street (9 min. walk)

Marcus Garvey Park: 6316 Mt Morris Park W (9 min. walk)

The Studio Museum: 429 W 127th Street (4 min. walk)

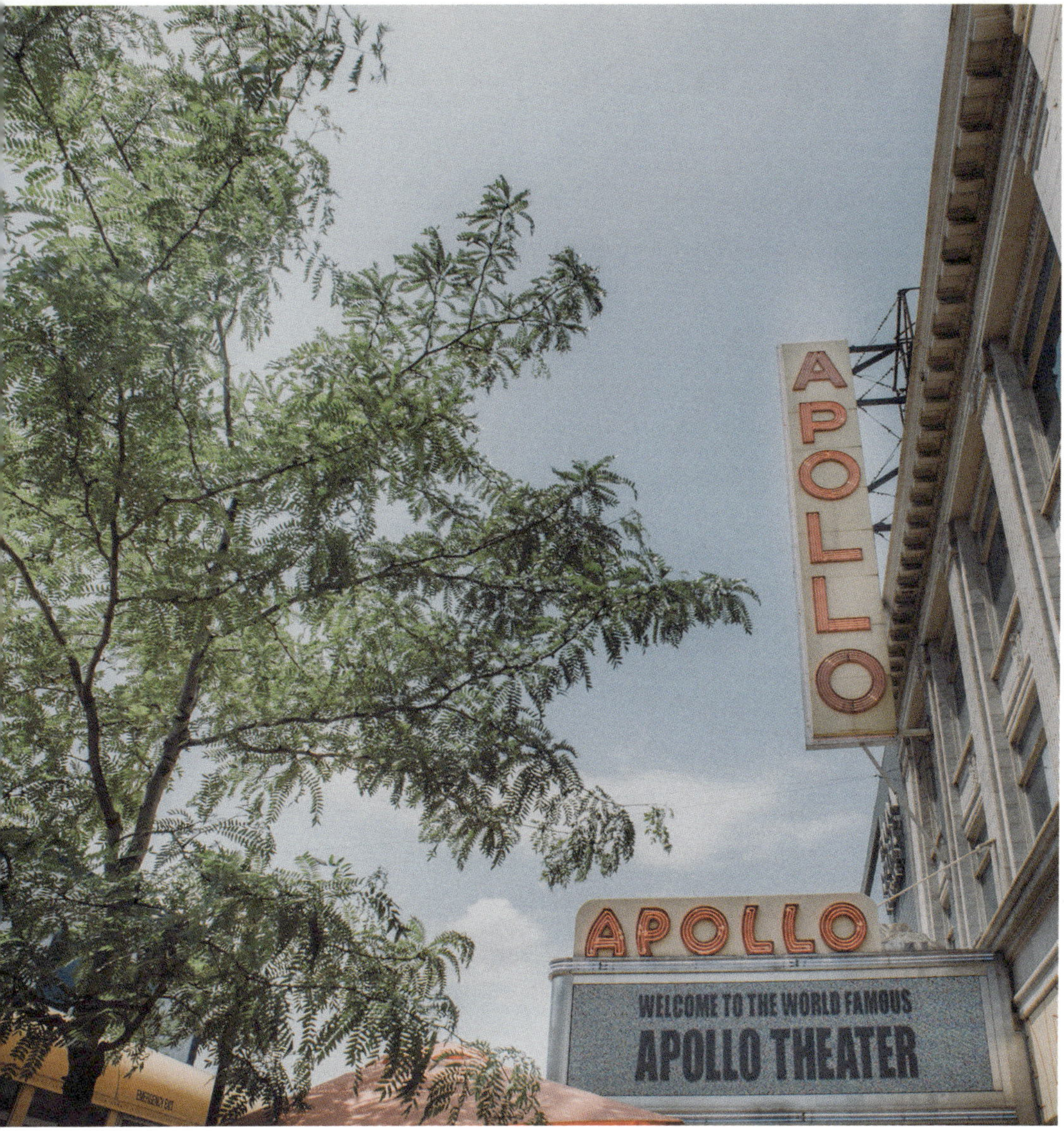

#apollotheater #apolloharlem #harlem #musichistory @apollotheater

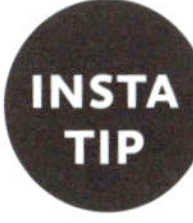

The Apollo Theater is often photographed at night but you can also take a nice picture of the iconic sign during daytime.

The text on the neon sign under the Apollo letters changes continually so wait until the "right text" appears.

69 COLUMBIA UNIVERSITY

Columbia University 116th Street & Broadway

HOW TO GET THERE
Subway 1 (red) to 116 Street - Columbia University Station

A huge, majestic and impressive university city in the center of a world capital. An estimated 30,000 students are enrolled in this university with the campus covering a surface area of 32 acres (14 hectares).

Columbia University is one of oldest colleges in the United States and one of the biggest landowners in New York City. Rockefeller acquired the land on which the Rockefeller Center of Columbus University now stands.

The campus comprises magnificent buildings and stunning gardens with beautiful sculptures. The impressive Alma Mater sculpture on the staircase of the Low Library is its most famous artwork. The bronze sculpture of the goddess Athena has come to symbolize the university. An owl is concealed in the folds of the goddess's skirt. Can you spot this symbol of knowledge and learning?

Perhaps the campus looks familiar? It has been featured in plenty of movies (*Ghostbusters, Spider Man*) and TV series (*House, Gossip Girl, Law & Order*) over the years.

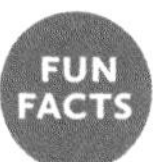

Before the university was built, there used to be a psychiatric institute here. Many of the underground corridors of this era still exist, connecting various buildings on campus.

The roaring lion at the beginning of every Universal Studio movie was the designer's tribute to Columbus University and his team, The Lions.

INSTAGRAMMABLE PLACES IN THE NEIGHBORHOOD

COFFEE Max Caffè: 1262 Amsterdam Avenue (7 min. walk)

FOOD Friedmans: 1187 Amsterdam Avenue (4 min. walk)
Ellington in the Park: Riverside Drive & W 105th Street (15 min. walk)

SEE Morningside Park: Morningside Drive (4 min. walk)
The Peace Fountain: 1047 Amsterdam Avenue (7 min. walk)
General Grant National Memorial: W 122nd Street & Riverside Drive (12 min. walk)

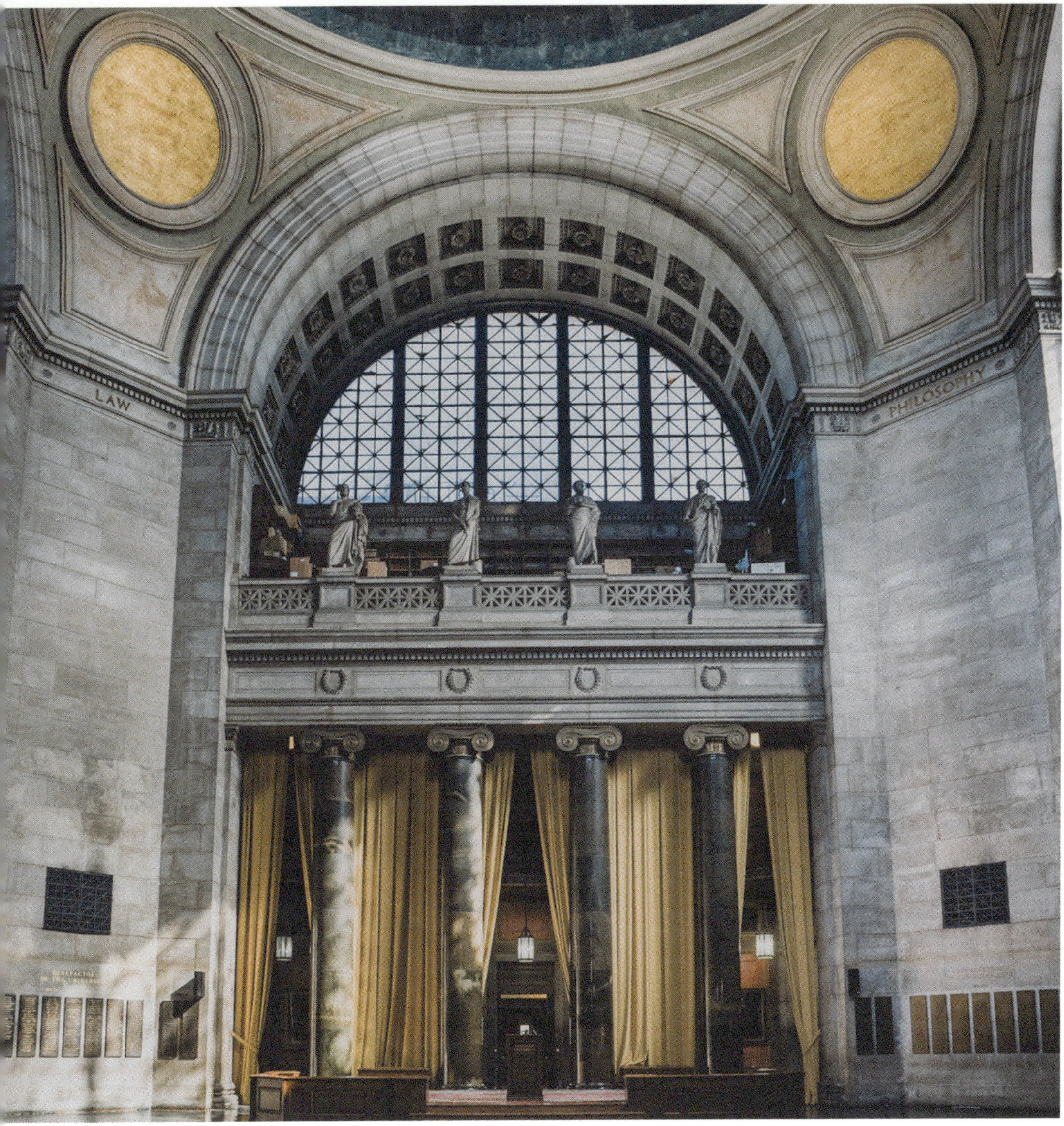

#columbiauniversity #columbia #university #almamater #harlem @columbia

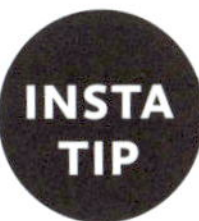

The building behind the large Alma Mater sculpture, the Low Library, is open to the public. This is also where the Visitor Center and the large auditorium where lectures and talks are given are located. To take a picture of this auditorium, you should display the gridlines of your camera, to ensure the horizontals are straight.

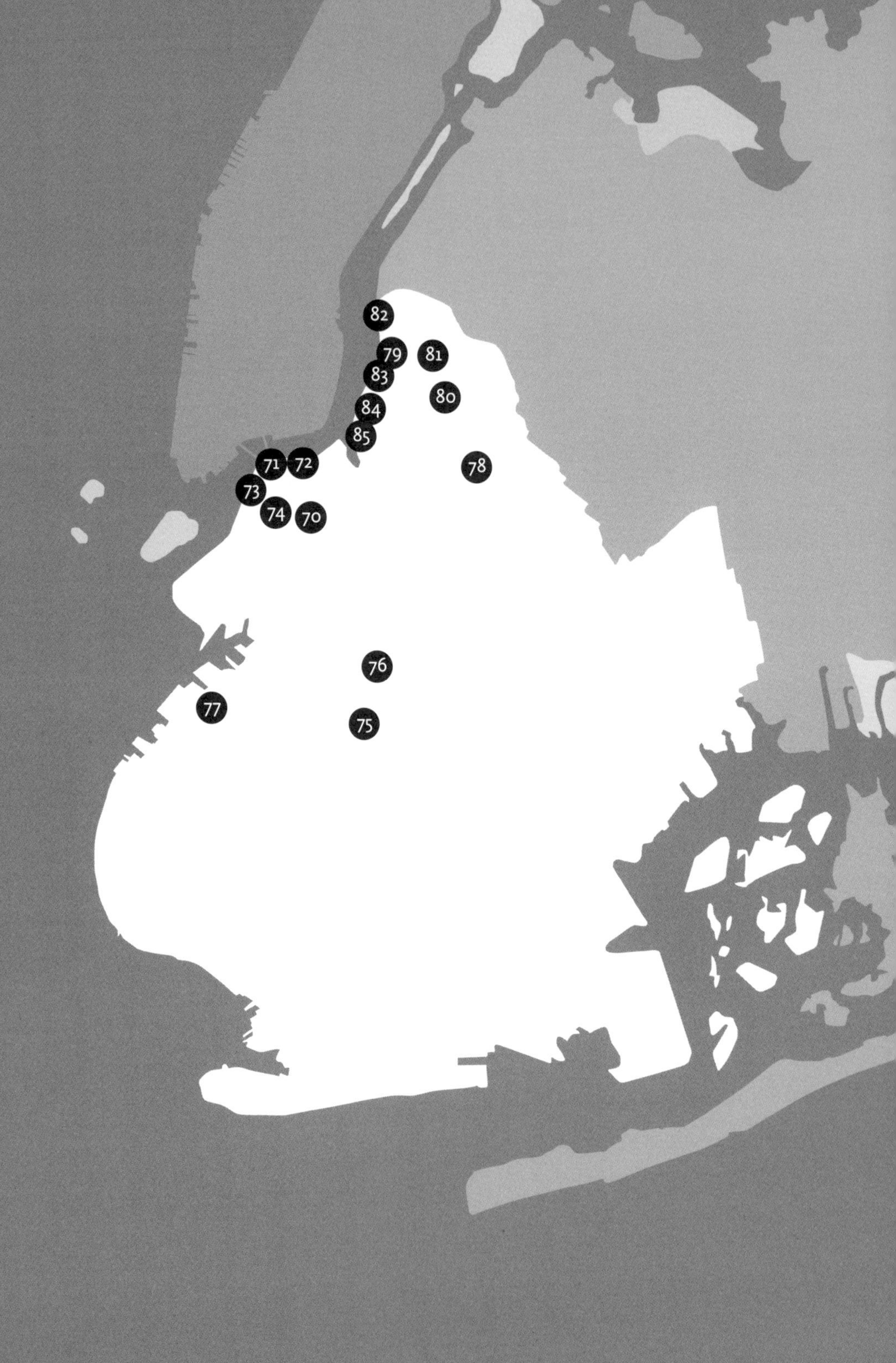
82
79
81
83
80
84
85
71
72
78
73
74
70
76
77
75

BROOKLYN

70 GOODBYE RHINOS

MetroTech Commons, Brooklyn

HOW TO GET THERE
Subway A or C (blue) or F (orange) to Jay Street - MetroTech Station

The Last Three is a monumental sculpture in the center of the MetroTech Commons. It was made by the artists Gillie and Marc and inaugurated on 15 March 2018. The artists wanted to make a statement about poaching, and the extinction of the white rhino. The gigantic sculpture has moved many people to tears.

The Last Three are Sudan, Najin and Fatu, the last three living northern white rhinos on earth when the sculpture was created. Sudan died on 20 March 2018, just one week after the sculpture was installed in the square.

Everyone can help raise awareness about the detrimental effects of poaching with the hashtag #goodbyerhinos when posting a photo of the monument.

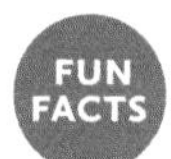

Although a rhino's horn is made of the same material as fingernails some people still believe that these horns can cure cancer, are a good panacea for a hangover and an excellent aphrodisiac. This belief is rooted in traditional Chinese medicine. As a result, rhino horns are sometimes more expensive than gold.

Gillie and Marc have completed more instagrammable public art in NYC. If you like the Rhinos, you should definitely check the Paparazzi Dogs at the Rockefeller Plaza, the Paparazzi Dogman and Paparazzi Rabbitgirl at 1221 Avenue of the Americas, The Table of Love at 237 Park Avenue and We Go Together at 9 Crosby Street.

INSTAGRAMMABLE PLACES IN THE NEIGHBORHOOD

COFFEE	Devoción: 276 Livingston Street (10 min. walk)
FOOD	DeKalb Market Hall: 445 Albee Square West (7 min. walk)
SEE	New York Transit Museum: 99 Schermerhorn Street (7 min. walk)
	Brooklyn Heights Promenade: Montague Street & Pierrepont Place (14 min. walk)

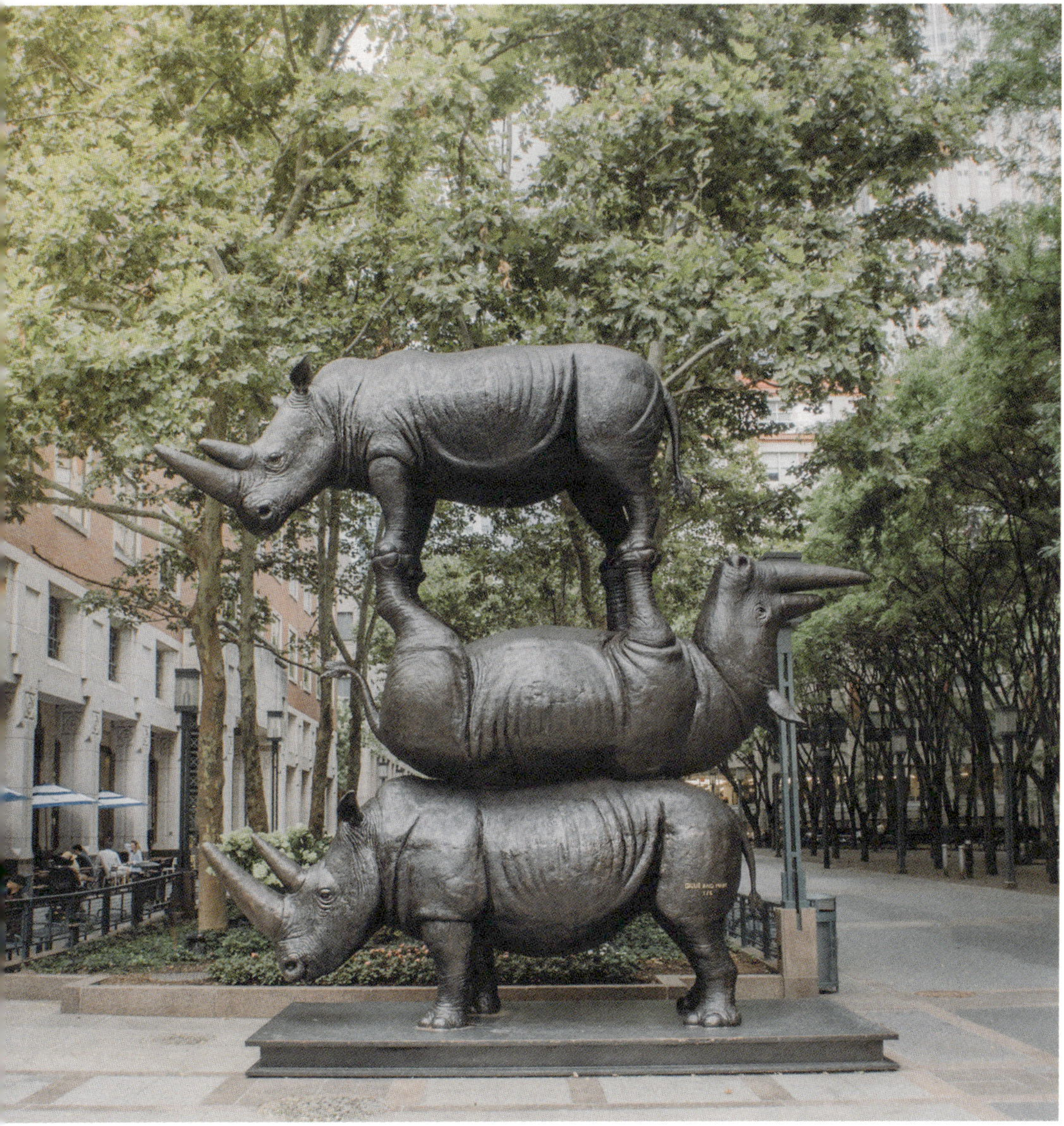

#goodbyerhinos #thelastthree #goodbyesudan #metrotech #publicart
@gilliandmarcart

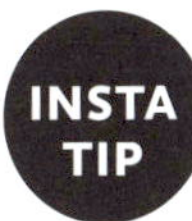

In order to get the whole state in your frame, take a picture from a position that is as low as possible. Make sure your camera doesn't tilt, or it will look like the statue falls over.

71 JANE'S CAROUSEL

Jane's Carousel
Old Dock Street

HOW TO GET THERE
Subway F (orange) to York Street Station

Subway A (blue) to High Street - Brooklyn Bridge Station

Jane's Carousel is a stunning antique carousel that was built in 1922. You can take a ride on one of the 28 lovely wooden horses and enjoy a magnificent view of the Lower Manhattan skyline in the meantime. The carousel is open year-round. Don't worry about the winter cold, as a glass structure surrounds the wooden carousel. The Brooklyn Bridge and the Manhattan Bridge are reflected in this jewel box-like structure, creating a rather photogenic combination.

The carousel is located between the two bridges. This neighborhood is also called Dumbo, or Down Under Manhattan Bridge Overpass. In the nineteenth and twentieth century, this neighborhood had plenty of industrial buildings. In recent years, however, Dumbo has become one of Brooklyn's hippest neighborhoods, with trendy shops and hotspots in the magnificently restored historical buildings.

This is also the place to be for romantic souls and photographers. The shore of the East River, in between the two bridges, is a very popular place for a snapshot of the spectacular sunset.

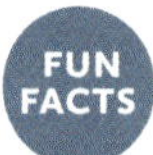

Jane's Carousel was the first carousel to be added to The National Register of Historic Places in 1975.

The plexiglass pavilion around the carousel cost more than the actual carousel itself and was designed by the architect Jean Nouvel. Its nickname is the 'Plexiglass Jewel Box'.

INSTAGRAMMABLE PLACES IN THE NEIGHBORHOOD

COFFEE	Brooklyn Roasting Company: 2 Main Street (2 min. walk)
FOOD	One Girl Cookies: 33 Main Street (2 min. walk)
	Grimaldi's Pizza: 1 Front Street (3 min. walk)
	Brooklyn Ice Cream Factory: 1 Water Street (3 min. walk)
SEE	Brooklyn Historical Society: 55 Water Street.
	St. Ann's Warehouse: 45 Water Street (1 min. walk)

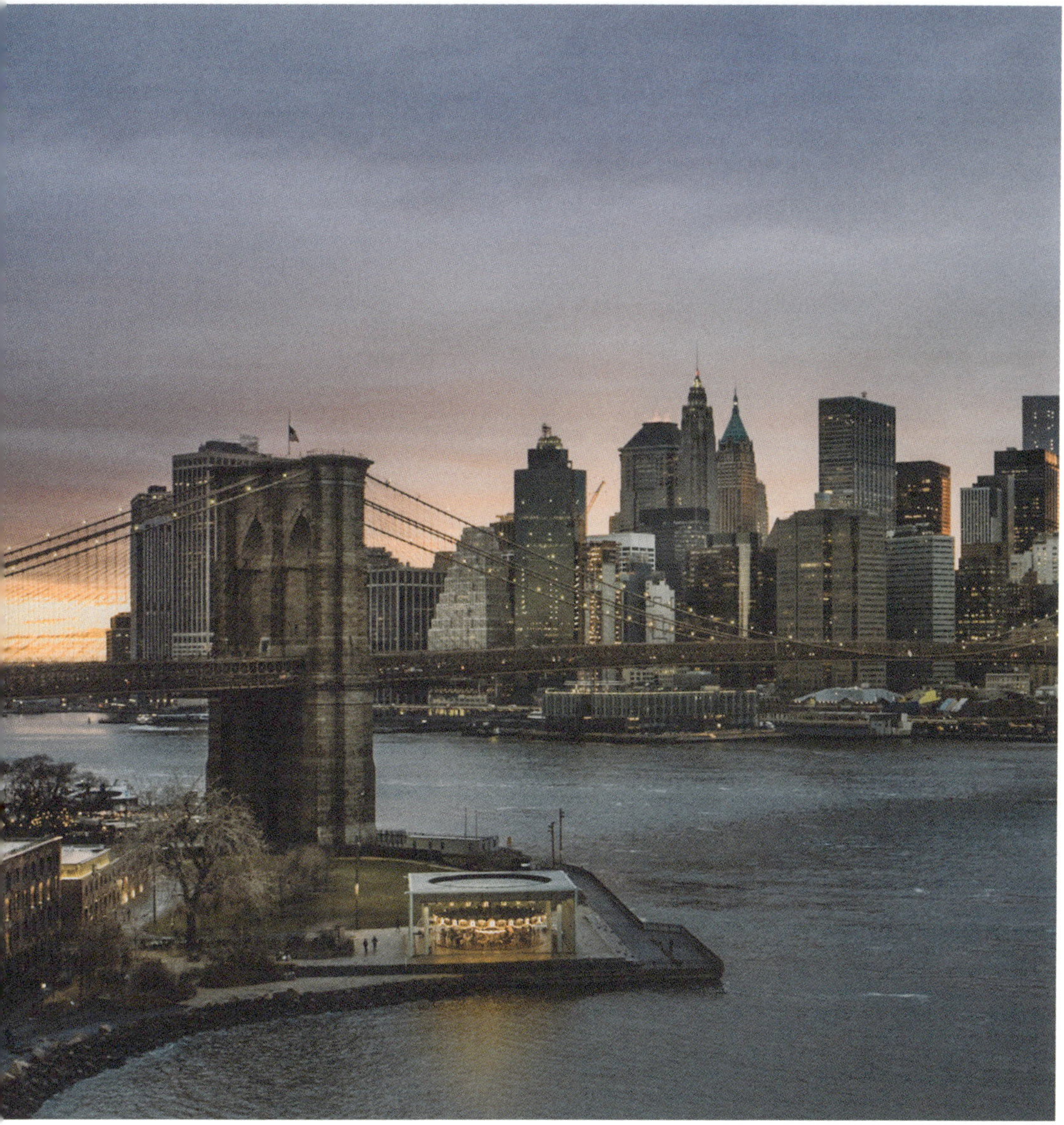

#janescarousel #brooklyn #dumbo #brooklynbridgepark @janescarousel

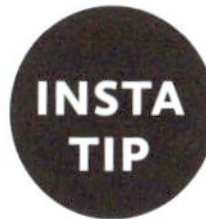

Enjoy incredible views of the Brooklyn Bridge, the Lower Manhattan Skyline and Jane's Carousel from the walkway on the Manhattan Bridge. This is an especially good location at sunset, when the sky still has some color in it.

⓻② TOM FRUIN'S WATERTOWER

Tom Fruin's
Watertower
20 Jay Street

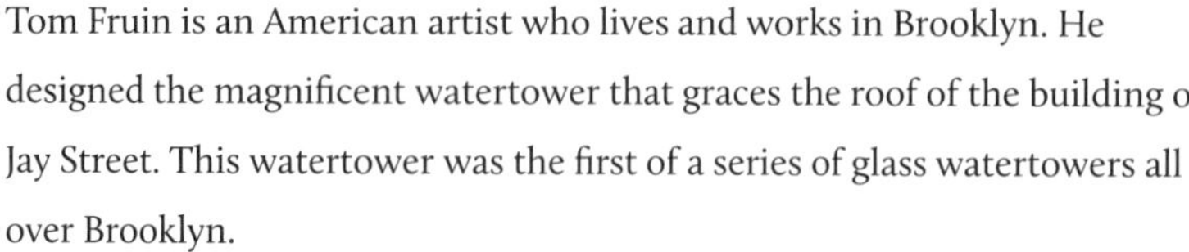

HOW TO GET THERE
Subway F (orange) to York Street Station

Tom Fruin is an American artist who lives and works in Brooklyn. He designed the magnificent watertower that graces the roof of the building on Jay Street. This watertower was the first of a series of glass watertowers all over Brooklyn.

The watertower is made of recycled steel and over 1,000 pieces of colored plexiglass and was inspired by the watertowers that are such an iconic feature of New York's skyline.

During the day, the sunlight that shines through the glass creates a kaleidoscope-like effect. At night, the watertower is lit from within. This light beacon pays tribute to New York's watertowers and Brooklyn's colourful community.

The best place to see the watertower is from the cycling path on the Manhattan Bridge or from the Brooklyn Bridge Park near Washington Street.

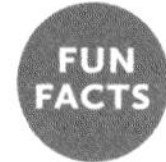

The reclaimed plexiglass fragments were sourced from various places all over New York including demolished warehouses, the remnants of signage, and so on. They were all recycled and integrated in this public artwork.

The artist Ryan Holsopple created the light within the watertower. Various light sequences light up the colorful windows from sunrise to sunset.

INSTAGRAMMABLE PLACES IN THE NEIGHBORHOOD

COFFEE	Brooklyn Roasting Company: 25 Jay Street (1 min. walk)
SHOP	Melville House Bookstore: 46 John Street (1 min. walk)
SEE	The Yes Murals: under The Manhattan Bridge, 1 min. walk from the York Street Subway Station
	The Cliffs at Dumbo: 99 Plymouth Street
	Brooklyn Historical Society: 55 Water Street
	Jane's Carousel: Old Dock Street

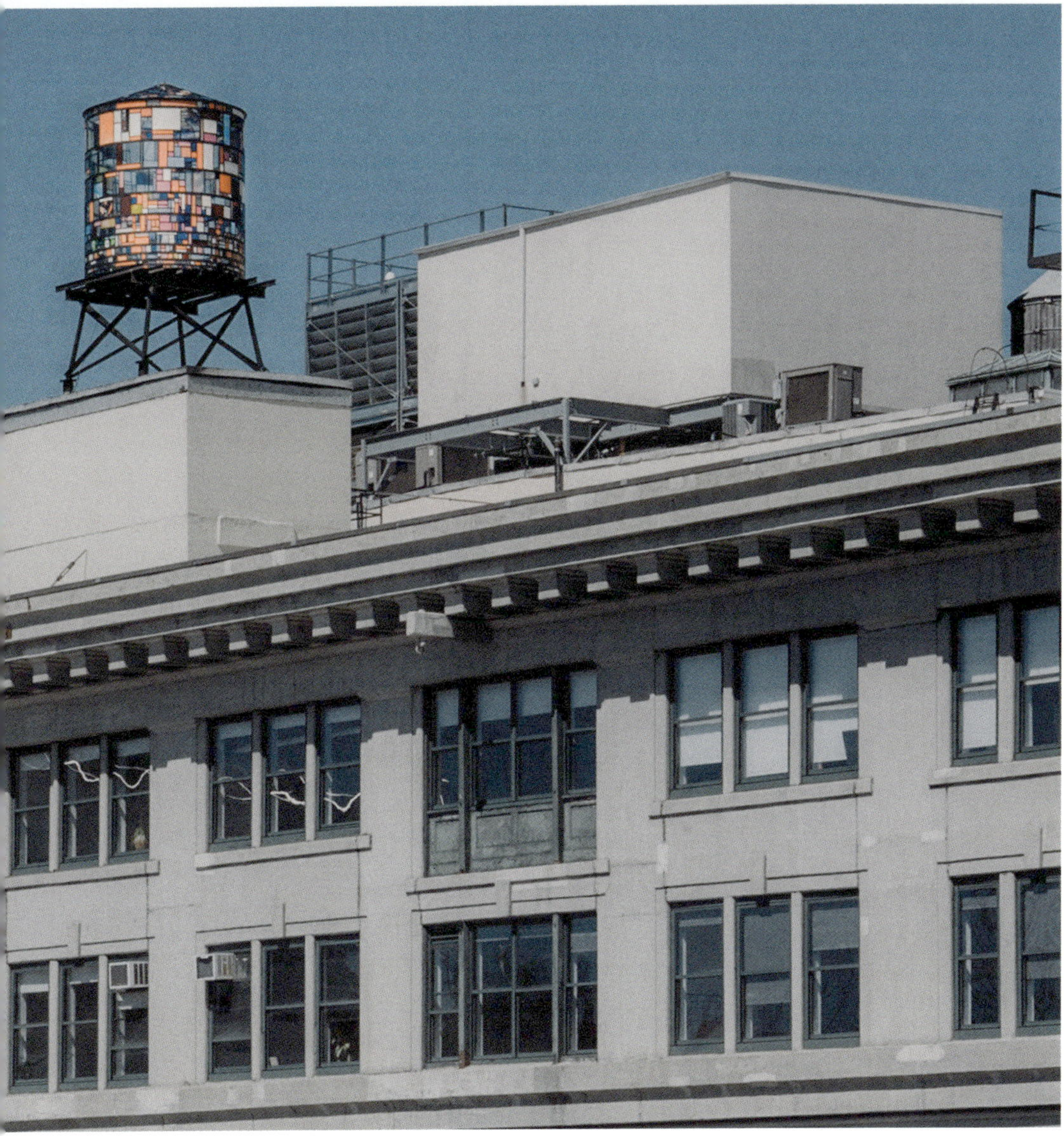

#tomfruinwatertower #tomfruin #brooklyn #dumbo #publicart @tomfruin

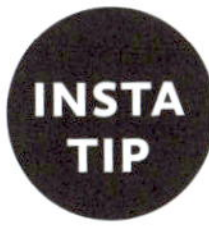

You can rent a bicycle and cross the Manhattan Bridge to take a picture of Tom Fruin's water tower. Also a great opportunity to take plenty of other impressive shots.

⑦③ BROOKLYN BRIDGE PARK

Brooklyn Bridge Park

HOW TO GET THERE

Subway A, C (blue) to High Street Station

Subway F (orange) to York Street Station

Subway 2, 3 (red) or 4, 5 (green) to Borough Hall Station

Brooklyn Bridge Park is a 85-acre (34 hectare) large waterfront park, spanning over 1.3 miles (2 kilometers) on the shore of the East River. Enjoy spectacular views of the Manhattan skyline, from the hills, pedestrian paths and gardens in the park, which extends from Jay Street near the Manhattan Bridge to Pier 6 and Atlantic Avenue.

In 1984, the piers, which were previously used for cargo ship operations by the Port Authority, were sold for commercial development. This was also when the idea of building a park here was first conceived. The master plan was published in 2000 and ten years later, the first two completed piers (Pier 1 and Pier 6) opened to the public.

The park was extended year after year. Since then many visitors find their way to the park, for a stroll or to participate in the many events and activities that are organized there. Brooklyn Bridge Park is a lively and dynamic park, which is both popular with locals and with tourists.

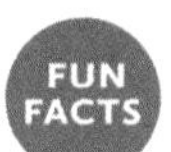

Only sustainable materials were used to develop the park, including salvaged material from all over New York. The park benches and the wooden decks were made using wood from the former warehouses on Pier 1. The Granite Prospect on Pier 1 was made using surplus granite blocks from reconstruction work on the Roosevelt Island Bridge.

The picturesque building of the Brooklyn Ice Cream Factory on Pier 1 is the former Marine Fire Boat Station.

INSTAGRAMMABLE PLACES IN THE NEIGHBORHOOD

DRINKS	Lizzmonade: Pier 1 Brooklyn Bridge Park Drive
FOOD	The Osprey: 60 Furman Street
	Forino at Pier 6: go to the rooftop!
SEE	The Granite Prospect at Pier 1
	Pier 2 Roller Rink: 150 Furman Street
	Brooklyn Bridge Park Pop-Up Pool: 150 Furman Street

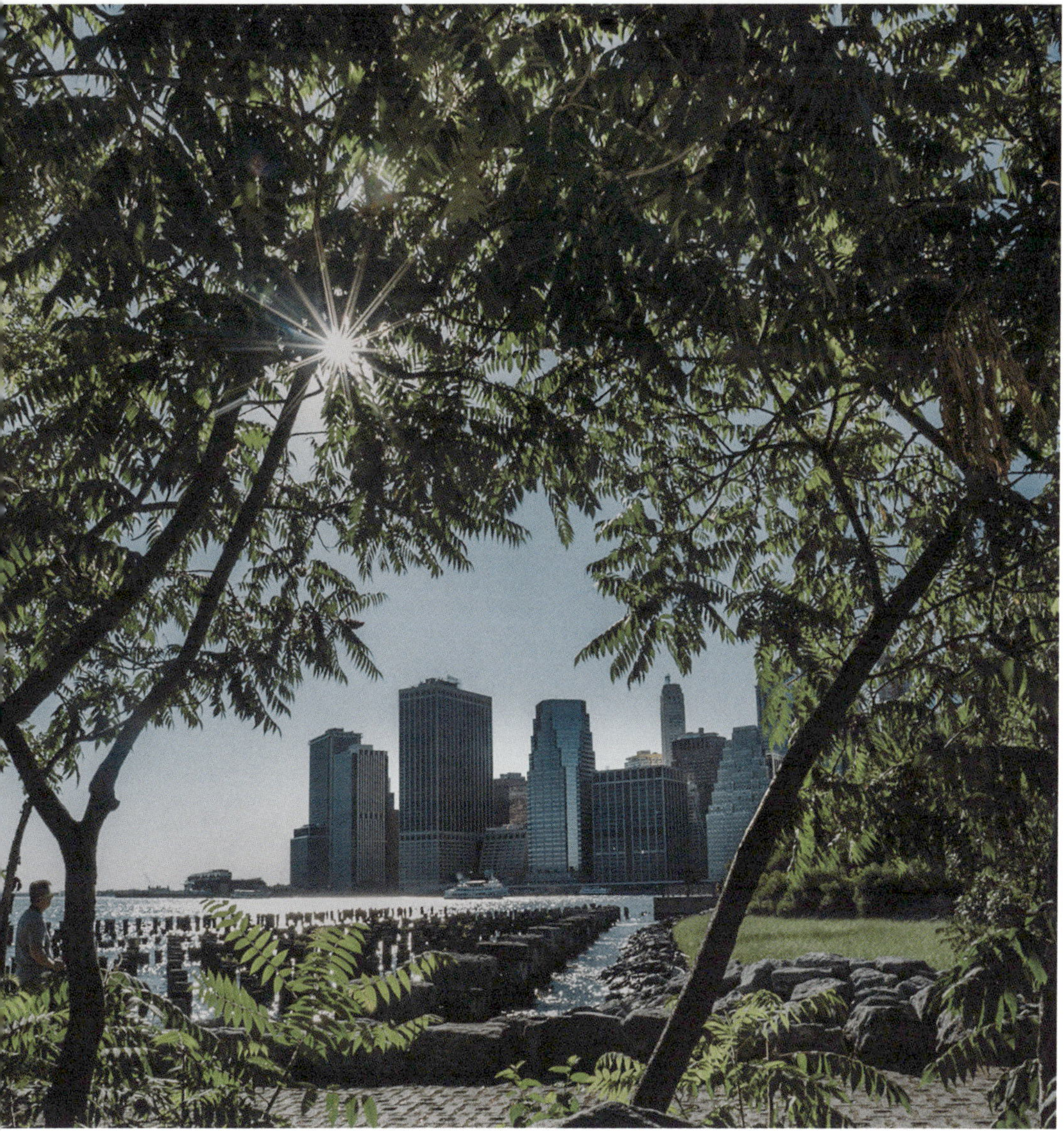

#brooklynbridgepark #brooklynbridge #brooklyn #nycparks @brooklynbridgepark

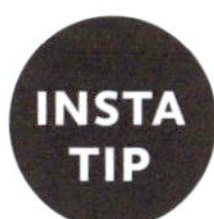

Between Pier 1 and Pier 2, you'll find the Old Pier 1. While you can no longer walk along the Pier, it provides a beautiful foreground for a picture with the Manhattan skyline in the background.

74 BROOKLYN HEIGHTS

Brooklyn Heights

HOW TO GET THERE

Subway C (blue) to High Street Station

Subway 2 or 3 (red) to Clark Street Station

Subway 4 or 5 (green) to Borough Hall Station

Brooklyn Heights is a residential neighborhood in Brooklyn, with lovely views of the Manhattan skyline and the East River. You can see Brooklyn Bridge Park and the skyline from the Brooklyn Heights Promenade.

Brooklyn Heights, an affluent residential neighborhood, is situated along the promenade and is known for its lovely brownstone rowhouses and several preserved wood houses. The excellent location and the unique houses have contributed to the eight-figure prices of homes in the neighborhood. Who knows, you may bump into one of the many famous residents, such as Tyra Banks, Sarah Jessica Parker, Matthew Broderick... Henry Miller, Marilyn Monroe and Truman Capote also lived here at one time. Brooklyn Heights is the first New York "neighborhood" to be added to the National Register of Historic Places.

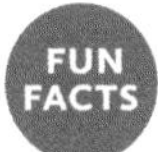

The "house" at 58 Joralemon Street is not a home at all. The façade conceals a subway vent and the emergency exit for the Lexington Avenue Line.

Häagen-Dazs was established in 1976 by two Polish immigrants, who opened their first ice-cream shop in Brooklyn Heights. You can still visit it at 120 Montague Street.

INSTAGRAMMABLE PLACES IN THE NEIGHBORHOOD

COFFEE Joe Coffee: 102 Hicks Street
Two For The Pot: 200 Clinton Street

SEE The Brooklyn Cat Cafe: 149 Atlantic Avenue
Truman Capote's House: 70 Willow Street
Brooklyn Heights Promenade: Montague Street and Pierrepont Place

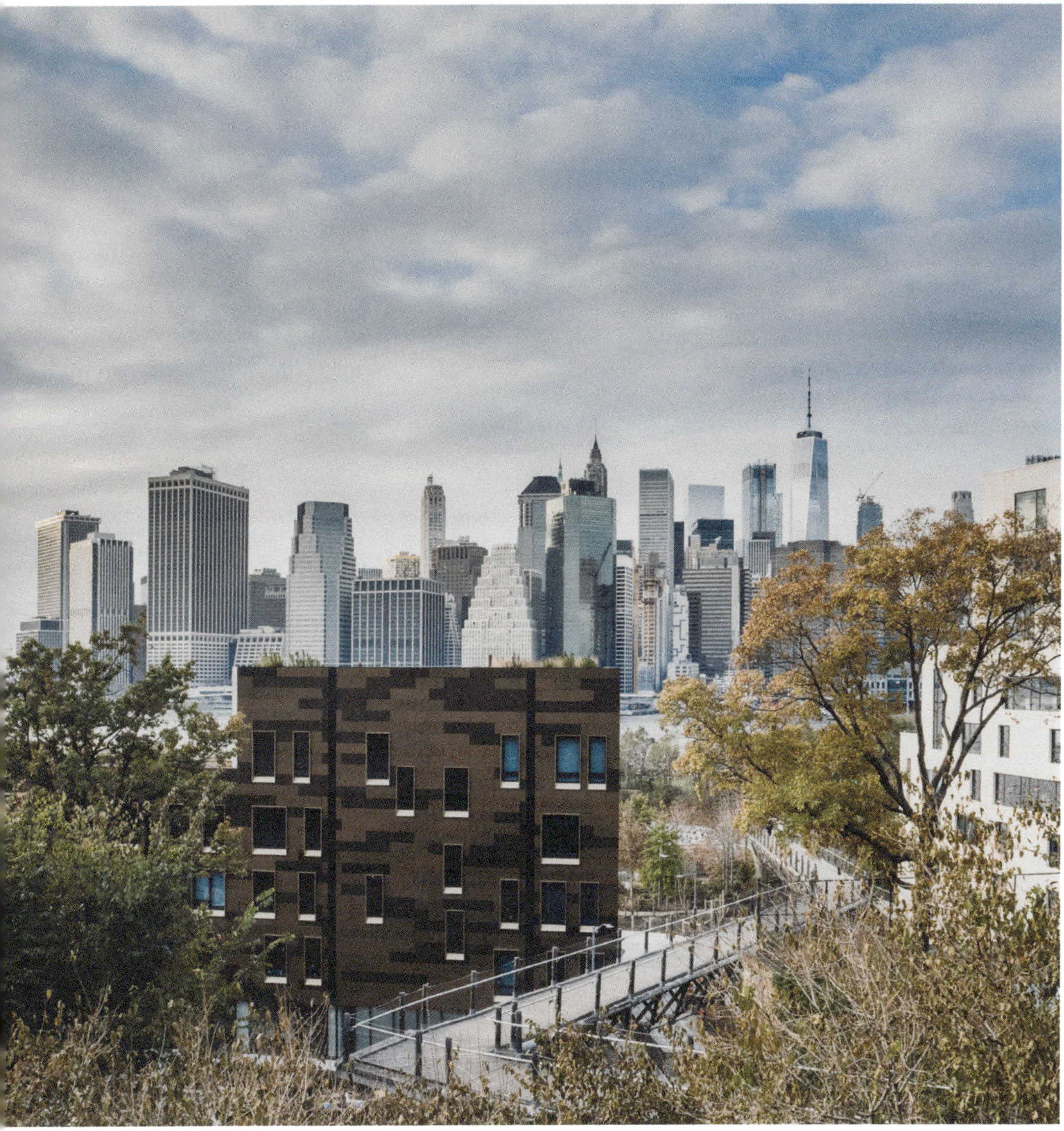

#brooklynheights #brooklyn #brooklynheights #streetsofnewyork

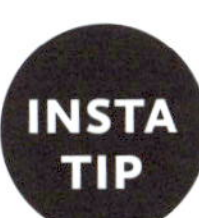

The Brooklyn Heights Promenade offers a fantastic view of the new buildings on the Brooklyn side and of the Downtown Manhattan Skyline. Add the pedestrian path to the shot, using it as a leading line to lead the eye to the skyline.

⑦⑤ SMORGASBURG PROSPECT PARK

Smorgasburg
Prospect Park

HOW TO GET THERE
Subway Q (orange) or S (grey) to Prospect Park Subway Station

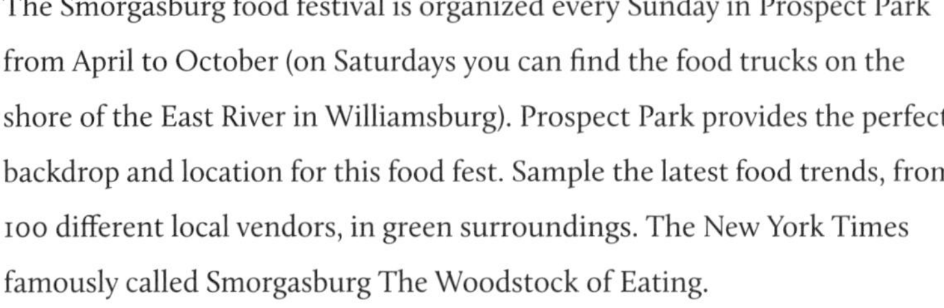

The Smorgasburg food festival is organized every Sunday in Prospect Park from April to October (on Saturdays you can find the food trucks on the shore of the East River in Williamsburg). Prospect Park provides the perfect backdrop and location for this food fest. Sample the latest food trends, from 100 different local vendors, in green surroundings. The New York Times famously called Smorgasburg The Woodstock of Eating.

A few photo faves:
- Spaghetti doughnuts from @pop_pasta.
- All juice, no cups from @johnsjuicenyc.
- The Vegan-Filipino inspired bites from @rubekitchen
- The Ramen Burger from @ramenburger

$

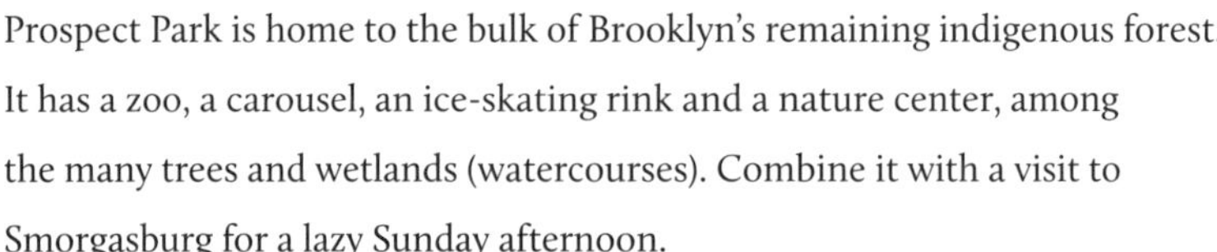

Prospect Park is home to the bulk of Brooklyn's remaining indigenous forest. It has a zoo, a carousel, an ice-skating rink and a nature center, among the many trees and wetlands (watercourses). Combine it with a visit to Smorgasburg for a lazy Sunday afternoon.

FUN FACTS

Prospect Park was designed by Frederic Lax Olmsted and Calvert Vaux, who also conceived Central Park.

Picnics were prohibited in Central Park in the 19th century but allowed in Prospect Park, which is why the park has always been a popular venue for people who like to eat out in nature. In the 1920s, the city installed 1,200 picnic tables in the park but on some days, things got so busy that the number of tables still proved insufficient.

INSTAGRAMMABLE PLACES IN THE NEIGHBORHOOD

COFFEE & FOOD	you're in the middle of the food and drinks walhalla!
SEE	Brooklyn Botanic Garden: 990 Washington Avenue (18 min. walk)
	Brooklyn Museum: 200 Eastern Peakway (20 min. walk)
	Brooklyn Public Library: 10 Grand Army Plaza (22 min. walk)

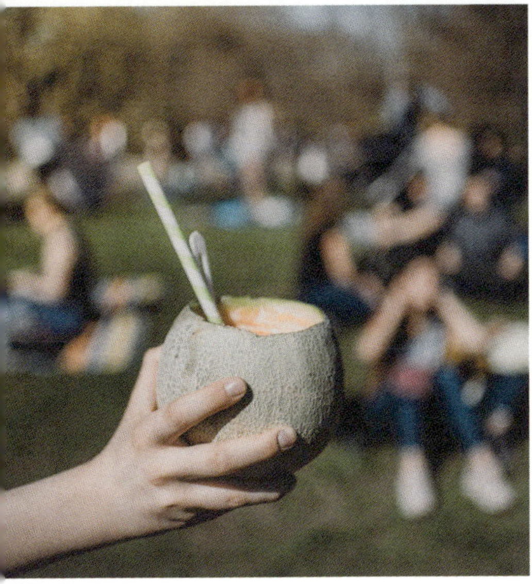

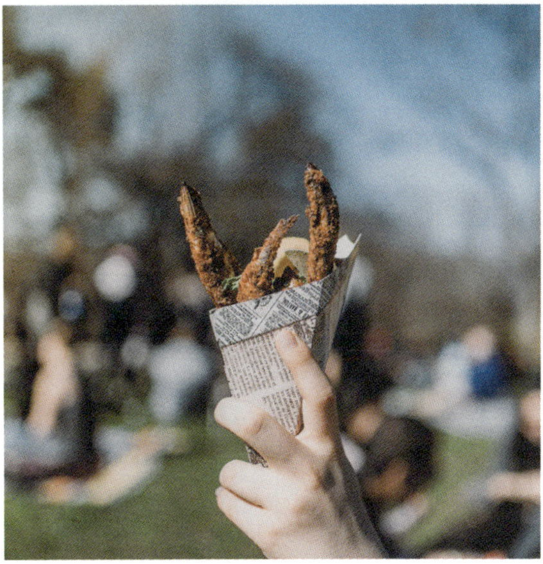

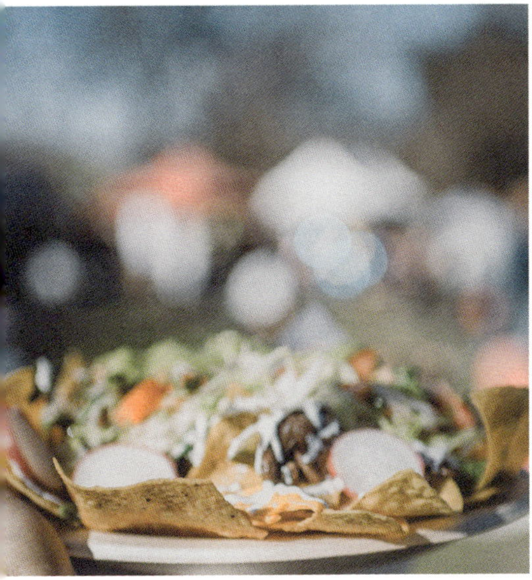

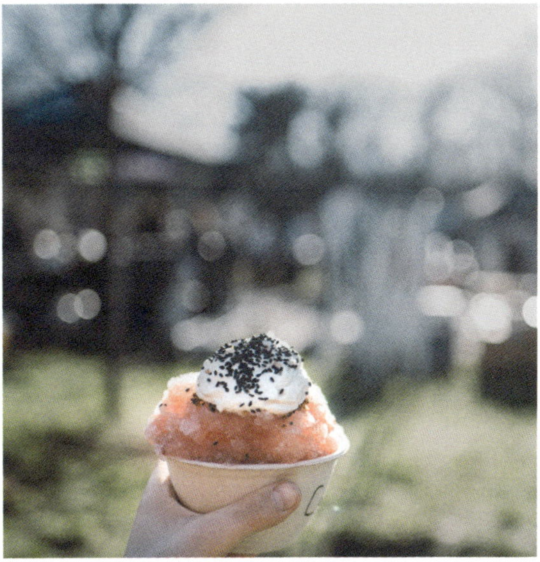

#smorgasburg #smorgasburgprospectpark #nyceats #prospectpark #brooklyn @smorgasburg @prospect_park

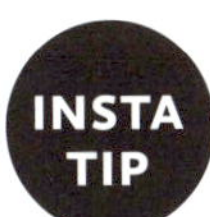

Use the focus functionality in the Instagram app to make your subject stand out from the background. Make sure to get close to whatever you are taking a picture of, and that there is a lot of space behind your subject for the best effect.

76 BROOKLYN BOTANIC GARDEN

Brooklyn Botanic Garden
990 Washington Avenue

HOW TO GET THERE
Subway 2, 3 (red) or 4, 5 (green) to Eastern Parkway Brooklyn Museum Station

Brooklyn Botanic Garden has more than 52 acres (21 hectares) of stunning gardens and is home to over 10,000 plant species.

When you step through the Eastern Parkway entrance, you will immediately get your first taste of the park's grandeur and beauty. The largest garden, the Osborn Garden, gives access to several smaller gardens. The woodland Native Flora Garden connects with the beautifully landscaped Rose Garden and the stunning Cherry Esplanade. When the cherry trees bloom (late March to early May), this large meadow transforms into a lovely pink forest.

The Japanese Garden is a beautiful hill-and-pond garden. The waterfalls, bridges, koi carp and turtles will make you briefly forget that you are in bustling New York... A tranquil green cocoon in a large and loud city.

The greenhouses are the place to be during the winter months. You can warm yourself and gaze at the amazing plant collections in The Warm Temperature Pavilion or The Tropical Pavilion. Still feel chilly? The Desert Pavilion with flowering cactuses will definitely warm you up.

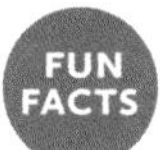

The tiny Bonsai Museum next to the greenhouses includes bonsais that are over 300 years old. One of the trees is even worth over a million dollars.

The sons of Frederick Law Olmsted, one of the architects of Central Park and Prospect Park, created the original design of the Brooklyn Botanic Garden.

INSTAGRAMMABLE PLACES IN THE NEIGHBORHOOD

COFFEE	Coffee bar in the Visitor Center
FOOD	Yellow Magnolia at the Brooklyn Botanic Garden
SEE	Brooklyn Museum: 200 Eastern Peakway (4 min. walk)
	Brooklyn Public Library: 10 Grand Army Plaza (10 min. walk)

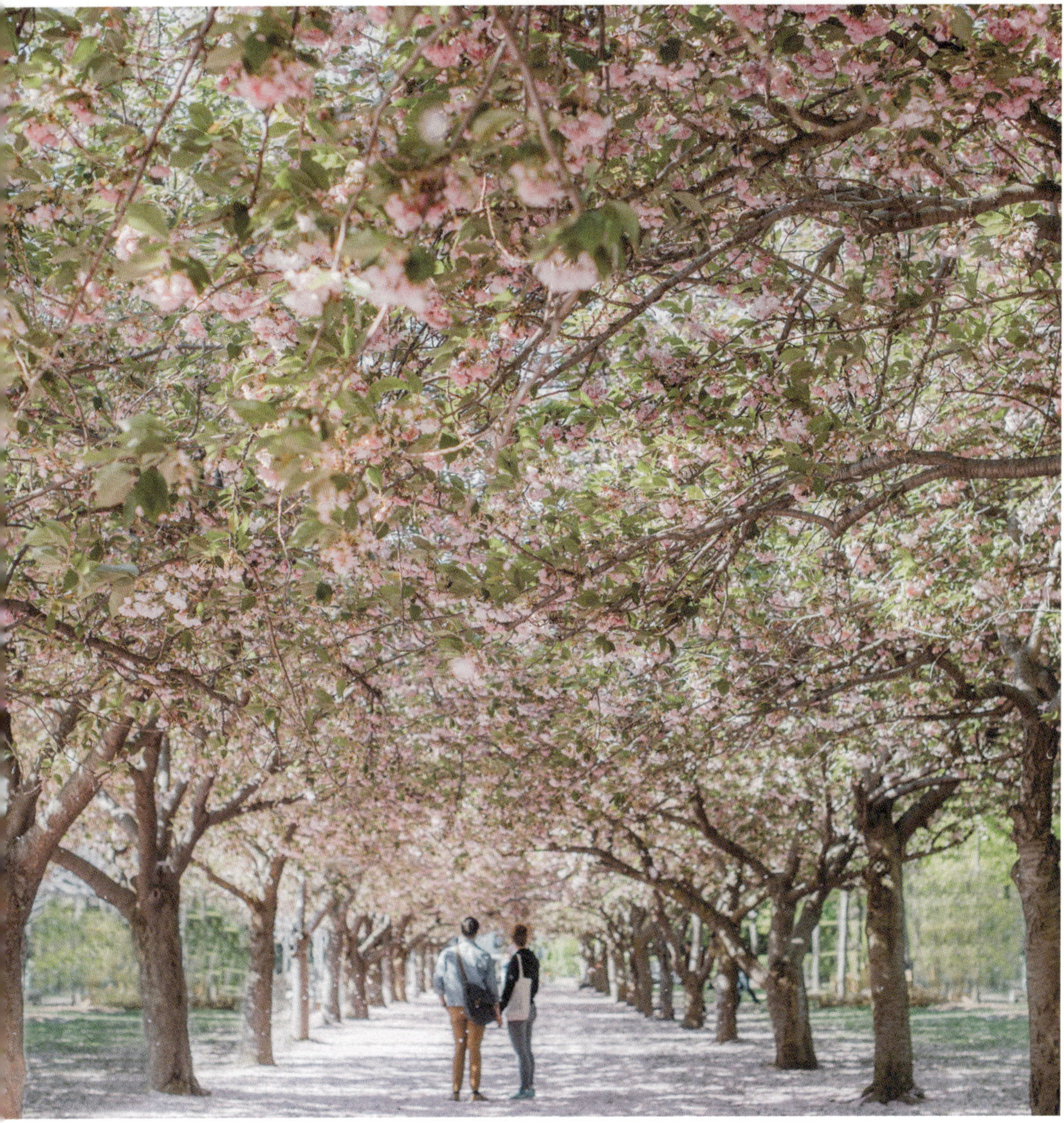

#brooklynbotanic #brooklynbotanicgarden #botanicgarden #brooklyn @brooklynbotanic

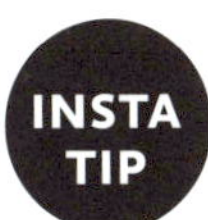

The website of the Brooklyn Botanic Garden informs you which flowers and trees bloom when. Most photographers like to visit the garden for the cherry blossoms in spring.

77 INDUSTRY CITY

Industry City
247 36th Street
Brooklyn

HOW TO GET THERE
Subway D, N or R (orange) to 36 Street Station

Industry City wants to be a hub for entrepreneurs and for arts and creative studios. The business park consists of six gigantic connected former warehouses. Each building spans an entire block. Industry City has space for up to 400 businesses, and each industry is represented here, including film, architecture, fashion and food, creating an exciting and diverse community.

You don't have to live or work in this neighborhood (Sunset Park) to visit this city. Everyone is welcome to explore the photogenic mix of retail, the arts and eateries here. The artfully landscaped garden, the hip food courts, the Frying Pan Bar with its game room... This is the perfect hangout. They also organize plenty of activities here, including open-air concerts, exhibitions, rooftop films and sunset yoga classes.

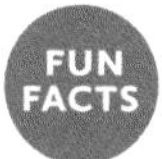

You can sample the most expensive cup in the US at The Extraction Lab in Industry City. The lab offers a coffee and tea experience and, according to its website, the world's best coffee. Filter coffees start at 4 dollars for a Toby's Estate Blend to a whopping 18 dollars for a Panamanian Brew. Feel free to check whether the experience lives up to your expectations...

Sunset Park, where Industry City is situated, is the largest historic neighborhood to be included on the National Register of Historic Places. Several individual landmarks were also added to the list including the Sunset Courthouse and St. Michael's Church.

INSTAGRAMMABLE PLACES IN THE NEIGHBORHOOD

COFFEE	*inside Industry City*	Alpha Dominate Extraction Lab
TEA	*inside Industry City*	Ninja Bubble Tea
FOOD	*inside Industry City*	Taco Mix
		Avocaderia
SEE	The Camille Walala Mural on the wall of the first building at 2nd Avenue (between 36th and 37th Streets)	

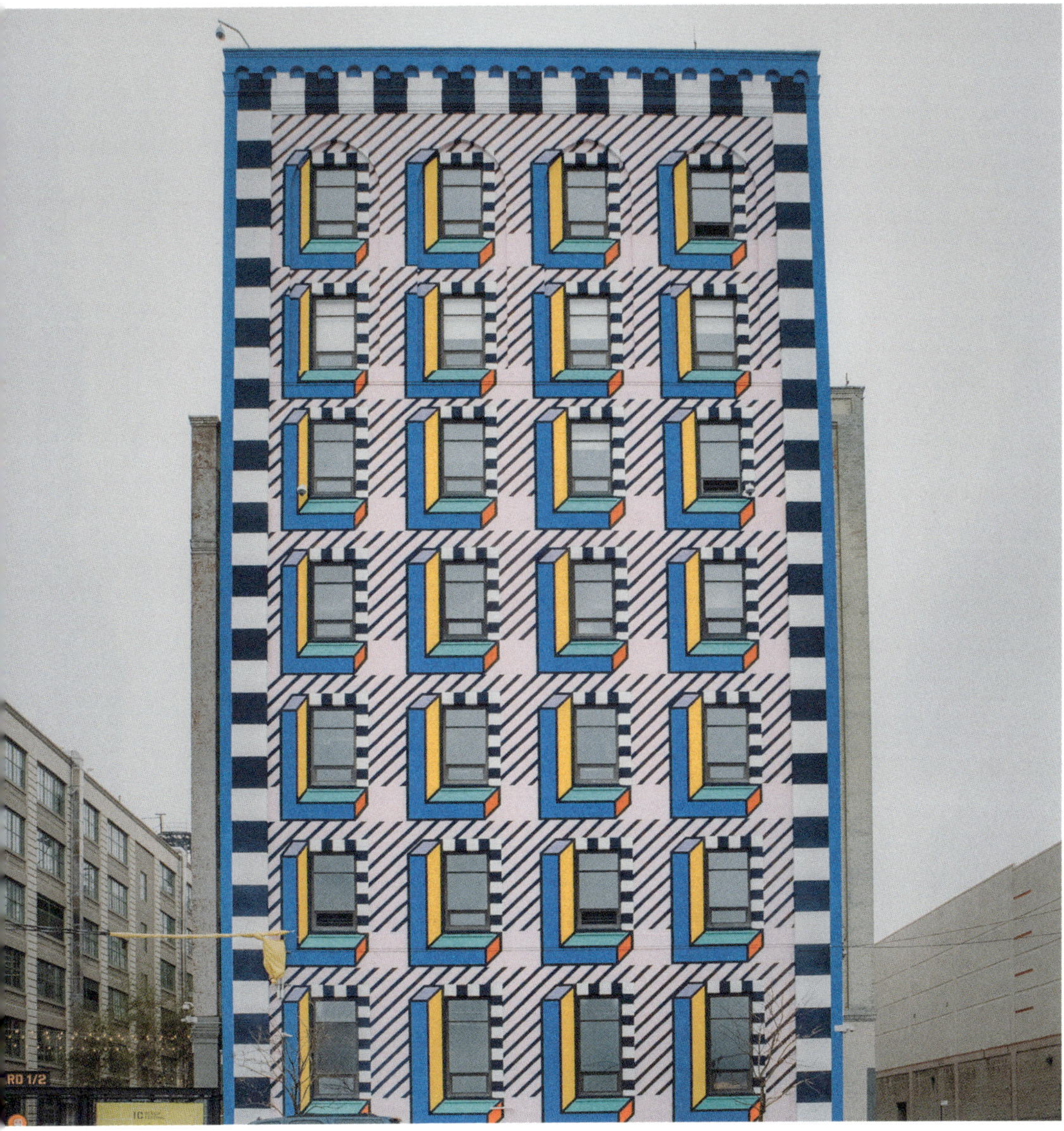

#industrycity #industrycitybrooklyn #brooklyn #sunsetpark @industrycity

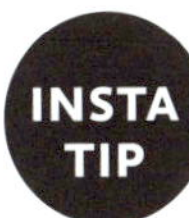

Camile Walala's mural on the first building of Industry City is pretty amazing. You can see it from 2nd Avenue.

You will have to move rather far back to get the entire building in one shot as it is so large. Go to the car park opposite the building for this.

78 THE BUSHWICK COLLECTIVE

The Bushwick Collective
St. Nicolas Avenue

HOW TO GET THERE
Subway L (grey) to Jefferson Street Station

The Bushwick Collective is a graffiti and street art project in Bushwick.

Joseph - Joe - Ficalora is the collective's founder and curator. He grew up in Bushwick, Brooklyn, which used to be grim and dirty neighborhood at the time. The only safe place was indoors, because of the gangs and robberies. His parents died when he was still quite young. These dramatic events inspired him to do something for his community, which is why he founded the collective to give the neighborhood a boost with street art. He contacted the owners of vacant buildings to find empty walls and was able to invite plenty of street artists to paint the walls of Bushwick. The project gradually evolved and now you can see 60 amazing murals there.

Nowadays Bushwick is a safe, family-friendly, hip neighborhood. This is largely because everyone involved sticks to a few ground rules: the murals must be family-friendly and not controversial. Neither the owners of the buildings, nor the artists are paid. As a result, the artworks are authentic and you can spend several hours exploring this gigantic free open-air museum.

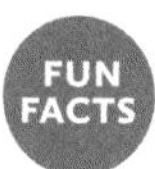

Bushwick has become a creative haven in recent years. Hundreds of artists have their studio here and there are over 50 (!) art galleries.

While there are plenty of pigeons all over New York, the pigeon population is larger in Bushwick where pigeon-keeping is a tradition that Italian immigrants brought with them from their homeland to Bushwick.

INSTAGRAMMABLE PLACES IN THE NEIGHBORHOOD

COFFEE	Domicile: 185 Howard Avenue
FOOD	Sea Wolf: 19 Wyckoff Avenue
	Maite: 159 Central Avenue
SEE	The murals on St Nicholas Avenue, Troutman Street and Wyckoff Avenue
	Kings County: Brewers Collective: 381 Troutman Street

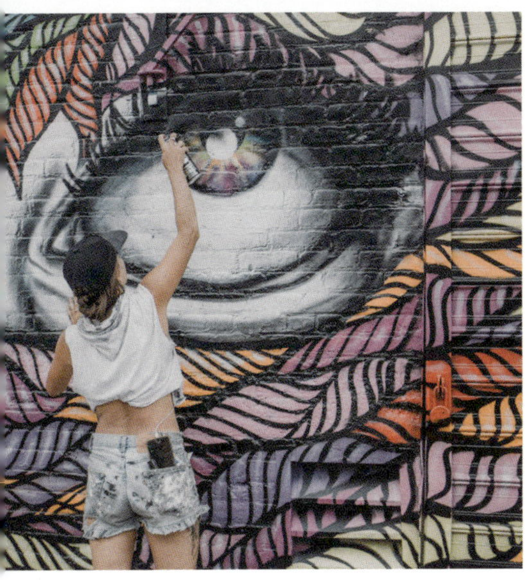

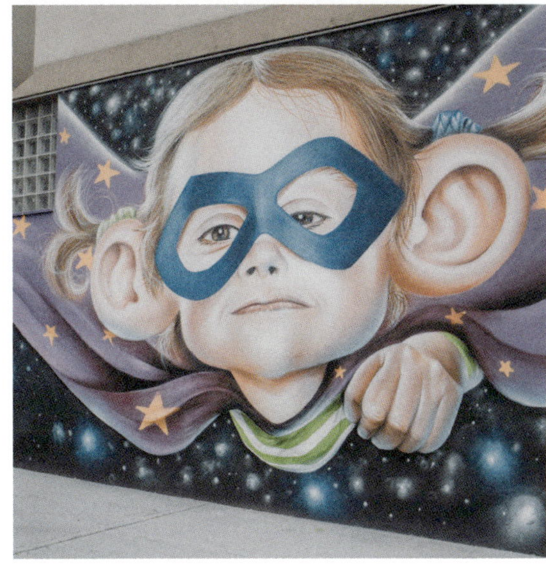

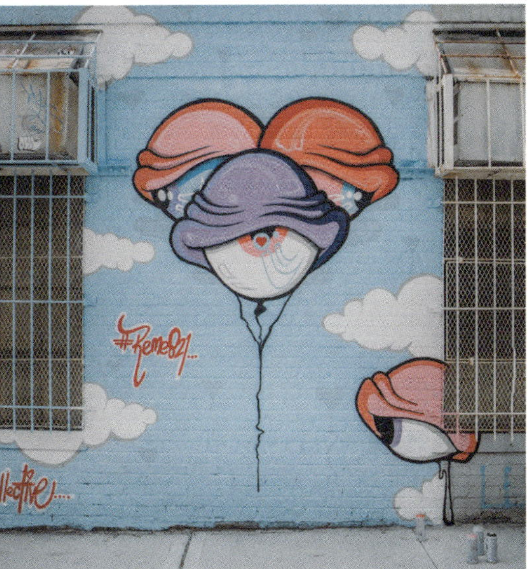

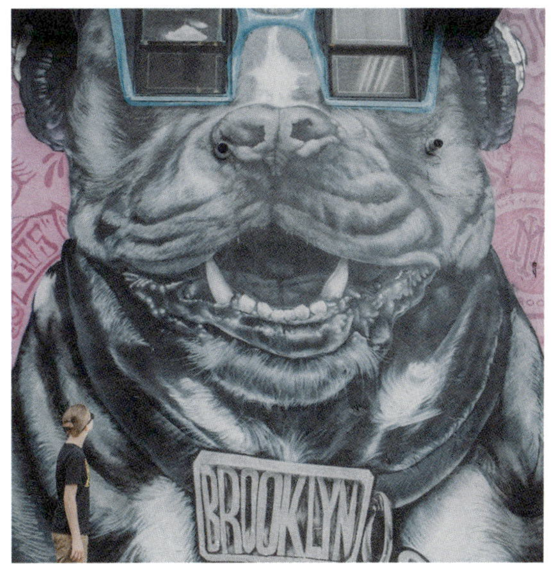

#bushwick #thebushwickcollectieve #nycstreetart #streetartnyc @thebushwickcollectieve

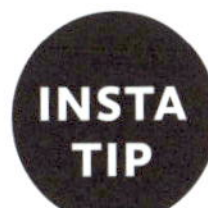

Include part of the surroundings in your photo to illustrate how large the murals are. Part of a window or a passer-by can help emphasize their dimension.

Don't forget to tag the artist when posting a pic of a mural. The artist's name and Instagram account are usually featured on the mural.

Clockwise: @reme_821 @urbanruben @findizzcreate @sipros_sipros

79 SMORGASBURG WILLIAMSBURG

Smorgasburg
Williamsburg
90 Kent
Avenue

HOW TO GET THERE
Subway L (grey) to Bedford Avenue Station

Smorgasburg is Brooklyn's weekend foodie heaven! Discover the latest trends and some New York classics, from 100 different vendors, at this weekly outdoor food fest.

In addition to Smorgasburg in Prospect Park (on Sundays), you can also visit Smorgasburg Williamsburg on the shore of the East River every Saturday. Smorgasburg is Brooklyn's weekend foodie heaven where you can discover the latest foodtrends from 100 different vendors. Unlike Prospect Park and its green surroundings, Williamsburg is a trendy neighborhood with stunning views of Manhattan's skyline.

Williamsburg is one of Brooklyn's most popular neighborhoods with the highest hipster factor in all of New York. It has a lively arts and music scene and a wide range of cafes, bars, restaurants and coffee shops. It is easy to see why Williamsburg is called Brooklyn's foodiest neighborhood, making it the perfect setting for Smorgasburg.

After choosing what you want from the dazzling array of fancy drinks and unique dishes, you can find yourself a spot on the shore of the East River, which also offers an amazing backdrop for your Foodstagram.

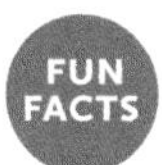

In 1638, the Dutch West India Company acquired Williamsburg from a tribe of Native Americans.
Williamsburg was more expensive than Manhattan.

All the vendors at Smorgasburg are locals. If you have discovered your new favorite dish you won't have to wait until next weekend, because every vendor has a shop somewhere in New York.

INSTAGRAMMABLE PLACES IN THE NEIGHBORHOOD

SHOP Artists & Fleas: 70 N 7th Street (3 min. walk)
SEE The Brooklyn Brewery: 79 N 11th Street (7 min. walk)
The North 5th Street Pier and Park: 105 River Street (6 min. walk)
Domino Park: 15 River Street (10 min. walk)

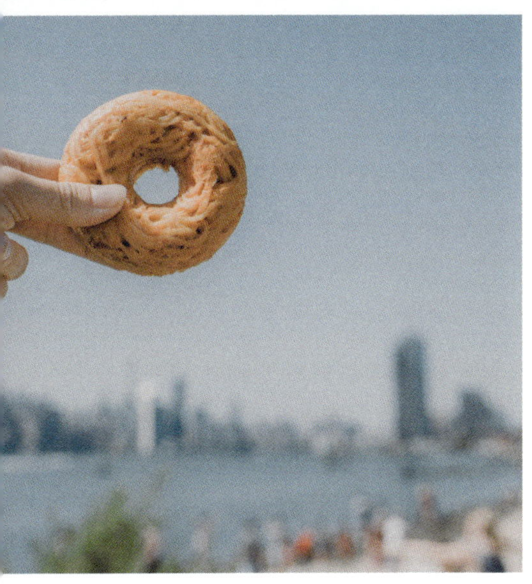

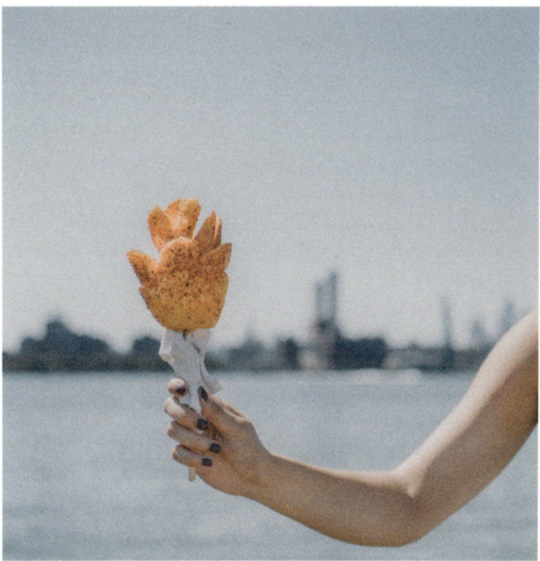

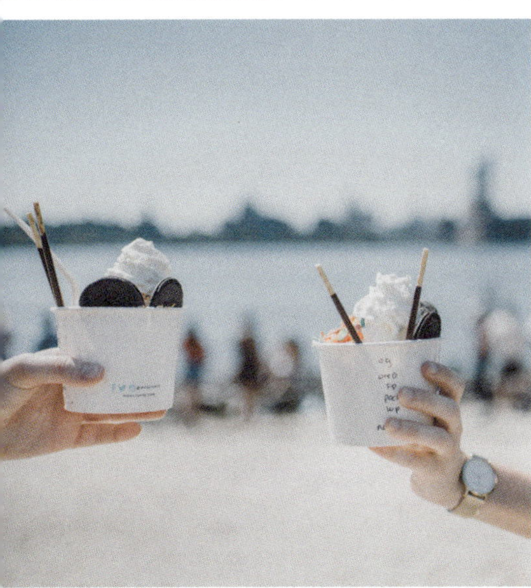

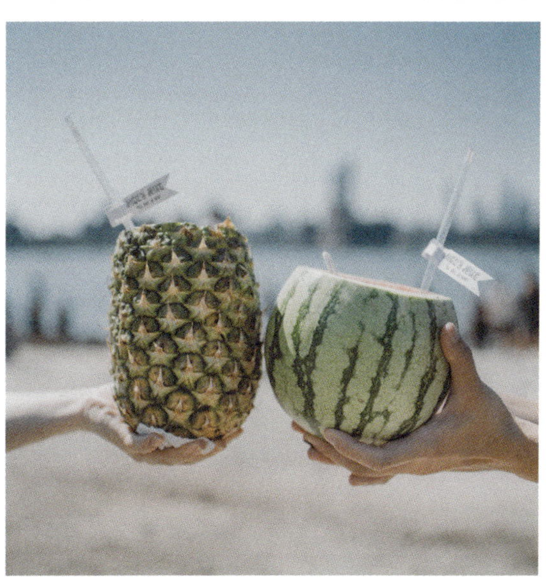

#smorgasburg #smorgasburgwilliamsburg #nyceats #williamsburg #brooklyn @smorgasburg

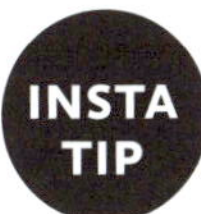

Smorgasburg in Williamsburg is organized along the East River. Take your food or drink to the shore for a photo with New York's skyline in the background.

80 THE SKETCHBOOK PROJECT

The Sketchbook Project
28 Frost Street

HOW TO GET THERE
Subway L (grey) to Bedford Avenue Station

The Sketchbook Project was launched in Atlanta in 2006, relocated to New York in 2009 and moved to its current location in the Brooklyn Art Library in Williamsburg since 2010.

Anyone who wants can participate in the project by ordering an empty sketchbook and sending back a full sketchbook. The library now has a collection of over 40,000 sketchbooks, with another 20,000 sketchbooks in its digital library.

The combination of physical art and the digital archive system has contributed to the worldwide dissemination of virtual inspiration. Artists from all four corners of the world have participated in the project, with contributions from 135 different countries.

Visitors can browse the permanent collection in the library, which essentially consists of shelves and shelves along the walls, lined with tens of thousands of sketchbooks. A changing selection of books goes on a world tour every year, in a mobile library, visiting various events and festivals.

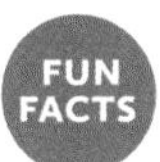

Every sketchbook on the shelves has its own unique barcode, which allows you to find out more about it: the artist's name, the book's origin, the materials used, etc. Use the digital system to find a sketchbook on a given subject or in a specific style.

INSTAGRAMMABLE PLACES IN THE NEIGHBORHOOD

COFFEE Oslo Coffee Roasters: 133 Roebling Street (9 min. walk)
FOOD Milk Bar Williamsburg: 382 Metropolitan Avenue (8 min. walk)
Cafe Colette: 79 Berry Street (9 min. walk)
SEE Mc Carren Park (5 min. walk)
Brooklyn Winery: 213 N 8th Street (6 min. walk)

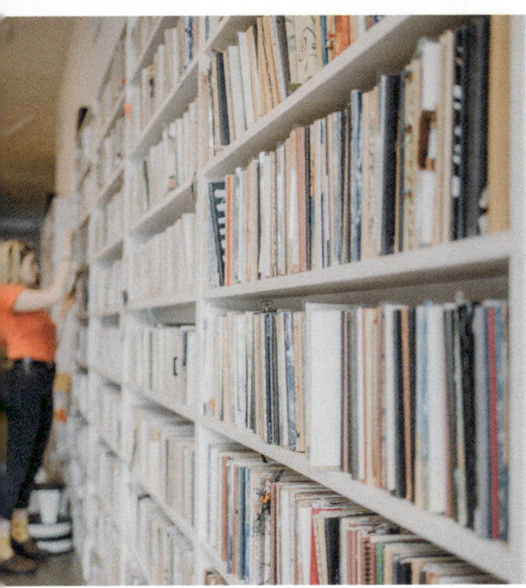
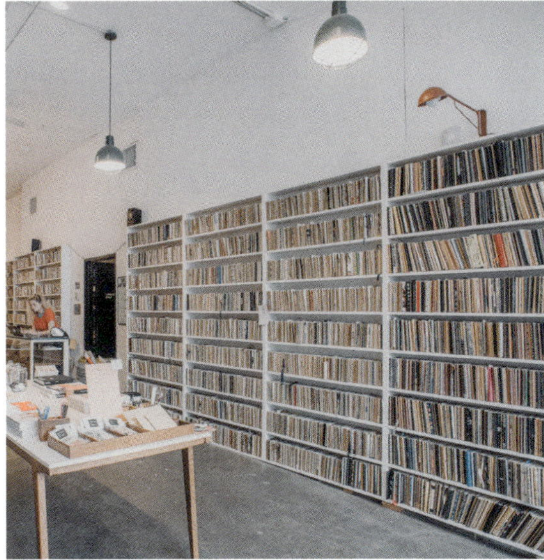
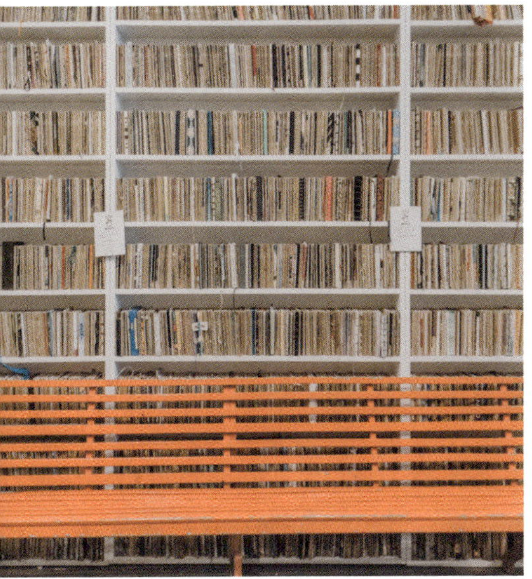
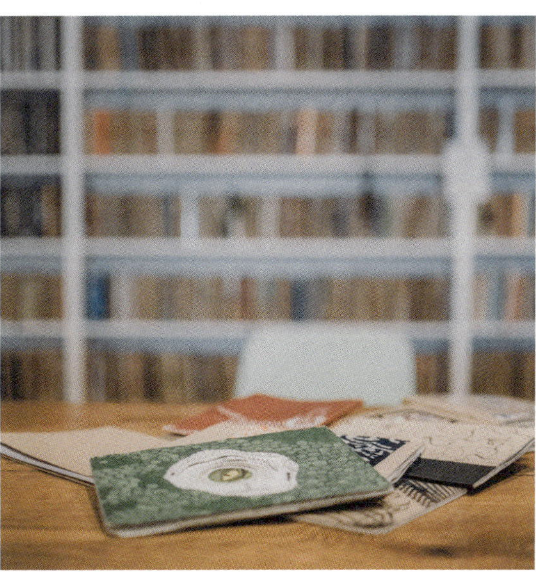

#thesketchbookproject #brooklynartlibrary #brooklyn #libraryofinstagram #sketchbookart @thesketchbookproject

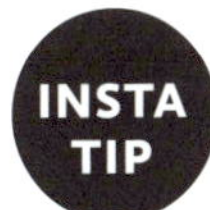

As all the sketchbooks in this library have the same dimension, this creates a repetitive pattern of lines, which you can use for your composition. Use the lines of the books and the shelves as your main subject, or as a backdrop. If you decide to focus on the diagonals, then do try to let your line start in a corner, for a more interesting shot.

❽ MISTER DIPS

Mister Dips
111 N 12th
Street

HOW TO GET THERE
Subway G (green) to Nassau Avenue Station

Subway L (grey) to Bedford Avenue Station

There is a park around the distinctive-looking Williams Vale Hotel, which you can access from the staircase on the corner of N 12th Street and Wythe Avenue. Once you have walked to the top, you will find yourself in a beautifully-landscaped aboveground park, with expansive views of Williamsburg and the unique architecture of the Williams Vale Hotel.

You can also find the Mister Dips airstream in this park. Mister Dips is the food truck of the team behind the upmarket, popular Williams Vale bar and restaurant, albeit a more budget-friendly option.

The menu features super photogenic soft serve cups and cones (with a dip, of course) and simple hamburgers with retro waffle fries (with and without cheese). They serve food from mid-April to October here.

The fun terrace is the perfect feel-good spot to enjoy the sunset on a warm summer evening, with the ideal burger-fries-ice cream combo, providing the perfect backdrop for a few great foodstagram shots.

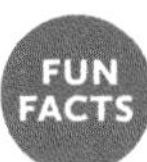

There is a deluxe rooftop bar on the 22nd floor of the Williams Vale Hotel, which serves special cocktails and boasts breath-taking views.

The hotel organizes a number of cultural events with emerging talent from Brooklyn. While the rooftop movies, meditation sessions and summer pool parties don't come cheap, the spectacular view is thrown in for free.

INSTAGRAMMABLE PLACES IN THE NEIGHBORHOOD

COFFEE	Du's Donuts & Coffee: 107 N 12th Street (1 min. walk)
FOOD	Kinfolk 90: 90 Wythe Avenue (1 min. walk)
SEE	Wythe Hotel: 80 Wythe Avenue (1 min. walk)
	Brooklyn Brewery: 79 N 11th Street (2 min. walk)
	Mccarran Park: Bedford Avenue and N 12th Street (3 min. walk)

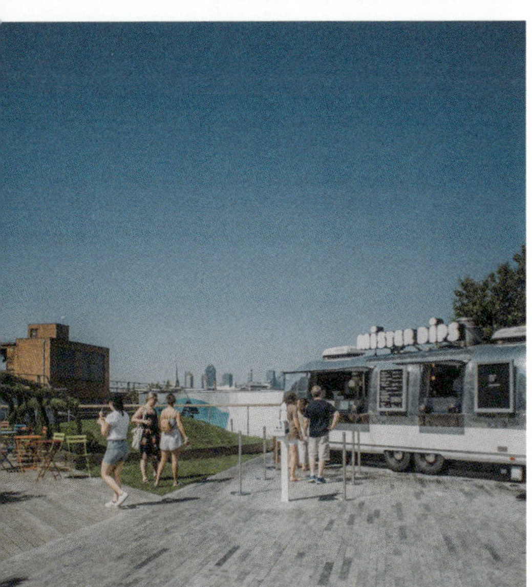

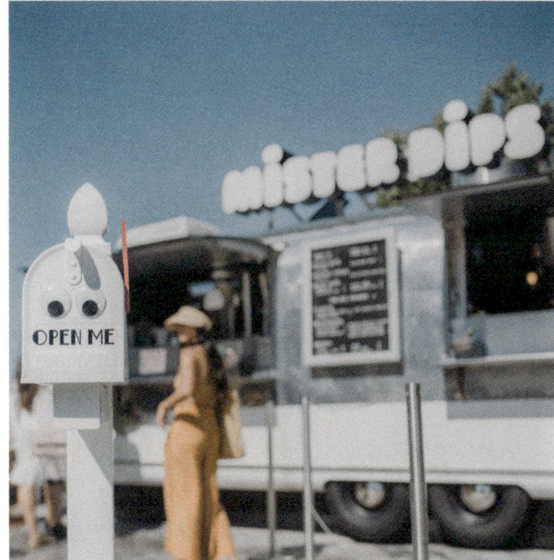

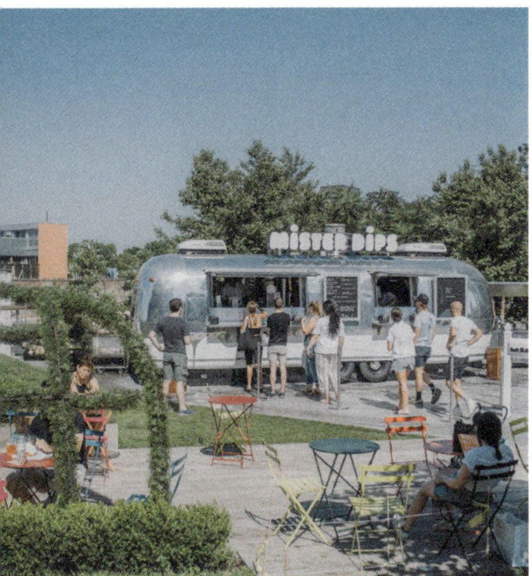

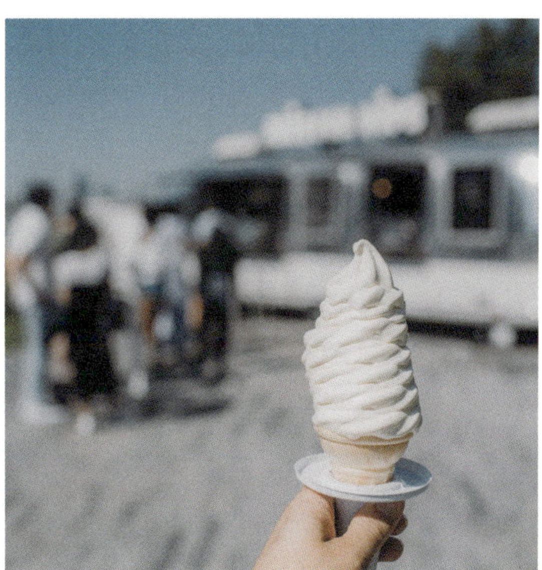

#misterdips #eatmisterdips #thewilliamvale #williamsburg #brooklyn @eatmisterdips @thewilliamvale

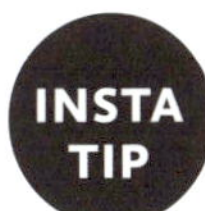

INSTA TIP

If you step away from the airstream, then you can include part of the skyline, the food truck and the colorful terrace in the frame.

82 WNYC TRANSMITTER PARK

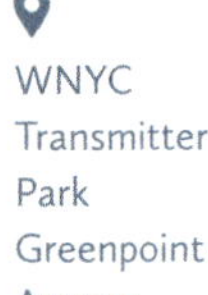

WNYC Transmitter Park
Greenpoint Avenue

HOW TO GET THERE
Subway G (green) to Greenpoint Avenue Station

The former home base of the WNYC Radio transmitters in Greenpoint has been transformed into a nice green oasis. The WNYC Transmitter Park is popular with locals, as it is a quiet park with plenty of space to play and lots of nature. It contrasts nicely with the walls of the former WNYC building, which is used as a canvas by street artists. The shore and the restored pier (which extends along the East River) are open to the public, offering spectacular views of Manhattan's skyline.

Greenpoint is one of Brooklyn's nicest neighborhoods. Old factories are transformed into ingenious residential buildings, studios for artists and hip event locations that attract young artists and designers. The result is a creative melting pot, in addition to the community of mainly Polish immigrants, with their traditional shops and restaurants.

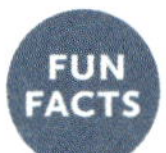

The WNYC radio station broadcasted its AM signal from this location from 1937 until 1990 when the transmitters were moved to New Jersey and the rooftop of the World Trade Center.

A few recent Netflix series were filmed on location in Greenpoint. Aziz Ansari in *Master of None* hangs out in several Greenpoint bars. You may also bump into Ellie Kemper or Titus Burgess while they are filming *The Unbreakable Kimmy Schmidt*.

INSTAGRAMMABLE PLACES IN THE NEIGHBORHOOD

COFFEE	Maman: 80 Kent Street (3 min. walk)
DRINKS	The Barge Bar: 3 Milton Street (1 min. walk)
FOOD	21 Greenpoint: 21 Greenpoint Avenue (1 min. walk)
SHOP	Word Books & Stationery: 126 Franklin Street (4 min. walk)
SEE	Brooklyn Expo Center: 72 Noble Street (5 min. walk)
	Sunshine Laundromat: 860 Manhattan Avenue (8 min. walk)
	A/D/O: 29 Norman Avenue (11 min. walk)

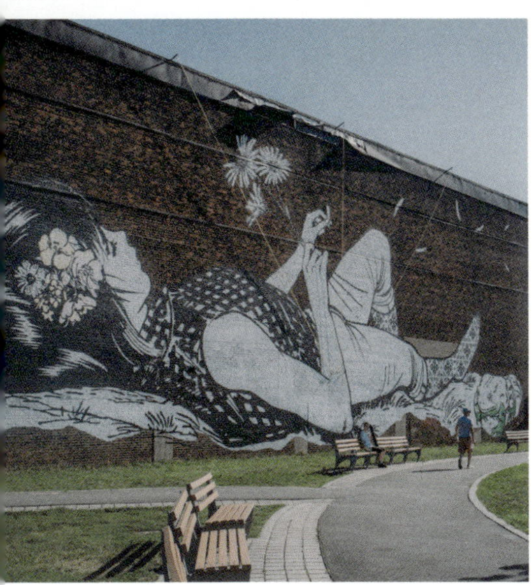

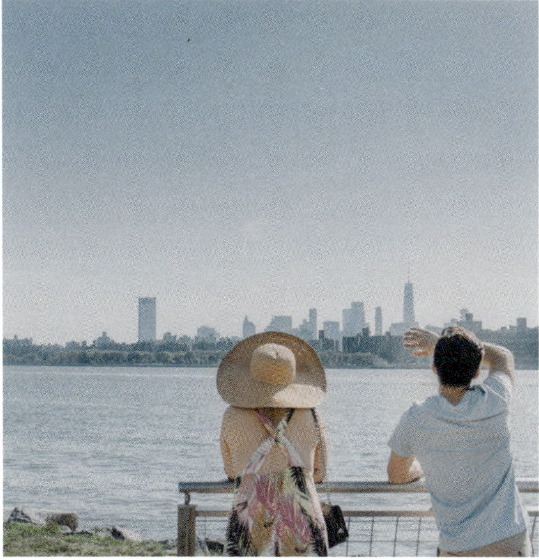

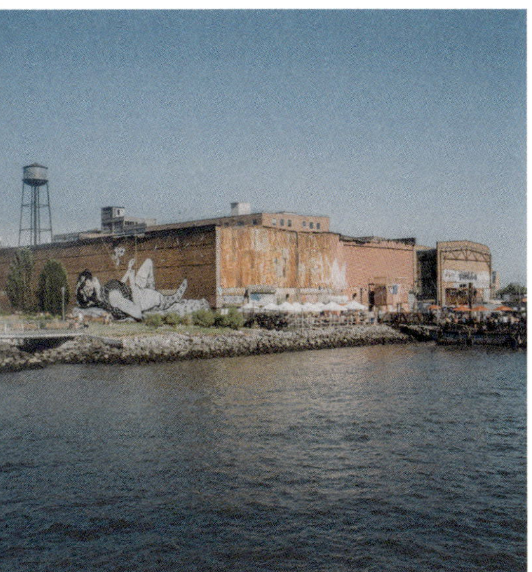

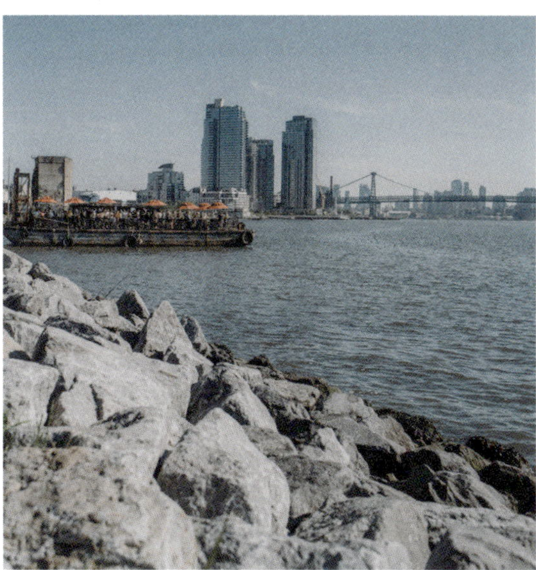

#wnyctransmitterpark #greenpoint #nycparks #eastriver #nycskyline @nycparks

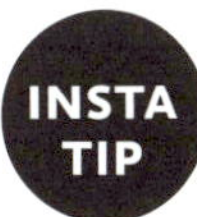

The pier that extends out of the park across the East River offers splendid views of the Manhattan skyline and Williamsburg Bridge. The perfect place to take pics.

83 THE OY/YO SCULPTURE

The OY/YO Sculpture
105 River Street

HOW TO GET THERE
Subway L (grey) to Bedford Avenue Station

Ferry ER (Wall Street/ Pier 11) to North Williamsburg

Deborah Kass's OY/YO artwork is a fun tribute to Brooklyn's multicultural community. The sculpture is installed in North 5th Street Pier and Park. If you stand in front of the sculpture facing Brooklyn, the sculpture reads "YO". Seen from the other side, facing Manhattan, "OY" appears. *Yo* means I in Spanish and *OY* is part of the Yiddish expression *oy vey*, an expression you use to express your dismay at a terrible situation (meaning something along the lines of "what a mess").

This artwork initially existed in the form of paintings and small sculptures. A Brooklyn-based real estate developer commissioned an 8-foot sculpture (2.4 meters) from the artist. Originally installed in Brooklyn Bridge Park, the sculpture was moved to North 5th Street Park in Williamsburg, where it has become a favorite photo spot for visitors waiting for the ferry.

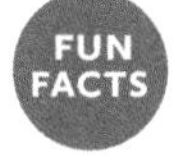

There is another unique artwork in the same park. Crescendo, a sculpture made of steel tubes and iron mesh, was created by the artist Mark Gibian. While it may not be as colorful as Kass's OY/YO, it is just as photogenic!

INSTAGRAMMABLE PLACES IN THE NEIGHBORHOOD

COFFEE	Gotan: 258 Wythe Avenue (6 min. walk)
ICE CREAM	Van Leeuwen Artisan Ice Cream: 204 Wythe Avenue (4 min. walk)
SHOP	Artists & Fleas: 70 N 7th Street (4 min. walk)
SEE	Nitehawk Cinema: 136 Metropolitan Avenue (8 min. walk)
	Williamsburg Bridge via the Continental Army Plaza (20 min. walk)

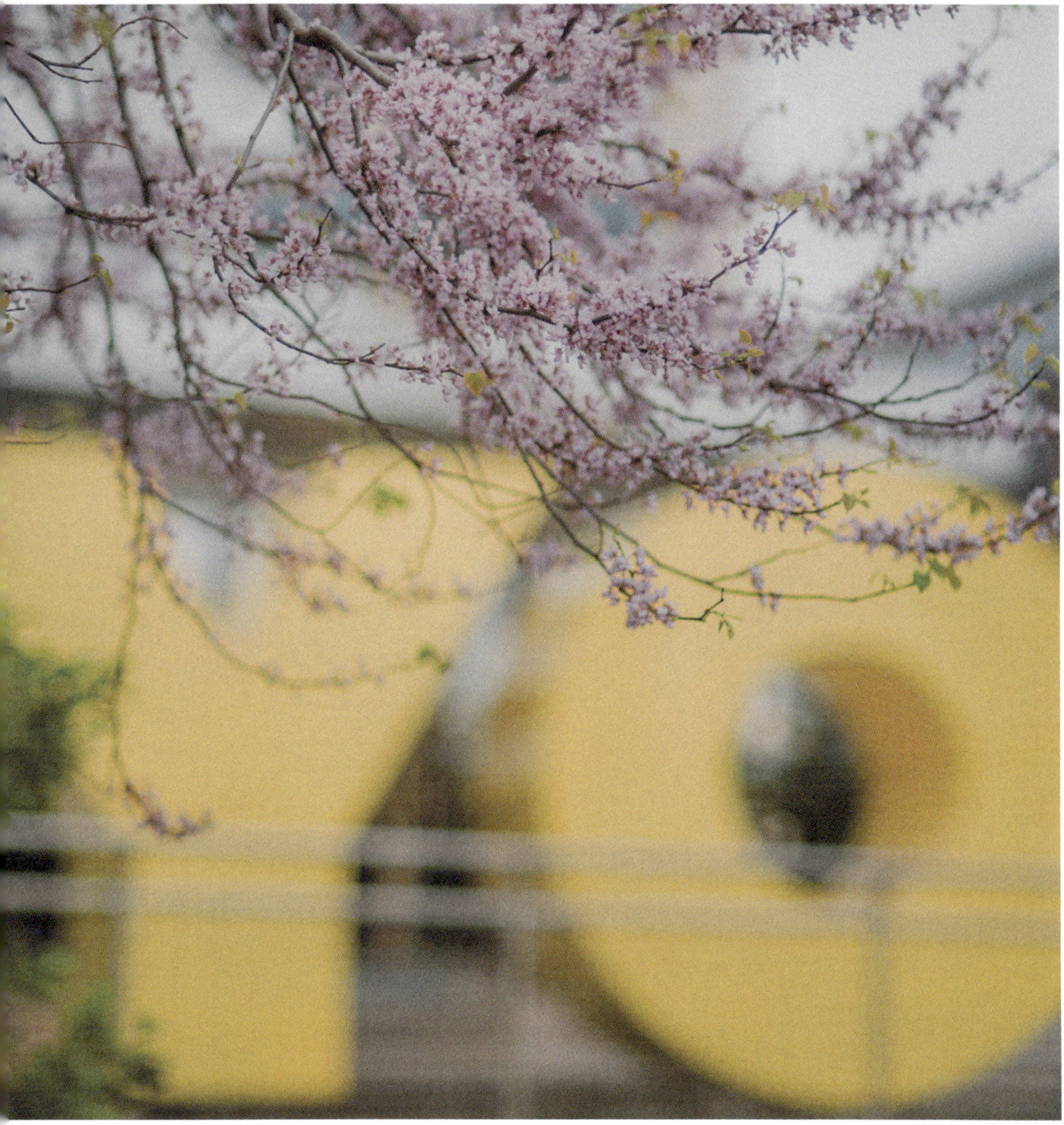

#oyyo #deborahkass #brooklyn #williamsburg #nycparks @nycparks

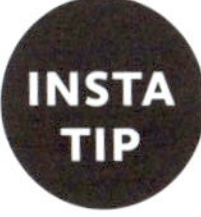

People usually like to take a photo of the sculpture with a person in, next to or under the letters. Instead of focusing on the artwork itself, you can also use it as a background color and contrast it with a subject (in this case pink blossoms) in the foreground. The letters are so large and distinctive that you can always recognize them.

84 DOMINO PARK

Domino Park

HOW TO GET THERE

Subway M (orange), J or Z (brown) to Marcy Avenue Station

Subway L (grey) to Bedford Avenue station

Ferry ER (Wall Street/ Pier 11) to North Williamsburg

A magnificent 5-acre (2.2 hectares) public park was created on the former site of the Domino sugar factory. The factory closed in 2004 and the public was only able to finally explore the quarter of a mile-long (400 meters) esplanade along Williamsburg's waterfront in early 2018.

The park's design pays tribute to the former factory. Old machinery is exhibited like art, two gigantic cranes have been incorporated in a raised pedestrian path and four cylindrical syrup tanks separate the flower meadows from the sports fields. The Artifact Walk informs visitors about the park's history.

Young children love playing in the factory-inspired playground and the enchanting lit dancing fountains. There is also a hip Mexican outdoor bar, a beach volley pitch as well as several beautifully-designed chill and relax corners.

The park caters to the hip and creative crowd that lives in Williamsburg and can get very busy, especially on the weekends.

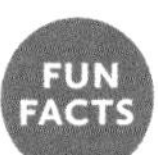

The entire site, with the factory buildings, dates from 1882. The factory was the world's largest sugar refinery at the time. The buildings are being converted into office and residential space.

In its heyday, the refinery processed more than half of all the sugar that was used in the United States.

INSTAGRAMMABLE PLACES IN THE NEIGHBORHOOD

COFFEE Freehold: 45 S 3rd Street (5 min. walk)

FOOD Tacocina: at the park

SEE North Brooklyn Farms: 320 Kent Avenue (5 min. walk)
Williamsburg Bridge Pedestrian walkway: Bedford Avenue (8 min. walk)
Nitehawk Cinema: 136 Metropolitan Avenue (5 min. walk)

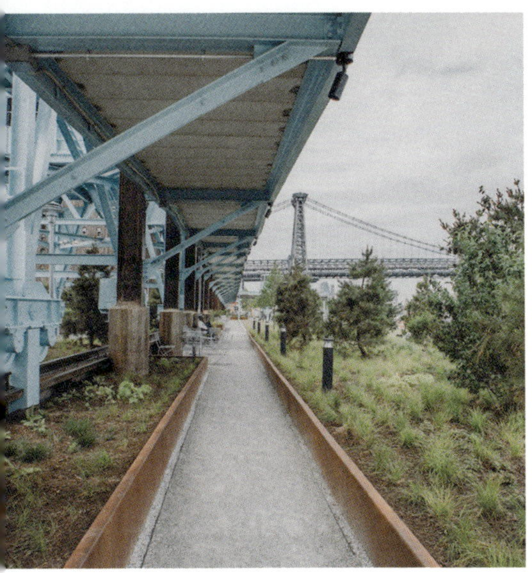

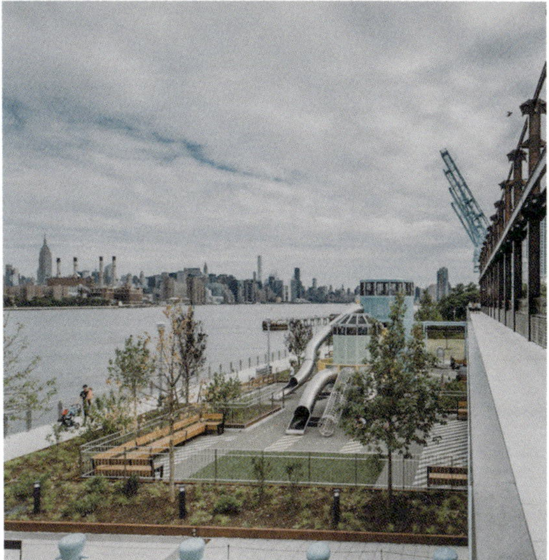

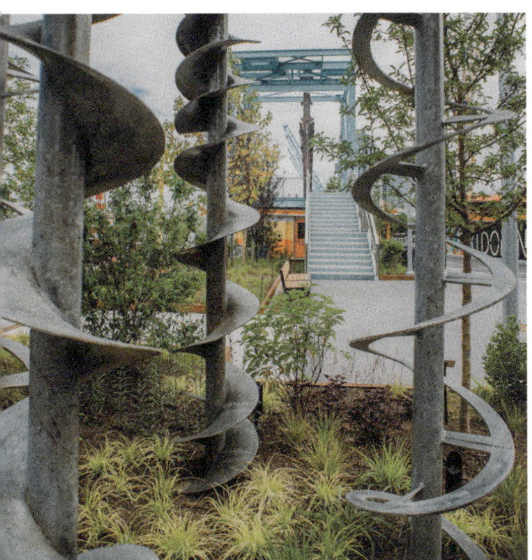

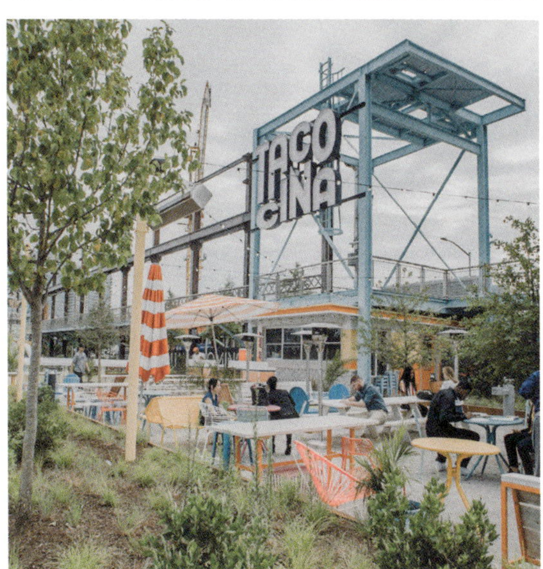

#dominopark #dominosugarfactory #williamsburg #brooklyn @dominopark

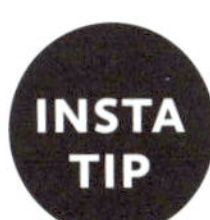

There are plenty of excellent photo opportunities in the park. You can even include Manhattan's skyline in your shot. Make the industrial art the star of your composition.

85 WILLIAMSBURG BRIDGE

Williamsburg Bridge

HOW TO GET THERE
Subway M (orange) J, Z (brown) to Marcy Avenue Station

Subway L (grey) to Bedford Avenue station

Ferry ER (Wall Street/ Pier 11) to South Williamsburg

The walkway starts in Bedford Avenue, between S 5th Street and S 6th Street (on the Brooklyn side). On the Manhattan side, you can leave or enter the walkway at the intersection of Delancey and Clinton (Lower East Side).

Every New York bridge has its own personality and the Williamsburg Bridge is no different. This bridge looks tough, because of its graffiti and tags but at the time, there is something endearingly cute about its pink ironwork.

The suspension bridge is 7,308 feet (2,227 kilometers) long and the walk from Williamsburg to Manhattan takes about half an hour. As this bridge is not considered as iconic as the Brooklyn Bridge, there are fewer tourists here. The walkway and the cycling path are both situated above the roadway and the subway tracks.

Walking or cycling across a pink bridge... will make you feel happy and sparkly. What's more, the unique views are thrown in for free. Thanks to the bridge's location, you can enjoy expansive views from the Brooklyn and Manhattan Bridges to the south all the way to the Queensboro Bridge to the north.

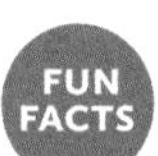

There are four public toilets on the bridge: two on the walkway and two on the cycling path. Unfortunately, they are no longer in use. Worth bearing in mind when you set out on your walk...

Unlike the other bridges, the Williamsburg Bridge has steel instead of stone towers, ensuring construction took only half as long as construction of the Brooklyn Bridge.

INSTAGRAMMABLE PLACES IN THE NEIGHBORHOOD

COFFEE Butler Bake Shop: 95 S 5th Street (3 min. walk)
FOOD Miss Favela: 57 S 5th Street (4 min. walk)
SEE Williamsburg Music Center: 367 Bedford Avenue (2 min. walk)
Domino Park: 15 River Street (8 min. walk)
North Brooklyn Farms: 320 Kent Avenue (8 min. walk)

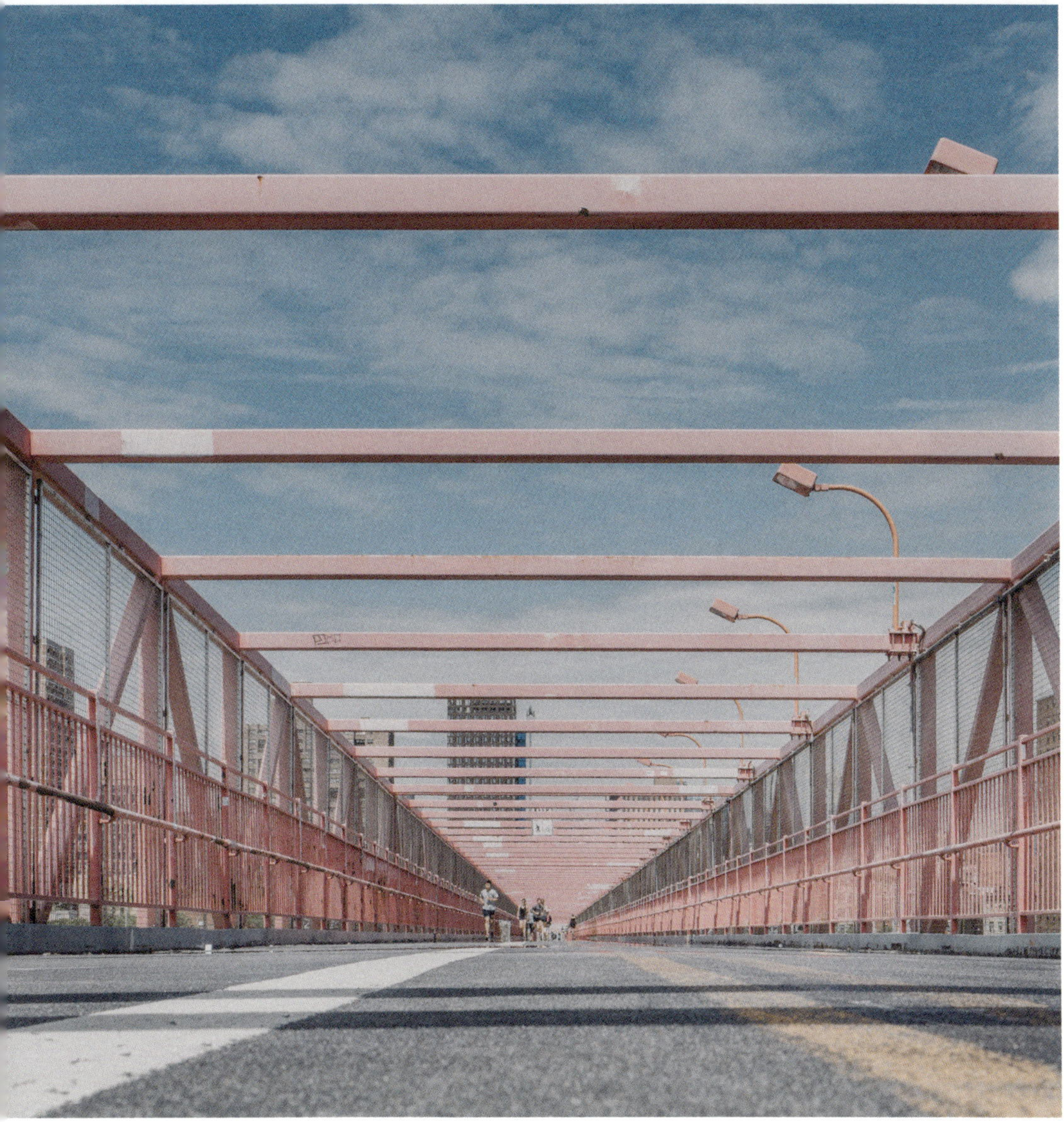

#williamsburgbridge #williamsburg #brooklyn #lowereastside #lavieenrose

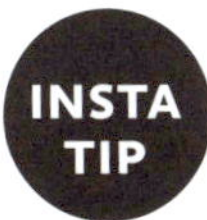

The iron structure is perfectly suited for symmetrical shots. Use your camera grid to ensure the verticals are straight.

I positioned my camera on the ground in the middle of the walkway for this shot.

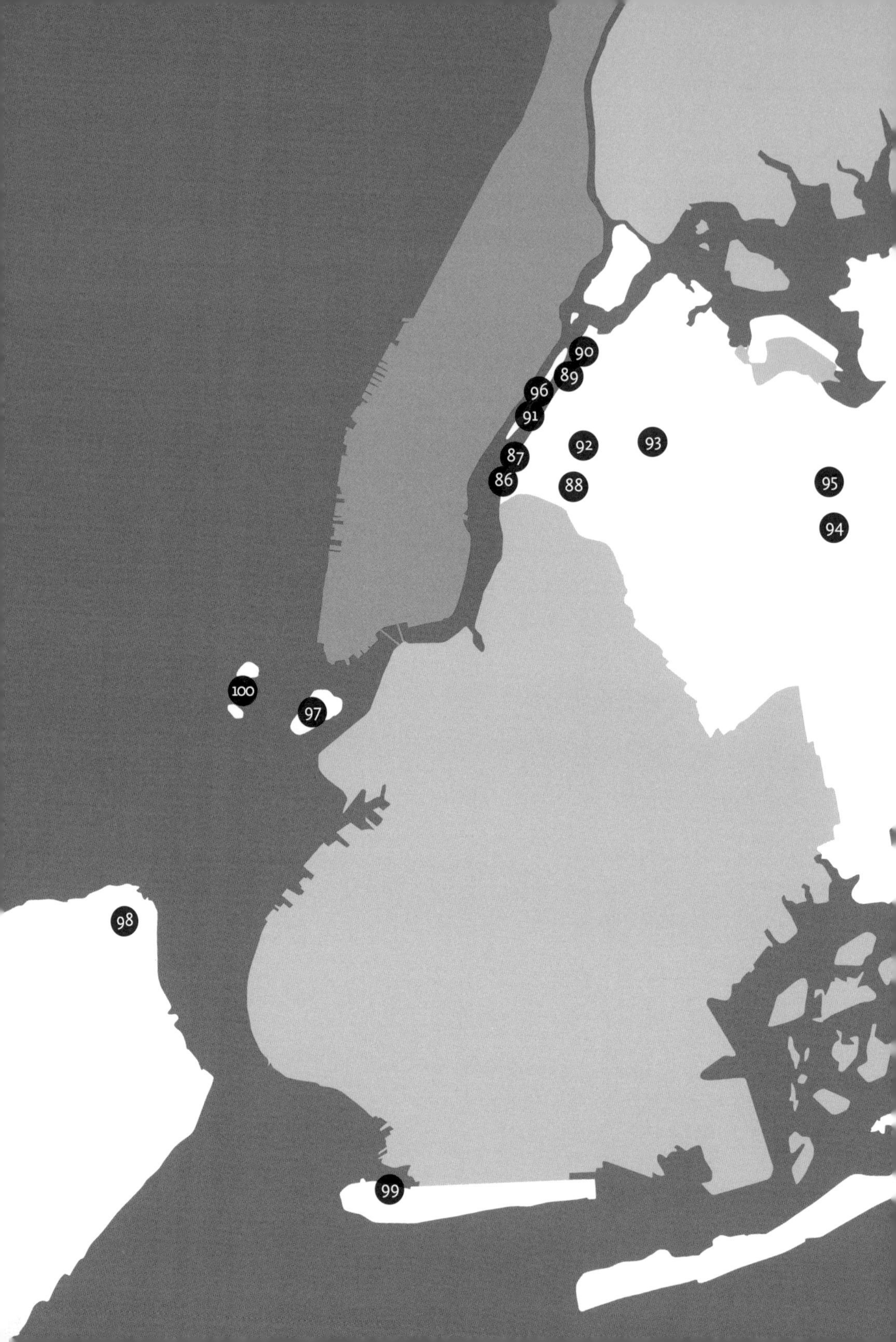

90
89
96
91
92
93
87
86
88
95
94
100
97
98
99

QUEENS & THE ISLANDS

86 GANTRY PLAZA STATE PARK

Gantry Plaza State Park 4-09 47th Road, Long Island City

HOW TO GET THERE
Subway 7 (purple) to Vernon Blvd - Jackson Avenue Station

Subway G (green) to 21 Street - Van Alst Station

Gantry Plaza State Park is in Long Island City (LIC) and is just one subway stop away from Grand Central (Manhattan). Nonetheless it feels like a different world here. No horns or sirens, but a 12-acre (4.9 hectare) riverside oasis that offers spectacular views of Manhattan's skyline. You can see the Chrysler Building, the Empire State Building and the United Nations Building at a glance from here.

Originally the park was a dock facility for cargo ships. Some of the industrial elements have been incorporated in the park's design. Every pier was given a new use. There is a pier with loungers, a pier with picnic tables and a pier with a long table which the fishermen use. The two large transfer bridges have also been preserved. They were once used for loading and unloading ships and train cars. Now these large black "gates" have become the symbol of Long Island City.

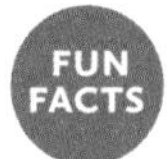

The park is a great place to catch "Manhattanhenge", when the setting sun is aligned with the east-west streets of Manhattan. This event only occurs twice a year for two days: the first time at the end of May and the second time in mid-July. On all other days of the year, the sunset is equally spectacular and photogenic here.

This is also a popular place on the 4th of July as the park is the perfect location to watch the fireworks from the boats on the East River to celebrate the national holiday.

INSTAGRAMMABLE PLACES IN THE NEIGHBORHOOD

COFFEE & FOOD	LIC Landing: 52-10 Center Boulevard (at the Ferry landing in the park)
	Black Star Bakery & Cafe: 2-10 50th Avenue
FOOD	Takumen: 5-50 50th Avenue
SEE	Pepsi Cola Sign: 4610 Center Boulevard

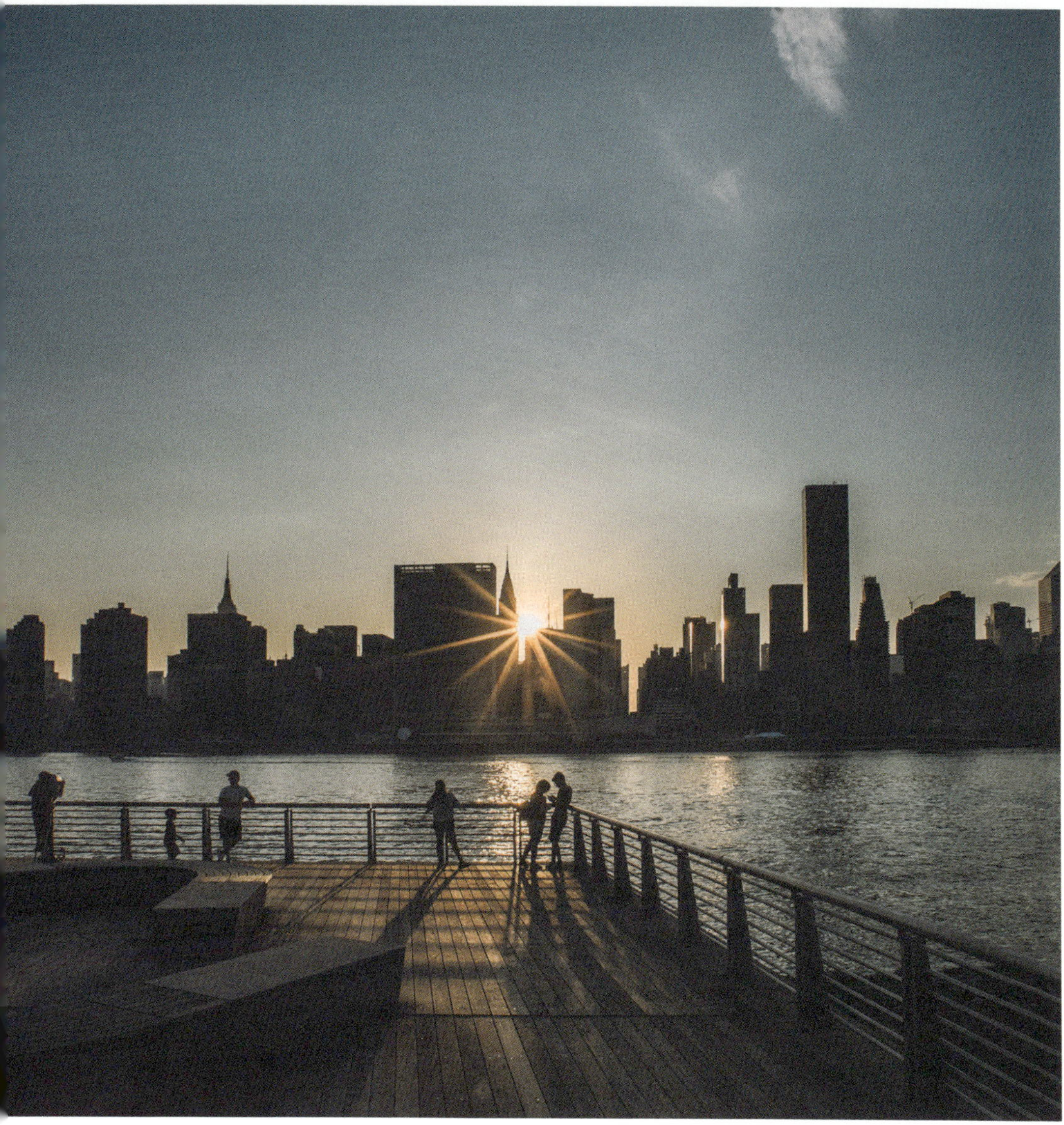

#gantryplazastatepark #gantrypark #longislandcity #hunterspoint #queens @nystateparks

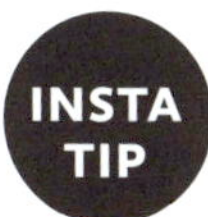

If you are in the park around sunset, you can capture the sunflare just as the sun sets between the buildings. It also casts a nice golden hue on the ground and reflects on the water surface.

87 PEPSI COLA SIGN

Pepsi Cola Sign
4610 Center Boulevard

HOW TO GET THERE
Subway 7 (purple) to Vernon Blvd - Jackson Avenue Station

Subway G (green) to 21 Street - Van Alst Station

There used to be a Pepsi bottling plant in the northern part of what is now Gantry Plaza State Park. A large sign was installed on the plant's roof in 1940. After the closure and demolition of the building in 1990, the neon billboard was preserved and reinstalled in 1998, when the park opened.

The Pepsi Cola Sign stands 20 feet (6 meters) above ground. The oversized bottle is 50 feet (15 meters) tall and the letters P and C span four floors. The impressive letters are made of steel and enamel and are lit with neon tubing. In the evening you can see this red beacon from Manhattan and Roosevelt Island.

While this is not a traditional landmark, the iconic neon sign became an official New York City Landmark in 2016, because of the vintage lettering and because it adds to the character of Long Island City.

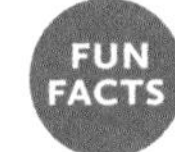

Legend has it that Joan Crawford (an Oscar-winning actress who married Alfred Steele, the president of Pepsi) had the gigantic Pepsi sign installed opposite River House (an exclusive residence in Manhattan) as a jab at the co-op residents (including a former Coke president) who had turned down her application.

The Pepsi Co. is still responsible for the maintenance of the sign and the land on which this sign is installed.

INSTAGRAMMABLE PLACES IN THE NEIGHBORHOOD

COFFEE Sweetleaf Coffee & Cocktails: 4615 Center Boulevard (2 min. walk)

FOOD Shi: 4720 Center Boulevard (3 min. walk)
Skinny's Cantina: 4705 Center Boulevard (3 min. walk)
Anable Basin Sailing Bar & Grill: 4-40 44th Drive (13 min. walk)

SEE Rockaway Brewing Company: 46-01 5th Street (4 min. walk)
Ferry to Roosevelt Island: Center Boulevard & 46th Avenue (1 min. walk)
LIC Flea & Food (every Sat. & Son.): 5-25 46th Avenue (4 min. walk)

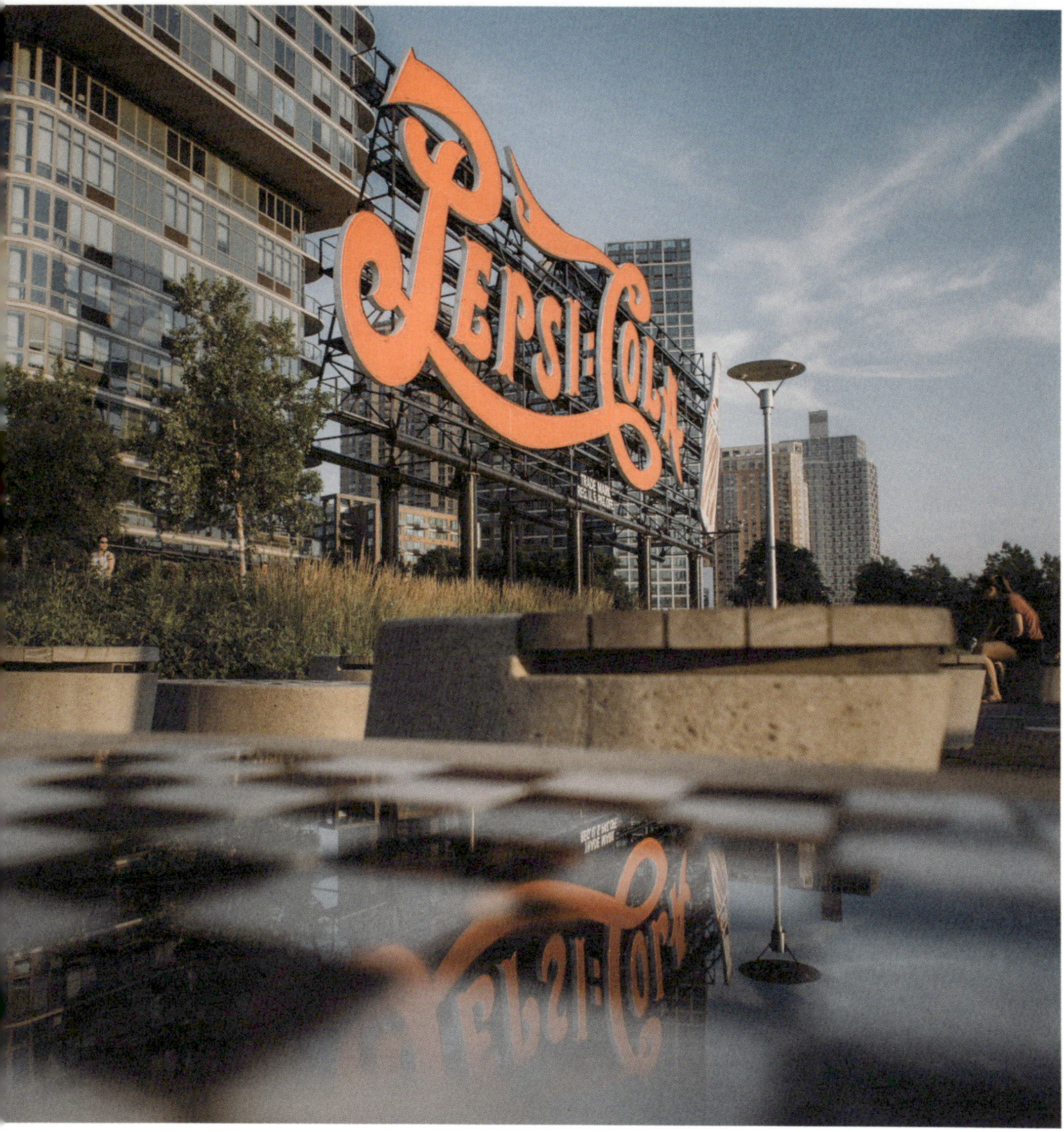

#pepsisign #pepsicolasign #longislandcity #gantryplazastatepark #queens

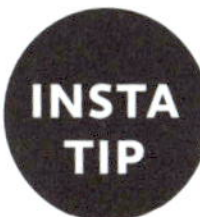

In this shot, the letters are reflected in the chess tables in the foreground. You must hold your camera as close to the reflective surface as possible to see a reflection.

88 MOMA PS1

MoMA PS1
22-25 Jackson Avenue

HOW TO GET THERE
Subway E (blue) or M (orange) to Court Square - 23 Street Station

Subway G (green) or 7 (purple) to Court Square Station

During the 1970's, the Institute for Art and Urban Resources Inc. discovered an old, vacant school building. The organization organized exhibitions in underutilized and abandoned spaces across New York and thought the school building was the perfect location for a Contemporary Art Center and in 1976 the MoMA PS1 was founded.

The building's original architecture and layout were preserved as much as possible. Walk through the old classrooms and stairwells that are used by artists for their location-specific art installations. Even the boiler room in the basement has been transformed by an artist.

The museum does not have a permanent collection but combines temporary exhibitions with a number of long-term installations.

In 1999, the center joined forces with The Museum of Modern Art (MoMA) to promote contemporary art and extend it reach.

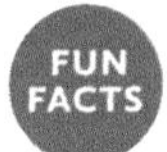

In addition to the exhibitions in the old school building, MoMA PS1 also regularly organizes projects elsewhere. The center has already held street performances in New York and created installations in Rockaway.

During the summer months, the outdoor sculpture area (the former playground) becomes a large dance floor for the annual Warm Up concert series. Up and coming DJs man the turntables here every Saturday afternoon for a tea dance.

INSTAGRAMMABLE PLACES IN THE NEIGHBORHOOD

COFFEE	Sweetleaf Coffee Roasters: 10-93 Jackson Avenue (6 min. walk)
COFFEE AND FOOD	Communitea: 11-18 46th Road (3 min. walk)
FOOD	M. Wells Dinette: 22-25 Jackson Avenue (located inside MoMA PS1)
	The Green Street LIC: 10-39 47th Road (6 min. walk)
	Court Square Diner: 45-30 23rd Street (2 min. walk)
SEE	Gantry Plaza State Park: 47th Road and Center Boulevard (12 min. walk)
	The Pepsi Sign: 4610 Center Boulevard (12 min. walk)

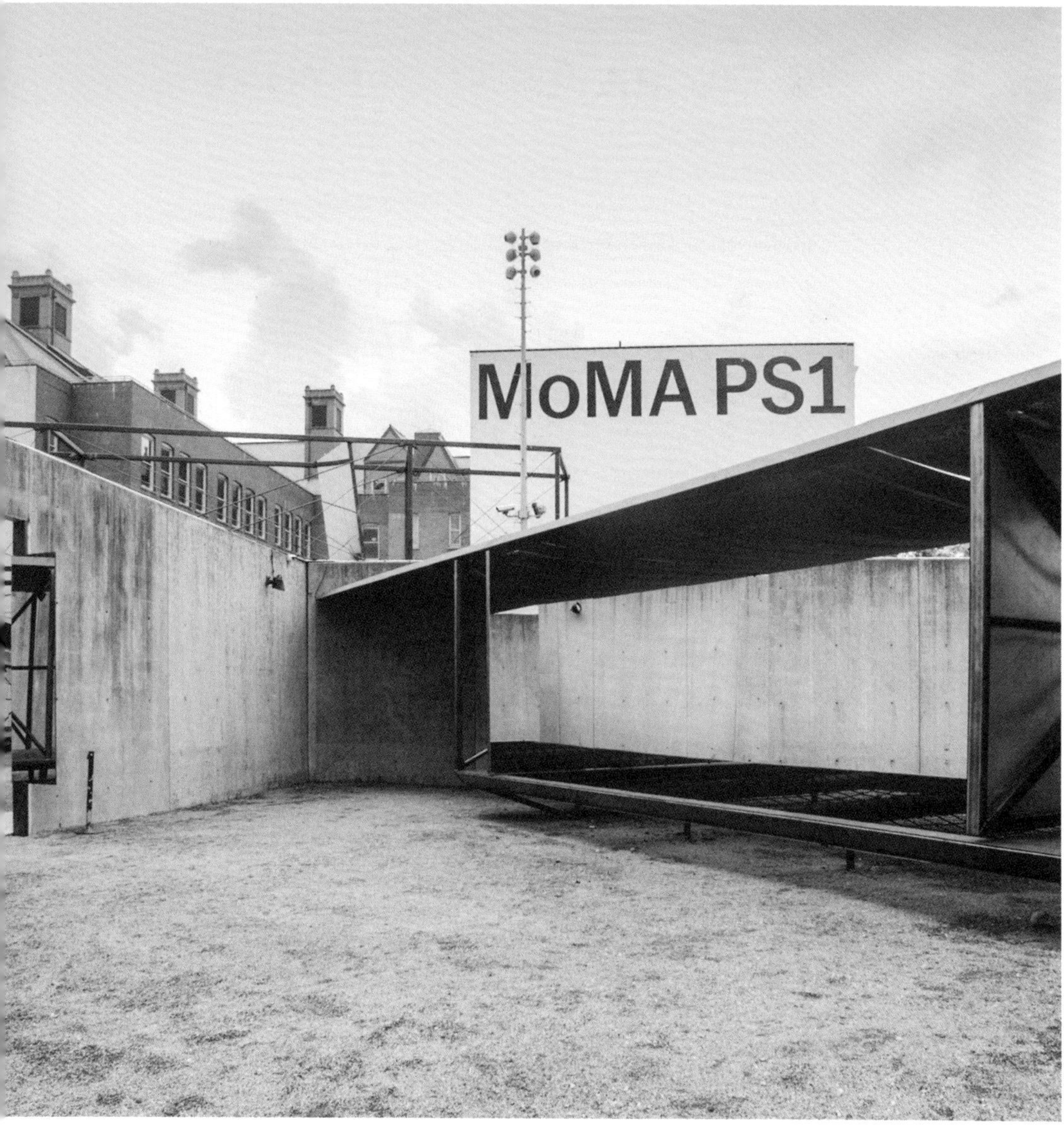

#momaps1 #moma #nycmuseums #longislandcity @momaps1

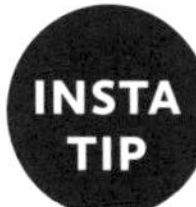

From the former playground, you can take a picture of the MoMA PS1 sign. There are temporary exhibitions in the courtyard. The artworks on display during your visit will influence the overall picture.

On this picture: featuring Hide & Seek by Jennifer Newsom and Tom Carruthers of Dream The Combine for The Museum of Modern Art and MoMA PS1's Young Architects Program 2018. @momaps1

89 SOCRATES SCULPTURE PARK

Socrates Sculpture Park
32-01 Vernon Boulevard

HOW TO GET THERE
Ferry to Astoria

Socrates Sculpture Park is a special place on the shore of the East River in Astoria, with a view of Roosevelt Island and the Upper East Side Skyline.

Until 1986, the park was an illegal dumping ground until an artist's collective, led by the sculptor Mark di Severo, transformed it into an open studio and exhibition space for artists and a community park for the locals. Nowadays Socrates Sculpture Park has become a unique outdoor museum with outstanding sculptures.

The permanent team develops various exhibitions every year. To date, over 1,000 artists have exhibited their work in the park, in a laidback bohemian ambience. In the summertime, the park also hosts (free) weekly cultural events and activities. The park is open 365 days a year.

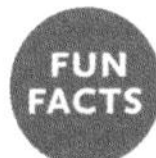

The park is named after the Greek philosopher Socrates as a tribute to the large Greek immigrant community in Astoria.

A stone fence surrounds part of the park. Some of the stones are old tombstones. Here and there you can make out an engraved name or letters.

INSTAGRAMMABLE PLACES IN THE NEIGHBORHOOD

COFFEE	Flor de Azalea Café: 902 34th Avenue (6 min. walk)
FOOD	Bel-Aire Diner: 31-91 21st Street (7 min. walk)
FOOD	Astoria Provisions: 12-23 Astoria Boulevard (10 min. walk)
SEE	The little Hallets Cove Beach: 31-10 Vernon Boulevard (1 min. walk)
	The Noguchi Museum: 9-01 33rd Road (3 min. walk)
	The Welling Court Mural Project: 11 - 98 Welling Court (8 min. walk)

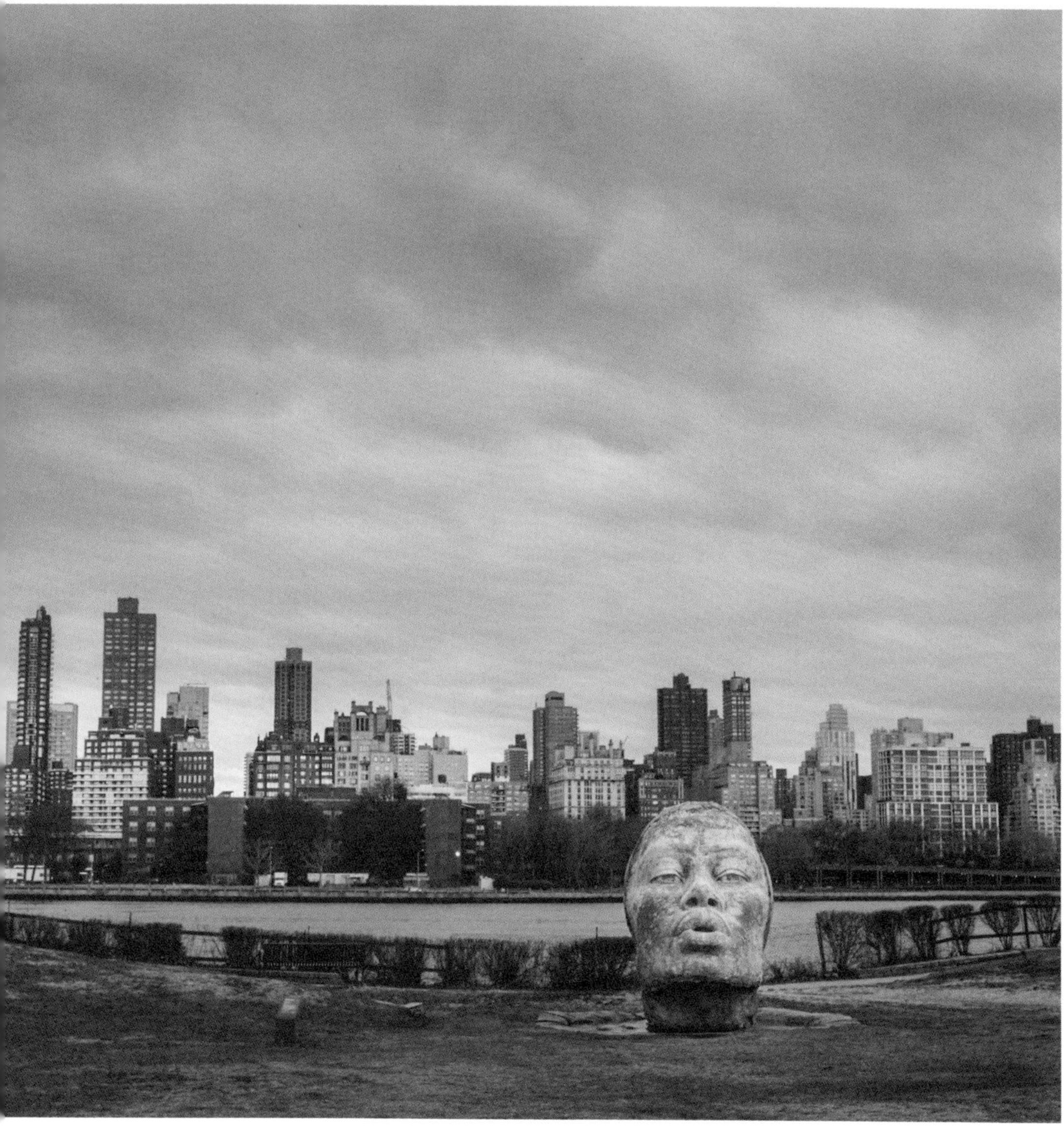

#socatessculpturepark #nycpublicart #astoria #queens #nycparks @socratessculpturepark @nycparks

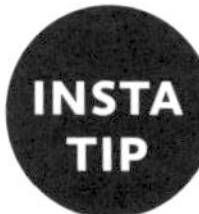

The park is located on the shore of the East River, as a result of which most of the artworks here have a panoramic skyline as a backdrop. Capturing this combination will add another dimension to your shot.

Don't forget to mention the artist if you post your photo online. Every artwork comes with a sign with more information. This sculpture by @tandafrancis is called Take Me With You.

90 WELLING COURT MURAL PROJECT

Welling Court Mural Project 11-98 Welling Court Astoria

HOW TO GET THERE
Ferry to Astoria

Like The Bushwick Collective, this street art project was established to bolster the community feeling, the attraction and the safety of this neighborhood. Local resident Jonathan Ellis decided to contribute to the neighborhood's upgrade with the Ad Hoc Art organization, using art. Wellington used to be a bare, industrial area, and has become a lively, colorful neighborhood since the first mural was created in 2009.

The project started in Welling Court, a small street in Astoria but since encompassed almost every block around this street. New color explosions appear in every intersection and on every corner and if you walk through all the streets, you can admire over 150 artworks.

Queens, and Astoria especially, is one of the US's most diverse neighborhoods. Astoria is home to more than 100 nationalities and this diversity is also reflected in the street art. This does not mean that political and/or difficult themes are sidestepped. On the whole, however, all the artworks have a positive vibe to them.

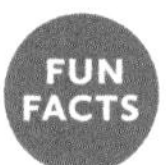

Every year, in June, during an annual event, a new batch of artworks is festively inaugurated. The new works are painted the week before the festival, the perfect opportunity to catch the street artists at work.

Queens has a longstanding tradition of street art. One of the most famous places for street art was 5 Pointz, the graffiti hotbed. 5 Pointz was an old 200,000 square foot (4.6 acres) large factory, all the walls of which were covered with hundreds of artworks by legendary graffiti artists. The old factory was demolished in 2014.

INSTAGRAMMABLE PLACES IN THE NEIGHBORHOOD

COFFEE	Astoria Provisions: 12-23 Astoria Boulevard (2 min. walk)
FOOD	Vesta: 21-02 30th Avenue (5 min. walk)
SEE	Socrates Sculpture Park: 32-01 Vernon Boulevard (8 min. walk)
	Astoria Park: 19th Street (10 min. walk)
	Athens Square Park: Corner 30th Street and 30th Avenue (10 min. walk)

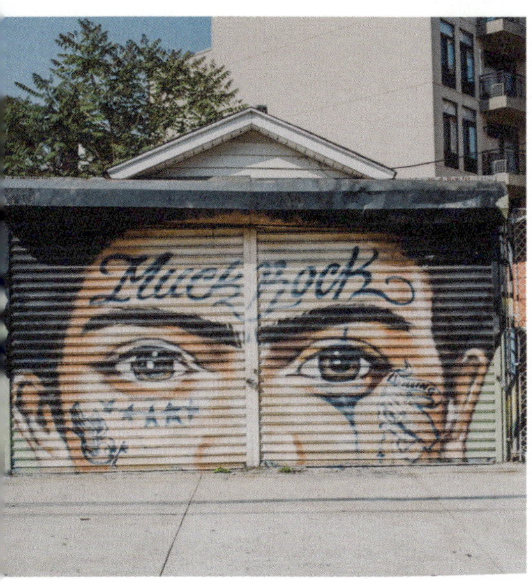

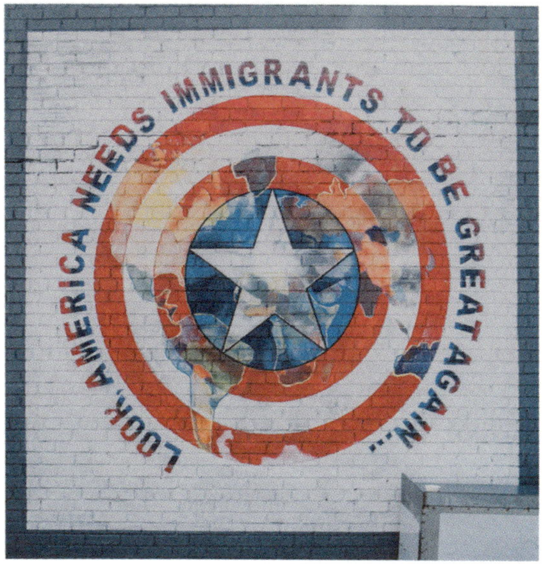

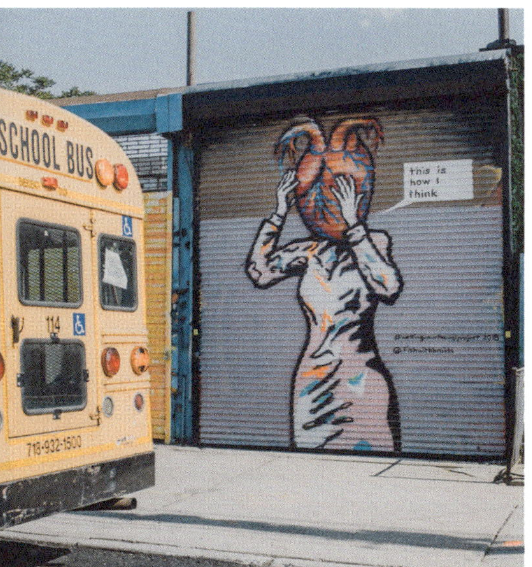

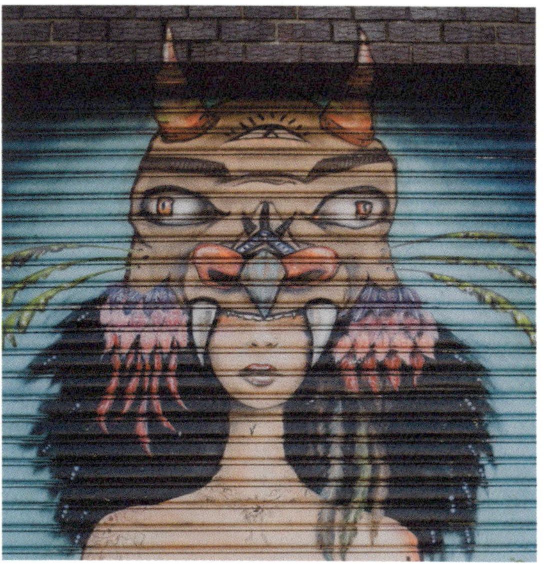

#wellingcourtmuralproject #adhocart #astoria #onemuralatatime @wellingcourtmuralproject

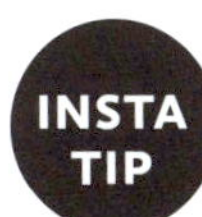

Incorporate part of the surroundings to highlight the huge dimensions of these murals. You can do this by adding part of the wall or a section of street.

Don't forget to tag the artist when you post a photo of a mural. The artist's name and Insta-account are usually featured on the artwork.

Clockwise: @muckrock @joaquinavilaart @fishwithbraids @aquarelaart

91 QUEENSBORO BRIDGE

Ed Koch Queensboro Bridge
You can find this walkway on the corner of Queens Plaza North and Crescent Street

HOW TO GET THERE
Subway 7 (purple) or N, W (yellow) to Queensboro Plaza

The Queensboro Bridge was built 20 years after the Brooklyn Bridge, to reduce congestion. It's also known as The 59th Street Bridge and its official title is Ed Koch Queensboro Bridge after the popular mayor Edward Irving Koch.

The bridge has a walkway and a cycling path on the north side, which is completely separate from the roadway. The walk from Queensboro Plaza to Manhattan is about 1.7 miles (2.7 kilometers) and takes about half an hour.

While the view from the bridge is perhaps less spectacular than the view from the Brooklyn Bridge, the view of Roosevelt Island midway across the bridge is quite unique. You can also wave at the passengers of the Roosevelt Island Tramway as they float by.

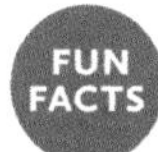

Sixteen bridges connect Manhattan with the surrounding areas, 12 of which have a walkway and a cycling path.

After years of decay, the renovation of the bridge started in 1987, costing more than 300 million dollars. A lot more than the total cost of the bridge's construction, 18 million dollars...

INSTAGRAMMABLE PLACES IN THE NEIGHBORHOOD

COFFEE Toby's Estate LIC Cafe & Courtyard: 26-25 Jackson Avenue (6 min. walk)
FOOD The Baroness bar + kitchen: 4126 Crescent Street (3 min. walk)
SEE Silvercup Studios: 4222 22nd Street (4 min. walk)
SculptureCenter: 44-19 Purves Street (6 min. walk)
Flux Factory: 39-31 29th Street (8 min. walk)

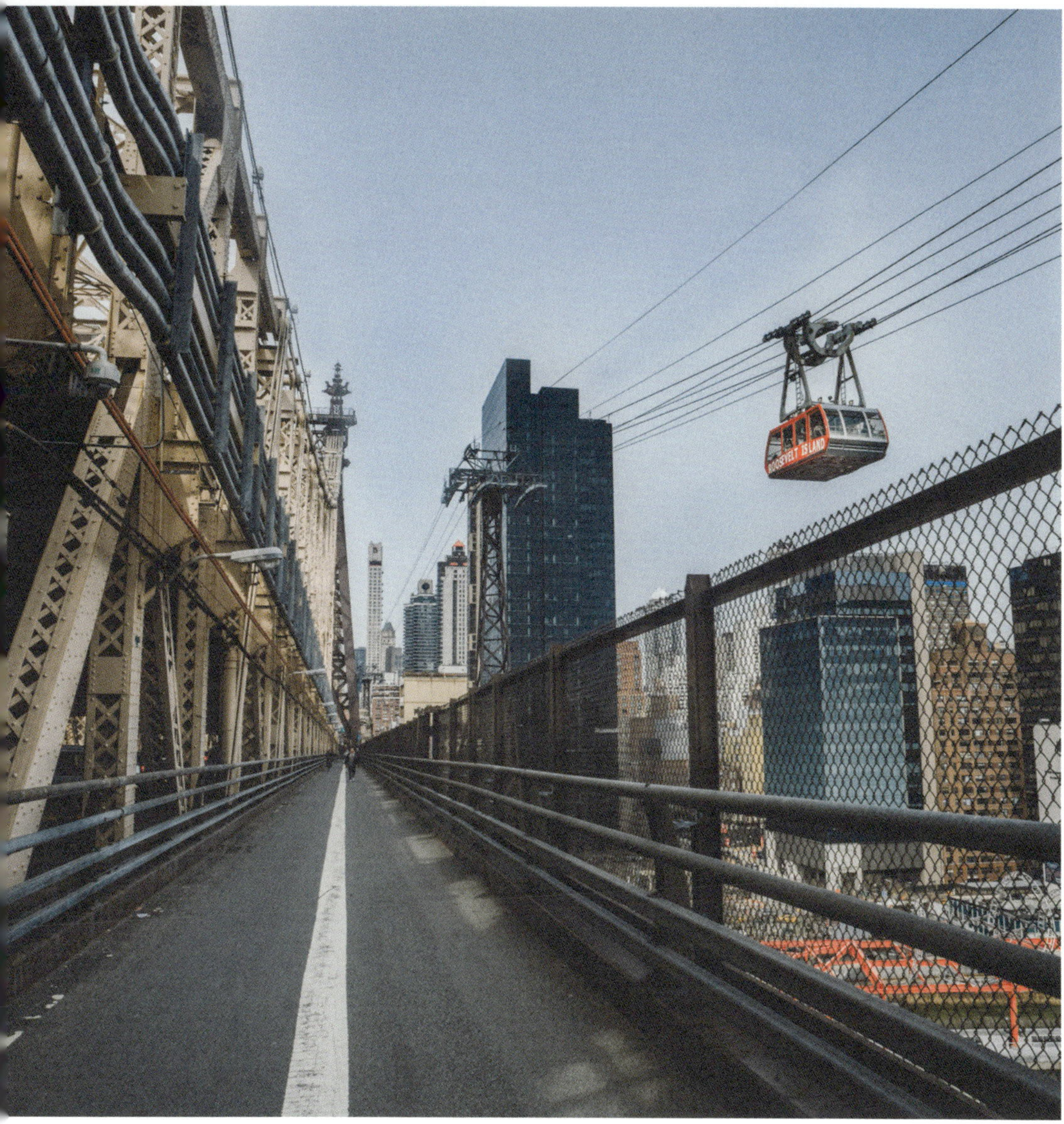

#queensborobridge #edkochbridge #59thstreetbridge #eastriver #rooseveltisland

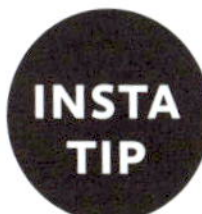

When walking past the cables of the Roosevelt Island Tramway, you could wait for a tram to pass (every 5 minutes approximately). Find a place where you can photograph the tram without interference in the background.

 SILVERCUP STUDIOS

Silvercup Studios 4222 22nd Street

HOW TO GET THERE
Subway 7 (purple) or N, W (yellow) to Queensboro Plaza

In 1983, Silvercup Studios moved into the former flour silos of the historic Silvercup Bakery. Silvercup Studios is the largest independent film and television production facility in New York City and the home base of plenty of classics. Sex and the City, The Sopranos, Gossip Girls and Mad Men are just a few of the series that were shot here.

Unfortunately, you cannot visit the studios but you can get a good idea of the ambience by walking around the building. And who knows, you may even bump into one of your favorite TV characters.

You cannot fail to notice the gigantic rooftop neon sign, which has become a Long Island City iconic. You may recognize it from the legendary last battle scene starring Christopher Lambert and Clancy Brown in *Highlander* (1986).

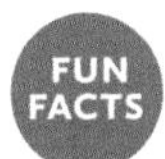

While the TV series *Friends* takes place in New York City, the series is recorded in the Warner Brother Studios in California. The Friends building is in New York however, at 90 Bedford Street in Greenwich. *Days of our Lives*, in which the Friends character Joey has a role, is shot in the Silvercup Studios according to the series.

The Maphook app and website has a map of locations where New York scenes of popular TV shows are filmed.

INSTAGRAMMABLE PLACES IN THE NEIGHBORHOOD

COFFEE — Birch Coffee: 40-37 23rd Street (6 min. walk)

FOOD — Ramen Shack: 13-13 40th Avenue (8 min. walk)

SEE — Queensboro Bridge: pedestrian entrence at Plaza North and Cresent Street (4 min. walk)

Queensbridge Park: Vernon Boulevard (12 min. walk)

Murals at 43rd Avenue between 21st and 22nd Street (3 min. walk)

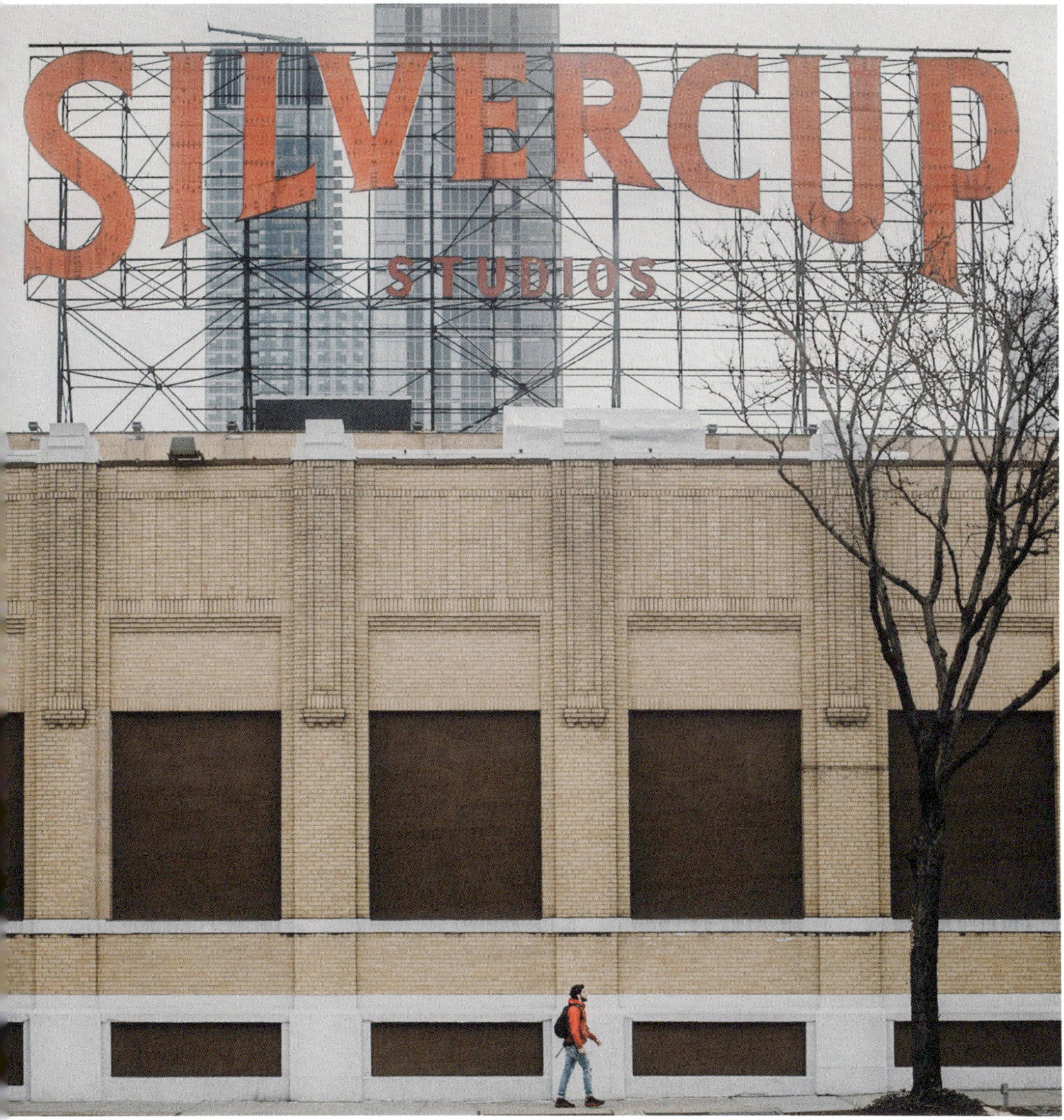

#silvercupstudios #nycstudios #longislandcity #queens

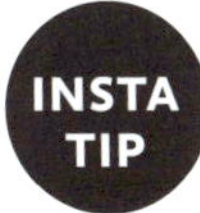

You can take photos of the iconic and photogenic sign from various angles. In 22nd Street you face the sign. If you travel to Queens Plaza Subway Station on the 7 train, you will drive past the back of the letters, so you can include part of Manhattan's skyline in your photo.

93 MUSEUM OF THE MOVING IMAGE

Museum of the Moving Image 36-01 35 Avenue

HOW TO GET THERE
Subway N or W to 36th Avenue Station

Subway R or M to Steinway Street Station

The Museum of The Moving Image is worth a visit because of the special content and its stunning architecture, film screenings and fun interactive activities.

The museum is located in the former building of the Kaufman Studios (the new studios are next door to the museum) and is the only museum in the United States to be entirely dedicated to film and television.

The three floors contain a unique collection of film-related artefacts, interactive corners where you can test special effects yourself, a retro video arcade where you can play a game for just 25 cents and take a look behind the scenes of classic and contemporary films.

The permanent Jim Henson exhibition is a trip down memory lane. It's so cool to come eye to eye with the original puppets of the *Muppets* (Kermit! Miss Piggy!) and *Sesame Street* (Elmo! Big Bird!). You can also see the authentic storyboards and sketches, impressive costumes and plenty of other interesting items from Jim Henson's archive there.

The museum is located off the beaten track and many tourists are unaware it even exists, but it is definitely a fun option for a visit whatever your age.

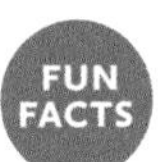

Every year, the museum screens more than 400 films in its own theaters. The Sumner M. Redstone Theater is a futuristic movie theater, with the latest technological features, a stunning design and a gigantic screen.

Astoria Studio (built in 1920) is America's oldest film studio and is the place where *Goodfellas*, *Sesame Street* and *Orange is The New Black* were shot. The studios are located next to the museum.

INSTAGRAMMABLE PLACES IN THE NEIGHBORHOOD

COFFEE	Coffeed: 37-18 Northern Boulevard (7 min. walk)
FOOD	Pye Boat Noodle: 35 13 Broadway (8 min. walk)
SEE	Brooklyn Grange: 37-18 Northern Boulevard (7 min. walk)
	Flux Factory: 39-31 29th Street (16 min. walk)

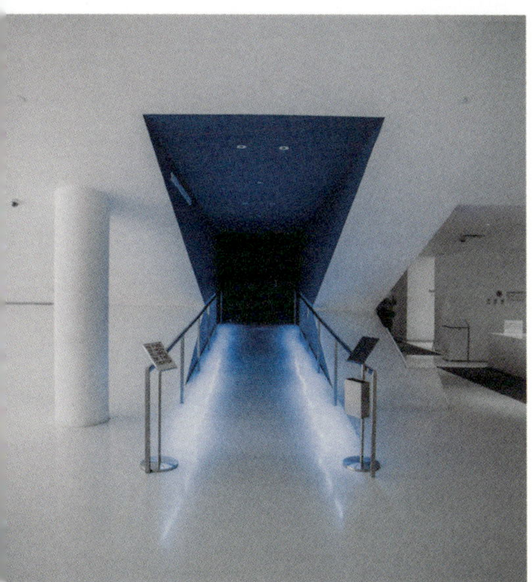

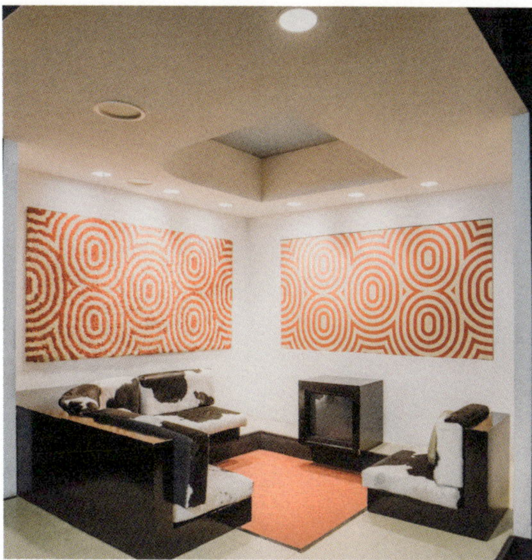

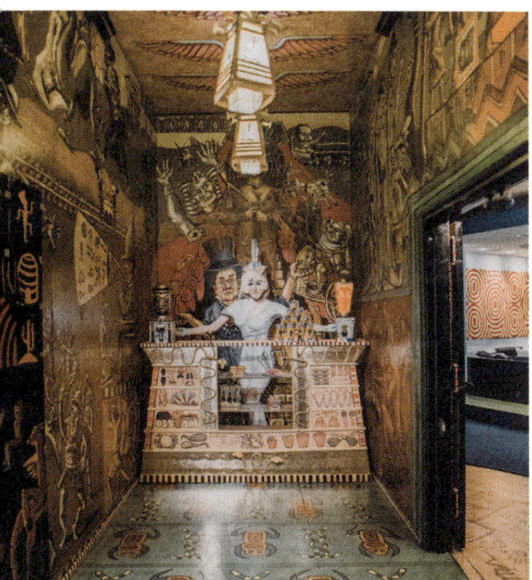

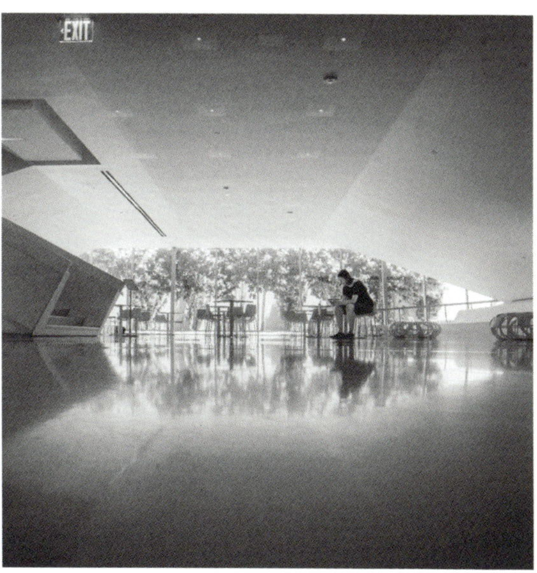

#museumofthemovingimage #movingimagenyc #queens #nycmuseums @movingimagenyc

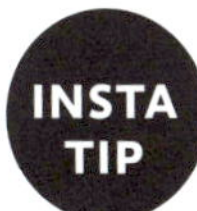

The museum has a lot of photogenic places and you can immerse yourself in various different atmospheres in the same building. In the entrance hall, you can capture some futuristic images while you can take some shots of scenes from the sixties on the upper floor.

Top right picture: Jim Isermann, "TV Lounge" (1988).

Bottom left picture: Red Grroms and Lysiane Luong, "Tut's Fever Movie Palace" (1988).

94 CORONA PARK

Flushing Meadows-Corona Park

HOW TO GET THERE
Subway 7 (purple) to the Mets - Willets Point Station

Flushing Meadows - Corona Park was created as the site for the 1939 and 1964 World Fairs. Some of the original features, such as the gigantic Unisphere and the New York State Pavilion are still there. The latter consist of three sections:

The futuristic and colorful Tent of Tomorrow.

The Observation Towers that resemble UFOs.

Theaterama, the home of the Queens Theatre.

The park is still used for major events, such as the annual grand slam, the US Open and the baseball matches of the New York Mets in the Citi Field Stadium. The locals also use it for picnics, swimming, jogging or a walk through the huge park.

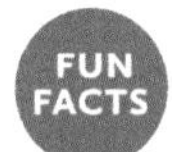

Time capsules were installed during both world fairs. You can find them next to the New York State Pavilion, but they may only be dug up 5,000 years after they were buried.

The 1939 capsule contains a pack of cigarettes and a message from Albert Einstein.

The 1964 capsule contains a Beatles album and an electronic toothbrush among others.

INSTAGRAMMABLE PLACES IN THE NEIGHBORHOOD

COFFEE & FOOD	Coffeed at the Queens Museum
SEE	The Tent of Tomorrow and the Observation Towers
	The Unisphere
	The Queens Museum
	Rocket Park Mini golf

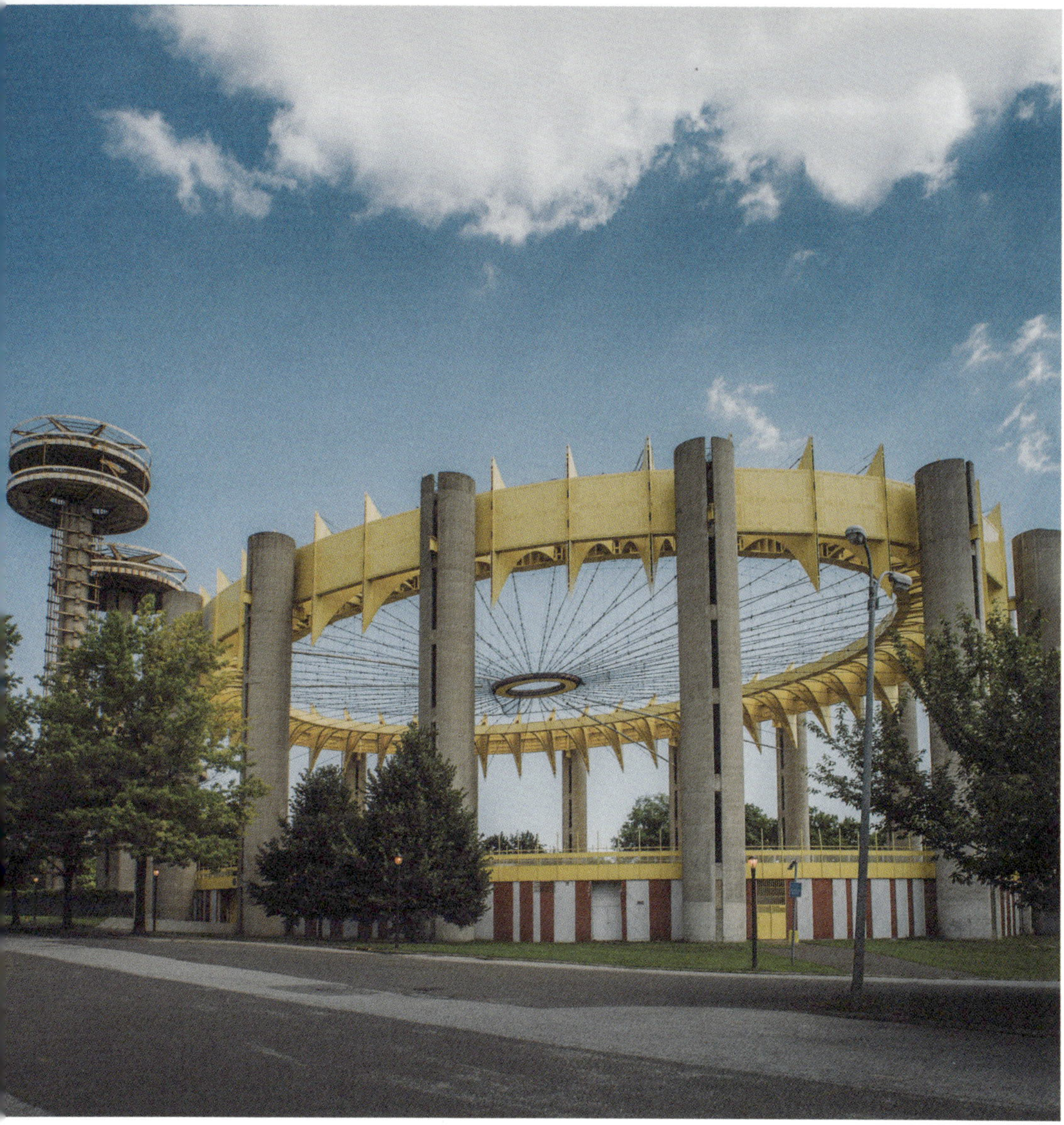

#flushingmeadowscoronapark #coronapark #worldfair #nycparks #queens @nycparks

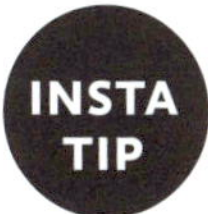

While the New York State Pavilion has a stunning design and color palette, it is very large. You will have to take your photo from a distance in other words. Try the Theaterama car park.

⓽⓹ UNISPHERE

Unisphere

HOW TO GET THERE
Subway 7 (purple) to the Mets - Willets Point Station

The Unisphere is the huge sphere in the center of Flushing Meadows-Corona Park. You can spot it from a distance, towering above the trees.

It was built as the theme symbol for the 1964 World's Fair, which was inspired by the Space Age and the umbrella theme of Peace through Understanding. It is 12 stories tall (140 feet or 42 meters), has a diameter of 120 feet (37 meters), weighs 700,000 pounds (350 tons), making it the largest sphere in the world. When driving from or to La Guardia or JFK, you can spot the gigantic globe along the highway.

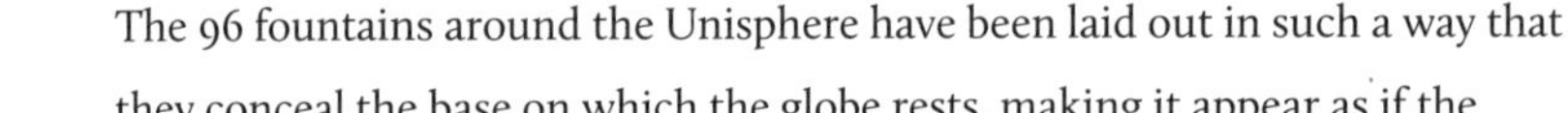

The 96 fountains around the Unisphere have been laid out in such a way that they conceal the base on which the globe rests, making it appear as if the sphere is floating in space.

The three large rings around the Unisphere refer to the first man in space, the first American in space and the first communications satellite.

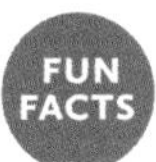

During the World Fair there were plenty of other interesting things to discover besides the Unisphere. Americans were introduced to Belgian waffles, there was a scale model of the Twin Towers (the World Trade Center) and the Vatican had loaned Michelangelo's *Pietà* for the occasion to be exhibited to the public.

The Unisphere has become an icon of Queens and is often featured in movies (including *Men in Black*), video clips (including *Mo Money* by the Notorious B.I.G) and games (such as *Grand Theft Auto*).

INSTAGRAMMABLE PLACES IN THE NEIGHBORHOOD

COFFEE & FOOD	Coffeed at the Queens Museum (1 min. walk)
FOOD	The Lemon Ice King of Corona: 52-02 108th Street (15 min. walk)
SEE	Queens museum (1 min. walk)
	The Tent of Tomorrow and the Observation Towers (3 min. walk)
	Rocket Park Mini golf: 47-01 111th Street (15 min. walk)

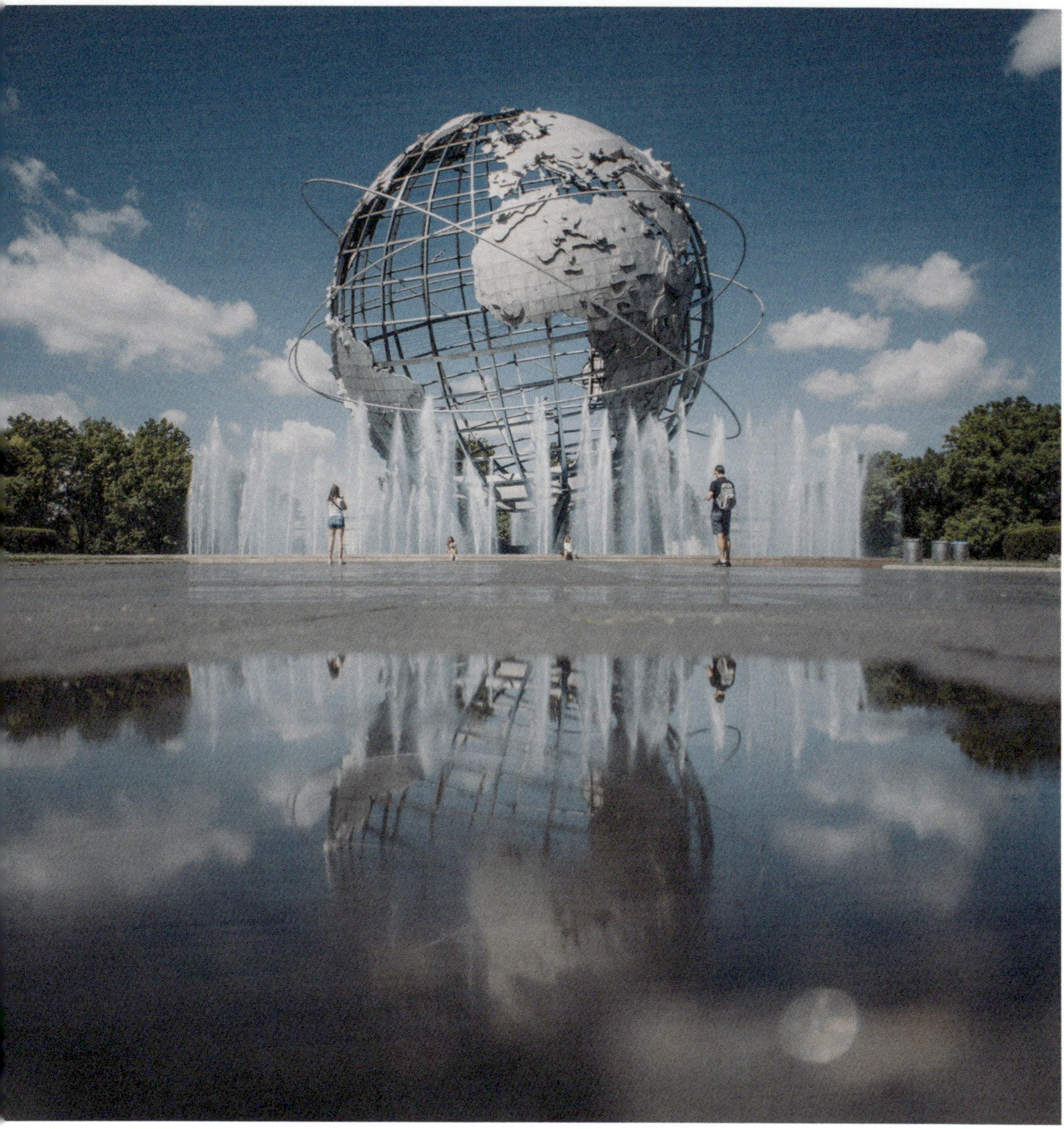

#unisphere #flushingmeadowspark #coronapark #nycparks #queens @nycparks

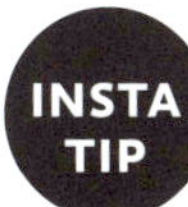

There's no denying that the Unisphere is gigantic which is why it is so difficult to capture its huge size. You can put this into perspective by positioning people at various distances in relation to the sculpture.

The closer your model stands to the sculpture, the smaller he or she will look (which emphasizes how big the sculpture actually is). The closer your model is to the camera, the larger he or she will appear, making the Unisphere look smaller.

96 ROOSEVELT ISLAND LIGHTHOUSE

Roosevelt Island Lighthouse

HOW TO GET THERE
The Roosevelt Island tramway at the corner of E 60th Street and 2nd Avenue

Subway F (orange) to Roosevelt Island

NYC Ferry from/ to Long Island City or Astoria (Queens)

Roosevelt Island is a small, narrow island between Manhattan and Queens. You can get there by subway or ferry, but the most interesting option is to take the Roosevelt Island Tramway, which floats above the streets of New York and over the East River. The trip takes a mere 2 minutes.

The Roosevelt Island lighthouse, also called The Blackwell Island Lighthouse, stands on the northernmost tip of the island. The small island was conceived by the architect James Renwick Jr., who also designed St. Patrick's Cathedral on 5th Avenue and the Smallpox Hospital on the other side of the island. The lighthouse was built in 1872 and was operational until approximately 1940. Afterwards the light from the city and the bridges was so bright that a lighthouse was no longer deemed necessary.

Franklin D. Roosevelt Four Freedoms Park and the ruins of the Smallpox Hospital are located on the southernmost tip of the island. A free shuttle bus tours the island, taking you from one end to the other. The views of the skylines of Manhattan and Queens, from the northern and southern tip of the islands, are magnificent.

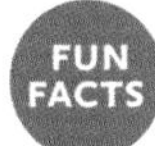

The lighthouse was built using rocks quarried on the island. Legend has it an asylum inmate constructed it. For many years, a saying was inscribed on the stone near the lighthouse: "This work was done by John Mc Cathy, who built the lighthouse from the bottom to the top. All ye who do pass by may pray for his soul when he dies".

In 1998, someone anonymously donated 120,000 dollars to complete the restoration of the lighthouse.

INSTAGRAMMABLE PLACES IN THE NEIGHBORHOOD

COFFEE & FOOD	there's only one coffeeshop (Starbucks) and a couple of restaurants on the whole Island! You can find them next to the subway station
SEE	The Manhattan Park Pool Club: 30 River Road
	The Franklin D. Roosevelt Four Freedoms Park
	The ruins of the Smallpox Hospital

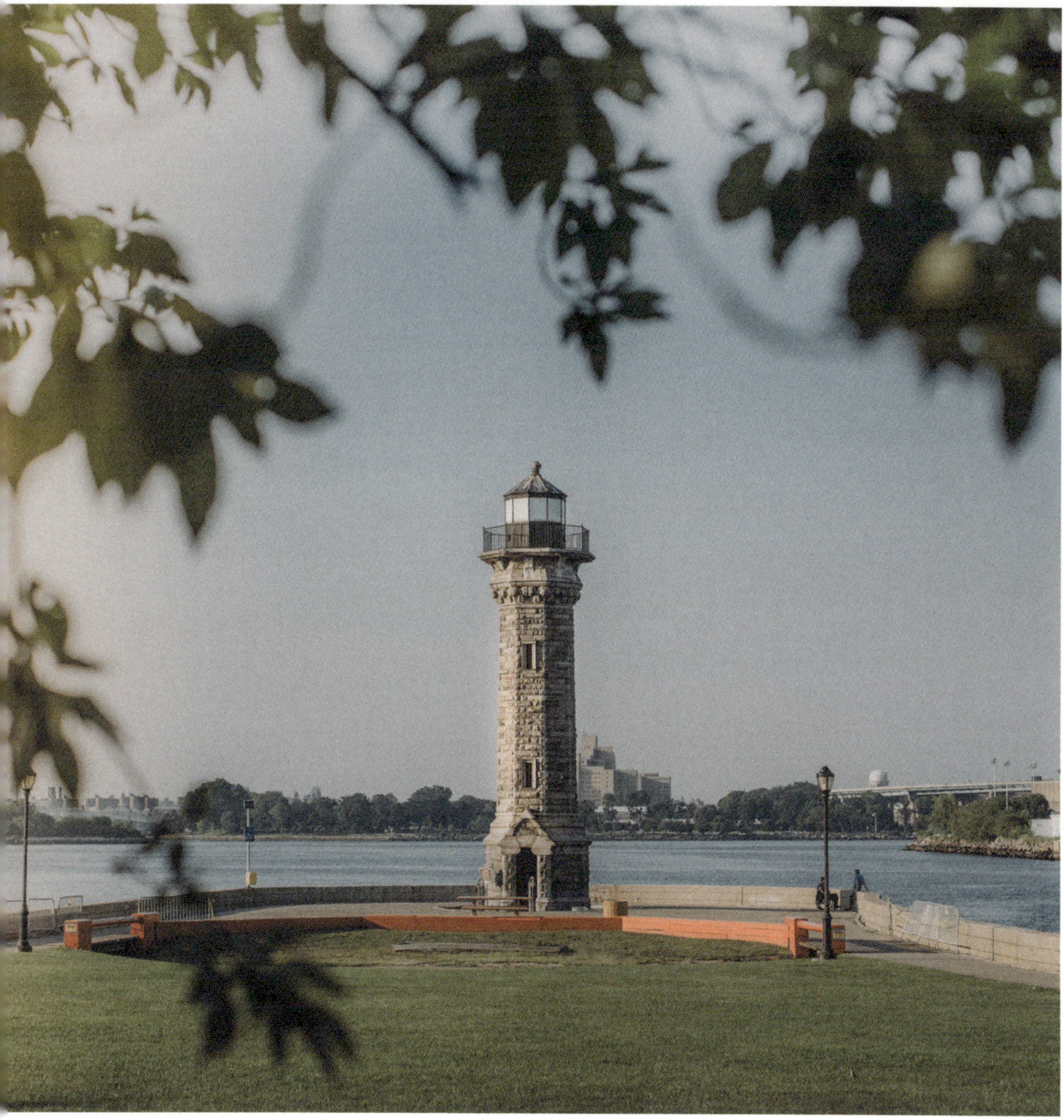

#rooseveltsisland #rooseveltislandlighthouse #blackwellislandlighthouse #nycskyline #eastriver

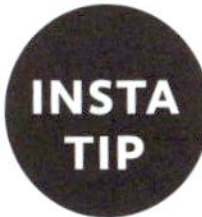

You can take a photo of the lighthouse in combination with the water in the background when standing in the middle of the grass in front of the lighthouse. If you are lucky, you may even catch a flight of geese as they take off, as they like to congregate on the grass.

97 GOVERNORS ISLAND

Governors Island

HOW TO GET THERE

Ferry from Battery Maritime Building (10 South Street) to Governors Island

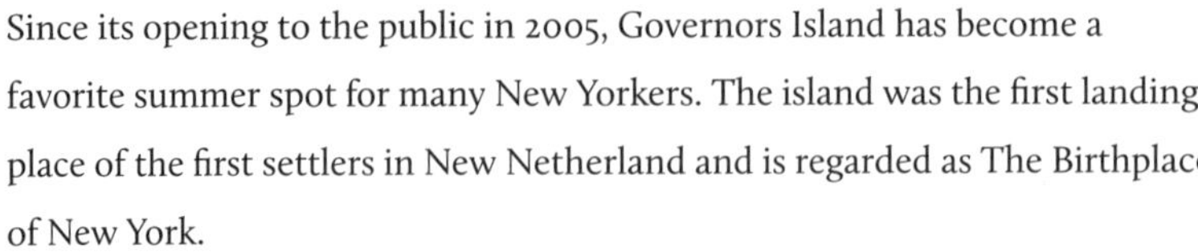

Since its opening to the public in 2005, Governors Island has become a favorite summer spot for many New Yorkers. The island was the first landing place of the first settlers in New Netherland and is regarded as The Birthplace of New York.

The island is only half a mile (800 meters) from the southernmost tip of Manhattan and it takes just a few minutes to get there by ferry from Downtown and yet it feels as if you have stepped into a different world. The phenomenal views of Downtown Manhattan and the Statue of Liberty remind you that you are indeed in New York City.

The large 172-acre park is car-free and perfect to explore by bike or on foot. There is a summer ice-skating rink, climbing wall or zip line for the more athletically inclined. If you prefer to relax, you can head to the lovely Hammock Grove or see one of the experimental art exhibitions you can find on the island.

You can only get to the island by ferry and only during the summer season (May to October) from 10 am until 6 pm.

FUN FACTS

Slide Hill is 40 feet (12 meters) above sea level and is a hill with various slides, including New York City's longest slide, measuring 57 feet (17.3 meters).

The various hills, Lookout Hill (70 feet), Slide Hill (40 feet) and Grassy Hill (25 feet), were built using reclaimed materials from the demolition of the buildings on the island.

INSTAGRAMMABLE PLACES IN THE NEIGHBORHOOD

COFFEE AND FOOD	Liggett Terrace (4 min. from the ferry landing)
DRINKS AND FOOD	Island Oyster waterfront bar (1 min. from the ferry landing)
SEE	Fort Jay (4 min. from the ferry landing)
	The Hammock Grove (5 min. from the ferry landing)
	The Hills (17 min. from the ferry landing)

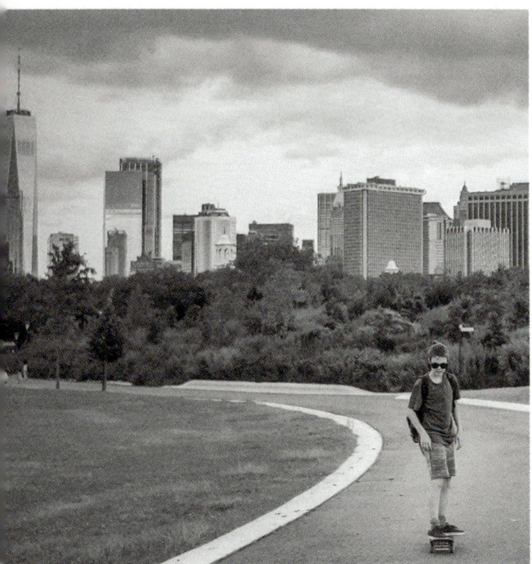
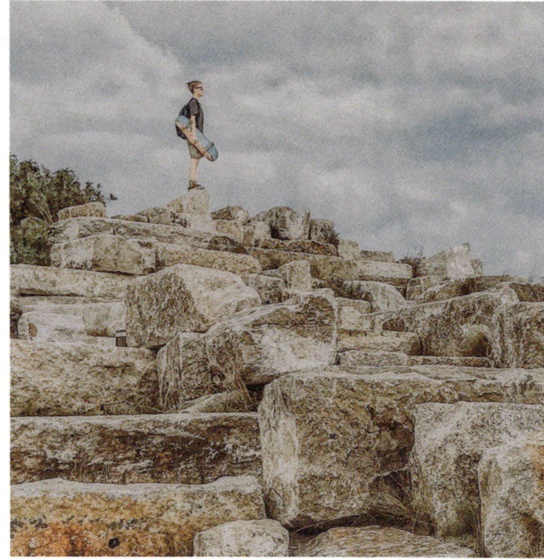
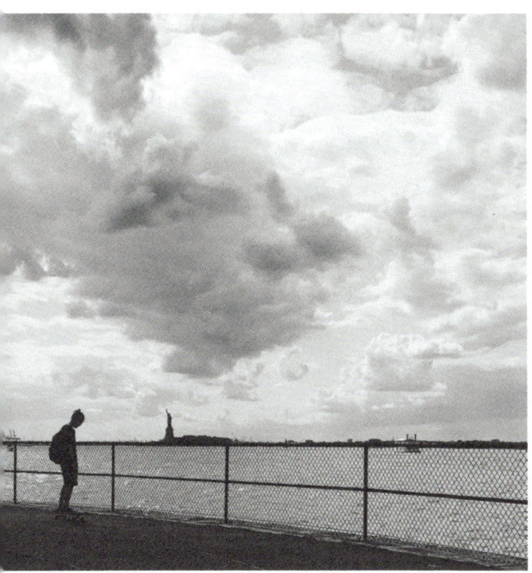
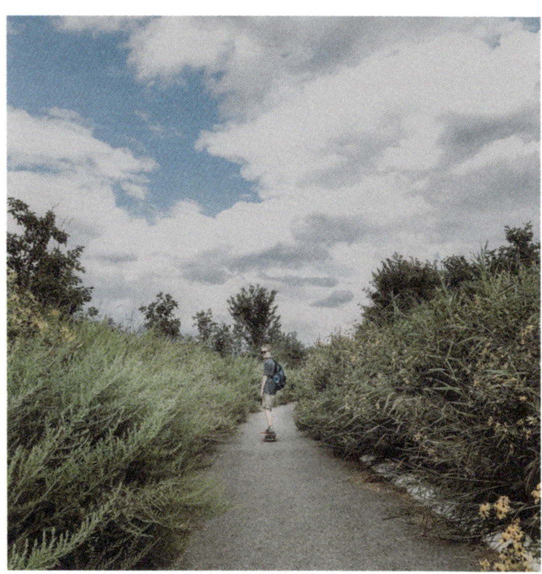

#governorsiland #manhattanview #nycsummer #hudsonriver #eastriver @governorsisland

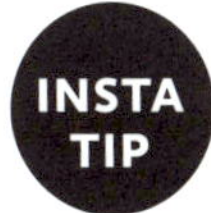

Governors Island has a lot of wonderful spots and views. The pictures above show the Downtown Manhattan skyline, the top of The Hill, the view of Lady Liberty and the road to the Hammock Grove.

98 STATEN ISLAND FERRY

Staten Island Ferry

HOW TO GET THERE

Subway 1 (red) to South Ferry Station

Subway 4 or 5 (green) to Bowling Green Station

Subway R or W (yellow) to Whitehall Street Station

Since 1906, the Staten Island Ferry transports commuters from Staten Island to Manhattan every day. The ferry service is operated by a fleet of nine ferries, which sail 24 hours a day, 365 days a year, offering 100 sailings every day.

In addition to transporting commuters, the ferry has also become very popular with tourists. The ferry is a great way to enjoy a free 25-minute, 5-mile (8 kilometers) journey between the two islands. Tourists mainly go for the phenomenal views of the Statue of Liberty, Ellis Island and the Lower Manhattan skyline rather than travelling to Staten Island. With 70,000 passengers daily, the Staten Island Ferry is one of New York City's busiest tourist attractions.

For many years, Staten Island was an unassuming residential borough but nowadays it is definitely worth exploring. The locals are working hard to make Staten Island more appealing, with the New York Wheel, the world's highest observation wheel among others. Foodies will also be happy to know you can visit the Flagship Brewery, near the ferry pontoon.

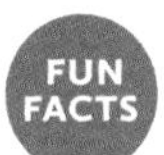

After the 9/11 attacks on the WTC Towers, the coastguard requested all boats to be used to evacuate people from Lower Manhattan. The entire fleet of the Staten Island Ferry was used to carry tens of thousands people to safety.

In the days after the attack the Staten Island Ferry was used to transport the emergency services and equipment to Lower Manhattan.

INSTAGRAMMABLE PLACES IN THE NEIGHBORHOOD

COFFEE There's a coffee bar on the ferry

Every Thing Goes Book Café: 208 Bay Street
(12 min. walk from the Ferry Terminal)

SEE The National Lighthouse Museum: 200 Promenade at Lighthouse Point
(3 min. walk from Ferry Terminal)

Hypno-Tronic Comics: 156 Stuyvesant Place
(9 min. walk from the Ferry Terminal)

Staten Island September 11 Memorial: St. George Esplanade
(6 min. walk from the Ferry Terminal)

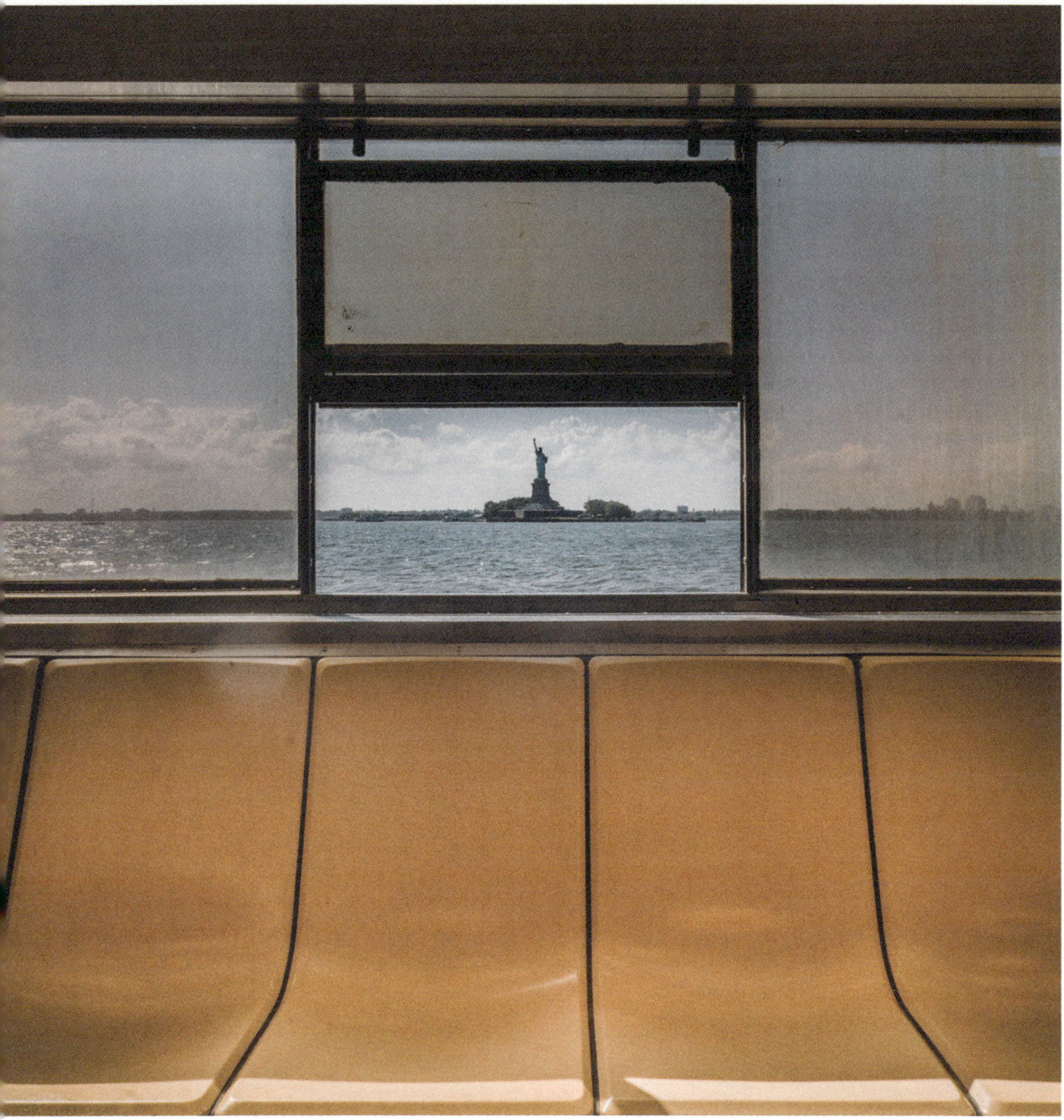

#statenislandferry #siferry #statenisland #manhattanskyline

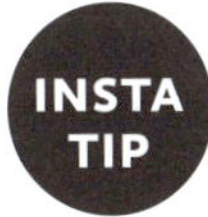

The typical colors of the ferry's seats and windows provide the perfect frame for a picture of the Statue of Liberty. The ferry sails at a leisurely pace so you have plenty of time to think about a beautiful composition and create that perfect shot.

99 CONEY ISLAND FERRIS WHEEL

Coney Island
3059 W 12th Street

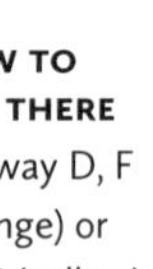

HOW TO GET THERE
Subway D, F (orange) or N, G (yellow) to Stillwell Avenue

Coney Island is a peninsular neighborhood that is part of the borough of Brooklyn with its own picturesque and kitschy personality. Coney Island is all about nostalgia. In the old days, it was mainly known for its wide beach and the many colorful carnival attractions.

During the summer months, New Yorkers flock to the beach to escape the hot, sticky city. The 3-mile (4.8 kilometers) sandy beach is big enough to accommodate the many sun worshippers and swimmers.

The boardwalk is lined with more than 50 (often retro) attractions. The (Insta) hits are the stunning retro Wonder Wheel and the iconic Coney Island Cyclone, a wooden rollercoaster, which has been catering to thrill seekers since 1927.

Events like The Mermaid Parade (end of June), Nathan's Hot Dog Eating Contest (4th of July) and summer activities such as the Coney Art Walls and the weekly fireworks on Fridays all contribute to the typical Coney Island ambience and make for some great Insta-stories.

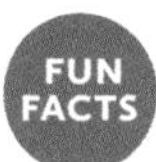

The world's first rollercoaster opened in 1884, in the location of the legendary Cyclone. In 1927, the wooden rollercoaster, which still stands here today, was built.

The Wonder Wheel was the wedding gift of a Greek immigrant to his future wife. Their son now operates the ferris wheel, which is still a popular choice to propose to the love of your life.

INSTAGRAMMABLE PLACES IN THE NEIGHBORHOOD

FOOD
- Nathan's Original Hot Dog Stand: 1310 Surf Avenue & 1229 Boardwalk
- Tom's Coney Island Diner: 1229 Riegelmann Boardwalk

SEE
- Coney Art Walls: 3050 Stillwell Avenue
- Steeplechase Park: 1739 Riegelmann Boardwalk
- The Cyclone Roller Coaster: 1000 Surf Avenue

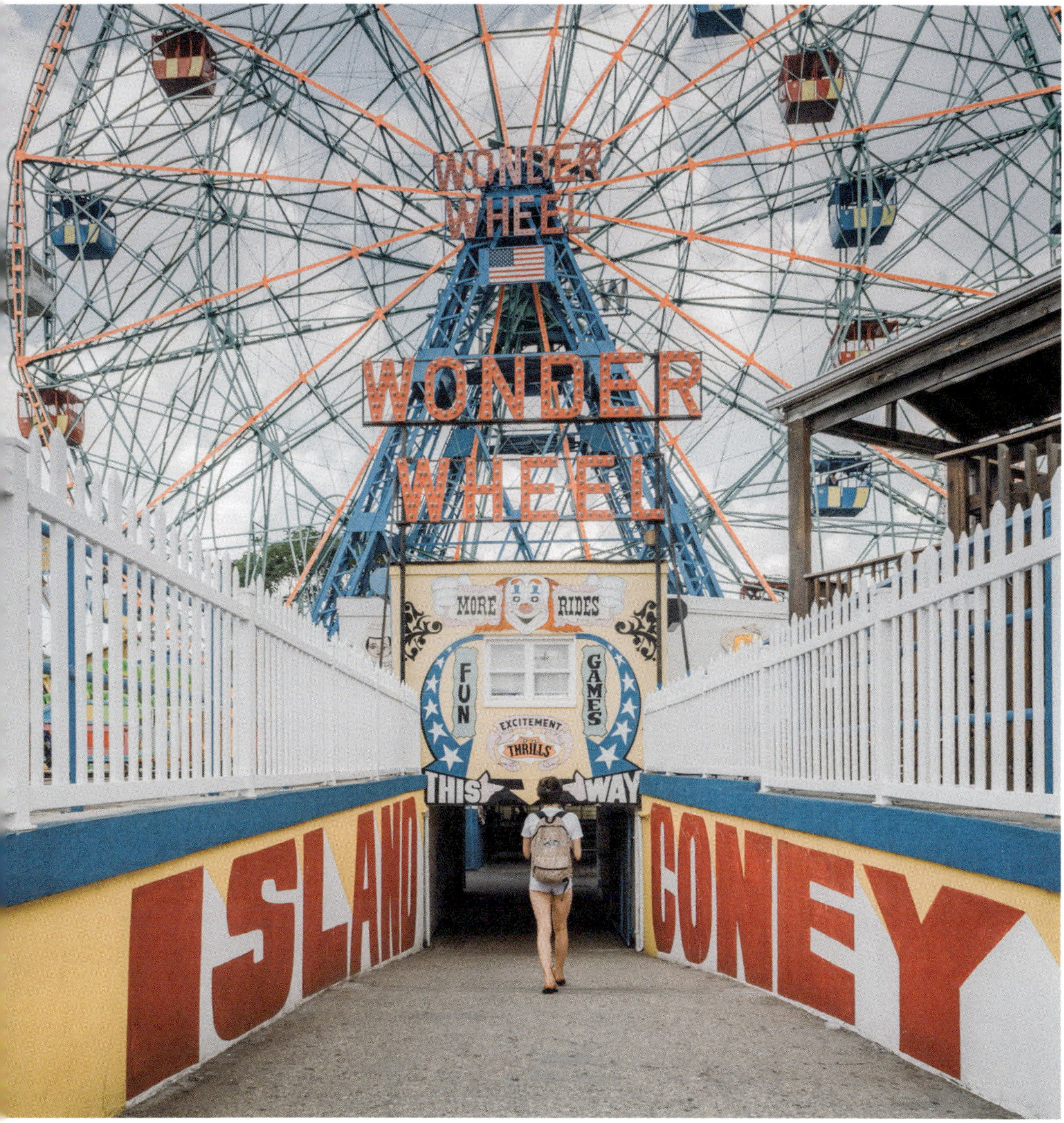

#coneyisland #coneyislandbeach #coneyislandfun #coneyislandboardwalk

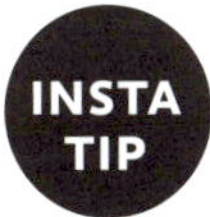

The entrance under the Wonder Wheel definitely is an Insta-hotspot. From here, you can capture the iconic ferris wheel, the retro atmosphere and the colorful character of Coney Island in one image.

100 ELLIS ISLAND/ LIBERTY ISLAND

Ellis Island/
Liberty Island

HOW TO GET THERE
Statue Cruises from Battery Park

Ellis Island is an artificial island, which was built as the gateway to America for new immigrants in the nineteenth century. Immigrants who moved to the United States were welcomed by the Statue of Liberty and underwent a medical examination on Ellis Island, before they were officially admitted to the country.

Since 1976, the island is open to the public and the border facility has become a museum where you can check whether one of the 12 million immigrants who entered America here was a family member of yours.

Ellis Island is situated next to Liberty Island. Together they form the Statue of Liberty National Monument, which you can visit with the Statue Cruises that leave from Battery Park.

The Statue of Liberty is known around the world as an icon of freedom. It was built to commemorate the Centennial of the American Declaration of Independence and was a gift from France to the United States. The 154-feet (47 meters) high base was built by the Americans, while Gustave Eiffel built the 150-feet tall (46 meters) statue.

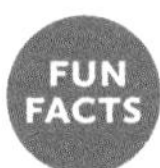

The two islands belong to the borough of New Jersey but are owned by the federal government and administered by the state of New York.

According to estimates, almost half of all Americans have at least one person in their family tree who entered the country at Ellis Island.

INSTAGRAMMABLE PLACES IN THE NEIGHBORHOOD

COFFEE & FOOD	Ellis Island Cafe and Statue of Liberty Crown Cafe
SEE	The Immigration Museum
	Ellis Island Hospital Morgue
	The Statue of Liberty

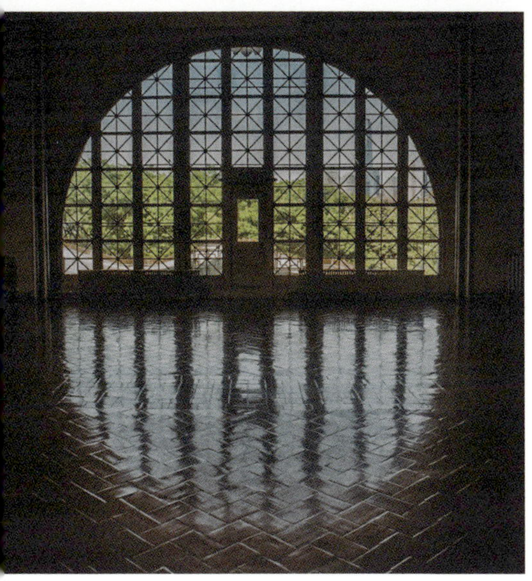

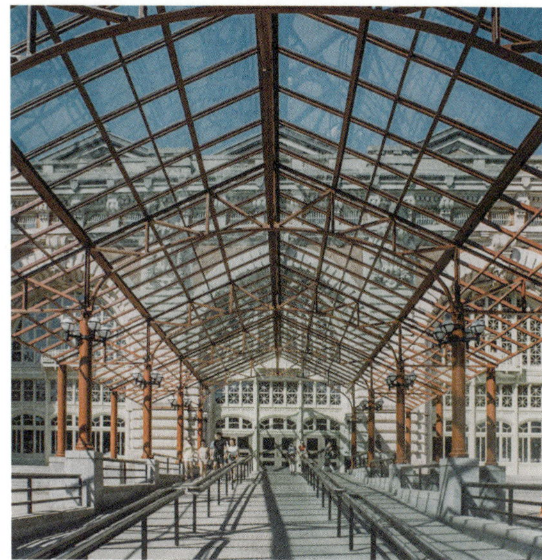

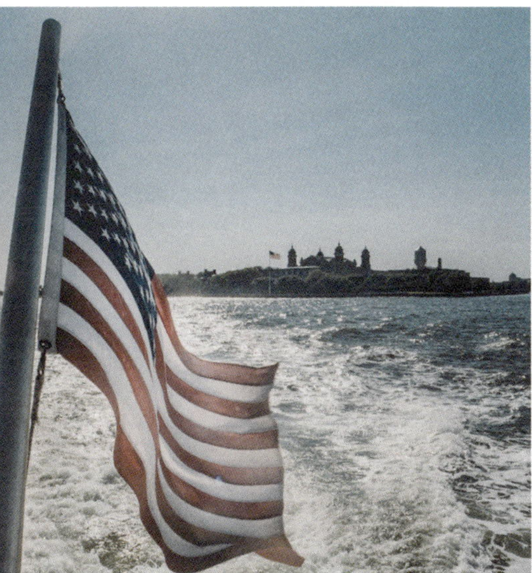

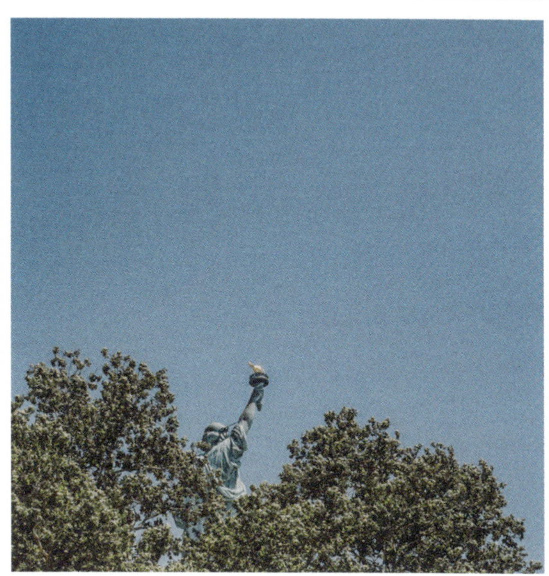

#ellisisland #libertyisland #ladyliberty #statueofliberty @statueellisnps

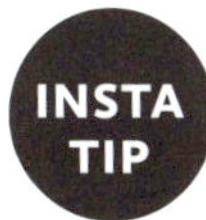

Both islands have a lot of Instagrammable spots. In the pictures above you can see the inside of the Ellis Island museum, the entrance of the museum, Ellis Island as seen from the Cruise and Lady Liberty peeping between the leaves.

INDEX

5 Pointz 198
9/11 Memorial 24
21 Greenpoint 180
43rd Avenue murals 202
58 Joralemon Street 164
A/D/O 180
Abraham Lincoln statue 64
Adam Clayton Powell Monument 150
Algonquin Lounge 86
Alice in Wonderland statue 124, 126
Alma Mater sculpture 152, 153
Alpha Dominate Extraction Lab 170
American Museum of National History 118, 128
Anable Basin Sailing Bar & Grill 192
Apollo Theater 148, 150
Arthur Ross Terrace 118
Artists & Fleas 174, 182
Astoria 198
Astoria Park 198
Astoria Provisions 196, 198
Athena sculpture 152
Athens Square Park 198
Atlas sculpture 97
Audrey Hepburn Mural 38
Balto Statue 122
Banks Skatepark 10
Bareburger 78, 104, 106
Barge Bar 180
Barnes & Noble 64
Baroness bar + kitchen 200
Battery 14, 18
Battery Garden Cafés 14
Battery Gardens 14
Battery Park 14
Bea 92
Beast Speedboat Ride 94
Beaver Street 16
Bel-Aire Diner 196
Belgian Beer Cafe Nomad 62
Belvedere Castle 128
Bethesda Fountain 120, 122
Bethesda Terrace 120, 121, 122
Bibble & Sip 90
Billy's Bakery 50, 68
Birch Coffee 10
Birch Coffee 106
Birch Coffee 136, 202
Black Star Bakery & Café 190
Black Tap 98, 102
Bloomingdale's 134, 136
Blue Bottle Coffee 84
Bluestone Lane 12, 46, 72
Bluestone Lane at the Church of the Heavenly Rest 130, 140, 142, 144
Bonsai Museum 168
Bosque Fountain 14
Bouchan Bakery 110
Bowery Mural 46
Bowne & Co. Stationers 28
Breads Bakery 44, 64
Broadway 92
Brookfield Place 20, 22, 26
Brooklyn Art Library 176
Brooklyn Botanic Garden 166, 168
Brooklyn Brewery 174, 178
Brooklyn Bridge 10, 158, 159
Brooklyn Bridge Park 10, 162
Brooklyn Bridge Park Pop-Up Pool 162
Brooklyn Cat Café 164
Brooklyn Expo Center 180
Brooklyn Grange 204
Brooklyn Heights 164
Brooklyn Heights Promenade 156, 164, 165
Brooklyn Historical Society 158, 160
Brooklyn Ice Cream Factory 158, 162
Brooklyn Museum 166, 168
Brooklyn Public Library 166, 168
Brooklyn Roasting Company 158, 160
Brooklyn Winery 176
Bryant Park 86, 88
Burger Joint at the Parker Meridian 84, 102
Bushwick 172
Bushwick Collective 172
Butcher's Daughter 40
Butler Bake Shop 186
Cafe Colette 176
Café Grumpy 50
Camille Walala Mural 170, 171
Canal Street 36
Central Park Reservoir 131
Cha Cha Matcha 34, 40
Charging Bull 18
Chelsea 50
Chelsea Hotel 50
Chelsea Market 52, 54, 58, 68
China Town 12, 32, 36
Chloe 96
Chloe's Soft Serve Fruit 64
Chopt 118
Chrysler Building 82
Circle Line 94
Circle Line cruise to Ellis Island and Liberty Island 14, 218
City Hall Park 10
Coffeed 204, 206
Colombe Coffee Roasters, la 66, 88
Columbia University 152
Columbia University auditorium 153
Columbus Circle 108
Columbus Park 36
Comme Des Garçons Boutique 50
Communitea 194
Complete Strategist 76
Coney Art Walls 216
Coney Island 216
Coney Island ferris wheel 216, 217
Conservatory Garden 132, 146
Conservatory Water 124
Cooper-Hewitt Design Museum 130, 140, 142, 144

Corona Park 206, 208
Court Square Diner 194
Crack is Wack Mural 148
Crescendo sculpture 182
Cresent Street 202
Cyclone Roller Coaster 216
Damrosch Park 114
David Geffen Hall Café 114
David Rubenstein Atrium 114
Dear Mama Coffee 146
Debbie Harry Mural 46
Dekalb Market Hall 156
Devocion 156
District, le 20
Dö, Cookie Dough
Confections 42
Domicile 172
Domino Park 174, 184, 186
Double Check 17
Double Dutch Espresso 150
Du's Donuts & Coffee 178
Duke Ellington Statue 146
Dumbo 10, 12, 158
Dylan's Candy Bar 134, 136
Earth Room 40
East River shore 174, 175
Eataly NYC 60
Economy Candy 30
Eggloo 12, 36
Eleanor Roosevelt Memorial 116
Elevated Acre 16
Ellington in the Park 152
Ellis Island 218
Ellis Island Café 218
Ellis Island Hospital Morgue 218
Empire State Building 74, 76, 78
Engineers' Gate 142
Every Thing Goes Book Café 214
Evolution Store 42
Fashion Institute of
Technology (F.I.T.) 74
Fearless Girl 18
Federal Hall 16
Financial District 16
Flagship Brewery 214
Flatiron building 60, 62
Flatiron Room 62
Flight Club 44, 64
Flor de Azalea Café 196
Flux Factory 200, 204
Ford Foundation Atrium 82
Forino 162
Fort Jay 212
Four Freedoms Park 210
Freedom Tower 22, 24
Freehold 184
Friedman's 58, 72, 152
Frying Pan 66, 94
Fulton Street 16
Gantry Plaza State Park 190, 194
General Grant National
Memorial 152
George Washington on
horseback monument 64
George Washington Statue 17
Gertrude Stein statue 88
Gina Mexicana 130, 140, 144
Ginny's Supper Club 148
Girl in the English garden
sculpture 133
Globe Sculpture 108
Goodbye Rhinos 156
Gotan 182
Gotham West Market 94
Gothic Bridge 130
Governors Island 212
Governors Island Ferry 14, 212
Graffiti Hall of Fame 132, 146
Grand Central 78, 80
Grand Central Oyster
Bar & Restaurant 80
Granite Prospect 162
Greenpoint 180
Gregory's Coffee 78, 86, 100
Grimaldi's Pizza 158
Guggenheim Museum
130, 138, 140, 144
Häagen-Dazs first ice-cream
shop 164
Hammock Grove 212
Hans Christian Andersen
statue 124, 126
Harriet Tubman Memorial 150
Hearst Plaza 114
High Line 50, 52, 54, 58, 66, 68, 72
Hills at Governors Island 212
Hope Sculpture 84, 98, 102
Hudson River Greenway
bike path 116
Hudson River Park 94, 66
Hudson Yards 72
Hudson Yards Gardens 72
Hypno-Tronic Comics 214
Imagination Playground 28
Immigration Museum 218
Industry City 170
Insomnia Cookies 56
International Center of
Photography Museum 46
Intrepid Sea Museum 94
Irish Hunger Memorial 20, 26
Irving Farm Coffee
Roasters 96, 138
Island Oyster waterfront bar 212
Jack's Stir Brew Coffee 28
Jackson Hole 134
Jacob K. Javits Center 72
Jacqueline Kennedy Onassis
Reservoir 130, 140, 142, 144
Jane's Carousel 158, 160
Jazz @ Lincoln 110
Joe Coffee 24, 164
Jump Into the Light
VR Cinema 30
Kellogg's NYC 64
Kinfolk 90 178
King's County Brewers
Collective 172
Kinokuniya New York 88
Korea Town 76
Labo, le 40
Lady Liberty Mural 34
Lasker Pool 132
Lasker Rink 132
Latte Art 18
Lego shop 96
Lemon Ice King of Corona 208
Liberty Island 218

Library Walk 86
LIC Flea & Food 192
LIC Landing 190
Life Underground 56
Liggett Terrace 212
Lincoln Center 106, 108, 114
Lincoln Center Public Plaza and Café 114
Literary Walk 120, 122
Little Bean Coffee 146
Little Beet 98, 100
Little Hallets Cove Beach 196
Little Italy 38
Little Italy Sign 34, 38
Lizzmonade 162
Loeb Boathouse 122, 124, 128
Loeb Boathouse Express Café 120, 124
Loeb Boathouse Lakeside Restaurant 120, 124
Lombardi's Pizza 38
Los Tacos No. 1 90
Love Sculpture 84, 98, 102
Low Library 152, 153
Lower Level Dining Concourse 80
Luchador, el 28
Ludlow Coffee Supply 30
Lyceum Theatre 92
M. Wells Dinette 194
MacDougal Street 42
Macy's 74, 76
Mahatma Gandhi's statue 64, 65
Maite 172
Majestic Theatre 92
Malcom Shabazz Harlem Market 148
Mall 120, 122
Maman 180
Manhattan Bridge 12, 159, 161
Manhattan Park Pool Club 210
Marcus Garvey Park 148, 150
MatchaBar Chelsea 56
Max Caffè 152
Max Neuhaus' The Hum 90
Mc Carren Park 176, 178
Meatball Shop 30
Meatpacking District 50, 52
Melville House Bookstore 160
Metrograph 32
Metrograph lounge and restaurant 32
Metropolitan Museum of Art 126, 128, 138, 140, 142
MetroTech Commons 156
Mickey Mural 46
Midtown Comics Times Square 90
Milk Bar 68
Milk Bar Williamsburg 176
Minton's Playhouse 150
Miss Favela 186
Mister Dips 178
Moma 84, 98, 100, 102
MoMA PS1 194
Momath 60
Momofuko 110
Morgan Library 78
Morningside Park 152
Mosaics of flying hats 60
Mulberry Street 38
Museum Mile 142
Museum of Arts and Design (MAD) 104, 106, 108
Museum of the City of New York 132, 146
Museum of The Moving Image 204
Nap York 74
Nathans Original Hot Dog Stand 216
National Lighthouse Museum 214
National Museum of the American Indian 14, 18
New York City Hall 10
New York Public Library 78, 86, 88
New York State Pavilion 206, 207
New York Stock Exchange 16
New York Transit Museum 156
New York Wheel 214
Ninja Bubble Tea 170
Nitehawk Cinema 182, 184
Noguchi Museum 196
NoLIta 38
North Brooklyn Farms 184, 186
Obelisk Cleopatra's Needle 138
Observation Towers 206, 208
Oculus 20, 22, 24
Old Pier One 163
Olmsted Flower Bed 122
One Girl Cookies 158
One World Observatory 22
Oslo Coffee Roasters 176
Osprey 162
OY/YO sculpture 182
Pain Quotidien, le 122, 126
Parliament 118, 128
Peace Fountain 152
Pennylane Coffee 82
Penrose 138
Pepsi Cola Sign 190, 192, 194
Pick A Bagel 126
Pier 1 162
Pier 2 Roller Rink 162
Pier 66 66
Pier 66 Maritime 94
Pier A Harbor House 14
Pier i café 116
Pietro Nolita 40
Pizza Beach 138
Plaza Hotel 136
Printed Matter, Inc 66
Prospect Park 166
Pye Boat Noodle 204
Queens Museum 206, 208
Queensboro Bridge 200, 202
Queensbridge Park 202
Radio City Music Hall 96, 98, 100
Ramen Shack 202
Ravine 132
Red Rooster 148, 150
Revson Fountain 114
Riverside Park 116
Rockaway Brewing Company 192
Rockefeller Center 84, 96
Rocket Park Mini golf 206, 208
Rooftop Bars NYC 62
Roosevelt Island 210
Roosevelt Island ferry 192
Roosevelt Island lighthouse 210

Roosevelt Island
Tramway 134, 198, 199, 208
Roosevelt Park 118
Rose Center for Earth
and Space 118
Saint Patrick's Cathedral 96
Saint Paul's Chapel of
Trinity Church 16
San Remo building 131
Sanctuary 116
Sculpture Center 200
Sea Wolf 172
Seaglass Carrousel 14
Serendipity 134
Seventy-ninth Street Boat
Basin 116
Sézane 46
Sézane L'Appartement 40
Shake Shack 10
Shi 192
Silvercup Studio's 200, 202
Simon Sips 92
Sketchbook Project 176
Skinny's Cantina 192
Skylight Diner 74
Smallpox Hospital ruins 210
Smorgasburg Prospect
Park 166, 174
Smorgasburg
Williamsburg 166, 174
Socrates Sculpture Park 196, 198
Soho 40
Sony Square 60
South Street Seaport 28
Sprinkles Cupcake ATM 134, 136
Sprinkles Ice Cream 136
Spyscape 104
St Malachi's, The Actor's
Chapel 92
St Nicholas Avenue, Troutman
Street and Wyckoff Avenue
murals 172
St. Ann's Warehouse 158
St. Michael's Church 170
St. Paul's Chapel of Trinity
Church 24
Starbucks Roosevelt Island 210
Staten Island 214
Staten Island Ferry 14, 214
Staten Island September 11
Memorial 214
Statue of Liberty 218
Statue of Liberty Crown Café 218
Steeplechase Park 216
Stone Street 16
Strand Bookstore 44, 64
Studio Museum 150
Stumptown Coffee Roasters 76
Sugerfina. 24, 110
Sunset Courthouse 170
Sunset Park 170
Sunshine Laundromat 180
Swedish Cottage Marionette
Theatre 118, 128
Sweetleaf Coffee & Cocktails 192
Sweetleaf Coffee Roasters 194
Table of Love 82
Taco Mix.Avocaderia 170
Tacocina 184
Tacombi Fonda Lolita 46
Taiyaki 34
Takumen 190
Tanner Smith's 104
Teardrop Park 26
Tenement Museum 30, 32
Tent of Tomorrow 206, 208
The Cliffs at Dumbo 160
The Green Street LIC 194
The Lego Store 60
The North 5th Street Pier
and Park 174, 182
Theater District 92
Think Coffee 72, 94
ThinkGeek 74
Time Warner Center 104, 108, 110
Times Square 84, 90
Toby's Estate LIC
Cafe & Courtyard 200
Tom Fruin's Watertower 12, 160
Tom Otterness sculptures 56
Tom's Coney Island Diner 216
Top of the Rock 77, 96
Top of the Rock 96
Truman Capote's House 164
Tudor City Overpass 83
Turnstyle Underground
Market 106, 108
Turtle Pond 128
Two Bridges 12
Two For The Pot 164
Umpire Rock 120
Union Square 64
Union Square Park 44
Unisphere 206, 208
United Nations Headquarters 82
Urbanspace Vanderbilt 82, 86
Van Leeuwen Artisan
Ice Cream 182
Vanderbilt Tennis Club 80
Vessel 72, 73
Vesta 198
Wall Street 16
Wall Street Bull 16
Washington Square Arch 42
Washington Square Park 42
Waterfall Tunnel 98, 100
Welling Court Mural
Project 196, 198
Whispering Gallery 80
Whitney Museum of
American Art 52, 54, 56, 84
Whole Foods Market 88, 110
Williams Vale Hotel 178
Williamsburg 174
Williamsburg Bridge 182, 186
Williamsburg Bridge
Pedestrian walkway 184, 186
Williamsburg Music Center 186
WNYC Transmitter Park 180
Wollman Rink 106, 120
Word Books & Stationery 180
World Trade Center 20, 26
Wythe Hotel 178
Yellow Magnolia 168
Yes Murals 12, 160
YouTube film studio 52

COLOPHON

NYC Guide for Instagrammers

TEXT & PHOTOGRAPHY – Silvie Bonne

You can find New York stories on Silvie's blog
www.silviebonne.be/blog
and on instagram
www.instagram.com/bonnesilvie

GRAPHIC DESIGN – Liesbet Van Cauteren
www.mino-studio.be

TRANSLATION – Sandy Logan

The addresses in this book have been selected after thorough independent research by the author. The selection is solely based on personal evaluation of the business by the author. Nothing in this book was published in exchange for payment or benefits of any kind.

D/2018/12.005/15
ISBN 9789460582264
NUR 513, 473

www.lusterweb.com
www.instagram.com/lusterbooks
info@lusterweb.com